The Purloined Islands

Caribbean-U.S. Crosscurrents in Literature and Culture, 1880–1959

Jeff Karem

University of Virginia Press
Charlottesville and London

University of Virginia Press

Printed in the United States of America on acid-free paper

First published 2010

9 8 7 6 5 4 3 2 1

Library of Congress Cataloging-in-Publication Data

Karem, Jeff, 1973-

The purloined islands : Caribbean-U.S. crosscurrents in literature and culture, 1880-1959 / Jeff Karem.

p. cm. — (New world studies)

Includes bibliographical references and index.

ISBN 978-0-8139-3086-2 (cloth : alk. paper) — ISBN 978-0-8139-3087-9 (pbk. : alk. paper)

1. American literature—Caribbean influences. 2. American literature—20th century—History and criticism. 3. American literature—Caribbean American authors—History and criticism. 4. Caribbean literature—20th century—History and criticism. 5. Caribbean literature—American influences. 6. Caribbean Area—In literature. I. Title.

PS159.C37K37 2011
810.9′9729—dc22

2010031486

This book is dedicated to my wife, Katharine,
whose thoughtful feedback and support have
improved both the book and my life, and to my
son, Ronan, whose encouragement was vital
in cheering me on to complete this book.

Contents

Acknowledgments

QUOTATIONS FROM the poems "O Carib Isle," "The Mermen," "Imperator Victus," and "Key West" are reproduced from *The Complete Poems and Selected Letters of Hart Crane* by Hart Crane, edited by Brom Weber. Copyright 1933, 1958, 1966 by Liveright Publishing Corporation. Copyright 1952 by Brom Weber. Used by permission of Liveright Publishing Corporation.

Quotations from the poems "Hoquet," "Shine," and "Trêve" are reproduced from *Pigments,* by León Gontran Damas. Copyright Présence Africaine, 1972. Used by permission of Présence Africaine Editions.

Quotations from the poems "Little Rock," "Tu No Sabe Inglés," and "Yanqui con Soldado" by Nicolás Guillén, are reproduced by the permission of Nicolás Hernández Guillén.

Quotations from the poem "Mississippi" are reproduced from *Cadastre* by Aimé Césaire, copyright Éditions du Seuil, 1961, reprinted as part of the series Points Poésie under the title *Cadastre suivi de Moi, laminaire,* 2006. Used by permission of Éditions du Seuil.

A preliminary version of part of chapter 3 was published under the title "Fear of a Black Atlantic? African Passages in *Absalom, Absalom!* and *The Last Slaver,*" in the anthology *Global Faulkner,* ed. Annette Trefzer and Ann J. Abadie (Jackson: University Press of Mississippi, 2009), 162–73.

The Purloined Islands

Introduction

U. S. AMERICANS have drastically overlooked the contributions of the Caribbean islands to the literary culture of both the Western Hemisphere and the United States itself. Although the Caribbean has often been an object of exotic or imperial desire, it has rarely been recognized by the United States as a collaborator or interlocutor in the development of New World history. This failure to recognize the Caribbean occurs in spite of the fact that intellectual and cultural movements of vital importance in U.S. literary history—pan-Africanism, pan-American modernism, the New Negro Renaissance—have substantial Caribbean roots. U.S. artists and intellectuals often have canonized themselves as the leaders of these movements and failed to acknowledge their debts to West Indian colleagues, effectively "purloining" the Caribbean. This study takes its name from Edgar Allen Poe's famous detective story "The Purloined Letter," arguing that, like Poe's letter, these contributions have been hidden in plain sight.

It may seem counterintuitive to discuss the Caribbean as "hidden" from the United States in 2011, after a year of intense focus on Haiti in the wake of its disastrous quake. However, the fact that only a natural disaster of calamitous proportions could draw U.S. attention to the Caribbean is quite revealing in itself. As the satirical online newspaper the *Onion* wryly proclaimed, "Massive Earthquake Reveals Entire Island Civilization Called 'Haiti.'" The humor of the article, of course, illustrates a deeper critique: the ignorance of the United States with respect to a significant nation in its own backyard, a gap in knowledge so profound that the island seems a forgotten relic. This blindness is all the more painfully ironic given Haiti's rich history as a New World civilization and the second-oldest democratic republic in the Western Hemisphere. The map accompanying the article in the *Onion* also skillfully satirizes another limitation of U.S. views on the Caribbean: the tendency to treat it solely as a tourist destination. The *Onion* map explains the location of the earthquake to readers by triangulating among vacation spots instead of national boundaries or geographic features: Sandals Resort, Las Tunas Hotels, Holguin Hotels, Casa Marina Resort, and Cotursa Santana Beach Resort.

Although "serious" media in the United States did ultimately train a substantive focus on the island after the quake, the earliest coverage revealed the relatively inconsequential position that Haiti held in media estimation. On January 12 seismologists reported that an earthquake of substantial magnitude (7.0, comparable to the San Francisco Bay earthquake of 1989) had occurred along the Enriquillo-Plantain Garden fault system in Haiti, and predicted grave consequences. The first day after the quake, however, U.S. media response was relatively muted. The *New York Times,* which would later give extensive coverage to the disaster, buried the story inside the front section. My local paper, the *Plain Dealer,* did the same, while granting front-page space to an article about the adverse side effects of watching James Cameron's *Avatar* in 3-D.[1] The *Plain Dealer* apparently assumed that Cleveland readers would have more interest in headaches caused by animated blue cat-people on a fictitious planet than in the suffering of fellow humans in an actual nation in their own hemisphere.

Contemporary U.S. ignorance about the Caribbean is not at all surprising given the centripetal, hyper-local focus of most U.S. media (especially on television) and the widespread lack of geographic knowledge among U.S. citizens. More surprising, however, is the relative blindness towards the cultures and peoples of the Caribbean that is evident in many U.S. scholarly and literary discourses, even among scholars doing comparative work in American literature. As a brief example, one might consider how U.S. scholars have approached the works of Paule Marshall, a Barbadian-American writer whose first novel, *Brown Girl, Brownstones* (1959), I will discuss at the end of this study. Critics almost invariably discuss Marshall's novels in relation to Toni Morrison's fiction, and they usually depict Marshall as somehow modeling her novels after Morrison's, even when the chronology makes such a claim precarious or impossible. For example, critics often treat Marshall's depiction of family conflict in *Brown Girl, Brownstones* as if it were an echo, rather than a forerunner, of Morrison's family in *Song of Solomon* (1977). Critics have also argued that Marshall's fiction "combines" or "ritual[izes]" Morrison's concept of "re-memory" from *Beloved* (1987) in *The Chosen Place, the*

Timeless People (1969) without even discussing the fact that Marshall's novel preceded Morrison's by two decades.[2] Significantly, such critics do not write that Marshall's fiction "anticipates" or "presages" Morrison's "re-memory" but assume, without discussion, that Morrison's concept has philosophical priority, even over writers, apparently, who came before her.

Comparative criticism of Marshall and Morrison almost always retroactively fits Marshall into a virtual "School of Morrison."[3] In such a grouping Marshall is not credited for her accomplishments on her own terms, but validated insofar as her novels perform "Morrison-like" work. Morrison's stature as a Nobel winner and her central role in the U.S. canon may make that gesture tempting, but one might rightly postulate that the more persuasive scholarly lens would be to consider how Morrison may have been building upon the seminal work of her predecessor. Even critics who aim to acknowledge Marshall's accomplishments frequently do so in a manner that marginalizes her, lamenting, for example, that Marshall "would have been Toni Morrison" had she started her career in the 1970s.[4] Such a statement discounts the possibility either that Marshall paved the way for a writer like Morrison, or that Marshall could stand alone in her own right as a significant author in the American canon.

A skeptical reader might ask whether this is just an "insider" subject for academic debate that should not concern anyone but specialists. After all, could we not just agree that all of this material is "American" or "African American" and cease historical inquiry into who did what, from where, and when? One need only pose a few hypothetical examples to suggest the problems with such an approach. How would scholars react to the proposition that Toni Morrison accomplished "Kincaid-like" work or echoed *The Autobiography of My Mother* (1996) in her depiction of mother-daughter relations in *Sula* (1973)? Or to a monograph that used Gabriel Garcia Marquez's fictional Colombian town of Macondo as a yardstick or analytic key for interpreting William Faulkner's Yoknapatawpha County? These propositions would likely provoke a host of objections, based not merely on issues of chronology, but of proper recognition and acknowledgment. Staring down centuries of Europhilia in arts and letters, Americanist scholars are often protective of their own sense of national cultural ownership. While there has been substantial progress toward recognizing the intranational diversity within U.S. literature (and indeed entire academic disciplines have emerged from that recognition), there has been much less willingness to countenance the international contributions to U.S. and American literatures, perhaps because doing so would threaten the centrality of the United States as an object of study.

I argue that a rigorously historicized consideration of U.S.-Caribbean literary crosscurrents is vital for several reasons. First, failing to examine the rich contributions of the Caribbean to American literary cultures leaves a distorted picture of New World history. Second, ignoring the perspective of the Caribbean leaves voiceless one of the most important regions in the American hemisphere. Third, subsuming Caribbean discourse into the U.S. literary field without acknowledgment extends the problematic pattern in U.S. literary history of appropriating the voice of others. This third consequence should be of particular concern to scholars, as the history of American studies since the 1950s has been construed largely as a narrative of reconsidering the narrow confines of the U.S. canon erected by F. O. Matthiessen, Richard Chase, and others. For example, one of the most important accomplishments of African American studies has been to demonstrate that much of what the United States has considered its "American" culture—narratives of ascent, the American trickster, jazz music, rock and roll—are derived from African American culture.[5] *The Purloined Islands* argues that scholars should be willing to extend that recognition at least one step further, to include the Caribbean and its contributing role to American and U.S. cultures.

That the Caribbean presence has been hidden in recent American studies scholarship is surprising given the long history of cultural exchanges between the United States and the Caribbean. Writers from the United States have long considered the Caribbean with a combination of fear and desire. Their depictions of the region have ranged from nightmarish portraits of black militancy, to imperialist visions of colonization, to ethnographic studies of traditional cultures. Caribbean authors, in turn, have viewed their northern neighbor with a mixture of interest and distrust. For them, the United States has represented both a source of economic opportunity and an engine of neocolonial power in the American hemisphere. Their interconnected histories of colonization, migration, slavery, and political struggle have thus thrust U.S. and Caribbean writers into a vibrant literary conversation across national borders, but this connection remains largely unexplored in contemporary American studies.

I propose to remedy this lapse by charting twentieth-century literary and cultural dialogue between the United States and the Caribbean from the close of the nineteenth century to the Cuban Revolution in 1959. This period was a time of extraordinary exchanges between the United

States and the islands, spawned by the violent U.S. occupation of Cuba and Haiti and by the cross-pollination effected by West Indian immigration to the United States. The crosscurrents that emerged were varied and numerous: shared literary influences, literal or virtual conversations among U.S. and Caribbean authors, travel writing about one another's cultures, and the use of one another's regions as mirrors or screens for imaginative literature.

During this period, many important U.S. authors—including William Faulkner, William Carlos Williams, James Weldon Johnson, Langston Hughes, Richard Wright, Zora Neale Hurston, Hart Crane, and Eugene O'Neill—either traveled to the Caribbean to write about the region or used it as a setting for their literary work. For their part, Caribbean writers like Claude McKay, C. L. R. James, W. A. Domingo, and Eric Walrond not only wrote about the United States, but immigrated there and became nationally significant contributors to U.S. literary culture. Cultural conversations were not bound by literal travel, either: many authors depicted the neighboring region in fiction, poetry, or drama as a foil for comparison, whether aesthetic, political, or cultural, with his or her own. Through an analysis of key literary and cultural sources in English, French, and Spanish, including a large body of little-considered archival evidence, this book will explore the cultural crosscurrents that were seminal in forming the twentieth-century literary cultures of the Caribbean and the United States.

Each of the five chapters of this study aims to illuminate a pattern of literary contact between the United States and the Caribbean. Chapter 1, "Birth of a Hemisphere: The Spanish American War and Caribbean Resistance Writing," examines how the expanding U.S. neocolonial presence gave rise to a critical dialogue among Caribbean writers about future relations with the U.S. It also traces how Caribbean writers contributed to the formation of pan-Africanist discourse during that period, even though W. E. B. Du Bois would later minimize their contributions as he assumed the mantle of the "father" of pan-Africanism. Chapter 2, "Fear and Fantasy: Haiti and the U.S. Occupation," traces the cultural and literary debates born of the U.S. occupation of the island from 1915 to 1934, including James Weldon Johnson's extensive partnering with Haitian friends to help restore their nation's sovereignty. I consider the large body of U.S. travel writing about Haiti, from the ethnographic to the sensational, and conclude with Haitian literary responses to the occupation. Chapter 3, "Expanding 'Our America': Caribbean Vistas in American Modernism," investigates how a wide range of canonical U.S.

modernists used the Caribbean as a setting or inspiration for literary projects that ranged from comic to tragic to salvific. In chapter 4, "Nationalizing Blackness in the New Negro Renaissance," the book's title takes on particular resonance, as I examine how West Indian authors from Anglophone islands contributed extensively to New Negro discourse, only to have those contributions appropriated and their origins obscured. At the same time that the works of celebrated West Indian authors such as Claude McKay were being used as cornerstones of the New Negro movement, their West Indian backgrounds were largely diminished, condescended to, or outright ignored for the sake of legitimizing and consolidating U.S. leadership of the New Negro movement. Chapter 5, "Translation and Cultural Critique between the Caribbean and the United States after the New Negro Renaissance," explores the development of more reciprocal partnerships in the 1940s and 1950s, ranging from Langston Hughes's translations of the Cuban poet Nicolás Guillén and his extensive anthologization of West Indian poetry, to the pattern of literary influence and friendship that developed between Richard Wright and George Lamming. I also examine how African American and black West Indian writers represented and revisited one another's regions in their literature in pursuit of locating their proper "home" in the American hemisphere. I conclude with a new reading of C. L. R. James's *Mariners, Renegades, and Castaways,* written in the liminal space of Ellis Island, in which I examine how James not only critiques the relations between the United States and the American hemisphere, but also demonstrates that the body politic of the United States is in a virtual diaspora, lacking the democratic citizenship that it believes to be its exceptional possession.

In addition to considering these specific examples of cross-cultural conversation, my investigation aims to fill a number of critical gaps in humanities scholarship that have arisen from trends in recently "globalized" American studies. Border studies scholarship, born of comparisons between the Latino cultures of the United States and Mexico, has accomplished vital comparative work in internationalizing American literary studies, but has been much less effective when applied to the Caribbean. Both early border studies works, like José David Saldívar's *The Dialectics of Our America* (1991), and more recent work, such as the essays collected in *José Martí's "Our America": From National to Hemispheric Cultural Studies* (1998), read the Caribbean primarily through a Mexican American paradigm, collapsing Cuban and Dominican identity into the looser heading of "Latino," and generally ignoring Anglophone and Francophone literatures altogether. Because the Caribbean islands have no land border with the United States, they do not fit well into border-studies models of continental migration, although some scholars have attempted to reframe the geography through models of a "greater South" or Caribbean basin. The history of substantial Caribbean immigration to northern metropolises outside the "basin," such as New York, Chicago, and Toronto, however, makes such geographic models precarious.

Scholars of ethnic studies in the United States have had more success in addressing the Caribbean by pursuing scholarship along hyphenated lines of identity (such as Cuban-American literature, Dominican-American literature, and Haitian-American literature), but such work has usually been highly localized and, more problematically, has often fallen victim to the U.S. tendency to essentialize national identities as originary principles, without considering the dynamism of cultures in the islands and of island-descended cultures in the United States. For scholars who have sought to pursue immigrant history along ethnic lines, the creolization within the Caribbean islands often defies those very ethnic categorizations, because European, African, Asian, and indigenous cultures have deeply intermixed in the Caribbean since the 1700s. The earliest comparative studies of African American and Caribbean cultures, completed in the 1970s, show the limitations of a strictly nationalist lens: scholars looked to the islands to assert an "ethnic unity" and to trace a fundamental "Black Consciousness."[6] Beyond their problematic essentialism, such critical gestures typically assimilated the complexities of Caribbean cultures into an African American critical paradigm.

Recent comparative or "new" American studies, even while professing a "globalized" perspective, still shows a tendency to interpret Caribbean authors via U.S. models while often ignoring those same authors' own literary reflections about the United States.[7] As Raúl Coronado pointedly observes of the vast majority of "new" American studies since the 1990s: "If Americanists have long celebrated post-nationalism, they have done little to move beyond the navel-gazing projects of seeing either how the US has understood the world outside itself or how the US has left its imperial trace throughout the world."[8] In failing to consider a reciprocal dialogue in the Americas, such as the extensive body of Caribbean discourse on the United States, many U.S. scholars miss the opportunity genuinely to expand American studies beyond more traditional national (and nationalist) boundaries. The very vocabulary within some branches of expanded American studies—such as "the greater South," for example—reveals an apparent failure to imagine a hemispheric model that does not consider the U.S. as the center.[9] Édouard Glissant has commented upon the parochial implications of U.S. intellectuals considering their south as *the* South: "One emphatically says 'the South,' with a capital 'S,' as though it represents an absolute, as though we other people of the south, to the south of this capitalized South, never existed."[10]

In this light, Susan Gillman's question "Have American studies gone imperial?" (referring to the voguish "discovery" of imperialism in American studies)[11] could be rephrased in a more polemical direction: can recent American studies move beyond replicating an imperial gaze? Gillman's own work on translation and transculturation in the American hemisphere, via her study of José Martí's adaption of Helen Hunt Jackson's *Ramona,* provides an apt illustration of how comparative Americanists can move beyond a U.S.-centric perspective.[12] However, Gillman's work is one of the exceptions that may prove the rule. Even critics with an avowed interest in transcending the nationalist limitations of a U.S.-centric view seem to fear the impact of fully reckoning with the complex connections between Caribbean cultures and the United States. For example, Heather Hathaway's outstanding *Caribbean Waves* fruitfully restores a Caribbean context to the works of Paule Marshall and Claude McKay, but seems afraid of its own implications. In contemplating McKay's sense of perpetual diaspora, whether in the United States or in the Caribbean, Hathaway fears that the marginalization McKay felt could synecdochically encompass the manner in which the United States and Europe have failed to recognize the Caribbean: "The question is frightening, for a positive answer would reveal the degree to which the Western world has marginalized an entire society in its midst."[13] Hathaway then retreats from that "frightening" possibility by eschewing differences in favor of finding "connection and reconciliation" between U.S. and Caribbean cultures.

One might rightly ask why accepting those differences is so disturbing. For many U.S. scholars, it appears to be unnerving to contemplate the possibility that there are cultures within the American hemisphere that, while illuminating in their parallels with the United States, are nonetheless distinctive in their own right. I would argue that the United States has not necessarily "marginalized" an entire society, but has borrowed from, benefited from, and appropriated from that society without a full sense of recognition or acknowledgment. It is the goal of this study to overcome that misrecognition not by assimilating those cultural contributions into a unitary "American" (read U.S.) field of study, but by considering the wide range of contributors to hemispheric dialogue between the United States and the Caribbean.

There are several studies that form a useful basis for this book. Paul Gilroy, Joseph Roach, Eric Sundquist, and John Carlos Rowe have given significant attention to cultural connections between the Caribbean and the United States, but each has done so in passing as part of larger arguments, rather than as a singular object of study. Gilroy's *The Black Atlantic* (1993) compares the Caribbean to other African-descended cultures in the Atlantic basin, but it focuses principally on triangulation among Africa, Europe, and America, rather than specific relationships between the United States and the Caribbean. Roach's *Cities of the Dead* (1996) examines connections among Caribbean and American traditions of cultural performance, but is primarily concerned with the colonial period through the nineteenth century. In *To Wake the Nations* (1998), Sundquist considers how the Caribbean affected discourses of race and nation in the United States across the nineteenth century, but he explores what the Caribbean has meant to the United States, and not the reverse. Similarly, John Carlos Rowe's *Literary Culture and U.S. Imperialism* (2000), which explores the Caribbean in the service of a larger argument regarding U.S. global hegemony, focuses primarily on how U.S. authors have interpreted the Caribbean.

My study finds its closest kin in the works of Wilson Harris, J. Michael Dash, and Vera Kutzinski, who have offered more reciprocal examinations of literary relationships, explicit and implicit, between the United States and selected Caribbean islands. Beyond their extensive accounts of intra-Caribbean literary history, Dash and Kutzinski have each examined a specific relationship between the United States and the Caribbean. Dash explores U.S-Haitian dialogue in *Haiti and the United States: National Stereotypes and the Literary Imagination* (1988); Kutzinksi has examined the relationship between Langston Hughes and Nicolás Guillén in a series of recent articles. Harris's cross-cultural readings of Melville, Faulkner, and Poe from a Caribbean perspective (he is from British Guiana) provide a model way to disrupt the homogenizing tendencies in both traditional and "global" American studies. According to Harris, "The paradox of cultural heterogeneity, or cross-cultural capacity, lies in the evolutionary thrust it restores to orders of the imagination, the ceaseless dialogue it inserts between hardened conventions and eclipsed or half-eclipsed otherness, within an intuitive self that moves endlessly into flexible patterns, arcs, or bridges of community."[14] Like Harris, I rely on heterogeneity and dialogue between the Caribbean and the United States as untapped resources. At the same time, my investigations are less speculative than Harris's. He traces the hidden and intuitive connections among New World writers, including ones that have not yet been fully realized by the authors themselves. I aim to uncover the "patterns, arcs, or bridges" that already exist between these Caribbean and U.S. literary traditions, but that have been hidden by subsequent history, canonization, or criticism.

The Purloined Islands aims to build upon the works of previous scholars to offer a general model describing literary and cultural exchanges between the United States and the Caribbean islands during the period of their greatest interaction, 1880–1959. This study is multilingual and strives to be reciprocal, exploring not only how writers from the United States have represented the Caribbean and how Caribbean writers have addressed their northern neighbor, but also how these literary exchanges have been mutually transformative. I will demonstrate that the crosscurrents between the United States and the Caribbean islands have been so strong and so interconnected that we can only understand the literary history of the United States if we understand that of the Caribbean, and vice-versa. Moreover, I argue that many cultural and literary developments that U.S. scholars have treated as essentially autochthonous intellectual property (such as pan-Africanism, the New Negro Renaissance, and pan-American modernism) have significant though often unacknowledged roots in the Caribbean. My aim, then, is not simply to trace literary or cultural genealogies, but to consider the Caribbean as a collaborator and contributor not only to hemispheric New World cultures, but to the "American" culture of the United States itself. As my title's allusion to Poe's "The Purloined Letter" suggests, the contributions of the Caribbean islands have been appropriated and nationalized by U.S. culture, hidden in plain sight.

1 Birth of a Hemisphere

The Spanish-American War and Caribbean Resistance Writing

THE U.S. VICTORY in the Spanish-American War in 1898 was a signal moment in both U.S. and Caribbean history. It marked the first time that the United States overtook Europe as a dominant power in the hemisphere, and the Caribbean experienced the onset of a hegemonic U.S. presence that would dominate the region until the Cuban Revolution in 1959. With the U.S. occupation of Cuba and Puerto Rico in the years following the war (and the guarantee of future interventions in succeeding decades that came from the Platt Amendment), a pattern of confrontation, migration, and exchange began that would shape the future of twentieth-century literature in each region. Perhaps because these Caribbean interventions formed the first major overseas, non-contiguous expansion of U.S. imperial power, the political and cultural response to this encounter was intense and multifarious.

Following the Spanish-American War, many Caribbean writers developed intensive plans for resisting U.S. hegemony and preserving cultural and political autonomy. In this chapter I consider the responses of late-nineteenth century Caribbean intellectuals to expanding U.S. power, with a particular eye towards the development of pan-American and pan-African ideologies. I will illuminate how Caribbean writers' critiques of U.S. hegemony established a foundation for the intellectual work of subsequent generations of Caribbean and U.S. authors. This chapter focuses on José Martí (from Cuba), Benito Sylvain and Anténor Firmin (from Haiti), and Henry Sylvester Williams and J. J. Thomas (from Trinidad). The history of Caribbean contributions during this period reveals that pan-Africanism, along with the unified sense of cultural resistance that would culminate in the New Negro Renaissance, was the product of collaborative and dialogic relationships throughout the Black Atlantic, born of mutual exchanges among U.S. and Caribbean writers. Martí,

Firmin, and Sylvain, in particular, established a critical discourse that examined both the local threat of U.S. dominion and the global implications of expanding Euro-American power. I conclude the chapter with an examination of the first Pan-African Conference, which inaugurated the discourse of pan-Africanism. Williams helped organize this event in 1900, and Caribbean intellectuals presented philosophical, cultural, and political arguments alongside a broad range of African and African American participants. W. E. B. Du Bois was a key collaborator at the conference, and I argue that the presentations of West Indian intellectuals like Sylvain contributed key components to Du Bois's subsequent global anti-imperialist vision, though he would ignore the role of this conference as he laid claim to the pan-African movement in the 1920s.

As substantive as Caribbean resistance discourse was at the turn of the century, U.S. scholars have paid relatively little attention to it.[1] Only Martí has effectively entered the canon of trans-national American studies, and that primarily through the attention of Latino studies scholars seeking a model for Hispanophone literature of the American hemisphere.[2] Even critics who acknowledge the importance of Martí's writings have typically positioned Du Bois as the father of American postcolonial discourse.[3] Overall, this chapter demonstrates that the work of Caribbean intellectuals anticipated and influenced subsequent resistance writing and critiques of American history in the United States during the New Negro Renaissance and thereafter. In this regard, I build upon J. Michael Dash's argument that fin-de-siècle Caribbean literature began the articulation of a modern, pan-Caribbean sense of identity. I would add to Dash's argument the contention that Caribbean discourse also shaped concepts of self, nation, and race in the United States, even as these influences would subsequently be occluded by writers and critics in the United States. In this context, the "purloining" examined in this chapter is the way in which U.S. intellectuals, particularly Du Bois, came to view the counter-discourses of pan-Africanism and anti-imperialism as U.S. cultural property, in spite of their shared origins in the Caribbean.

The Boundaries of José Martí's "Our America"

José Martí's contributions to Caribbean resistance have been well-explored by many scholars, so my treatment of him will be briefer than my attention to his colleagues from Trinidad and Haiti, who have been more neglected by critics. The recurrent focus on Martí in recently "worlded" American studies has sometimes had the effect of establishing him as the representative place-holder for "the other America" in comparative studies. To position Martí in this way is tempting given the astonishing range of his writings, as well as his participation in the first Cuban War for Independence, but doing so has the unfortunate effect of making him an exceptional figure and hiding the contributions of others. Although he was respected by his peers (his Haitian contemporary Firmin called him "l'incomparable Martí" and revered him as a Cuban patriot), one must take care not to over-represent Martí as a singular voice of Caribbean resistance or dialogue with the United States.

Martí was incomparably prodigious as a journalist: no other Caribbean intellectual of his time traveled so extensively throughout and commented so extensively upon the United States. At the same time, Martí (in contrast to Firmin and Sylvain) never developed his sketches into an extended study or monograph of U.S.-Caribbean relations. Martí's writings accomplished the important cultural work of successfully revealing to Latin America the dazzling developments and shameful inadequacies of the United States during the Gilded Age. He also aimed to advance a progressive, integrationist agenda within what he termed "nuestra America" [our America]. Because of these grounding ideas, Martí has been celebrated in recent decades as an uncannily modern forefather of postcolonial and dependency theory. At the same time, there are significant boundaries to Martí's "modern" sensibility. His critiques of U.S. dominion, while gesturing towards the future, were strongly rooted in nineteenth-century traditions of romantic racialism and conventional notions of "national character" (Latin vs. Anglo; European vs. American). Other Caribbean intellectuals in his context, such as Thomas, Sylvain, and Firmin, articulated theories of interconnection between the United States, the Caribbean, and Africa that more closely anticipate the reconceptualizations of black and New World identity that would emerge across the twentieth century, including key tenets of postcolonial theory.

Martí's writings about the United States can be divided into two genres: his extensive body of articles written for Latin American newspapers while in exile in the United States, and an equally impressive body of political manifestos and pamphlets surrounding the Cuban War for Independence. Martí's articles about the United States were extensive in subject and widely disseminated. Over the course of his decade of reporting from the United States (1881–91), Martí contributed to *La Nación* in Buenos Aires, *La Opinion Nacional* in Caracas, *La Pluma* in Bogóta, and *El Partido Liberal* in Mexico City. Within these articles, there seems to be virtually no critical subject or journalistic genre left untouched. Martí wrote over three dozen sketches of "representative men" of the

United States, in the manner of Plutarch or Emerson, ranging from poets (Longfellow, Whittier, Whitman), to novelists (the Alcotts), to politicians (General Grant, Samuel Tilden, Chester Arthur), to outlaws (Jesse James). Martí was particularly impressed by Whitman, whom he viewed as not only the boldest and most visionary poet of the United States, but also as the pinnacle of "el hombre natural," a crucial term of praise in Martí's vocabulary used to validate the organic, autochthonous intellectual (in opposition, for example, to Europhilic aesthetes).[4] In terms of events, Martí seems to have been ubiquitous, as he described in detail the national conventions of the Republican and Democratic parties, senate campaigns, the Yorktown centenary celebration, Grover Cleveland's inauguration, the christening of the Brooklyn Bridge ("menos bella que grande"[5] [less beautiful than grand]), and the dedication of the Statue of Liberty. With regard to controversial subjects, he addressed "el problema Negro," political corruption, protectionist debates, the rise of iron and sugar magnates, labor conflicts ("la revolucion del trabajo"[6] [the labor revolution]), Indian wars, Chinese labor on the West Coast, and immigration conflicts in New York. On the cultural front, he discussed not only highbrow U.S. art and literature, but also popular holiday traditions—Christmas trees, Hanukah, and the puzzling figure of Santa Claus—and popular entertainments, such as Coney Island and Buffalo Bill's Wild West Show.

Over the course of his reporting, Martí shifted from initial admiration of U.S. traditions of liberty and idealist energy towards a sense that materialism and imperialism had corrupted the soul of the country. In 1881, during his first year as a correspondent for *La Opinion Nacional,* Martí commented upon the paradoxes embedded in the United States: "In the annals of history, nothing equals the marvelous prosperity of the United States. Whether or not the lack of deep foundations [and] . . . the absence of the feminine spirit, the origin of artistic sensibility and the complement to a nation's soul, will harden and corrupt the heart of that astonishing people, time will tell."[7] Martí's critique of the United States as lacking an artistic sensibility or possessing only a simple materialistic energy echoes a wide range of discourse inside the United States, from Ralph Waldo Emerson to Henry Adams.

Martí's greatest concern regarding materialism in the United States was that the multiplication of wealth had led to massive inequalities. In the summer of 1883, two years after his first visit to Coney Island, Martí returned to the same scene to consider the surrounding slums in the vicinity and criticized the urban landscape with intensely baroque imagery: "A boa constrictor would not leave the poor children of New York as the city summer does: as gnawed, as peeled, as drained and dried. Their little eyes seem like caverns, their skulls, the bald heads of old men, their hands, bunches of dried grass. They crawl along like worms; they breathe in groans. And I say that this is a public crime, and that it is the obligation of the State to remedy this unnecessary misery!"[8] This passage exemplifies the rhythm of Martí's most potent critiques: vivid, evocative imagery of a cultural or moral wrong, followed by a specific call for political action by the public and the state.

Given his moral framework and belief in public responsibility, Martí was especially incensed by the treatment of African Americans and Indians in the United States, not only because of the continued discrimination in the form of Jim Crow and reservations, but also because of a systematic failure of the government to help these populations. He found a startling contrast between the moral obligation of reparation towards African Americans and the actualities of their experience post-Reconstruction: "There already shines fully, in these children of fathers cursed by slavery, the character and intelligence of free men. They are owed, of course, what is owed to them, reparation for the offense; but instead of raising them up from the misery into which they were thrown, in order to rid them of that miserable and unpleasant appearance, they [the people of the United States] make use of that unjustly inflicted appearance in order to refuse to treat them like men!"[9] Martí's advocacy for reparation and integration of African Americans into the U.S. body politic is characteristic of his desire that cultures in the Americas, insofar as possible, assimilate and fuse into one. Thus he did not argue for Native American sovereignty, but for an eradication of the stereotypical images of savagery ("un concepto falso del indio" [a false concept of the Indian]) as well as freedom from "la rapacidad de los agentes" [the rapacity of the government agents] under the reservation and Bureau of Indian Affairs system.[10] Reporting on the Lake Mohonk convention, Martí likened the activist Helen Hunt Jackson to Harriet Beecher Stowe and approved of the political momentum that brought Grover Cleveland to investigate failures within the bureau. Martí also called for the extension of U.S. citizenship to Native Americans, along with the opportunity for education and training in trades outside the reservation.

Martí's incisive critiques of the U.S. Bureau of Indian Affairs aligned him with many Native American writers—most notably Luther Standing Bear, who would reflect on the failures of the reservation system in succeeding decades—but his sense that Native American culture must evolve to join the national central culture marked him as more Eurocentric in focus. According to Martí, the greatest ill of the reservation was not that it hampered indigenous cultural traditions, but that it stifled their development: "The Indian is dead, with that vile system that extinguishes his personality: man grows with the exercise of his own self, as a wheel gains speed as it rolls; and when he does not exercise himself, like the wheel, he rusts and rots."[11] Although Martí was not hostile to indigenous culture—indeed he positioned himself as an ally to it in this article—his vision of the Indian needing to "develop" differed strongly from the sovereignty desired by Native American intellectuals and leaders of his time. Although Martí critiqued U.S. hegemony over Native Americans, he typically did so by privileging modernity and "progress" over the traditions and history of the very indigenous peoples he championed. As I have argued elsewhere, Martí's vision often had blind spots with regard to indigenous cultures.[12]

Besides criticizing the systematic oppression of African Americans and Native Americans, Martí grew increasingly critical of the level of violence in the United States, both in popular unrest and in judicial responses to it. Most pointedly, the Chicago Haymarket bombing in 1886 (allegedly by immigrant anarchists), along with the bloodthirsty hanging of possibly innocent men in retaliation, convinced Martí that something was threatening the core of the United States: "This Republic, because of its excessive worship of riches, has fallen from the ties of tradition into inequality, injustice, and the violence of monarchical countries."[13] Given Martí's sense of New World exceptionalism, the claim that the United States was becoming as unjust and as violent as "monarchical countries" (i.e., Old Europe) was especially damning.

In spite of this critique, Martí still held out hope during the 1880s for the integrity of U.S. ideals and a remediation of the failures that compromised them. He drew particular inspiration from the dedication of the Statue of Liberty, which he saw as a reaffirmation of the United States' commitment to welcoming the oppressed: "Liberty, your hour has arrived! The entire world has brought you to these shores, pulling the cart of victory. Here you are like the dream of a poet, great as the space from the earth to the sky. . . . Look: everyone shows the joy of those coming back to life! Is not this people, in spite of its coarseness, the house of respite for the oppressed?"[14] The pros and cons of serving as a "house of respite" would prove a controversial subject in the United States at the turn of the century, but the steady flow of European immigrants also began to provoke questions in Martí about the future stability of the nation. For example, when Martí turns his attention to the labor movement in the United States, he is sympathetic to the workers' demands, but clearly repulsed by the ethnic make-up of the labor unions: "Without the reins of patriotism, which can do so much even for the lowest men, that mix of Irish, of Scottish, of Germans, of Swedes, of people who eat meat and drink beer . . . goes quickly and without restraint, without any restraint but fear or instinct or self preservation, to conquer whatever they believe to be theirs."[15] Martí's distaste for beer-drinking and meat-eating habits may be humorous for the contemporary reader, but his larger sense that these essentially non-Anglo white immigrants lacked patriotism and could not be blended into the U.S. citizenry shows a surprising turn in his reasoning, given his own confidence that Spanish, French, African, and Indian strains would blend seamlessly in the Caribbean. Indeed, as Martí moves on to predict the future of the United States in his famous essay "La Verdad Sobre Los Estados Unidos" ["The Truth about the United States"], he grounds his critique on a basis that was as much cultural as political: "I do not predict, but rather guarantee, that which can be observed in the United States: that reasons for union are not drawing together but loosening as people attempt to resolve their problems, which are multiplying; instead of blending into a national polity, the localities are becoming divided and inflamed; democracy, instead of becoming robust and saving itself from the hate and misery of the monarchies, will become corrupt and diminished, and hate and misery, menacingly, will spring up again."[16] Although Martí would certainly not have wished to see himself in the company of later U.S. racial scientists like Lothrop Stoddard and Madison Grant, his belief that assimilation of some immigrants would be impossible, along with his fear that conflicted ethnic interests would permanently divide the U.S. body politic, is hauntingly similar to elements of subsequent nativist philosophy in the United States.

Perhaps because of his fears of cultural disintegration, Martí worked to establish cultural and political distance between the United States and Latin America in his writings, often on culturally nationalist terms that were deeply rooted in the nineteenth century. As much as Martí was confident of the integration of Indian and African-descended cultures into "nuestra America," he perceived clear distinctions between the Anglo-American culture of the north and the eminently superior Spanish culture of Latin America. Although Martí explicitly disavowed the category of race as having any reality—"no hay razas" [there are no races], he writes in "The Truth about the United States"[17]—he was clearly concerned with questions of cultural miscibility and based many of his judgments on assumptions about "national character."

Most such comparative discussions from Martí hinge upon a contrast between Yankee vulgarity and what one might call "Latin exceptionalism." In an account of New York beachgoers, for example, Martí critiques the practice of burying oneself in the sand as evidence of an unhealthy culture: "They throw themselves into the sand, and let themselves be covered, and buffeted, and mashed, and surrounded by the hot sand, because that is thought to be healthful exercise and because it offers singular opportunities for superficial intimacy, vulgar and loud, for those apparently prosperous and affectionate people."[18] Like many observers of foreign cultures, Martí perceives small personal practices (recreation in the sand) as evidence of larger issues of national character, and he draws the conclusion that this contented burial is an analogue for the complacency of the American spirit, which grasps after money but little else: "Other peoples—and us among them—live absorbed by a sublime interior demon, who pushes us forward towards the tireless pursuit of an ideal of love or glory. . . . Not so for those tranquil spirits, troubled only by the longing for a fortune."[19] In the context of late nineteenth-century debates regarding race, nation, and national destinies, perhaps the most important phrase here is "other peoples," which implies that the United States and Latin America are not merely divided by distinct historical and political formations, but by a difference in the *volk* itself.

I raise these points regarding Martí's romantic racialism and elitism not to diminish Martí's centrality as an anti-imperialist writer or pan-American visionary, but to rehistoricize scholars' understandings of his interventions in debates about New World hemispheric politics. Many pan-Americanists, following the lead of Roberto Fernández Retamar, have romanticized Martí as a populist in the manner of Guevara or Castro, and have rechristened Martí's vision of "nuestra America" to incorporate the colonial and postcolonial peoples of North America.[20] Careful attention to Martí's political judgments against the United States reveal that his philosophy does not always develop in the smoothly progressive and populist direction represented by contemporary pan-Americanists, who have typically situated Martí as a theoretical spokesman for all the oppressed of the New World. Although part of Martí's critical discourse against the United States anchors itself in a defense of marginal and oppressed groups, an equally sizable portion rests in an elitist critique of U.S. culture.

Martí's Vindication of Cuba

Martí's critiques of U.S. internal division possessed powerful implications in the context of U.S. debates in the 1880s about annexing Cuba. His exposés of internal conflict within the United States offered the implication, both to readers from the U.S. and those from the Caribbean, that the last thing the United States should do is to step beyond its continental boundaries to incorporate other peoples who would further complicate their internal dynamics. His insistence on critiquing North American ethnic traditions may have been in response to a similar tendency in annexation debates, as many U.S. papers framed the controversy of Cuban annexation as a problem of blending distinct peoples and racial destinies. In Martí's career, this debate is best encapsulated in a pamphlet entitled "Cuba y Los Estados Unidos" [Cuba and the United States] published in New York in 1889. This pamphlet reprints two U.S. newspapers' articles on the question of Cuban annexation, along with Martí's response, "Vindicación de Cuba" [A vindication of Cuba].

The two U.S. papers, the Philadelphia *Manufacturer* and the New York *Evening Post,* each advocated caution regarding annexation, albeit for different reasons. The *Post* offers a technocratic critique of the impact of such a move on U.S. export/import balances, protectionist laws, and other trade policies, while the *Manufacturer,* despite its name, seems more concerned with culture than commerce. While acknowledging that Cuba seems a natural prize to desire—"She is so close to Florida that Nature seems to indicate her affiliation with the dominant nation on this continent"[21]—the *Manufacturer* fears "the question of whether our race would not degenerate under a tropical sun" (330). Even more pointedly, it expresses racist distrust of both the Spanish and African populations on the island:

> They are helpless, lazy, deficient in morals, and incapable by nature and experience of fulfilling the obligations of citizenship in a great and free republic. Their lack of virile strength and self-respect is shown by the apathy with which they have submitted to Spanish oppression for so long. . . . As for the Cuban Negroes, they are clearly at the level of barbarity. The most degraded Negro in Georgia is better prepared for the presidency than is the ordinary Cuban Negro for American citizenship. (228, 230)

In this context, Martí's "Vindicación" moves towards a vision of separate destinies for Cuba and the United States:

> It is probable that no Cuban who has any honor in him desires to see his country united with another where those who guide public opinion share respect for worries excusable only by political braggadocio or confused ignorance. . . . They admire this nation, the greatest of those ever built by liberty; but they distrust those unfortunate elements that, like worms in the blood, have begun in this marvelous Republic their work of destruction.[22]

Given the body of racist discourse directed against Cuba and Latin America from the United States, it makes sense that Martí framed his criticisms of the United States in a parallel language of nation, cultural destiny, and corrupted blood, with the prediction that it is the United States that is slated for disintegration. In this passage he rebuts U.S. racialists on their terms: it is the United States, not the Caribbean, that is culturally degenerate and whose collective health is in jeopardy. In doing so, however, Martí tacitly reinforces the framework of that debate by relying upon the concepts of blood and decay, leaving the concepts of national health and cultural degeneracy unchallenged.

Indeed, a commitment to the traditional pairing of nativity and nation inhabits (and perhaps inhibits) Martí's most cited and visionary essay, "Nuestra America." As much as José David Saldívar and others (including myself) have sought to view this essay as an act of coalition-building across a North-South divide in order to recognize a common "our" in both regions, close examination of the language reveals a much less cosmopolitan vision of diasporic unity and a more traditional sense of birthright and homeland. Comparing Cuba to a mother (as he did in the precursor to "Nuestra America," "Madre America" ["Mother America"]), Martí asks the rhetorical question: "Well, who is the real man? He who stays with his mother to cure her of sickness, or he who puts her to work where she cannot be seen and lives off her sustenance in powerful lands with a thin worm of a tie, cursing the womb that bore him, parading the sign of a traitor on the shoulder of his coat?"[23] Martí's image of the "thin tie" (referring to U.S. fashions) as a sign of betrayal evokes not only national betrayal, but also emasculation through the aping of dandyish customs. In a different metaphoric vein, Martí fears an epistemological betrayal from exilic youth: "To who-knows-where those youths go into the world, with Yankee or French spectacles, and they aspire to lead a people they do not know."[24] These commentaries aptly anticipate the debates surrounding assimilation, mimicry, and double-consciousness that would come to be at the heart of twentieth-century postcolonial discourses. At the same time, Martí's solution to exilic situations, in this article, is not even pan-Americanist, but profoundly nationalistic: the exile should return to the motherland, be loyal, and not betray her. Indeed, in comparing Cuba to the mother to be protected, he invokes traditional associations of race, sexuality, and national purity that Vera Kutzinski well traces in *Sugar's Secrets* (1993).[25] Thus, Martí framed the coming threat to "Our America" in an embodied, personal image: "But another danger perhaps chases our America, which does not come from within, but rather from the difference in origins, methods, and interests between the two continental powers, and the hour will soon come when she will be approached by a grasping and groping people, demanding intimate relations, who do not recognize her and disdain her."[26] In "demand[ing] an intimate relationship," the United States thus emerges not simply as an imperial power, but as a violator of the mother. Accordingly, Martí concludes this vision with a prediction that if Cubans and others of "nuestra America" resist, the United States will withdraw its "hand" from the region.

J. J. Thomas's *Froudacity:* Triangulating among Britain, the United States, and the West Indies

J. J. Thomas, from Trinidad, was similarly committed to comparing U.S. and Caribbean political systems at the dawn of the Spanish-American War, but he reached more optimistic conclusions, perhaps because he was more distanced from U.S. hegemony, but also perhaps because he had a different sense of how race and national character interacted. Like Martí, Thomas was interested examining the role of the United States in a triangular geopolitical competition with the Caribbean and Europe. Unlike Martí, Thomas saw a more inspiring example in the United States, particularly in aspects of Reconstruction, though he was quite critical of delays in abolishing slavery and of the disenfranchisement of African Americans. In *Froudacity, or West Indian Fables by James Anthony Froude* (1889), Thomas presents one of the most important articulations of Black Atlantic cultural sovereignty and solidarity in the nineteenth century.

Froudacity accomplishes a tremendous amount in its slim two hundred pages: it refutes English imperialist representations of the West Indies, critiques white supremacy, offers a nascent pan-Africanist vision, and develops a pragmatic vision of multi-ethnic Caribbean identity less invested in romantic racialism than that of Martí. The book has received very little critical attention, in spite of these achievements. The primary aim of *Froudacity,* particularly in its early chapters, is to refute the racist, imperialist vision that James Froude articulated in the travel narrative *The*

English in the West Indies; or, The Bow of Ulysses (1888). Froude's title refers to the famous scene in the *Odyssey* in which no one but the titular hero can manage the great bow at his homestead in Ithaca. Froude uses this scene as a political metaphor for the necessity of English governance in the islands: the natives (especially the blacks) were not strong enough to "bend the bow" and govern themselves. Froude's central thesis is clear and paternalistic: "The negroes of the West Indies are children, and not yet disobedient children. . . . If you enforce self-government upon them when they are not asking for it you may . . . willfully drive them back into the condition of their ancestors, from which the slave trade was the beginning of their emancipation."[27]

Froude's proleptically Orwellian construction of colonial government as freedom and slavery as emancipation would seem to put his prose as beneath contempt by 1888, but his voice was prominent in the literary field, and hence necessitated refutation. Although he is no longer part of any serious canon of English letters—perhaps due in no small part to Thomas's devastating critique—Froude was a preeminent English travel writer in his time, comparable in his stature to V. S. Naipaul or Paul Theroux at the end of the twentieth century. Consequently, Thomas deemed it vital to refute this cultural slander.

The early chapters of *Froudacity* may well account for the lack of critical attention, for they are very much "inside baseball" discussions of how Froude misreads local politics, customs, and geographic details of the islands he visits. As the volume develops, however, Thomas moves to a Popean satire of Froude's follies, with arch responses to the Englishman's absurd presumptions. For example, Froude credits English slavery for producing good manners among blacks on the islands: "The name of slavery is a horror to us; but there must have been something human and kindly about it, too, when it left upon the character the marks of courtesy and good breeding" (134). Thomas's response is a sarcastic reductio ad absurdum of Froude's compliment: "Granting the appreciable and ethical value of hat-touching, the smirking and curtseyings of those Blacks . . . we fail to discover the necessity of the dreadful agency [i.e., slavery] we have adverted to, for securing the results on manners which are so warmly commended" (134). Thomas was even more pointed in rebuking Froude's allegations regarding witchcraft on the islands. According to Froude, "In spite of the priests, child-murder and cannibalism have reappeared in Hayti, but without them things might have been worse than they are, and the preservation of white authority and influence in any form at all may be better than none" (164). Thomas's response reverses the polarity of

Froude's judgment, rendering the Englishman superstitious for his naïve faith in white skin: "We discern in the foregoing citation the exercise of a charity that is unquestionably born of fetish-worship, which, whether it be obeah generally, or restricted to a mere human skin, can be so powerful an agent in the formation and retention of beliefs" (164).

With such moments of "reverse anthropology," Thomas not only accumulates witty refutations of Froude's fallacies, but also develops an active defense of island culture, the equality of the races, and the consequent right to West Indian self-governance. The nuances and details of his vision, as well as the succeeding theories anticipated, are quite astounding, particularly for such a small volume. At least eleven years before the first Pan-African Conference, Thomas offered a nearly pan-African vision with respect to the American hemisphere. In reclamation of the noble lineage of West Indian blacks, he enumerates the powerful tribes from which he and his brethren are descended: "We have had the Madingoes, Foulahs, Houssas, Calvers, Gallahs, Karamenties, Yorubas, Aradas, Cangas, Kroos, Timnehs, Eboes, Mokes, Bibis, and Congoes, as the most numerous and important of the tribal contribution of Africa to the population of these colonies" (142). Thomas also shows an awareness of what Gilroy would later term "the Black Atlantic" in his sense that there is a kinship between Africans of the continent ("intra-Africans") and their descendants around the world (which he terms "extra-Africans") (179). With his eye on the fate of empires, Thomas extends his vision globally and historically to prophesy that Froude's sense of English destiny is insecure and will not stand the test of time:

> We see that in the past different races have successively come to the front, as prominent actors on the world's stage. The years of civilized development have dawned in turn on many sections of the human family, and the Anglo-Saxons, who now enjoy pre-eminence, got their turn only after Egypt, Assyria, Babylon, Greece, Rome, and others had successively held the palm of supremacy. And since these mighty empires have all passed away, may we not then, if the past teaches aught, confidently expect that other racial hegemonies will arise in the future? (180)

Thomas offers a vision of black destiny that would become familiar across the twentieth century (especially with the rise of Marcus Garvey), but nonetheless complicates this vision with an intense awareness of the multicultural, hybrid dimensions of the islands, which he also values in *Froudacity.* One might say that Thomas was an Africanist but not an Afrocentrist. In contrast with both black and white discourses of the nineteenth century that condemned miscegenation, Thomas accepted the mixing of races as the result of "natural affection" (184), and dismissed concerns over *mulatez* and *mestizaje:* "The blending of races is not a burning question. . . . Time and Nature might safely be left uninterfered with to work out whatever social development of this kind is in store for the world and its inhabitants" (70). In terms of pragmatic politics, Thomas advocates for a "West Indian Confederation"[28] in which all distinct groups would have equal franchise after the cessation of Crown control: besides blacks, "the duly qualified Spaniard, Coolie, Portuguese, or man of any other non-British race, will each thus have a vote, the same every Englishman or any other Briton" (146).

For scholars interested in transnational convergences of power in the hemisphere, Thomas offers even more innovative material in his globally-minded defense of West Indian sovereignty and black equality. Thomas triangulates among the cultural and political histories of England, the islands, and the United States. Some of his attention is aimed in an intra-Caribbean direction, as he contrasts the lack of cultural enfranchisement in the British colonies with those under French and Spanish dominion: "Are Negroes under the French flag not intensely French? Are the Negroes under the Spanish flag not intensely Spanish?" (115). Thomas also alludes to Haiti as a powerful cautionary tale about the limits of European power (52). Looking north, Thomas uses the United States as a foil for his analysis of British domination. In representing connections between the U.S. and the islands, Thomas sees the United States as a land of serious contradictions for African-descended peoples. Thomas had clearly learned about the innovations of the Reconstruction period, from the Civil Rights Act to the brief blossoming of black officeholders and enfranchisement in the South, and he discusses these achievements in *Froudacity.* Indeed, C. L. R. James argues that Thomas's work on the subject was a crucial precursor to W. E. B. Du Bois's *Black Reconstruction in America* (1935), which emerged more than forty years later.[29] As impressed as Thomas was with the opportunities of Reconstruction, he was also aware of the racist backlash that emerged during that period in the United States. Thomas laments that African Americans "were hunted down from city to city as few felons would be, and finally done to death—'serve them right!' being the grim commentary regarding their fate for having sought to usurp the ineffable privilege of whitesmanship" (116–17). Thomas acknowledges that the United States had an explicit system of legal discrimination unlike the West Indies, but then uses this fact to cast the Reconstruction reforms in even more notable contrast to Crown policies in the islands, where Britain had not attempted any such enfranchisement:

> Mr. Froude, being so deferential to skin-prejudice will doubtless find it strange that such a measure as the Civil Rights Bill should have passed a Congress of Americans. Assuredly with the feeling against the coloured race which custom and law had engrafted into the very nature of the vast majority, this was a tremendous call to make on the national susceptibilities. But it has been exactly this that has brought out into such vivid contrast the conduct of the British statesman, loudly professing to be unprejudiced as to colour, and fair and humane. (117)

Thomas notes that there was only one black officeholder in the islands—Chief Justice Reeves of Barbados—in contrast to the blossoming of African American politicians in the United States during Reconstruction:

> Hence it is that in only twenty-five years America can show Negro public officers as thick as blackberries, while Mr. Froude can mention only Mr. Justice Reeves as a sample of the "exceptional" progress under British auspices. . . . Verily, if in fifty long years British policy can recognize only one single exception . . . , the inference must be that British policy has been not only systematically, but also too successfully hostile to the advancement of the Ethiopian subject thereto. (118)

Elsewhere in *Froudacity,* Thomas draws rhetorical strength and buttressing evidence for his case for equality from the accomplishments of African Americans, and he cites them as kindred, from spiritual leaders like Josiah Henson and Sojourner Truth (171) to political leaders and writers like Frederick Douglass, Henry Highland Garnet, Alexander Crummell, and Edward Wilmot Blyden.

Thomas thus envisioned the post-emancipation United States as a place of greater black opportunity compared to the apparently "freer" islands (which had been emancipated decades earlier), but also as a place with a history of greater racial violence and legal discrimination. Thomas's wrestling with the complex racial legacy of the United States anticipated vital cross-cultural dialogue in the twentieth century between U.S. and Caribbean writers.

Anténor Firmin's Proposal for a Haitian-U.S. Hemispheric Partnership

The question of how the United States would resolve its questions of internal racial conflict took on an especially urgent tone for Caribbean writers in the wake of the Spanish-American War. Crucial terms of the U.S.-Spanish peace, especially the Platt Amendment, provoked substantive discussion from Caribbean intellectuals, who rightly perceived that European dominance was on the wane and U.S. influence on the rise. Black Caribbean writers and leaders feared that their region's racial politics would be redrawn along harsh U.S. lines if the Caribbean became merely a satellite to its northern neighbor. Foremost among these was Anténor Firmin, a Haitian in exile who published widely in anthropology, history, and politics. By 1889, Firmin had already secured himself a substantial place in European intellectual circles as one of only two black members of the French Société d'anthropologie. In 1885 Firmin published a landmark anthropological study entitled *De l'égalité des races humaines* [*On the Equality of the Human Races*], which was an explicit rebuttal to Comte de Gobineau's *Essai sur l'inegalité des races humaines* [*Essay on the Inequality of the Human Races*]. According to Carolyn Fluehr-Lobban, who has done humanistic scholarship a great service in bringing Firmin's work back into print, Gobineau's pseudoscientific justification of white superiority shaped the dominant paradigm of European anthropology and social theory in the nineteenth century (particularly that of Herbert Spencer); influenced U.S. racial scientists of the twentieth century, such as Louis Agassiz, Lothrop Stoddard, and Madison Grant; and had a profound influence on both Richard Wagner and Adolph Hitler.[30] Firmin's refutation of Gobineau was outstanding in its time for relying not on abstract a priori theoretical suppositions (e.g., a belief in "natural" racial supremacy), but on a rich range of historical evidence and sociopolitical data. Firmin's conclusions were audacious in their time and remain fresh today. Firmin argued for the basic equality of potential among all races: "Human beings everywhere are endowed with the same qualities and defects, without distinctions based on color or anatomical shape. The races are equal; they are all capable of rising to the most noble virtues, of reaching the highest intellectual development; they are equally capable of falling into a state of total degeneration" (450).

Firmin's positivist methodology not only influenced subsequent Caribbean intellectuals like Sylvain, but formed an apt precursor to the rigorous sociology that Du Bois employed in landmark studies like *Black Reconstruction in America*. Firmin's work also anticipated Afrocentric and pan-Africanist thought in arguing for a monogenic (single origin) narrative of human civilization, with a crucial role played by black African culture, particularly via Egyptian civilization and its connection to the Greeks. Unlike many subsequent pan-Africanists (particularly

Garvey), who validated the "purity" of Africa as an anodyne to the white race, Firmin was skeptical not only of the value of racial purity but even of its possibility: "Observing that human beings have always interbred whenever they have come in contact with one another . . . the very notion of pure races becomes questionable" (64).

Although *On the Equality of the Human Races* does not speak extensively to questions of U.S.-Caribbean interaction, it shows a hemispheric awareness of the vital interactions between the United States and the Caribbean. Firmin cites both Stowe and Douglass in making his case that New World slavery enforces an inferior social status on African peoples rather than reflects their existing potential (331). In one of the later chapters of the volume, "The Role of the Black Race in the History of Civilization," Firmin points to Haiti's successful war for independence from Europe, as well as his nation's support for Latin American liberator Simón Bolívar, to argue that black Haitians had a crucial role in promoting liberty in the New World.

Following the U.S. victory over Spain, Firmin took a very active role in engaging with the United States in both politics and in writing. As Fluehr-Lobban notes, in his role of Minister of Foreign Affairs for Haiti, Firmin worked with Frederick Douglass (U.S. Minister Resident and Consul General to Haiti at the time) in 1891 on the question of granting specific harbor rights to the United States at the town of Môle St. Nicolas. This plan fell through because neither Douglass nor Firmin seemed willing to create a beachhead for U.S. imperialism on the island (xl–xli). Indeed, this entire episode, in which the *U.S.S. Philadelphia* sat anchored offshore awaiting the chance to take possession of the harbor, anticipated in miniature the U.S. occupation that would take full force in 1915. Firmin also met with Martí in 1893 in Cap Haïtien to discuss how the Antilles might fit into the latter's pan-Americanist visions—an exchange that Brenda Gayle Plummer explores in her comparison of Firmin's pan-Africanism to Martí's pan-Americanism.[31] In the wake of his awkward diplomatic exchange with Douglass, Firmin resigned his post. He was reassigned to Paris in 1900, but returned to lead an insurgency that called for a reduction of foreign interests in the island and a diminished role for the Haitian military. Firmin was unsuccessful and fled to St. Thomas, where he produced his final body of writings, which engaged directly the questions of U.S.-Caribbean relations in the New World.

Although Firmin was quite supportive of Caribbean participation in a pan-American republic in his final body of letters from St. Thomas, he had a much more nuanced sense of engagement—both attraction and repulsion—with the United States during the first part of his exile. When Theodore Roosevelt came to occupy the presidency after the assassination of William McKinley, Firmin wrote a mammoth study (five hundred pages) about the future of relations between the United States and Haiti, entitled *M. Roosevelt, président des États-Unis et la République d'Haïti* [*Monsieur Roosevelt, President of the United States*] (1905). This text, although little studied today (Plummer mentions it only briefly), provides not only a complex portrait of how a progressive Caribbean intellectual viewed the United States, but also a prophetic vision of Haitian-U.S. cooperation that could lead the hemisphere into the twentieth century. In *M. Roosevelt* Firmin simultaneously advises Haitians to strengthen their military to preserve their sovereignty (so as to stave off, by implication, U.S. intervention in Haiti comparable to that in Cuba) while arguing that his nation should partner with the United States to lead the hemisphere. Firmin grounds his case in a careful renarration of U.S. history in the first half of the volume, followed by an equally systematic account of Haitian history. Firmin argues that the United States and Haiti are parallel nations that, while disparate in power, could stand shoulder to shoulder as revolutionary republics that have protected the New World from European intervention.

Firmin begins his volume by referring to "la question americaine," which is itself an effective retroping of a phrase usually applied by Europe and the United States to their "problem" zones, as in the "Negro question," the "Cuba question," and so forth.[32] Firmin acknowledges a fear that "the advent of a new host at the White House [means] a threat to our national autonomy,"[33] but also aims to educate Haitians about "a great people with whom we have so many points of contact, material and moral."[34] Lest this estimation seem an overly generous view of his northern neighbor, Firmin recognizes from the start of his book that a central challenge in understanding U.S. history is that a nation founded in the name of liberty could be simultaneously committed to militaristic expansion (and, hence, subjugation of others) from its earliest days—a paradox that would not be substantively explored by U.S. historians until much later in the twentieth century. A crucial goal of *M. Roosevelt,* according to Firmin, is "to grasp how a people given to the dignity of liberty and of equality put their energy into conquering others, empowered by these enlightened ideas, seeing them as the source of all social well-being and progress."[35] For Firmin, it is this peculiar combination of idealism and imperial ambition—which he sees as reaching its apogee in Roosevelt—that makes the United States such a formidable neighbor.

Firmin thus observes that the military threat from the United States is real, but argues that reckoning with that possibility will be beneficial for his country, which he had come to view as lax: "And it will be a new merit for Roosevelt if his beautiful and healthy energy, after having inspired in us a salutary fear, makes us find our way again after having long abandoned our national destiny."[36]

As the language of "destiny" suggests, Firmin aims to complicate, and perhaps co-opt, the U.S. claims to Manifest Destiny. He notes that, much as the U.S. declared its independence and sought to offer a model republic in contrast to European monarchy, Haiti fought to achieve its own sovereignty, and could serve as a model of black autonomy for the world: "For Haiti this ideal is the sublime effort of a small nation to rehabilitate an entire race."[37] Firmin views these apostolic missions of the United States and Haiti as not simply parallel, but as mutually intertwined, particularly insofar as the U.S. had failed to enfranchise fully African Americans, and thus had compromised its own ideals.

As Firmin elaborates his historical comparisons across the volume, he finds "points of contact" and shared values, as well as shared problems that would benefit from mutual aid between the nations. As he does so, he pays careful tribute to the highest ideals treasured by the United States, even as he subtly suggests parallel lessons that the U.S. should learn from its own history. For example, in recounting the history of U.S. independence, Firmin honors the founding fathers, especially Washington ("the immortal name that will always awaken in our spirit sentiments of respect and of admiration"), and refers to the Declaration of Independence as "a sacred thing."[38] Firmin couches his appreciation of the American Revolution in a discourse of natural justice that suggests the rectitude of past and future defenses of Haitian sovereignty: "No one will recoil before the sacrifices necessary for the defense of a cause in which one has recognized justice."[39]

But almost immediately after concluding his discussion of the U.S. Revolutionary War, Firmin turns to the "Negro Question" in U.S. history. While giving credit to the United States for abolishing slavery, particularly to Lincoln and the Republican Party, Firmin argues that the U.S. needs to resolve its own issues of race prejudice and segregation before it can truly become a leading force in the civilized world: "Undoubtedly, a problem remains to be resolved, before the American people can really assume the leading role among civilized nations. I must speak of the troubling question of granting Afro-Americans the prerogatives of citizens and social equality, which are so ardently contested throughout all of the South of the United States."[40] Firmin was in correspondence with Booker T. Washington, and he had traveled through the United States, so he was well aware of the unequal treatment of African Americans there. Perhaps because he offers such admiration for U.S. ideals elsewhere in the book, Firmin is particularly scolding when the U.S. fails to live up to them. Firmin further contends that the prejudiced whites of the South are unpatriotic, and that it is they, not African Americans, who threaten the integrity and potential of the country: "It is impossible to create, in white South Carolina or Alabama, for example, the sentiment of national solidarity capable of suppressing racist repulsion. . . . The brain of this descendant of the ancient slaveholders is now held in the tight circle of the superannuated doctrines of Morton and Gliddon."[41] In implicating racial scientists like Morton and Gliddon in this problem, Firmin skillfully reveals that it is not simple regional ignorance that results in race prejudice, but antiquated and irrational dogmas circulated within the United States.

No doubt because of his awareness of the power of prejudice in shaping policy, Firmin feared that the Monroe Doctrine might be applied unjustly to invade Haiti as a black nation. Firmin comments that "the question of race dominates fatally the problem of Haiti's destiny,"[42] and he notes that "after that famous doctrine, what interests Haitians the most in their relations with the United States, is the question of race or color prejudice."[43] Perhaps surprisingly for contemporary scholars, Firmin does not object to the Monroe Doctrine per se; as he declares, "I will gladly repeat the words of the President of the United States, 'I believe with all my heart, in the Monroe Doctrine.'"[44] Instead, he objects to its improper application. For Firmin, the U.S. invasion of Cuba was not in accordance with the Monroe Doctrine because the United States was not protecting the hemisphere against new European intervention (Spain was, after all, an old colonial power), but seizing a part of the Americas for itself. Firmin satirically represents McKinley's intervention as a misguided romantic quest, with the president fancying himself a Wagnerian hero, Lohengrin: "He must have felt that he was a good man, a loyal knight, Lohengrin, protector of the weak, calling for help for desperate Cuba."[45]

In discussing future relations between Haiti and the Roosevelt administration, Firmin expresses great admiration for the president as a man of both action and ideas, with a sense of cautious optimism that the relationship could be one of partnership rather than domination. Commenting that "the true American has never had a fear of pursuing risks, when the prize to be won has been sufficiently worthy,"[46] Firmin predicts that it would be difficult to prevent U.S. incursion if the president set his mind to it, given Roosevelt's forceful character, "a combination of intellectual initiative, of sporting discipline and moral development, all of which are hard to find in the same individual."[47] More philosophically, Firmin observes that Roosevelt has deployed a noble but highly mutable ideal for governing U.S. foreign policy: "le plus grand bien" [the greatest good] (182). Firmin offers a brief mention of the U.S. hegemony over the Philippines as a cautionary example of how difficult it can be to check U.S. expansion under this ideal: "Who could deny that 'the greatest good' for the citizen of the Philippines is liberty, with political franchise, and that he should prefer it to independence under the malfeasance of a national oligarchy?"[48]

This seemingly straightforward rhetorical question has multiple layers of meaning and aptly embodies Firmin's complex views regarding U.S. policy. At one level, it pays tribute to the "greater good" effected by the U.S. intervention. At another, the possibly ironizing quotes around "the greatest good," as well as Firmin's sense that the U.S. intervention cannot be effectively "denied," suggest the dangerous inevitability of intervention under those idealistic auspices. Firmin also makes clear that this "greatest good" is problematic because it comes at the price of independence. What would make U.S. intervention so potent and dangerous was that Roosevelt possessed both great military force and an idealistic narrative to justify use of that force. In the context of Haiti, the last phrase—"independence under the malfeasance of a national oligarchy"—seems a jab at the Haitian government that had sent him into exile, which he perceived as a corrupt oligarchy itself. In this light, Firmin's cautionary citation of the Philippines suggests that if Haitians do not maintain an effective government and military presence for themselves, the United States will have not only the military means but the ideological justification to invade their nation.

Turning away from specific discussions of Roosevelt and the hemispheric geopolitics of his day, Firmin devotes the second half of *M. Roosevelt* to recounting Haitian history, which he develops in parallel to his previously elaborated version of U.S. history. Citing each country's revolutionary history and republican origins, Firmin perceives "déstinées dependant" [dependent destinies] (285). Returning to the language of exceptionalism used at the start of the book, he argues that each nation has a responsibility to protect sovereignty in the hemisphere and to share in furthering the development of "le deux Ameriques" (216)—a formulation that echoes Martí's formulation of "nuestra America" (versus "theirs"), but also draws those Americas closer together. Although Firmin observes many continuities in the second half of his book, he also notes the radically different origins of each revolution—a difference that speaks highly of the Haitian patriots. After suggesting that scholars should treat the revolutions in parallel, he also suggests that there should be a degree of "proportion" in estimating the subsequent successes or failures of each nation (287). The founding fathers of the U.S. were highly educated landowners trained in the Enlightenment traditions of humanism and science, and made a conscious choice to leave Europe to found colonies of their own design. In the case of Haiti, however, "one finds all the conditions of those predecessors exactly reversed."[49] The black population of Haiti came from a slave trade that forced people away from their native countries and combined them with foreign peoples, "strangers forced together from diverse places in Africa, often as distant as the space that extends from Portugal to the Ural mountains."[50] Firmin argues that it would be illogical to expect the same results from those revolutions in the long term (287), but that it is a tribute to the Haitian people that they founded a republic under conditions that were the reverse of the privileged opportunities afforded to Europeans in North America. Firmin makes this case not only in order to give proper credit to the extraordinary achievement of Haitian independence, but also to offer a bulwark against claims that the subsequent political turmoil on the island constituted evidence of racial inferiority or an inability of Haitians to govern themselves.

As Firmin moves toward the conclusion of *M. Roosevelt,* he calls for a cooperative relationship between the United States and Haiti, grounded in mutual interest, investment, and shared democratic history. He asserts that neither nation had yet reached its full potential: "But Haiti is nothing more than the leading nation of the blacks and the United States still has not seized its destiny within the Western hemisphere."[51] Rather than abridging Haiti's autonomy, the United States and Haiti should work "cote à cote" [side by side] to develop both their nations and the American hemisphere (478), and should recognize that each has something to offer the other. Haiti, most obviously, needed its sovereignty to be respected, and could benefit from an influx of U.S. investment and capital. In turn, Haiti could provide the United States with an example of black democracy and integrated society that could transform the U.S. South into a patriotic part of the nation once again. Cooperation between African Americans and Haitians would ensure that "the states of the South will be filled with a larger civilization."[52] In this regard, Firmin cites his relationship with Frederick Douglass as evidence of the fruitful possibilities of cooperation between African Americans and Haitians.

Firmin was certainly not the first to advocate for partnering between African Americans and black West Indians—Edward Blyden and Martin Delany each did so as well—but he skillfully placed his proposal in a mutually pragmatic context to make it palatable to a skeptical U.S. audience. Clearly recognizing that expanding the influence of African Americans through such a partnership would offend "les blancs du Sud" [the whites of the South] and thus strengthen the Democrats, Firmin reassures Roosevelt and politically likeminded readers that black solidarity, enhanced by a Haitian influence in the United States, would solidify the legacy of Lincoln and guarantee the future success of the Republican party. Such astute awareness of the internal complexities of U.S. electoral politics shows not only Firmin's considerable (albeit optimistic) acumen, but also the wide range of rhetoric he employs to solidify a U.S.-Haitian partnership. In the closing pages of his book, Firmin argues that an intervention would be contrary to the interests of the United States, cautioning that one must balance "the benefit of such acquisition . . . in comparison with the considerable expenditures, in human lives and in money."[53] Beyond cautioning the U.S. reader, he advises the Haitian people to prepare themselves for the possibility of a U.S. invasion, and to remember the tactics and traditions that brought them victory against the French: "Hand in hand, we will press our backs against the slopes of our protecting mountains, putting our shoulders together, united for the common prosperity, as for the common defense."[54] Unfortunately, Firmin's less optimistic predictions regarding the necessity of Haitian defenses would prove truer that his vision of partnership. He may have been correct to note that "Haïti n'a rien a craindre de M. Roosevelt" [Haiti has nothing to fear from M. Roosevelt] (463), but Haiti would have much to fear from M. Wilson, as history would show.

Henry Sylvester Williams, W. E. B. Du Bois, and the Pan-African Conference of 1900

The case of Henry Sylvester Williams is particularly illustrative of the "purloined" gifts of the islands. Owen Mathurin has well illustrated Williams's contributions to Pan-Africanism in a biographical study, but subsequent critical understandings of the movement have still neglected Williams and the first Pan-African Conference, which he organized.[55] Born in Trinidad, Williams trained as a doctor and served his community in that capacity for many years, but gradually turned his attention to political and cultural activism. Influenced by Thomas's *Froudacity* and Firmin's *De l'égalité des races humaines,* he published his first tract, "The People's Case," in 1899, to advocate for Trinidadian self-rule and democratic government. Williams's intellectual life at the turn of the century provides an apt model of the cultural crosscurrents central to my study. Not only was he active within the Anglophone Caribbean communities in the islands and in London, he also corresponded with French-speaking Haitian intellectuals like Benito Sylvain and Bishop James T. Holly (a leader in the Episcopal Church in Haiti). Holly himself was a leader of Caribbean-U.S. collaboration: he worked with Martin Delany to organize a convention in Cleveland, Ohio, in 1854, and argued vigorously for black emigration from the United States to Haiti. Williams wrote to Sylvain to organize the first Pan-African Conference in 1900. He also corresponded with and met Alexander Crummell, pastor of St. Luke's Episcopal Church in Washington, D.C., and first president of the American Negro Academy; Du Bois attended the conference at Crummell's suggestion.

This conference brought together a significant body of West Indian, African, and African American intellectuals to present and discuss philosophical, cultural, and political arguments about the status and future of African and African-descended peoples throughout the world. The roster of attendees was a veritable who's who of global black leadership at the turn of the century. Besides Williams, Du Bois, and Sylvain, the attendees included the famous composer Samuel Coleridge-Taylor, J. F. Loudin (director of the Fisk Jubilee Singers), Bishop Alexander Walters (of the African Episcopal Methodist Church in the U.S.), and Firmin himself.[56] Bishop Walters presided over the proceedings and provides the most thorough account of the conference in his autobiography entitled *My Life and Work* (1917). Participants passed resolutions regarding labor conditions, civil liberties, and black property, including a critique of U.S. segregation.

Du Bois was elected to chair a committee tasked with addressing the nations of the world on behalf of the conference. He co-authored, along with Williams, Walters, and the Reverend Henry B. Brown, a manifesto entitled "To the Nations of the World." It proclaimed that "the problem of the Twentieth Century is the problem of the color line," which Du Bois famously reiterated in *The Souls of Black Folk* (1903). According to Mathurin, this address was signed not only by Du Bois, but also by Williams, Walters, and Brown (70). While it is not possible to recapture all the details of collaborative production that resulted in "To the

Nations of the World," it emerged from the conference as a document supported by multiple sides of the Black Atlantic. Although Du Bois's re-presentation of this idea in his own work is now the most famous statement of the "problem of the color line," it was a shared declaration in its textual provenance, and both Walters and Sylvain described "To Nations of the World" as a collaborative product.[57]

Walters's description of the reception of the conference reveals the singularity of its historical moment. After submitting a petition to the British government regarding abuses in South Africa, the conference officers received a reply from a ministry official named Bertram Cox, Esq., writing on behalf of Neville Chamberlain and the queen to reassure the conference that "she [the queen] was graciously pleased to command him to return an answer to it on behalf of her Government" and that "Her Majesty's Government will not overlook the interests and welfare of the native races" (257). The conference also received official invitations from many London dignitaries, including members of Parliament and the Lord Bishop of London himself (262–63). Walters also wrote that following their circulation of the conference resolution to other black leaders after the conference, the officers received "numerous letters . . . from different parts of the world commending the work of the Pan-African Association and the National Afro-American Council" (263).

Overall, the West Indian presence at the conference was dominant. Besides Sylvain and Williams, contributors included C. W. French (St. Kitts), John E. Quinlan (St. Lucia), William Meyer and Richard Phipps (Trinidad), and George J. Christian (Dominica). Although there are not full copies extant of each of their contributions, the program listings are available, and the very titles reveal that the West Indian intellectuals, as much as Du Bois, were globally minded in their emphases and were helping to develop a greater diasporic black community across varied geographies. French's "Conditions Favoring a High Standard of Humanity," Sylvain's "The Necessary Concord to be Established between Native Races and European Colonists," and Christian's "Organized Plunder and Human Progress Have Made Our Race Their Battlefield" each pointed towards a globalized sense of blackness. Taken together, these presentations, along with "To the Nations of the World," offered a globalized program of black uplift that preceded the New Negro Renaissance and the Pan-African Congress of 1919 by almost two decades.

Given these lively collaborations at the conference, one might expect Du Bois to acknowledge the shared production of this pan-African vision, but that was not to be the case. Du Bois makes a passing reference to the first Pan-African Conference in *Darkwater*,[58] but he never substantively discussed his participation, nor did he describe the contributions of West Indian intellectuals to pan-Africanism. Within his *Autobiography*, Du Bois makes no mention of the conference at all. In reporting on his travels to Europe in 1900, he mentions only his time at the Paris World's Fair, and gives the appearance that he returned to the United States having invented the idea for a pan-African gathering entirely on his own: "I had emerged with a program of Pan-Africanism, as organized protection of the Negro world led by American Negroes. But American Negroes were not interested" (184). Du Bois was similarly reticent about his collaboration with West Indians at the Paris Exposition itself. His award-winning presentation at the exposition on African Americans and their achievements was part of a program organized by Firmin entitled "The Equality of the Human Races," which was intended to illustrate the central thesis of his anthropological study.[59]

Du Bois did finally credit Williams with inventing the term "pan-African" almost 40 years later, in *The World and Africa* (1946), but the tone of Du Bois's description still insists on his legitimacy as the effective originator of pan-Africanism. Du Bois did not even mention Williams by name (a fellow New Negro author noted that Du Bois had a faulty memory when it came time to give credit by name to colleagues, especially from the West Indies[60]), and he minimized the importance of the conference:

> It was not, however, until 1900 that a black West Indian barrister, practicing in London, called together a Pan-African Conference. This meeting attracted attention, put the word "Pan-African" in the dictionaries for the first time, and had some thirty delegates, mainly from England and the West Indies, and a few colored North Americans. . . . This meeting had no deep roots in Africa itself, and the movement and the idea died for a generation.[61]

Du Bois's last sentence could be more properly restated as "died for me for a generation," as he did not return his attention to the matter until 1919, when he called a new Pan-African Congress on his own terms. Williams, Firmin, and Sylvain each worked to spread pan-Africanism in the two decades after the first conference, as will be discussed at the close of this chapter.

Du Bois was not only silent about the conference, but about the West Indies more generally throughout his career (save for his battle with Marcus Garvey, which will be discussed in chapter 4). In his *Autobiography*, Du Bois does discuss his family's significant roots in the Caribbean: his great grandfather James Du Bois was a British royalist who left the

American colonies for the Bahamas, where his grandfather was born. That grandfather lived in Haiti from 1821 to 1830 and returned there at the onset of the U.S. Civil War in 1861.[62] Beyond those bare-boned facts, however, Du Bois does not touch on the islands at all: his visits to Jamaica and to Haiti, his numerous encounters with Caribbean intellectuals in New York or at Pan-African Congresses, or even his shared philosophical concerns with Caribbean intellectuals during his lifetime.

Du Bois's silence was likely rooted in a personal and nationalistic stake in "owning" pan-Africanism, a movement that, in his words, should be "led by American Negroes." To be sure, Du Bois's contributions to pan-Africanism were deep and vital, but it is misrepresentation to label him as the "father" of pan-Africanism. A need to maintain that fiction of paternity may have accounted for Du Bois's almost unbelievable silence about the West Indies and West Indian intellectuals in his own writing. Scholars have contributed to this silencing as well. Many accounts of pan-Africanism erroneously cite the pan-African Congress of 1919 (which was called by Du Bois) as the first such gathering, when the conference of 1900 holds that distinction. Tellingly, in the chronological appendix to the newly authoritative edition of Du Bois's *Autobiography,* the editors confuse these two gatherings, and credit Du Bois, not Williams, as the convener of the first Pan-African Conference (248). One hopes this is simply a clerical error, but it is nonetheless troubling that authoritative U.S. accounts of pan-Africanism have edited out the contributions of Caribbean writers. Even Manning Marable, whose biography of Du Bois aims to relocate him within a tradition of global black leftist activism, represents the conference in reductive terms: "Only thirty-two delegates attended this meeting, radical representatives of the black diaspora's radical petty bourgeoisie"[63]—a stunning diminishment of a conference that gathered black intellectuals and government officials from the United States, Africa, England, and the West Indies.

Du Bois's elision, if not erasure, of his collaborative connections to Caribbean intellectuals is all the more notable given his interest in affirming other global ties, such as his links to the European university system (which Paul Gilroy has well documented) or, later, his ties to Russia, Asia, and Africa.[64] Indeed, in his most extensive autobiography, Du Bois dedicates far more time to situating himself amongst European intellectuals than to exploring his early and subsequent exchanges with West Indians, and he discusses his travels to almost everywhere in the world *but* the Caribbean. Perhaps because of Du Bois's complex self-representation vis-à-vis the Caribbean and early pan-Africanists, even the most comprehensive Du Bois biographer, David Levering Lewis, is confused in his handling of the conference and its legacy. Lewis acknowledges Williams's innovation in developing the conference and the term "pan-African," and he discusses the importance of the conference for Du Bois, noting that he "was in the company of racial equals for a change."[65] Lewis also observes that Du Bois was puzzlingly silent about his cohorts at the conference in his subsequent writings—Du Bois "seems to have forgotten about Williams"—but then subsequently credits Du Bois as the paterfamilias of pan-Africanism, commenting that Du Bois returned to the United States "with the satisfaction of having fostered a new movement" (251). Lewis's shifting approach to the West Indian presence at the Pan-African Conference—ranging from recognition of Williams, to tacit acceptance of Du Bois's amnesia, to crediting Du Bois as the emergent force—recapitulates in miniature Du Bois's own reaction to that signal moment in his career. One might rightly claim that, in the wake of the first Pan-African Conference, Du Bois arrogated to himself the cultural capital of representing pan-Africanism, while distancing himself from debts to his Caribbean collaborators.[66]

Benito Sylvain's Global Vision from the Caribbean

Beyond these knotty questions of collaboration and influence, Du Bois was certainly mistaken to claim that the pan-African movement "died for a generation" after the Pan-African Conference in 1900. In the wake of the conference, Firmin, Williams, and Benito Sylvain each worked to encourage the spread of pan-African ideals. As I discussed earlier in this chapter, Firmin's *M. Roosevelt* advanced the case for Haiti as the exemplary republic to lead African and African-descended peoples into the twentieth century. In 1900, Sylvain and Williams attended the Anti-Slavery Congress in Paris, France. In correspondence with T. Thomas Fortune (who later partnered with Marcus Garvey), Williams planned a tour of Jamaica, Trinidad, and the United States to establish branches of the Pan-African Association and, in 1910, he published the first issue of *The Pan African.* In addition, during that interval, one of the most radical exponents of pan-Africanism and black uplift, the West Indian Hubert Harrison (from St. Croix) would promote a wide range of globally-minded, internationalist activism that combined pan-Africanism, the labor movement, and socialist ideology, which I will discuss in chapter 4. Sylvain, for his part, carried forward the pan-African cause in his travels through Africa and in his political and economic writings. Inspired both by the Conference and the ideals of Firmin, Sylvain developed an extensive treatise on the future of African-descended peoples in the twentieth century. Sylvain's *Du sort des indigènes dans les colonies d'exploitation* [On the fate of indigenous peoples under colonial exploitation] (1901), along with what Firmin published in exile in the wake of the conference, provided a crucial line of continuity between nineteenth-century pan-African thought (of both the U.S. and the Caribbean), and the much-acknowledged flowering that would emerge in the New Negro Renaissance. In fact, the comparative anthropological and political works of Firmin and Sylvain presaged the postcolonial discourse that would emerge during the 1960s, as they diagnosed and classified the effects of varied colonial practices throughout the non-Western world. As much as Du Bois is rightly credited for his role in rethinking the centrality of Africa to geopolitics (especially in *The World and Africa* [1946]), he was relatively silent during most of his career on the full range of geography that we would now term the Black Atlantic, especially in comparison to Sylvain and Firmin.

Sylvain, in particular, was committed to comparing the experiences of colonized peoples in Africa with those in the Caribbean and Latin America. Toward this end, *Du sort des indigènes dans les colonies d'exploitation* builds upon Firmin's anthropological argument for the equality of human races to analyze the history of U.S. and European colonization of Africa and the American hemisphere. Maintaining a commitment to Firmin's anthropological, positivist perspective on race, Sylvain positions himself in this volume as a defender against the "calmonié" [calumny] of black inferiority. Sylvain's study offers a series of comparative histories exploring European and U.S. colonial practices, with particular emphasis upon how they have systematically suppressed the potential of African-descended and indigenous peoples in their colonized territories. He classifies colonizers into three categories: "(1) conscious enslavers . . . [who] are vampires more or less disguised as men; (2) unconscious enslavers who, without mistreating the indigenous out of prejudice, intend to keep them perpetually in the condition of social inferiority; (3) the rare apostles of true civilization, who have the just and generous conception of the role of colonizers."[67] Perhaps the sharpest barb in this critique, beyond the vampiric comparison, is the suggestion that colonizers who support systems of social inferiority are nonetheless "enslavers" just as are those who are explicitly exploitative in their systems.

In comparison to later postcolonial critics such as Frantz Fanon, Sylvain was not only sanguine about but insistent upon the value of some degree of assimilation. Recognizing that a refusal to allow African-descended peoples access to tools of uplift and education would relegate them to subservience or to the status of "une souvenir ethnographique" [an ethnographic souvenir] (253), Sylvain is emphatic that colonizers not withhold their resources from the colonized: "Pour bien coloniser, il fault civiliser" [in order to colonize well, one must civilize] (327). At the same time, Sylvain skillfully suggests that the task of "civilizing" also applied to the colonizers themselves. "Pour bien coloniser, il faut civiliser," is an ambiguous maxim because of its grammar: who is to be civilized, the colonizer or the colonized? Indeed, when Sylvain enumerates the vices that "civilisateurs" need to extirpate, he lists some of the expected tropes applied to native peoples, such as "backwards or barbarous customs" and "ignorance," but also "pride" and "greed"—traits associated with the colonizers, which they need to purge from themselves (327).

Much like Firmin, Sylvain drew upon positivist science and evolutionary theory to defend equality and to counter the racist science of Herbert Spencer. Sylvain's rebuttal of Spencer anticipated Du Bois's refutation in *Dusk of Dawn* (1940) by almost forty years. Rebutting Spencer on his own Darwinist terms, Sylvain argues that recognizing the equal rights of all peoples is a necessary step in humanity's evolution. To attempt to stop this process is both unethical and unnatural: "Civilization is the state of evolution, an essentially dynamic state, which permits organized societies to ensure the moral perfection of man."[68] Consequently, for Sylvain, color prejudice is not only irrational, but also an impediment to the evolution of world civilization: "Therefore, what is the obstacle that hinders the application of these principles of equity and of wisest politics? The most stupid and hateful of social prejudices: what we call the prejudice against color."[69]

Sylvain used the United States as a primary evidence of how color prejudice inhibits progress. He mentions Stowe in his study to remind his readers that the debilitating effects of slavery have already been well established: Stowe "has sufficiently dramatized the horrible scenes of slavery that we can cease to insist on the depressing effects of servitude."[70] Sylvain cites Douglass's writings extensively, notably his struggle with the "slave breaker" Covey in his *Narrative,* to demonstrate that degradation is a reversible process. Moreover, he uses Douglass's ascent as evidence that there is a bounty of potential within African Americans, West Indians, and Africans that ought to be developed. While crediting Douglass as "the greatest orator from the United States" Sylvain wonders what he would have been able to achieve "if instead of having spent the most fertile years of his youth in the heart of slavery, he had been sent to the University of Cambridge, Oxford, or West Point."[71] Sylvain thus argues that the segregationist tendencies in white colonialism reveal a fundamental hypocrisy: if U.S. and European whites were really so confident of black inferiority, then they would not feel obliged to bar the way to higher education or other opportunities. The fact that they uphold those barriers shows that white colonizers are more dedicated to suppressing civilization than to spreading it: "The fears of the civilizers give the lie to their promises."[72]

As Sylvain's case draws to a close, the United States becomes more fascinating for his vision, for it embodies extremes of opportunity and oppression without equal in his experience—an observation that will recur in many Caribbean authors' writings about the U.S. Sylvain extensively describes the means by which southern states, post-Reconstruction, tried to suppress black votes—physical intimidation, poll taxes, literacy tests (418–19)—all of which show a fear of black political action, rather than a faith in African Americans' racial inferiority. Sylvain also notes that the United States is the only nation in the world with a substantial number of lynchings—a shameful case of American exceptionalism: "Nowhere in the world manifests a character of violence more hateful than the United Sates: lynchings, which occur almost daily, with scenes of incredible savagery."[73]

Sylvain struggles to explain how such savagery in the South could coexist with a body politic that also acknowledges the national importance of figures like Washington and Douglass. The best explanation he can offer is that the South was not founded by religious men or by descendants of the Enlightenment, but "by criminals, by freed or escaped convicts, and by prostitutes" (420)—a theory that, while not wholly correct, effectively renders the white South, not African Americans, as the problematic "other" that the United States must struggle to assimilate. Even with these criticisms, Sylvain argues, perhaps overly optimistically, that most of the United States, which had previously consigned African Americans to slavery, had come to embrace them as citizens: "In a generation, contact with Americans has made them into citizens."[74] Sylvain marvels at the paradox that, while racial violence is subjugating blacks in the U. S. South, African Americans and Africans are gathering in New York City to learn from American democracy: an "assembly of Africans comes, to the heart of New York, in a popular meeting room aimed at teaching American democracy, to vindicate the rights of citizens."[75]

Du Bois and other writers during the New Negro Renaissance would explore this contradiction in detail, positing Harlem as the "Zion" in the midst of a nation steeped in color prejudice, but Sylvain's prescient account of the twinned opportunities for racial progress and racist suppression in the United States reveals his awareness of a complex dialectic that would continue to unfold across the twentieth century. More broadly, Firmin's and Sylvain's texts give the lie to Du Bois's claim that pan-Africanism lay dormant for a generation after the first Pan-African Conference. While the ideals of pan-Africanism reached a crucial flowering in New York during the New Negro Renaissance (and in no small part thanks to the contributions of another generation of West Indian authors, which I will discuss in chapter 4), the seeds were planted collaboratively with writers from the Caribbean.

2 Fear and Fantasy

Haiti and the U.S. Occupation

If the Spanish-American War and the Platt Amendment made Cuba the Caribbean island of greatest contention for the United States at the turn of the century, geopolitical and economic anxieties arising from World War I made Haiti the most substantial focus of U.S. attention in the Caribbean in the early part of the twentieth century. The occupation of the island from 1915 to 1934—an explicit "purloining" on behalf of U.S. business and political interests—provoked an intense national interest in all things Haitian, ranging from debates about the merits of U.S. intervention, to sensational popular interest in voodoo, to ethnographic fascination with Haitian folk culture.

U.S. interest in Haiti in the post–World War I period had important precedents in the nineteenth century. As the first black republic in the Americas (following Toussaint L'Ouverture's defeat of the French in 1798), Haiti served as an icon of freedom, a source of fear, and an object of colonial desire among nineteenth-century U.S. writers. Eric Sundquist has demonstrated how Haiti during that period became a nexus for conflicting imperial fantasies and fears: from the pro-slavery Knights of the Golden Circle, who sought an expanded plantation empire in the Caribbean, to James T. Holly's plans for Haiti to be the "Eden of America," to isolationists who feared that "Caribbean nations would be the cradle for revolutions aimed at the United States."[1]

At the close of the nineteenth century, U.S. struggles with Spain to grasp the remaining parts of the Spanish Empire placed Cuba and Puerto Rico at the center of U.S. occupations in the region, while Haiti remained largely overlooked. A succession of coups between 1912 and 1915 refocused U.S. attention on the island, particularly given the growing U.S. commercial interest in the island's resources and concerns that Haiti would fall into a European (especially German) sphere of influence. After the death of Haitian president Vilbrun Guillaume Sam, who favored political and economic ties to the United States, the Wilson administration sent the Navy to seize control of the island. This occupation provoked intense literary debate and resistance within both the United States and Haiti.

In *Haiti and the United States* (1997), J. Michael Dash carefully examines literary responses to this conflict, and the most striking aspect of this period is the extraordinary range of literature. On the part of U.S. writers, the responses were usually revealing of U.S. fantasies—what the authors wanted to project onto the island—rather than any reliable account of Haitian culture itself. As Dash notes, "Like the Orient, Haiti emerges as an inexhaustible symbol designed to satisfy material as well as psychological needs."[2] From racist travel writings about Haitian savagery, to anthropological accounts invested in the purity of folk ritual, to sympathetic defenses of Haiti in the *Crisis* and *Opportunity,* U.S. writers saw the island as a locus for both dreams of solidarity and nightmares of contamination and miscegenation. For their part, writers from Haiti sought to critique the occupation on similar grounds of purity, representing the occupation of the island not only as an infringement of sovereignty, but as a figurative violation of the national body politic.

Because of political circumstances, the field of discourse about Haiti was highly asymmetrical. U.S. citizens had ready access to the island and publishing opportunities that Haitians did not. The U.S. Navy controlled the island by martial law, censored the press, and imprisoned dissenting journalists for sedition, so Haitian literary resistance existed under severe duress. As a result, the most extensive critiques of the occupation were published outside Haiti or after the occupation ended in 1934, when Haitians could publish their opinions without fear of U.S. reprisal. Consequently, this chapter cannot be as fully reciprocal as I would like. I will examine the Haitian novelistic responses to the occupation at the end of the chapter, but the bulk of the material in this portion of my study comes from U.S. sources. This imbalance does not reflect my own preferences, but the stark inequalities of the occupation. Chapter 5 will examine the broader range of Caribbean responses to the United States that emerged after the occupation ended.

In this chapter I will add to and expand upon Dash's important work by using archival research to reveal the considerable fissures and complexities within the generalized sense of either solidarity or anxiety present in U.S. representations of Haiti. Dash is surely right in his claim that, historically speaking, "if the Haitian revolution was white America's nightmare, it fulfilled the passionate dream of black Americans" (11). At the same time, African American writers like Zora Neale Hurston and James Weldon Johnson disagreed substantively about that "dream" and were conflicted about what Haiti represented, not only among themselves, but also within their own works. By examining the multiple drafts of these writers' works on the Caribbean, their private correspondence, and their personal journals, I reveal complex contradictions that were not explicit in their published works. The insistent revisions that these writers made in their depictions of Haiti suggest just how symbolically and ideologically central the island was to their projective imaginings about the future of the hemisphere. The range of political debates, popular cultural representations, and ethnographic journeys to the region suggest that, for many branches of U.S. literary culture, the 1920s and 1930s marked a time when, to rephrase the words of David Levering Lewis, "Haiti was in vogue."

Before turning to the complex cultural work evident in New Negro writers addressing the island, it is vital to consider the popular responses to Haiti in mainstream media and travel literature during the occupation period, for they reveal the "horizon of expectations"[3] against which one might compare the more complex works. Within cinema, fears and fascination with voodoo gave rise to sensationalistic films, such as Victor Halperin's *White Zombie* (1932), which used representations of Haitian voodoo and the zombie not only as ingredients for gothic cinema, but as a richly metaphoric resource for contemplating issues of sexual control, racial "contamination," and the nature of modern labor.[4] *White Zombie* not only inaugurated a cinematic subgenre (the zombie film), but also initiated the horror trope of the white traveler being vanquished by native ritual and mystery in the Caribbean. As significant as *White Zombie* was, there was an even greater outpouring of popular travel literature and soldier's memoirs about the island during the occupation. With the notable exception of ethnographic literature aimed at an academic audience, travel writing about Haiti almost always fell into sensationalistic traditions. U.S. writers often posited a dichotomized vision of the island: they contrasted the feuding elite, who seemed more European and cultivated than most people in the United States, with the black peasantry, who seemed to embody "primitive" Africa unlike anyone else in the New World.

U.S. attitudes toward either class showed a mixture of contempt and admiration, although the latter sentiment seemed to be used to create a feeling of "fair and balanced" reporting. White U.S. writers, whatever their class allegiances, seemed to find neither the elite nor the peasantry fit to rule. In this regard, Haiti offered an excellent microcosm for comparative political economy, as writers could justify U.S. occupation with seemingly opposing motivations. On the one hand, they represented the Haitian peasantry as too simple, ignorant, and superstitious to govern themselves. On the other, they depicted Haitian elites as too "European" in all the negative senses of the word: decadent, corrupt, fraught with internecine quarreling. In this respect, U.S. occupation emerged as the "middle way" of common sense, virtue, and prudence. Not unlike recent defenders of the U.S. occupation of Iraq, writers claimed that only U.S. intervention would keep the island from tearing itself apart. All of these rhetorical strategies served, as Dash notes, to "justify America's 'civilizing mission'" (22).

The one line of U.S. discourse that took Haiti seriously as a sovereign nation emerged in African American periodicals, letters, and political discussion. Most African American intellectuals disapproved of the occupation and perceived it as a colonialist act, although they varied in their degree of attention to the issue. These authors also sometimes disagreed as to what would be the best means for restoring sovereignty to the nation and whether or not a campaign to restore Haitian autonomy would complement the goal of securing African American civil rights. Although Dash describes the relationship between African American writers and Haitian patriots as one of "instinctive solidarity" (45), some responses showed a concern that Haiti might be both a brother and an "other" with respect to African Americans, particularly when the subject of voodoo arose.

James Weldon Johnson's Advocacy for Restoring Haitian Sovereignty

More than anyone else in the United States, James Weldon Johnson was at the center of public and private discourse surrounding the question of restoring Haiti's sovereignty. Even before the U.S. occupation, Johnson wrote with concern about the political instability in Haiti, anxious the island's troubles would reflect badly on "the Negro." After lamenting that "the only real independent Negro state in the world has not yet achieved stable government," Johnson also noted, "the condition in Mexico [i.e., the Mexican Revolution] stops the ever ready critics from pointing their fingers and declaring that the stage of affairs in the Island Republic is due to the innate incapacity of the Negro for self-government."[5] Johnson went on to mention civil instability in Venezuela, Colombia, Nicaragua,

Honduras, and Guatemala to demonstrate that the political turmoil in Haiti was not a problem of Negro self-determination, but a larger characteristic of the region. In this respect, one sees the risks for Johnson and other NAACP leaders in aligning themselves with the Haitian cause. As much as the island's history as a black democracy and current state as a victim of U.S. imperialism demanded attention, Johnson and his colleagues did not want a systematic identification with Haitian culture and politics to emerge from NAACP assistance and advocacy. Once the occupation occurred, Johnson was highly sought after by all parties for his expertise in addressing "the Haitian question," particularly because of his diplomatic experience (he had served as an embassy official in both Venezuela and Nicaragua) and influential political connections. Johnson was besieged with requests for references, connections, and insights from forces both for and against the occupation. He was in regular contact with entrepreneurs, traders, journalists, and Haitian politicians and strove to find a delicate balance among their demands. For example, Johnson used his connections with the West Indies Trading Company to provide an introduction and garner a presidential audience for a *Chicago Tribune* journalist, James O'Donnell Bennett, so that he could "find out the truth concerning the Haitian situation."[6] Within the political sphere, Johnson wrote to his friend Lemuel Livingston on behalf of Joseph Jolibois *fils,* who had been imprisoned by the U.S. authorities for sedition because of his articles opposing the occupation.

Johnson strongly believed that the occupation was a violation of Haitian sovereignty, particularly after visiting the island as part of an NAACP delegation in 1920. That same year, Johnson published two substantial articles on the situation in Haiti based upon his visit: an extended commentary in the *Nation* and a more compact version in the *Crisis.* Throughout these essays Johnson crafted his rhetoric about the island to connect with the interests of his distinct audiences for each publication. In the *Nation,* Johnson first traces a chain of political connections and interests that accounted for the intervention—one that fits an uncanny pattern of U.S. intervention on behalf of corporations since the Spanish-American War. Positing the question as to why the United States is interested in the island, Johnson offers a clear and succinct answer: because "National City Bank of New York is very much interested in Haiti" (2:207). With extremely careful attention to diplomatic communiqués and legal documentation, Johnson shows the essential features of the occupation to be impositions that Americans would never tolerate on their soil and should not in their name, including martial law, forced labor (the *corvée*), and the holding of the Haitian government's finances in receivership by National City. Most pointedly, he describes the situation as "government of, by, and for the National City Bank" (2:218) and notes that the United States was persecuting rebels who were quite similar to our founding fathers: "The America of the Revolution, indeed the America of the Civil War, would have regarded Charlemagne [a 'caco,' or local guerilla leader] not as a criminal but as a patriot" (2:214). Drawing on more recent history, he compares the U.S. actions on the island to Germany's invasion of Belgium that started World War I (2:227).

As thorough as Johnson's political critique is, his commentary on Haitian culture and its collision with American color prejudice shows the deepest investment of his rhetorical energies. Johnson saw Haiti, even in its turbulence, as providing a useful foil for contrast with the problems of racism and discrimination in the United States. Johnson praises the urbanity of the Port-au-Prince elite—"Cultivated people from any part of the world would feel at home in the best Haitian society" (2:225)—and he contrasts the conditions of rural Haitians with the low standard of living for the U.S. underclass. In villages, "An aesthetic touch is never lacking—a flowering hedge or an arbor with trained vines bearing gorgeous colored blossoms. There is no comparison between the neat plastered-wall, thatch-roof cabin of the Haitian peasant and the traditional log hut of the South or the more wretched American suburbs" (2:225). Significantly, he makes no mention at all of voodoo or other folk ritual, which was an object of fascination for so many other writers, black and white, in their experience of Haiti.

Both in his commentary for the *Nation* and in that for the *Crisis*, Johnson is especially worried about an unwanted American "import" to the island: "Americans have carried American hatred to Haiti. They have planted the feeling of caste and color prejudice where it never before existed" (2:217). Writing in the *Crisis*, Johnson makes a compact summary of the problems of the occupation, and offers an urgent plea to his African American readers for their support, aiming to show them what was at stake for all persons of color in the fate of Haiti. He begins by recognizing that the troubled political history of the island made it tempting for African Americans to keep their distance from the subject: "Even intelligent colored Americans are apt to feel indulgent or embarrassed over the subject of Haitian history" (2:245). He reminds his readers, however, "It is a people of Negro blood, who has produced a Christophe and a Dessalines, who have given to the world one of its greatest statesmen, Toussaint L'Ouverture, who have behind them a history of which they have every right to be proud, that are now threatened with the loss of their independence; that have now fallen not only under American political domination, but under the domination of American prejudice" (2:246). In evoking the subtler threat of prejudice, as opposed to explicit political dominion, Johnson clearly aims to shift the grounds of argument away from international law and diplomacy (as he focused upon in the *Nation*) towards the sphere of cultural and racial sympathy for the *Crisis* audience. He comments that "a great deal of this prejudice has been brought about because the Administration has seen fit to send southern white men to Haiti" (2:251), redirecting readers' attention towards a subjugation much closer to home. He closes by rallying his readers to the cause of restoring Haiti's sovereignty, both for the sake of their brethren and for themselves: "The colored people of the United States should be interested in seeing that this is done, for Haiti is the best chance that the Negro has in the world to prove that he is capable of the highest self-government" (2:252).

Over time, Johnson's criticism of the U.S. occupation grew more intensive, and he eventually engaged publicly the spectacular allegations of cannibalism and voodoo that many U.S. writers saw as justifying the "civilizing" presence of the United States. In a speech to the NAACP in 1924 entitled "Haiti and Our Latin American Policy," he sought to unveil that the "real reasons" for the U.S. occupation were "dollars and cents," as opposed to the national "rationaliz[ation]" of the campaign as "true benevolence and unadulterated altruism." Johnson argued that the claim that German business interests needed to be seized for national security was merely an excuse to advance U.S. economic interests in the region, and exposed as a libel the claim that Haitian "anarchy," "barbarism," and "cannibalism" necessitated Anglo-American intervention. With a wry turn, Johnson contrasted allegations of cannibalism with the actuality of lynching atrocities on U.S. soil, and posed almost a Swiftian rhetorical question: "Which is worse, to eat a human without cooking him—as is alleged to be the custom in Haiti—or to cook him without eating him—as is known to be the custom in Mississippi?"[7]

Along with this public advocacy, Johnson assisted Haitian patriots by advising and encouraging them in a long series of private correspondence throughout 1920 and 1921. Johnson's private exchanges with Haitian patriots opposing U.S. occupation were much more complex and extensive than his published writing on the subject. Over the course of little more than a year (March 1920 to March 1921), Johnson corresponded with dozens of Haitian intellectuals, professionals, and government officials, and even penned a manifesto for the Haitians to use to rally support for their cause. Within these letters, Johnson echoed his public commitments to Haitian sovereignty even as he sought to establish some distance between the work of the NAACP and that of the Haitian patriots. Upon his departure from Haiti and after his return to the United States in the summer of 1920, a number of Haitians, including Bertomieux Danache, Etienne Mathon (a former secretary of state), and Arthur Holly (a doctor and specialist in voodoo), wrote to Johnson to express gratitude for his visit[8] and to alert him to the fact that U.S. control on Haiti was tightening, rather than loosening. In a letter of 7 August 1920 Danache informed Johnson that the U.S. occupation government had dismissed the ministers of state, transferred the national bank to a U.S. bank, and was attempting to pass a law restricting Haitian property rights.[9]

In August, Johnson wrote back to his Haitian contacts to encourage them on multiple fronts. Johnson reassured Georges Sylvain (a lawyer and poet who was extremely active in Haitian politics) that he had been in conversation with Senator Warren Harding and that "a change was at hand," and he told Danache to advise President Philippe Dartiguenave to "stand firm."[10] In September Johnson took an even more active step towards partnership with the Haitian cause by helping to develop, along with Mary White Ovington, an NAACP auxiliary to help Haiti, the Friends of Haitian Freedom.[11] Johnson wrote to Emile Faubert, of the Haitian Consulate in the United States, to lay the groundwork for this cooperation.[12] It was clear in his correspondence that Johnson perceived advocacy by the NAACP on behalf of their Caribbean brethren to be a crucial milestone among organization's achievements. He confided to Ovington, "It looks as though the trip to Haiti will result in one of the biggest things the Association has ever done. It appears as though we are going to have the pleasure of seeing a consummation of our efforts."[13] In subsequent letters that month to Sylvain and Mathon, he reassured them that a government investigation of military abuses in Haiti was about to commence. Johnson also exhorted: "This is a critical moment for Haiti. Now, if ever, all the Haitians need to unite and stand together for the good of their country."[14] With statements like these, Johnson made clear that, for all the help he believed the NAACP could provide, the Haitian citizenry itself had the right and responsibility to take charge of restoring their nation's sovereignty.

The question of what role African Americans in the U.S. should play in advocating for Haiti would become an increasingly tricky issue within Johnson's correspondence. The Haitian response to Johnson's advocacy was quite enthusiastic, perhaps overly so for Johnson. The lawyer Alfred Henriquez informed Johnson that Haitians had read his articles and embraced him as their most prominent U.S. advocate: "Your name runs on all lips."[15] Arthur Holly was even more lavish in his praise: "Your name is mentioned as that of a Saviour. On every tongue and in all circles 'Johnson' is likened to that of a second Toussaint L'Ouverture, to that of a Messiah."[16] Johnson never directly responded to this elevated positioning by his Haitian friends, but the change in tenor in his subsequent correspondence with them was nonetheless revealing. While still avowing his commitment to the Haitian cause, Johnson came to emphasize more and more the need for self-reliance on the part of Haitians, distancing himself from a messianic role. On 5 November 1920, Johnson sent pamphlet versions of his articles from the *Nation* with letters to Louis Borno (the newly elected President), Georges Sylvain, and Chrystome Rosemond that strongly encouraged them take charge of their advocacy and to set up a delegation to visit Washington, D.C., to plead their case: "The whole Haitian question has now been opened up. The American people know the facts. The government is on the defensive. It is now necessary for Haitians themselves to finish the work that has been commenced. They can now make their voice heard. . . . The elections are over; the Republican party is victorious. This gives Haiti a great opportunity, but the Haitians themselves must take advantage of it."[17] After corresponding with Pauleus Sanon (former secretary of foreign affairs) and Borno about the details of the delegation, Johnson made clear that he saw his current role as ending: "As I said in a former letter it is now for the Haitians themselves to achieve the victory. I have done what I could."[18]

Johnson's role was not at an end, however, and further complexities would change his relationship with the Haitian patriots. The government investigation (the Mayo Commission) failed to issue any punishment for those who had committed abuses against the Haitian civilian populace, and the expected progress towards restoring sovereignty from the Harding administration never materialized. Perhaps in response to his sluggishness, some Haitians began to correspond with Johnson about eschewing overt diplomacy for more clandestine means of resistance, and these suggestions seemed to alter Johnson's subsequent conversations with his Haitian friends. In an extensive letter of 10 December 1920 Holly described the failure of the Mayo Commission to redress U.S. abuses, and he proposed a more vigorous partnership between the NAACP and Haitian patriots. In a shift from the republican language of patriotism and sovereignty circulating in previous correspondence with Johnson, Holly suggested that future cooperation proceed in terms of blood allegiance and African unity. Addressing Johnson as "Brother," Holly argued that "self-determination" ought to follow racial lines in Haiti, and he deployed a rhetoric of racial authenticity to discredit centrist movements on the island. Holly argued that Johnson and the NAACP needed to make a distinction between members of the domestic Haitian ruling class who were "blancophiles" and the "true Africans." Holly questioned whether or not it would be wise, once sovereignty was restored, for blacks and whites to have "equal rights" on the island, because so much had been denied to the Africans that they deserved special redress for their suffering. At the end of the letter, Holly took Johnson into his utmost confidence, inviting him to join a different kind of brotherhood:

> I have a secret Order being S.I., the mission of which is to direct the secret forces of the people towards a happier goal. I have been counselor of many Presidents. In other words, I am an "occultist." If you have had time to read my book on the Voudo cult, you must have gotten to that conclusion. I am now actively working toward any alliance with Afro-Americans. . . . Surely you cannot refuse to be of help towards anything tending to ameliorate the condition of colored people, whether in the U.S. or in Haiti.[19]

In broaching the idea of uniting political resistance with voodoo, Holly was certainly not advocating for anything radically new in Haitian history. As C. L. R. James details in *Black Jacobins,* folk ritual was central to the revolution. For Holly to suggest that Johnson and his brethren support not only a political wing of the NAACP in Haiti, but also extend assistance to a secret voodoo society, was an invitation without precedent, however. It would certainly do nothing to strengthen the position of African American advocacy in the United States for them to ally themselves with Haitian spiritualism. Indeed, many Haitian intellectuals had tried to distance themselves publicly from these rites, as they played into dominant U.S. and European assumptions about primitivism on the island. Johnson responded to Holly with his typical tact, but with a note of polite demurral and silence on the subject of voodoo: "I have your most interesting letter of the 10th and I have noted very carefully all of the information which you have given me."[20] Johnson did not discuss secret societies or voodoo in response to Holly, and the tone of his letter (and of others to Haitians in the wake of Holly's proposal) shows more and more distance between his U.S. advocacy and Haitian solidarity movements. While Johnson had previously made clear that the Haitians had a culminating role to play in securing their sovereignty, he now made explicit the sense that they had a greater responsibility for this activism than their U.S. allies, perhaps with the implication that they should not expect salvation from the NAACP. He wrote to Holly that "the whole Haitian situation is now more in the hands of the Haitians than in the hands of their friends in the United States."[21] On the same day that he wrote back to Holly, Johnson communicated the same point to a number of his other Haitian correspondents.

Because neither Harding nor the Mayo Commission had provided any resolution to questions of military abuses and plans for restoration of sovereignty, Haitian patriots would go on corresponding with Johnson throughout the following year (1921), but Johnson continued to distance himself further from the cause. The subject of voodoo arose only once more, and Johnson met it with an even more interesting silence than in his letters to Holly. Sanon wrote to Johnson in January of 1921 to ask if he could write an article to repair the association of Haitian resistance with voodoo that had been drawn in the U.S. press:

> I would like, before closing this letter, [to] call your attention upon a matter which is of great concern for us since a few days. With the return to the United States of the Naval Court of Inquiry we have come by reading some New York papers, to the impression that a campaign of detraction has started against the Haitian people by charges of voodooism and even cannibalism. . . . May I rely upon you for a word in "The Nation" in order to make justice of this bad history?[22]

Perhaps because of what Holly had suggested, Johnson did not volunteer to write such an article, nor did he even address the request in subsequent correspondence with Sanon. It would be an overstatement to say that the issue of voodoo permanently drove Johnson away from pursuing solidarity with the Haitians, as he did maintain regular correspondence and write pieces of advocacy throughout 1921, but he clearly did not return to the same level of involvement that he had prior to Holly's proposal.

Johnson subsequently shifted the focus of his advocacy to public venues (such as a letter to the *Chicago Tribune*[23]), or correspondence within U.S. government channels.[24] When Johnson did write to Haitian intellectuals during the remaining occupation, he was still supportive of their cause, but he did not engage in private discussions, preferring instead to advocate via platform and manifesto. For example, in August and September of 1921, he corresponded with Sanon and Sylvain regarding the case of Jolibois, the imprisoned journalist. While assuring the Haitians that they could count on support from the NAACP and other U.S. advocacy groups like the Society for the Independence of Haiti (formed at the *Nation* on 2 August 1921), Johnson's rhetoric encouraged them to establish their own solidarity and restore their own sovereignty. One might say that Johnson eschewed the language of interventionist partnering—he declined to return to the island and refused suggestions of serving as a representative there—in favor of inspirational partnering. Writing to Jolibois, he advised him to embrace his struggle: "I wish to say finally that the men who have suffered and sacrificed for Haitian liberty should feel that they have been privileged."[25] He wrote to Sanon that "we trust that all Haitians will unite in this matter in which no sacrifice can be too great."[26] This inspirational idea reached its strongest tenor in a manifesto that he sent (via his friend the journalist Ernest Gruening) to be circulated among Haitian patriots. The address extended Johnson's calls for unity and sacrifice, exhorting Haitians to complete the task of regaining their sovereignty immediately:

> This is a critical hour for Haiti. What her future and destiny shall be hangs in the balance. The time demands wisdom, courage, the burying of factional strife, the sacrifice of personal ambitions, and a devotion to the highest ideals of patriotism. As a friend of Haiti, I call upon you to rise to the opportunity. It is time for the patriots of Haiti, for all who love their country, to unite upon a plan and a line of action. . . . Do not be deceived by temporary and expedient advantages. Bear in mind the ultimate future of Haiti and Haitian children yet unborn. The men who will stand today unselfishly, courageously, and with clear vision will be remembered as the fathers of the new Haiti, and there can be a new Haiti more glorious than the old.[27]

Johnson's rhetoric is as much exhortative as supportive, and its central theme offers a charge of responsibility to the people of Haiti, as it unequivocally addresses the second person and asks for "you" to take a stance, and Johnson eschews any mention of "I" beyond his issuing a "call." He clearly and effectively distances himself from the expectation of "saviour" or "Toussaint" that had circulated a year before. Neither is there any mention in the address of explicit help on the island from the NAACP, though Johnson would continue to work in private back in the United States. Part of this rhetoric must have been a function of simple pragmatism. Johnson certainly would not have wanted to give his friends the false hope that he and the NAACP could serve as a deus ex machina. Given the history of sovereignty on the island, Johnson would no doubt want Haitians to maintain their tradition of self-determination by having the primary role in liberating themselves from the occupation.

Johnson's address to the patriots marked the last substantial piece of Haitian correspondence from him. For the remainder of the occupation, Johnson would remain relatively silent. Rosemond and others wrote back later in 1922 to update him about their activism, but they did not receive a response.[28] On the eve of the end of the occupation, Jolibois wrote to Johnson for help, but Johnson politely referred him to his successor at the NAACP, Walter White: "I think it would be better if you wrote directly to Mr. Walter White, who is the executive secretary of the NAACP."[29]

I have taken care to trace the evolution and modulation in Johnson's public advocacy and private advice because they embody some of the key dissonances at the heart of Haitian–African American contact. Johnson's dedicated advocacy during 1920 and 1921 shows his solidarity with the Haitian cause, as well as his political acumen in assisting his Haitian friends. At the same time, it became clear in his correspondence that there were both personal and strategic reasons for Johnson and the NAACP to maintain a recognizable distance from the vernacular sides of the Haitian struggle. That the eloquent and productive Johnson was so silent on the subject of voodoo, which was clearly the most commonly circulating subject surrounding Haiti in the popular press, suggests his concern at the idea of African American "brotherhood" being taken a step too far in that direction.

The "Magic" of Haiti: Voodoo and Dance as Cultural Resources

During the occupation, most discourse on Haiti in the United States focused not on political questions but cultural ones, especially those pertaining to folk and voodoo cultures, which seemed both desirable and threatening gateways towards new spiritual and unconscious realms. The ur-texts for considering voodoo practice during the occupation were Blair Niles's *Black Haiti* (1926) and William Seabrook's *The Magic Island* (1929). Niles's layperson travel approach to the narrative broadly engaged issues of culture and politics on the island, while Seabrook offered a much more thorough ethnographic account of voodoo practices, in such detail that Haitian writers like Philippe Thoby-Marcelin have cited him as an influence upon their work.

Niles's account of her Haitian travels anticipates Hart Crane's and Waldo Frank's calls for American rejuvenation through contact with the

Caribbean. Niles, in general, writes as a New World Romantic who respects the sovereign history of Haiti, but nonetheless perceives it as a cultural resource from which the United States should not separate itself. She critiques the Monroe Doctrine as "high handed in form and spirit" and calls instead for Haiti, the United States, and other nations born of revolutions to forge a "brother Federation of the American Democracies."[30] Niles also devotes considerable energy to disabusing readers about rumors of cannibalism and savagery on the island. She derides Americans as the credulous and superstitious ones in the Haiti-U.S. relationship, for their belief in "the sinister Haiti of distorted tales of cannibalism, of the inflated myth of the 'goat without horns,' of the hatred of black for white, of the importance of going armed" (151).

As much as Niles aims to rescue Haiti from the most dire allegations of savagery, it is clear from her narrative that she values the island more for its elemental, "primitive" culture than for its civilization. When Niles describes her first dance scene on the island, she falls into rhapsodic prose, stretching back to primeval history: "Then . . . it is no longer the year 1925. It is the sixth day of creation; the day when 'male and female He created them.' And under the high moon, we watch the creatures of creation dance. . . . They dance to the long voodoo drum, the voice of which so profoundly stirs them that its use has been made illegal" (22). Perhaps because of her awareness of the martial laws against folk practices (the occupation government had banned them, fearing that they would incite violence and revolt), Niles is elegiac as she observes the dances: "Soon there will be no longer on this aging planet any such innocent dance of creation" (29). Given Niles's emphasis on folkways, she laments the cultural transformations wrought by the United States more than the occupation itself: "It is all important that Americanization should stop with order and science; it must not stifle the song in hearts that yet remember how to set life to music. For that is their priceless gift. No other race has created a joyous heaven" (154).

Niles devotes her most excessive and romantic rhetoric towards a racialist celebration of Haitian culture. She compares the "denatured African" of the United States unfavorably to the "singularly vital" African of the island (102) and even declares that the true spirit of Africa, "violated" by European colonization, has been reborn in Haiti: "The god said that Africa was not to be broken, not to be annihilated, but that she would re-live, there where the expedition was come to an end. She would be young and strong and more invincible. For what after all mattered the place where the children were going to create a new country!"

(131). With this optimistic language regarding Haiti's "gifts" and regeneration, Niles echoes the traditions of Romantic racism, but with a sense of exceptionalist projection onto Haiti that would come to characterize almost every U.S. writer's approach to the island, whether celebratory or critical.

In contrast to the rhapsodic celebration of Haitian folk culture in Niles's writing, Seabrook crafted a comparatively measured study of voodoo traditions and spirituality in *The Magic Island.* Relatively silent on the question of the occupation itself, though critical about the importation of racial prejudice to Haiti,[31] Seabrook, like Niles, rejects the horrific stereotypes emerging in the popular media about the island. He refutes the claim that cannibalism is part of voodoo, attributing this belief in the U.S. to "a misleading tale current among the white Americans in Haiti" regarding three deceased marines. Seabrook specifically explains that the one sect that uses human bodies in its rituals, the *cultes des morts,* is an unorthodox group feared by other Haitians, and that "this *culte des morts* practices neither human sacrifice nor murder, but molests only the dead" (321). Drawing comparisons to witchcraft in medieval Europe, Seabrook argues that such sorcery is not the primary spirituality of the island, but a "twisted by-product" of an otherwise beautiful religion: "Voodoo in Haiti is a profound and vitally alive *religion*—alive as Christianity was in its beginnings and in the early Middle Ages when miracles and mystical illumination were common everyday occurrences . . . Voodoo is primarily and basically a form of worship" (12). He places the apparently strange ritual of possession by a *loa* and frenzied dancing into a broader context, drawing comparisons to the rites of Dionysus and Adonis and to David's celebrations in the Old Testament: "No need for me to insist here on the absolute subjective reality of this phenomenon. It has been common to all religions during periods of deep, mystical faith" (41). Seabrook echoes Niles in justifying Haitian practice with damaging commentary about modernity: "Of what use is any life without its emotional moments or hours of ecstasy? They were reaching collective ecstasy by paths which were not intrinsically peculiar to their jungle ancestors, but which have been followed by many peoples, some highly civilized, from the earliest ages, and will be followed to the end of time or until we all become mechanical, soulless robots"(42). Even as Seabrook rebuts one strain of stereotypical representation—depictions of Haitians as savages—he inaugurates a new strain of cliché about Haiti that will be taken up by subsequent writers: a romanticized image of the pastoral purity of the folkways, which must be preserved, by implication, from the corruptions of modernity. Commenting on the practice of animal sacrifice, Seabrook declares, "Better a black *papaloi* in Haiti with blood-stained hands who believes in his living gods than a frock-coated minister on Fifth Avenue reducing Christ to a solar myth and rationalizing the Immaculate Conception" (62).

If one of the implications of Seabrook's voodoo portrait is that Haitian folk tradition provides a source of energetic folk belief that must be harnessed before the *papaloi* falls into the "rationalizing" mode of the "frock-coated minister," then many other U.S. writers were eager to follow his lead. In this respect, Haiti emerged in Seabrook's and Niles's texts as a cultural resource for rejuvenating the flagging energy of the West—a gesture of some respect perhaps, but with the United States, not Haiti, as the object of concern. Indeed, one might argue that the silence of sympathetic observers like Seabrook, Niles, and later Melville Herskovits on issues of Haitian sovereignty, with a simultaneous interest in capturing Haitian traditions, represents a different kind of exploitation of capital, this time in the cultural realm. Dash notes that even for those writers with a reverence for Haitian tradition, their concerns regarding the United States presence were not political, but fit into a politics of ethnic purity and authenticity: "Their fear that Haiti might become culturally contaminated far outweighed any apparent concern with either the nature of Haiti's problems or how they could be solved" (31).

Is It Good to Be the King? The Strange Case of Faustin Wirkus

If Nile's and Seabrook's works offered their readers a primitivist fantasy of premodern "innocent" culture on the island, the case of Faustin Wirkus provides a more specifically narcissist fantasy for U.S. male readers. Wirkus was a U.S. marine mentioned in Seabrook's text as "the white King of Gonave," a small island under Marine control. Seabrook discussed Wirkus's political and cultural mastery of the island, offering almost a reversal of the Kurtz narrative in *Heart of Darkness*. Seabrook received so much fan mail and requests for information about Wirkus that he and his publisher decided to offer the marine a contract for a narrative of his own, which was cowritten by Taney Dudley and introduced by Seabrook. Seabrook's introduction, unlike his own study, catered quite explicitly to fantasy, opening with an almost Austenian declaration that imperialist desire is essential to masculine character: "Every boy ever born, if he is any good, wants, among other things, to be king of a tropical island."[32]

Wirkus's account of his "kingship" provides a more conflicted view of Haiti than the narratives of Seabrook and Niles. Although he describes the island as a place of Edenic possibility, Wirkus also figures it as a place of sorcerous danger. His first steps on the island show these opposing tendencies. He writes that upon landing at Port-au-Prince, "We simply felt we had been delivered into a land of evil enchantment" (18), but that he also expects regenerative possibilities in Haiti: "One heard, even in those early days, of the mysterious island of La Gonave and other distant places where the natives were as yet unspoiled" (31). With this language Wirkus evokes a "New" New World discourse, echoing the language of Columbus and other explorers/conquerors. Upon arriving at Gonave, Wirkus marvels at the natural beauty of the island: "It seemed to me that I had wandered into a Garden of Eden entirely out of the world from which I came . . . a Black Eden" (149). Like Prospero, however, Wirkus is intent on transforming the island and making it his own. Rendering himself as Promethean, he describes his first great accomplishment as bringing the gift of fire safely into houses in Gonave via his introduction of the chimney. According to Wirkus, it was said of him, "The lieutenant was a wonder worker—a sorcerer" (78). Even more prophetically, the queen of the island, Ti Memenne, says to him, "If the *bon Dié* wills, I may tell you that you will one day come here to stay and rule" (161). Wirkus then undergoes a voodoo baptism when Ti Memenne declares, "The time has come, now, to-night, when we are to make you the king of La Gonave" (274) and he is enthroned to the chants of "Le Roi, le Roi, le Roi!" (275).

Even as Wirkus embraces his role as king, he makes clear that his partnership with the queen, Ti Memenne, is strictly professional. Indeed, Wirkus seems to avoid the Haitian female body altogether, unlike his colleagues. Wirkus informs readers that many marines used native women as live-in translators, but drops a hint as to other relations in describing them as "sleeping dictionaries" (74). Wirkus, in contrast, orders a native woman out of his house when she misinterprets his request for translation help as an invitation to a relationship. When Wirkus does pursue a friendship with a Haitian woman named Marie, he loses her to a Syrian delivery man who steals Wirkus's gift and offers it to Marie as his own. The author finds this to be a blessing in disguise, however, because Marie takes the present as such a token of love that she marries the man. Wirkus comments, "I am not sure that I was in a mood to appreciate the aid which he had unwittingly given me in a grave situation" (126). These discussions reveal an anxiety about the capacity for Haiti to transform or contaminate the U.S., specifically the U.S. male, through cultural contact and miscegenation.

Indeed, Wirkus decides at one point to go on leave and travel back to the United States because, "I felt that I was, as we had a way of saying in the Marines, on the way to 'go native'" (106). At the same time, Wirkus keeps coming back to Gonave, as if he has discovered his true self there. It is only when President Louis Borno orders him to leave, described in a chapter tendentiously titled "Out of Eden," that Wirkus returns to the United States permanently. Writes Borno to Wirkus, "Haiti is a republic. I am its president. It is unthinkable that there should be a kingdom within a republic or a 'king'" (329). Wirkus gives Ti Memenne the last word on the subject in the narrative, however, and her words provide a description of a future reunion that is both predictably paternalistic and unexpectedly erotic in its implications: "You will always be king of La Gonave, wherever you go, no matter how long you must stay away from your children. There will never be another king but you. Not even after you join me in God's banana garden, will you cease to be king of La Gonave" (332). Wirkus subtly depicts "Queen" Ti Memenne as Eve, the fellow ruler of "God's banana garden" in the mystic beyond. Although Wirkus was anxious of too much intimacy with Ti Memenne earlier in the narrative, this conclusion suggests that he was not altogether comfortable settling for a permanent distance from her either.

Haiti as the Valley of Ethnography for the United States

Subsequent U.S. writers showed a similarly complex dialectic with respect to the Haitian body. For writers with an ethnographic interest, such as Melville Herskovits, the Caribbean peoples were an object for scientific consideration, an unspoiled natural resource for contemplating rituals and traditions free from external influences. Herksovits, already distinguished as an anthropologist by 1937 for his work on the Dahomey peoples of West Africa, completed a landmark study, *Life in a Haitian Valley,* based on his field research in Mirebalais. Although critics of the Western anthropological gaze have argued that his approach to Haiti is imperialist in spite of its scientific goals, Herskovits aims to break from (and rebut) previous U.S. interpretations of the island. Indeed, he begins his study with the caveat that readers should discard what they had previously thought of the island. Faulting Froude, Seabrook, Niles, John H. Craige, and Wirkus, Herskovits laments that Haiti has been a victim of "condescension and caricature," "distortion[s] of fact," and "the most striking misrepresentations."[33] Most notably, Herskovits seeks to dispel mistaken and sensationalist accounts of voodoo, cannibalism, and other libels extant in previous texts about Haiti. In contrast to previous studies of Haiti, Herskovits strives to apprehend the island on its own cultural terms, both in its connection to West African cultural traditions and in its syncretic connection to French imperial legacies. The majority of Herskovits's study is not of great relevance for those interested in U.S.-Caribbean literary relations, except insofar as it reveals the nature of the U.S. anthropological gaze and what Haiti represented for anthropologists. Although Herskovits describes Haitian culture as a product of intermixture ("a cultural mosaic" [244]), he is primarily interested in the island as a laboratory control group or an object lesson, a vessel for access to pure cultural material from Africa: he notes, with admiration, that "life in the valley of Mirebalais continues the course it has followed for the past two hundred years" (11). Based on this assumption, Herskovits sets out to trace patterns of continuity by determining the precise African tribes from which the Haitians appear to be descended. Herksovits's use of the mosaic as a metaphor to account for Haitian cultural intermixture reveals his anthropological assumptions about the nature of culture. The image of a mosaic supposes that the original cultural materials have not transformed each other but are fused fragments that possess their original substance. In rebuttal to the dominant metaphor of the "melting pot," Herskovits ambitiously uses Haiti to track down the fragments that have been rearranged in a new pattern in the New World.

Perhaps aware of the need to establish a broader-based connection between his structuralist readings of Haitian history and ritual, Herskovits concludes *Life in a Haitian Valley* with a short chapter entitled "Some Wider Implications" (292). His first comments in this regard are clearly aimed at his professional colleagues, as he offers Haiti as an object lesson to show that Haitians have not "been overwhelmed by European tradition" (297). Moving towards the United States, Herskovits uses Haiti to rebut the claim that black culture is essentially an inferior imitation of white culture, "that Negro music, Negro speech, Negro games, and Negro folk beliefs stem from European sources" (302). Herskovits posits the island as a refutation of such racist truisms: "Once again reference to Haiti is to be made: to the fact that in economic life, in social organization, in religion, in music, and dance, Africa has not disappeared. . . . Cannot the same be said of all areas of the New World where Negroes are gathered in great numbers?" (302).

Herskovits does not draw many tangible conclusions regarding African Americans in the United States from this proposition, but he suggests that considering the African legacy will be crucial for future developments in race relations within the U.S.: "May it not be true that the Negro in the United States has preserved some vestiges of his aboriginal heritage even in outwards institutionalized forms; that in his attitudes, points of view, and characteristic responses to social situations the factors of his dual heritage have not been entirely lost?" (302). One might rightly criticize Herskovits for epistemological presumptuousness—the implicit claim that white anthropologists and other academics hold the key to understanding the African heritage of the U.S. Negro—but his study clearly broke new ground in the 1930s in arguing for both the integrity and the continuity of African cultures in the New World. Herskovits seems conflicted at the end of his volume as to the possibly essentialist implications of his study, and fears that "proponents of programs of action rather than seekers after knowledge" may misappropriate his findings (303). Most pointedly, Herskovits fears that extremists might use his findings to claim that African Americans are inassimilable into the mainstream of U.S. culture because of their African roots and can never be equal citizens. To counter this possibility, Herskovits reminds readers that English, German, Scandinavian, and Polish immigrants all show a "carry-over" of their European heritage in the United States, and he puts New World descendants of Africa in parallel to these groups: "Any distinctively African traits of behavior retained by the Negroes cannot be claimed to make him a unique phenomenon; this merely marks him as a group no different from all the others that go to make up the citizenry of the United States" (304). Although Herskovits never directly engages with the political question of U.S.-Haitian relations, he nonetheless effects a powerful shift by moving Haiti away from the role of cautionary, exceptional example (e.g., a savage country in need of civilizing) towards a normative representation of cultural functions in the New World. If the study of Haiti led Herskovits to argue for parallel cultural capacities and legacies between Africans and Europeans in the New World, then Haiti provided a powerful object lesson indeed.

The Purging Puritan: Edna Taft's "Rediscovery" of Race in Haiti

At the opposite end of the discursive spectrum from Herskovits is the work of Edna Taft. The most prominent travel narrative about the island by a white woman from the United States, Taft's *A Puritan in Voodoo-land* (1938) offers richly erotic imagery of seduction and struggle, sometimes sublimated into accounts of the landscape. As her ship pulls into

Port-au-Prince, Taft observes, "As I lay there I became conscious of a peculiar, insinuating, subtle odor—all-enveloping—that drifted stealthily from the shore, pervading everything. It was an indefinable scent, repellent yet alluring. To me it symbolized the soul of this fascinating, yet frightening, country."[34] This contradictory feeling becomes even more fraught when Taft visits a series of balls with the elite of the island. Her friend Felicité Toussaint explains to Taft that as a single, pretty white woman, she is naturally a centripetal force to be admired and envied in Haitian society: "A white woman—especially an American—attracts our Haitian men very much, indeed. A white skin is nearly irresistible to them. Haven't you noticed the popularity of the paler Haitian women over those cursed with a dark skin? *Eh bien,* these Haitian girls hate you as a rival" (39).

Haitian women consider Taft a rival, in no small part, because her dance card at society events is full and far-reaching: she is comfortable dancing and socializing with men of all colors on the island, which is an aspect of the narrative that would likely scandalize and titillate her readers in the 1930s. Taft, who hailed from a family of former slave-traders and seems, in part, to want to expiate that past via this visit, recalls the criticisms of her racist Uncle Elijah: "'Remember,' he had said, 'if you mix with those Haitians socially, you'll have to shake hands with 'em, eat with 'em, dance with 'em. I think your papa would turn over in his grave'" (43). A matronly American woman also tells her, "I am positive your family would disapprove highly of your friendship with these Haitians. And your father would turn over in his grave. These Haitians are nothing but niggers. Don't you realize that?" (94). With these allegations of racial treason surrounding her, it is all the more surprising, then, that Taft is quite willing to admire the male Haitian body when the opportunity presents itself. Writing of her favorite dance partner, Platon Vieux, she offers a classical description: "He was like a tall, broad-shouldered bronze statue. Phidias or Praxiteles would have gloried in such a model, for Platon Vieux had a splendid athlete's body. . . . Platon's features were fine and delicate; his eyes were a deep cornflower blue, and the sheen of his smooth black hair was like that of a raven's wing" (43). Their relationship never progresses beyond dancing, but Taft's description allows her to maintain a platonic distance while elaborating an aesthetic (though strongly objectifying) admiration. Platon Vieux seems especially attractive to Taft because of the transgressiveness of his beauty, especially from a U.S. perspective. Defying ready categorization both in terms of race and gender, Vieux is neither black nor white (bronze), and he combines masculine strength (his athlete's body) with feminine grace (his fine features, hair, and eyes).

Male writers from the United States would offer a similar admiration of the paradoxical mixture of robust physicality and delicacy in Haitian women, but Taft more often located latent rivalry or hostility within the Haitian female. Although Edna starts to befriend the elite Haitian ladies, she renders them as possessing the latent rage of a black revolution. When dining with a notable family of decaying gentility, the Charmeurs, Taft drops into a reverie during dinner that is as violent as it is abrupt: "It was easy for me to believe *Grand'mère* the reincarnation of one of those murdering blacks who had chopped off white people's heads, burnt white people alive, put them between planks and sawed them in two, during the bloody days of Haiti's horrible struggle to get free from France. . . . It did not require much imagination to fancy that *Grand'mère* wanted to put *me* between planks and saw me up" (100). The ease with which Taft, who is otherwise reaching out in friendship to the Haitian elite, flies into this fantasy, reveals the depths of distrust and associations of racial violence undergirding U.S. perceptions of the island. As with Wirkus, some of this distrust extends even to herself. Although Taft recurrently disparages the sound of voodoo drums in her narrative, taking solace in the sound of church bells instead—"the voice of God chiding the voice of evil" (27)—she finds herself tempted by the "relentless rhythm" (115) of the drumming. Eventually, she fears she will surrender herself to the dance:

> The perpetual rhythmic thumping of the drums, the endless monotony of the chanting, the ceaseless serpentine motion of the haunches, the uncertain flickering of the torches, the sweat-laden, *clairin*-reeking air, the swimming sea of ecstatic black sweating faces—all these finally got under my skin. An almost overpowering desire, akin to hypnotic suggestion, came over me, and I had to fight myself to refrain from leaping among the blacks and dancing too. . . . We stole away silently, but the mad, intoxicating rhythm of the Voodoo drums still followed us. (212–13)

Over the course of her narrative, Taft makes a separate peace with voodoo and comes closer to the measured admiration that Niles and Seabrook had for it as a spiritual system. She acknowledges that "cannibalism is a very rare occurrence" (249) and mentions the presence of human sacrifice in many other world religious rituals—including those of the Phoenicians, the Druids, and the Aztecs—and in the legend of Abraham and Isaac. In a comparison clearly intended to shock her "respectable"

U.S. readers, Taft suggests that consumption of human flesh ("the goat without horns"), when it occurred, was less a barbaric ritual than "a solemn communion of the worshippers" akin to Christian communion (250).

Even with this relatively enlightened approach to the question of Haitian spirituality in the abstract, Taft seemingly cannot help a distrust of it at the personal level. With all of her admiration for Haitian gentility and refinement, Taft nonetheless closes her book with fears about what is inside the Haitian racial stock, particularly the mulattoes: "Fiery Latin and turbulent African blood boiled fiercely in their veins. There was no check to either their mad, carnal passions nor their lust to destroy when emotions of anger raced through their bodies. The insidious climate abetted the heritage of illegitimacy and violence" (371). Although Taft is speaking here in particular of the legacy of racial violence born from Dessalines's massacres, her depiction of Mdme. Charmeur at dinner shows her fear that violence is always lurking under the surface. Indeed, a small episode with a one-time friend of hers epitomizes this doubled dynamic. As she begins her tour of the society balls in Port-au-Prince, Taft befriends, along with Felicité Toussaint, another high-born mulatto beauty, Camille Symphorien. Camille, more than anyone else Taft meets, dismisses the presence of voodoo on the island as the superstitious fears of outsiders, and is a model of Francophilic charm. Taft is shocked then, when Camille steps out of a carriage and accidentally drops an object from under her dress: "What had fallen from Camille Symphorien's pocket was a *ouanga* bag [a voodoo charm to curse or to protect]. . . . Camille Symphorien never spoke to me again" (85).

An Occupier Conflicted: Repulsion and Nostalgia in John H. Craige

A doubled portrait of urbane refinement with dark rituals underneath would become a trope of many depictions of Haiti, particularly in the works of John H. Craige. Craige was a U.S. Marine commander during the occupation, in charge of the domestic police force, and a clear believer in the need for U.S. occupation and "civilizing" of the island. Craige was also the most published and widely disseminated U.S. author describing the occupation. As a Marine commander, he had considerable privilege in investigating the island, and he penned two works in sequence to describe his years during the occupation, *Black Bagdad* (1933) and *Cannibal Cousins* (1934). Throughout these texts Craige offers a predictably exculpatory, even celebratory, account of what the United States had accomplished in Haiti and on behalf of Haitians. In *Cannibal Cousins,* he describes the intervention in Haiti as a "queer, misbegotten experiment in American altruism" and represents the United States as suffering from the experiment: "Those were the days when we were getting ready to save the world for democracy with no profit to ourselves and at a cost that we are still paying."[35]

Like Wirkus, Craige at first revels in his own sense of power, comparing himself to a "white emir" and declaring that to the Haitians, "I was king, sultan and dictator rolled into one. My word was the Law and the Prophets, the Beginning and the End. It came over me gradually, and sometimes took my breath."[36] Like Taft, Craige claims that beneath the veneer of gentility of the island, voodoo lurked at every turn. This belief provides a sensationalist suspense to his narrative—who can he trust? who will betray him?—as well as an implicit sense of the cultural corruption that justifies whatever measures the United States might take, including martial law, censorship, and political imprisonment. In his opening chapter to *Cannibal Cousins,* he explains a fundamental duality of Haitian life, as he perceives it: "In the streets of her capital the impossible and the incredible walked bodily abroad in the full light of day. Cosmopolite and cannibal rubbed shoulders. The silk hat of the savant and the knotted wool of the witch-doctor met in daily intercourse, and each found nothing remarkable in the other" (17). The full meaning of the title "cannibal cousins" becomes clear later, when Craige describes an unlikely pairing of descendants from the great Haitian hero, General Jean Louis Bellegarde. A friend reveals to Craige that two of the general's great-grandsons are present in the street. One is Papa Cadeus, a noted voodoo priest who had just been arrested for murder and cannibalism because of a stash of bones in his home: "Most of these were the bones of children. All had been cooked. Some bore the marks of human teeth" (124). The other great-grandson is Dantès Bellegarde, of whom it "is said that he is to be the next Haitian Minister to Washington, your Capital. Quite a marvelous fellow. Think of classing a man like that with savages. He's come a long from Africa, what?" (145). That Craige devotes such attention to this anecdote—indeed, makes it the title of his book—suggests a desire to implant fear and even a gothic horror in his readers. Tellingly, this kinship does not simply pose a challenge in Haiti for Craige, but seems to extend back to the United States itself, as the cousin to the cannibal is slated to become an emissary to Washington, D.C., suggesting that national contamination of the U.S. is forthcoming.

Given his commitment to fear and horror, Craige provides especially sensationalist accounts of Haitian violence and voodoo. He depicts voodoo sacrifices to the exclusion of any other ritual practice: nothing peaceful or beneficent is ever associated with voodoo in Craige's texts. A friend of his summarizes this vision: "The voodooist believes in a different type of God. The God he worships is a big negro with supreme power, no morals, and an unlimited appetite for rum, women, whoopee, and blood. . . . Many of the voodoo gods like human flesh and blood. Men, women, and children are sacrificed to them, their blood drunk and their flesh eaten" (98–99). In *Cannibal Cousins,* he describes a general eaten by a *caco* (rebel leader) hoping to gain powers via sympathetic magic. The *caco* Benoit is made to say, "How would it be if I could get your courage, your intelligence, your understanding?" (73). The fact that Craige can offer such blithe assertions in the wake of travel writers who have spent more time with folk culture than he (even his fellow marine Wirkus is relatively skeptical about the prevalence of cannibalism) reveals just how much this was part of conventional wisdom in U.S. public discourse.

When Craige turns his attention to the women of Haiti, he is similarly objectifying in his assessments. As in his other descriptions of the "magic" of the island, he finds the Haitian women of Port-au-Prince irresistible, even heart-stopping: "There were women whose lithe beauty brought the heart into the mouth. Blonde and golden, copper and ebony mingled together, clothed alike in the latest creations of Worth and Paquin and wearing jewels that would ransom a king" (*Cousins* 161). Although Craige acknowledges the beauty of the urban female class in Haiti, he seems to regard the female peasantry as little more than livestock: "Rape, I believe, implies lack of consent. I never heard of a case where consent was lacking in Haiti's black belt" (*Cousins* 124).

Craige might have felt some anxiety that his harsh depictions exceeded even conventional expectations, as he shows an awareness that there were other books competing to represent Haiti. His response was to claim more masculine ground for himself and disparage the others (though not by name) as effete and out of touch:

> American writers of books on Haiti, and other foreign countries for that matter, usually formulate their books at home. Then the ambitious author tucks a powder puff in his sleeve and dashes off for a visit to the country to be written about. He garners a few "adventures," picks up some local color, associates

> with the literate classes, reads their books, then goes home to dash off the book he had in mind when he set out. He wants to write a pleasant book. . . . The result is a "lovely book," but a book describing idealized Americans such as the author is familiar with, not real natives of the country of whom he knows next to nothing. (23)

Craige, in contrast, takes special pains to offer unlovely scenes, many of which seem designed to offer violent cautionary tales. He tells the story of a small-town U.S. soldier from below the Mason-Dixon Line, appropriately named Lieutenant South, who enters the military with an overdeveloped hunger for military adventure: "He had been carefully brought up, and was prim, precise and exact. . . . He was better than the average gendarme officer and, at first, he reveled in the life. With a boy's thirst for romantic trappings he bought himself elaborately ornamented boots of Spanish leather and carved holsters of the new, low-necked Cheyenne type" (88). South slowly decays during the occupation, in no small part because of his Manichean puritanism: "He believed in a personal God and a very real personal devil. The drums always seemed to him to be the voice of the Evil One, always booming in his ears, threatening him, tempting him" (89). The drums eventually drive him into violence and madness: "Drums boomed continuously. South heard strange stories of the superstitions of the negroes by whom he was surrounded. The sun began to get to him. . . . Drums were confiscated by the carload but other drums took up the chorus and the booming kept up its rhythmic, interminable throb" (89). South retreats into bouts of catatonic singing of Christian hymns, alternating with violence against Haitians and his fellow Marines, and he is ultimately relived of his command. Although this portrait is in no way flattering of the Haitians, it does suggests the hubristic futility of South's desire to extirpate evil or to supplant the Haitian drums with Christian hymns, with accordingly skeptical implications for the capacity of the United States to transform the island.

On the other political extreme, Craige tells the tale of a marine raised with a progressive sense of equality, whose naïveté with respect to race causes a distinctly different downfall than that of South. The counterpoint to the avenging South is Mike Morris: "Mike belonged to one of those sects that teaches the brotherhood of man. . . . When he was a boy, he went to a fine school where they taught him a lot of nonsense about non-resistance. They were preparing him for a cannibal's pot, although, of course, they didn't know it" (100). Morris is slain and eaten by a *caco* named Papillon. The net result of comparing Morris's and South's cases is a sense from Craige that American ideals—in either extreme—find a common grave in Haiti. This portrait makes Craige's Haiti a very different kind of place than that depicted in the fantasies of Niles, Taft, and Wirkus. Indeed, Craige seems to regard Haiti as a tutor that has disabused him of his previous ideals. Commenting upon his upbringing in a Quaker school, he notes: "The friends taught me that all men are brothers and all races of men are equal in endowment. I left school a believer in the noble but unsound doctrine of intellectual Liberalism which insists that all men lack but the opportunity to rise to equal heights. Experience with savages proved to me that this wasn't true" (128). Craige's "experience" leads him to horrifically racist conclusions about Haitians, including such statements as, "A man who is born with a semi-ape's brain cannot rise in life's competition. That was the kind of brain ninety per cent of the Haitian peasants seemed to have" (133). When combined with his portrait of Morris's death, Craige's racist judgment of Haitians offers not only a critique of what he terms the "Negro enthusiasts" and "negrophile publications" (e.g., the *Nation*) in the United States (*Cousins* 77), but also a justification for the racial system at home. In passages like these, Haiti seems less important to Craige as an exotic space in itself (for whatever end), than as an object lesson to reflect back to the United States.

At the same time, even as Craige expresses confidence in his racial and cultural superiority, there arises in his texts a fear of Haitian power, along with a sense that nothing in his tradition can combat it. When he offends the American-born voodoo priestess Kitty Smith, he finds an *ouanga* left on his doorstep (presumably from her) to curse him. Craige then finds himself feeling "nerves," psychosis, and rheumatism. He consults his library, but neither the great minds of the West—"Freud, Jung, Adler, Kafft-Ebbing"—nor the Eastern practice of "Yogi self-discipline" assist him (*Black Bagdad* 271). Only when a voodoo doctor friend of his, Calide, offers him a good-luck *ouanga* does he recover. Tellingly, upon his return to New York City, he still cherishes the charm, and seems to have made a shrine for contemplation:

> I carefully preserve my wanga.
>
> Its gay silk and beads and feathers are faded and dust-stained now. It looks odd and exotic and it stands on a tall voodoo drum in a corner of my study. There is a big drum, a genuine *Arada* nearly six feet tall. The stains on it are, I was told, from the blood of the Goat Without Horns. . . .
>
> At times, when the light is switched off and the moon shines through the window, they seem less incongruous. I can sit and look at them through half-closed

> eyes and imagine that I can see voodoo altars lit by the lurid glare of smoking torches. I can hear the thump of drums, the shrieks of the crowds and the pattering feet of dancers. Or sometimes, I can hear the shots and blows of Haiti's revolutions. Or the thunder of surf on the white coral reefs. (275)

This closing gesture shows a crucial scene of imperial nostalgia.[37] Craige implicitly laments the discrepancy between the magic he experienced in Haiti and the banal calm of his life back in the United States. He even cherishes a residue of cannibalism—the blood of the "goat without horns"—on his Arada drum. In such passages, the language of the most overtly racist travel writing cannot help but remind us of some of the mystic celebrations of Niles, Seabrook, and Taft. Even for Craige, Haiti ultimately proved irresistible as a space for imaginative projection and rejuvenation: a "magic island," indeed.

Zora Neale Hurston's Sensational Populism in Haiti

Zora Neale Hurston would seem, at first glance, to be a polar opposite to Craige in her writings. Hurston arrived in Haiti not as a representative of the U.S. Marine Corps, but as a prominent African American writer of the younger "New Negro" generation, with extensive training in ethnography and anthropology. Sent by Franz Boas to collect folk songs, rituals, and other traditional practices, Hurston made careful and detailed observations of Haitian voodoo, with great respect for the power of Haitian vernacular culture. At the same time, she showed a sensationalist gaze comparable to that of Craige, and she also emerged as a supporter of the U.S. occupation. Her observations were published as the travel narrative *Tell My Horse* (1938), and the complex cultural and national politics in the volume have consistently bedeviled scholars.[38] To make matters even more complex, Hurston's narrative illustrates a curious dialectic of silence and exposure, as she purports to offer the most intimate details of voodoo culture while simultaneously alluding to secrets that she dare not reveal.

In its overall handling of questions of political and cultural sovereignty, *Tell My Horse* shows almost a reverse emphasis from James Weldon Johnson's ideological approach to Haiti. Whereas Johnson distanced himself from almost any aspect of Haitian vernacular culture in favor of discussion of politics and history, Hurston's writings focused on the folk and their mystic rites almost to the exclusion of any explicit consideration of the political situation on the island. Careful examination of the archival record reveals that this dichotomous perspective in *Tell*

My Horse is deliberate, as the very passages that have caused such debate among critics are the places where Hurston exerted the greatest and most careful efforts at revision. I argue that Hurston explicitly crafted and revised the manuscript to foreground the contrast between traditional bourgeois politics and populist resistance, with the goal of using the example of Haiti to privilege the latter. This perspective has the conservative effect of leaving the U.S. occupation uncritiqued, but it is also radical in casting a skeptical eye on traditional "Talented Tenth" politics. Hurston's complex position is consistent with her contention in other works that it is through vernacular culture, rather than conventional politics, that African-descended peoples of the New World can best keep their traditions and advance their interests. Rather than turning away from her "cultural populism," as Duck argues (142), Hurston's revisions show her desire to use Haiti as a "staging ground" for her populist argument that black elites (whether in Haiti or the U.S.) are, in some cases, as great an obstacle to black uplift and cultural sovereignty as white elites.

The first round of deletions that Hurston made to her typescript of *Tell My Horse* shows the author to be isolating the island as a case study of the problems of intraracial politics. Hurston eradicated reference to whites from her first draft of the manuscript, thus representing Haiti as an entirely black island, where whatever power struggles occur are primarily internecine rather than cross-racial. On the first page of her typescript for the chapter entitled "The Next 100 Years," for example, Hurston originally made mention of "the white colonials" in describing the social structure and caste system of the island.[39] The typescript shows that she crossed out mention of them, and indeed, white colonials do not make any significant appearance in that chapter or elsewhere in *Tell My Horse*. Instead, Hurston grounds her political and cultural reportage on the axis of comparison between the mulatto, light-skinned elite and "the blacks," so much so that, according to Hurston, Haiti has "always been two places" (VII ts., 2). In notable contrast to the heroic celebration of the revolution evidenced in works like C. L. R. James's *The Black Jacobins,* Hurston argues that the elite did not fight for the good of all black Haitians, but for their own class privilege: "They fought only for themselves" (VII ts., 1). Hurston's critique of the Haitian upper classes suggests her desire for a more radical revision of Haitian politics than a simple restoration of sovereignty, which would return the island not to the people themselves, but simply to a domestic elite rather than a U.S. one.

Several of the most substantive early additions to the manuscript foreground Hurston's commitment to a populist radicalism. In diagnosing

Haiti's problems, for example, Hurston first writes, "In the past, Haiti's curse has been her politicians." Her typescript shows a handwritten insertion of "as now" after "in the past," showing that she wanted to ensure that her indictment had current force (VII ts., 2). Showing perhaps the early Marxist leanings that led her to support the publication of *Fire!* with Claude McKay and Langston Hughes (in their earlier, more explicitly radical days), Hurston created a holograph addition to her typescript (found on the back) that, in its embrace of expanded political participation, sounds as if it could have been written by her rival Richard Wright, who would later struggle with these same questions after his visit to the island. Hurston writes:

> They [the new generation of politicians not from the elite] felt that they must do those things which will prove that they deserve their freedom. It was said over and over that they are weary of the type of politician who does everything to benefit himself and nothing to benefit his country, but who is the first to rush to press to "defend" Haiti from criticism. These "defenses" are the only returns that Haiti receives for the money he [the politician] is allowed to squander and the opportunities for national advancement that he ignores or prostitutes to his own advantage. These men [of the new generation] do not want Haiti apologized for. They want to make these apologies unnecessary. So they are now laying the groundwork for greater unity and progress in the future.[40]

Elsewhere, Hurston calls this new generation the true "Race Men" of Haiti, suggesting a desire to realign, rather than discard, racial politics on the island.

Hurston took special pains to revise her manuscript to emphasize that the current Haitian government was in the hands of "the type of politician who does everything to benefit himself and nothing to benefit his country" (VII ms., 5). The president himself, Sténio Vincent, is subjected to fierce, recurrent criticism in *Tell My Horse.* Nearly every passage that deals with the president shows revision and insertion by Hurston, and in each case it is to exacerbate, never to mollify. For example, early in the holograph manuscript, when evaluating the president's representation of politics in Haiti, Hurston inserts the addition, "His lies were that bold and brazen" (VII ms., 8). In a subsequent addition to the manuscript, she amplifies her critique by putting his deception in a historical context, adding, "Like many other Haitian ex-presidents have done" (VII ms., 12).

The few times that Hurston erases criticisms from the manuscript show her to be revising for the sake of respecting the Haitian populace at large or the private life of the president's family. For example, in the holograph manuscript Hurston added a large section covering personal gossip regarding the president's sister, misappropriation of funds, and allegations that he was preparing to flee the country with her under the guise of seeking medical treatment in France, but this was omitted in the typescript.[41] In a broader vein, Hurston asserted in the holograph manuscript that, prior to the U.S. intervention, "there were people who did not have a government of any kind to cover their nakedness so that they could come out of doors at all" (VII ms., 9). Perhaps because this image of nakedness might have been shaming to the people themselves, or because it created an image of an ungoverned populace, Hurston deleted this in the typescript and final versions. In any case, this deletion showed that Hurston did not feel comfortable asserting that the Haitians had no government. Indeed, in other contexts her claim seems to be precisely that the problem was not the lack of government, but the presence of a corrupt and selfish one.

Unfortunately, Hurston did not reckon with the ways such antidemocratic tendencies would certainly not be helped by the U.S. occupation, which spread corruption and nepotism of its own, but it is clear from this and other revisions that she had chosen a different target than did Johnson and the NAACP in examining the island. Hurston does credit the younger generation of Haitian politicians for having more noble aims than those of their predecessors. As opposed to simply preserving a "government," Hurston argues that a new generation is "trying to make a nation" (VII ts., 7). While Hurston is certainly no Garveyite, she invokes the language of nation (with its connection to birthright) to argue for a different vision of Haitian unity. In this light, an ethnographic interpreter accused of justifying the occupation may well reveal herself to be the most radical of all in her claim that the Haitian republic has not yet been the black nation that it could be.

As Hurston redirects the reader's gaze away from the urban domestic elite (the class she blames for the island's current troubles), she also elects to show a very different set of loyalties to the Haitian people, specifically to the vernacular cultural practices from which Johnson and others had shied away, including voodoo. Hurston's crafting of her voodoo scenes shows special care within the holograph manuscript and typescript, and this attentiveness suggests just how important she found these practices to be. The nature of her prose, particularly the materials prefacing and surrounding the voodoo scenes, shows that Hurston's interest in voodoo extends beyond ethnography and into politics. Hurston's revisions to the voodoo scenes also show a remarkable commitment to the supernatural and the miraculous. In many cases she added details to show the efficacy of the voodoo, the effect of which was, in part, to legitimate the practice and show it to be a substantive and valued ritual. For example, in depicting a reanimating ritual, Hurston simply describes the ritual practice in her first typescript: "As he finished chanting this the third time, a stone fell to the floor." (XII ts., 4). On the back, she later added an insertion to reveal the effect of the ritual, so that the full sentence reads, "As he finished chanting this the third time, the body of the dead man sat up with its staring eyes, bowed its head and fell back again and then a stone fell to the floor." This addition makes vivid the embodied nature of voodoo and forces the reader into a more explicit confrontation with the miraculous.

In most of Hurston's revisions to her voodoo scenes, she shows a careful double voicing that draws an explicit comparison between folk practices in Haiti and the United States, but with a critical distance that implicitly rebukes those Haitian practices. By the time Hurston had published *Tell My Horse,* for example, expectations of human and animal sacrifice were already abundant in popular depictions of the island. Consequently, Hurston staged such scenes with particular care. For example, a late addition to her typescript offers a model conversation on the subject of the treatment of animals:

> "Why do you Americans always speak of our cruelty to animals?" the editor of Le Matin asked me. "You are cruel also. You boil live lobsters."
>
> "Yes," I said, "but the people who sell them would not be permitted to drag them by the legs from Massachusetts to Virginia, nor to half-skin them on the way."
>
> "It's all the same," he shied away from actuality and went on.[42]

Hurston's dialogic approach to this question of animal sacrifice typifies her handling of folk practice in much of *Tell My Horse.* Her friend at *Le Matin* is given the opportunity to offer a critique of U.S. hypocrisy in which he points out the pain inflicted by a quintessential American cooking technique, and the fact that Hurston offers him this line indicates her desire to show how the United States is not nearly so "civilized" in its treatment of animals as it thinks. Conversely, Hurston is able to reframe the distinction in a reassuring light by depicting the cruelties of voodoo in exaggerated terms—dragging the animal from state to state or "half-skin[ing]" it on the way. Hurston represents her colleague in an embarrassing light by depicting him as "sh[ying] away from actuality," but that very phrase is also doubled, as it could apply to the U.S. reader as well.[43] One could easily argue that those in the United States who critique Haitian folk practice for its cruelty to animals "shy away from the actuality" of what occurs in the United States with respect to animals (one might recall, for example, Matt Bonner's mule in *Their Eyes Were Watching God*).

Such double voicing is fundamental to Hurston's depiction of Haitian folk culture. She invites the reader to recognize voodoo as something exotic and frightful, but also to understand it as a coherent folk practice that has value beyond being material for horror stories. In this respect, Hurston herself accomplished some "shying away" within her own manuscript, as she deleted some details that would have made the folk practice of sacrifice too explicit for the reader. For example, in one holograph addition describing a traditional folk altar, Hurston crossed out a line in her typescript that specified what she witnessed there: "The place of honor was given to a black stone that was attached to a heavy chain, which was itself held by an iron bar whose two ends were buried in the masonry of the wall. A well used cunette was before the stone that had the same look of age and memory as an ancient gibbet. ~~The dog gasped out his last upon it a little later~~" (XIV ts., 6). The fact that Hurston added this entire scene late to her manuscript shows her belief that she needed to reveal the apparatus of sacrifice to the reader, even as her deletion from that very addition shows her hesitancy to disclose too much. Hurston was similarly ambivalent about revealing details about the secretive and violent voodoo cult known as the Sect Rouge: she appended a lengthy description of the sect to her first holograph manuscript, but subsequently crossed it out.[44]

The vacillation between exposure and secrecy increases for Hurston as she draws closer to more inflammatory issues within voodoo, such as the summoning of spirits, zombies, and human sacrifice. Many of Hurston's additions on these subjects seem to have been as much for the sake of storytelling as for ethnographic correctness. For example, in another ritual scene, Hurston mentions in the manuscript that "there was a whisper that an evil spirit had materialized." On the back of that page, she inserts an extra passage for gothic effect:

> From appearances, this might well have been true, for the face of the man had lost itself in a horrible mask. It was unbelievable in its frightfulness. But that was not all. A *feeling* had entered the place. It was a feeling of unspeakable

> evil. A menace that could not be recognized by ordinary human fears, and the remarkable thing was that everybody seemed to feel it simultaneously and recoiled from the bearer of it like a wheat field before a wind. (XII ms., 5)

With such baroque narrative details, Hurston creates a dynamic of horrific exposure for her readers, one that well suited the horizon of expectations surrounding Haiti produced by the works of Craige and Taft. Indeed, in many textual revisions and additions Hurston seems intent on capitalizing on the dominant impression of Haiti in the United States as a dark and adventurous carnival. On the subject of zombies, for example, Hurston depicts herself as poised on the brink of discovering a horrifying secret that could have destroyed her:

> The two doctors expressed their desire to gain this secret [of the drug that induces the zombie state], but they realized the impossibility of doing so. These secret societies are secret. They will die before they will tell; they cited instances. I said I was willing to try. Dr. Legros said that perhaps I would find myself involved in something so terrible—something from which I could not extricate myself alive—and that I would curse the day that I had entered upon my search. Then we came back to the case at hand. (XIII ms., 14)

In such passages Hurston is undoubtedly playing into sensational expectations regarding voodoo that had appeared previously in U.S. popular culture over the 1920s and 1930s, but she is careful not simply to let the voodoo in her overall narrative be reduced to exotic spectacle. Indeed, even as Hurston details the sensational excesses most likely expected by a U.S. audience—from grave robbing, to human sacrifice, to cannibalism—she makes clear that these are the practices of villainous, renegade sects such as the Vinbrindingues, the Sect Rouge, and the Mondongues. In addition, in true adventure narrative form, Hurston describes the presence of heroic voodoo societies, such as the Societe de Couleve, which is allied with nationalists like Dr. Arthur Holly (who had proposed a secret voodoo partnership to Johnson) and is dedicated to "the extermination of the Sect Rouge and the devil worshippers in Haiti" (XVII ts., 1). Beyond avoiding a depiction of mainstream voodoo as evil, Hurston argued that such sensationalist portraiture was a political strategy of the elite. In the holograph manuscript Hurston added a substantial defense of voodoo before she turned to any details of the practices:

> The politicians, to cover up their mistakes, have also seized upon this device. As someone in America said of whisky, voodoo has more enemies in public and more friends in private than anyone else in Haiti. None of the sons of

> voodoo who sit in high places have yet had the courage to defend it publicly, though they know quite well and acknowledge it privately that voodoo is a harmless pagan cult that sacrifices domestic animals that are killed and eaten every day in most of the civilized countries of the world. So since voodoo is openly acknowledged by the humble only, it is safe to blame all the ills of Haiti on voodoo. I predict that this state of affairs will not last forever. A feeling of nationalism is growing in Haiti among the young. They admire France less and less, and their own Negro patterns more. (VII ms., 12)

Hurston describes how voodoo is a safe object for blame, as it is the province of the "humble," but she also argues that in its association with those classes, it offers a way to break away from a Europhilic mindset.

In her handling of Haitians' imitation of white power, Hurston offers some of her most subtle but resonant criticism. Into the holograph version of chapter XI, Hurston inserted an entire episode that almost uncannily prefigures Homi Bhabha's notions of mimicry and colonial power:[45]

> At Ansa-a-galet I met the black marine. A sergeant of the Garde d'Haiti lived in the house beside mine and I kept hearing "Jesus Christ!" and "God damn!" mixed up with whatever he was saying in Creole. When he became friendly enough to converse, I told him that I had heard him and said that it was remarkable to hear the ejaculations from him. "Oh," he said, "I served with the Marines when they were here." "I see," I replied facetiously, "then you are a black Marine." "But yes," he replied proudly, "I am a black Marine. I speak like one always. Perhaps you would like me to kill something for you? I kill that dog for you!" It was a half-starved dog that had taken to hanging around me. "No, no, don't kill it! Poor thing!" He put his pistol back in his holster. "Jesus Christ! Goddamn! I kill something!" He swaggered. I learned afterwards that he had told all of his friends and associates that he was just like an American Marine because the femme Americaine had recognized his likeness at once. Perhaps in this time he has promoted himself to Colonel Little. (XI ms., 3)

This passage provides one of the best examples of double-voiced satire within *Tell My Horse*. One the one hand, Hurston clearly pokes fun at the pretensions of this Haitian and allows his imperfect mimicry to offer the reader easy comic relief. On the other hand, the nature of the performance suggests Hurston's own discomfort with the violence of the occupation. The fact that this man's English is largely swearing, and that he wants to shoot something (even a helpless dog) to prove his worth as a "black Marine" suggests that the U.S. military presence has offered lessons not in "civilization," but in profanity and gratuitous violence. Hurston never confronts the United States directly, but filters a criticism of male violence (present in most of her work) through relatively safe ridicule of this Haitian other.

Hurston's respectful, if not reverent, portraits of humble voodoo ritual are all the more striking for their contrast with her portraiture of Marine-imitating Haitian soldiers and Francophilic elites. Even as Hurston takes pains to ridicule and critique the government of the island and its bourgeois pretensions (even revising intensely to make her language harsher, bordering on libelous in the case of the president), she is equally committed to faithful, dramatic portraiture of vernacular voodoo customs, bringing to light and valuing a ritual practice that is not publicly embraced. In this respect one might call her text both intensely anti-Haitian, in terms of the political status quo and its government culture, and equally pro-Haitian, in her defense of and privileging of folk traditions.

One of the ways that Hurston sought to support her critique of Haitian self-rule was to suggest that even in its republican state, issues of class division—notably, those between the elite light-skinned Creole class and the rural, folk class of darker-skinned blacks—forestall any true sense of democracy. Although such political analyses are relatively scarce in *Tell My Horse,* compared to ethnographic reportage, they are some of the most carefully edited passages, which suggests that Hurston had a strong sense of their importance. Regarding the question of democratic participation on the island, Hurston at first drafted in her typescript a comparison that depicted Haiti's governance as dissonant with U.S. republican ideals, but then edited it to make a more general (and perhaps inflammatory) indictment of the lack of democracy on the island itself: "Haitian class consciousness and the universal acceptance of the divine right of the upper crust is a direct denial of ~~a republic of the United States variety~~" (VII ts., 2). In a handwritten insertion on the typescript, the phrase "the concept of democracy" replaces the language of "republic."

At first glance, this might seem like a small or even irrelevant change, but I would argue that this revision gets to the heart of Hurston's cultural politics with respect to Haiti. Shifting the language from "a republic of the United States variety" to "the concept of democracy" seems a retreat into political abstraction. Indeed, one may well wonder if Hurston chose not to evoke a direct comparison between U.S. republican ideals and Haitian governance because the occupation itself was highly dissonant with respect to republicanism (i.e., it suppressed it). At the same time, the revised phrase offers a sharper indictment of a more basic failure on the island of Haiti as Hurston sees it: the lack of respect for the vox populi, irrespective of the U.S. presence. Such political comparisons may have an aura of "collaboration" with the occupation, and they do indeed provide a kind of alibi, if not explicit justification, for the U.S. intervention. At the same time, Hurston offers a more radical critique of democracy itself on the island, suggesting, through her vernacular research into the sources of Haitian culture, that the anti-democratic, elitist government has deeper roots that, by implication, pose a more longstanding threat to the majority of Haitians than the U.S. occupation. The crucial issue for Hurston, it seems, is the location of true sovereignty and who has the greatest right to rule. When one considers the distrust of governmental authority present in other works by Hurston (such as her depiction of the horizontal violence and repression effected by Joe Starks in *Their Eyes Were Watching God*), it seems just as likely that Hurston's distrust of the local authorities is grounded in a more radical notion of popular democracy than in simple imperialist designs.

Haitian Literary Responses to the U.S. Occupation

Although Hurston's validation of the U.S. intervention was not shared by the cadre of Haitian writers emerging during the occupation, her attention to folk life finds strong parallels in the tradition of what Dash terms the "peasant novel" emerging during the 1930s and 1940s in Haiti.[46] The homegrown Haitian literary response to the occupation was inhibited and delayed because of U.S. martial law and censorship of journals and publishers, but a vibrant group of young novelists emerged right after the occupation to re-present their nation to the world, and on terms different than those of previous Haitian writers, who had privileged the elite. Jacques Roumain, Philippe Thoby-Marcelin, and Maurice Casseus each penned seminal novels that gained world attention for their participation in an emerging global discourse on *negresse* and negritude, even as they couched their fiction in intensely localized settings in Haiti. Their commitment to localism showed a strong desire to root nationalism in cultural sovereignty distinct from the United States or Europe as a point of reference.

Maurice Casseus's *Viejo* (1935) is one of the key sources of the "peasant novel" tradition in Haiti. Although the novel is written primarily in French, it has a strong multilingual and cross-cultural focus. Casseus makes extensive use of Creole dialogue and folk customs, along with explanatory notes for traditional Francophone readers. He also includes Spanish and English dialogue, as he skillfully examines relations between

Haiti, Cuba, and Harlem. Given the politically fraught nature of what Casseus was examining—his work touches upon more raw nerves of geopolitics than does the work of Thoby-Marcelin and Roumain—it is not surprising that *Viejo* did not have any extensive reception in the Anglophone world. There was no translation of it into English during its print history, and it does not appear to have been translated in succeeding years. This lacuna is regrettable, because Casseus's vision of Caribbean independence and archipelagic interaction not only rebuts U.S. imperial designs under the Monroe Doctrine, but also politely distances the fate of Haitians and Cubans from the advocacy of African Americans in Harlem, who are viewed with admiration but nonetheless as "other" with respect to the Haitian people.

From the start of his novel, Casseus intertwines his protagonist's love for his native land with his loyalty to his first lover: "Mario dreamed about his childhood. All the perfumes of his homeland, the old days spent under the beautiful sun, rising to his nostrils. The dark corridor that opened over the sea, there, when for the first time, he remembered having known the flesh and embrace of a little seller of oranges within the pigsty of the stinking marines' breath. Olive . . . her name was Olive."[47] As the novel develops, Casseus achieves a doubled plot of political and romantic struggle that connects, implicitly, the struggle for sovereignty against occupation to the fraught question of whether or not Olive will choose a white man or an elite Haitian over Mario. Upon his return from Cuba at the start of the novel, Mario observes a disturbing tableau in the center of Port-au-Prince: "But from the Casernes Dessalines an alarm broke out, that rose like a rampart around the floating flag of the forty eight states. Only then did he remember: the American was master here, but not of him. Liberty or Death! The irony of that flag floating in the clear morning, and across from it the whites mocking it with their sarcasms."[48] Casseus's rendering of this scene reveals that the U.S. presence in this Haitian national space is a hypocritical betrayal of the United States' own revolutionary history. The slogan of the U.S. patriot Patrick Henry has been grotesquely mocked by the imposition of a flag (as well as death) in suppression of Haitian liberty. A "viejo" [old man] who witnesses Mario's reaction to Dessalines's statute comments, "Yes, a colonizer, a colonizer again, with whom one doesn't even want to bargain over the price of land."[49] Similarly, Mario finds that his favorite dance hall has become contaminated, not only by Americans, but by the scent of American tobacco—a crop cherished as part of indigenous Caribbean agriculture and a symbol of independence since the nineteenth century, as

Vera Kutzinski has illustrated.[50] Writes Casseus, "The atmosphere tightened chests with the bitter odor of American tobacco, and also of that acrid smell of wet armpits."[51] Casseus even renders the U.S. male body itself as grotesque in the form of the most prominent white character, Cap. Cap is a former Marine officer who was dismissed for hitting a superior during the occupation and has joined the life of Port-au-Prince as a perpetual drunk and lecher. He grasps after Olive in much the same way that the Marines are holding Haiti.

At first, Mario's hold on Olive seems secure. She reassures him, "Sweetie, I will get rid of Cap, and return."[52] Mario confides to his closest friend, Claude Servin, that he could not survive if Olive were to betray him: "I didn't know how I could have been able to live with that thought, there, in my head, that image continually before my eyes, of Olive my woman, that I love more than all the world, sleeping with that dirty white man."[53] By the end of the novel, however, Mario learns that Olive has cheated on him with a "p'tit blanc" ["poor white"] (145). This betrayal threatens to overwhelm Mario, given what Olive meant to him in the past, particularly in his associating her with the land and his childhood. Mario's friend Claude Servin counsels him to move on and not to depend on the frail relations between men and women for his stability: "Comrade, you must not go over this problem, for the story of man and woman is always the story of the pig in the mud."[54]

Mario does survive Olive's betrayal, in no small part because he has learned, from his time in Cuba to the present, to depend upon a deeper, almost maternal sense of cultural nourishment: his negritude, what he calls the "chant primitif" (24), particularly as registered in music and dance. Casseus's depictions of dance and drumming draw fruitful parallels among African-descended musical traditions. When Mario first enters into the frenzy of dancing in Port-au-Prince, he has a reverie connecting many musical traditions: "Mario faints, and on his heart presses the weights of a black continent with all its deserts, its grains of sand, its Pyramids, with all the waves of the dark Nile, the dirty froth of the Mississippi that scraped the banjo. A hand lifts him up, tosses him up into the air filled with jazz band, with the congo-paillette, with the slow blues and with the pignitte led by Mario in a black suit and white gloves."[55] This global sense of African presence clearly shows the influence of Langston Hughes's "The Negro Speaks of Rivers" upon Casseus; indeed, Mario later ridicules the government for their snub of Hughes ("le plus grand poète nègre" [the greatest black poet]) and Walter White during a testimonial before the prime minister (114).

Mario's identity is transformed by these repeated dances, and he celebrates the change: "The night closed up, and glistened in the tubes of his veins. Mario of yesterday replaced by the Mario of today, newly born."[56] Mario apostrophizes the dance itself:

> Chant, chant drums of the blacks! Go on, sing to me the black couplet. You are not the music of the whites, the long flute of silver nor the varnished violin. Go on, sing the song that swarms in your stomach. That's it, that's it! I want your heart, for your hiccups are shadows like black skin and the breath of my Guinea! Ah! You are my mother, drum, you are my father, drum, you are my brother, and it is you that I will hold when I lie down soon with my black beloved.[57]

Mario's reverie suggests that through music he has discovered his black identity, as well as a new sense of extended kinship, which perhaps helps prepare him to overcome the loss of Olive. Most powerfully, through his embrace of the music, Mario not only feels reconnected to Africa, but appreciates himself as a bond between Old and New Worlds: "Africa! It is the marsh's acrid stench that your unknowable mask breathes, all these hysterical bodies. And Mario is a liaison!"[58] That Casseus celebrates this linking role for Mario makes this novel's negritude not simplistically Afrocentric in its handling of black culture (there is no one pure origin here), but valuing of the distinct African-descended identities in the New World. In a similar spirit of "liaison," Mario and his friends recall a cosmopolitan range of black heroes as they plan to work for Haiti's "seconde independence," inspired by L'Ouverture, Dessalines, Pétion, and Booker T. Washington (86, 88).

Even as Mario and his comrades evoke with pride the names of African Americans like Booker T. Washington, they do not believe that their salvation will come from African Americans, nor do they look to Harlem as the inspiring Zion envisioned by New Negro authors. Servin reports upon Harlem, but the metropole is represented as a place of ecstatic excess that, though tempting and diverting, is not a fruitful site for Caribbean resistance. Servin celebrates the complex gorgeousness of Harlem: "The noisy joy of dim faces, noisy and sad, pleasure without wine, faces without sun, disguised with charcoal, antechamber to trampled-upon Africa, but music hall of a race mad with the joy refused to them, dynamic poetry, sensual sweetness of Harlem, debauched with lights and colors, festival of the rainbow as long as your parties and your nights, Harlem!"[59] In spite these attractions, Servin resists the temptation of the excess, and feels the call for home: "However, I have returned here, comrade, for in spite of all the riches of Harlem, all the beauties of Harlem, there is something that you cannot resist, and it is the imperial call of your land, when it has a hold on you, it lodges in your heart, as if it sounded on a ringing gong, each hour, each minute, each second, ah! It's terrible like that, comrade!"[60]

In keeping with the sense that it is to the black kin of the Caribbean, rather than to Harlem, that Haitians should turn for support, Mario uses a chant he learned in Cuba to rally his friends as he makes his final march towards the town square to redeem Dessalines's statue. As the drums urge the marchers onward, Mario sings in Creole: "*Alamba, Alamba, toutt' corps'm cé corps mama*" (155–56) [Alamba, Alamba, all the body is the body of my mother]. This chant makes explicit the union between body, motherland, and nation, but it is also, paradoxically, translated and translatable. Mario is translating into Creole something he learned in Cuba (and Casseus also provides a translation into continental French at the bottom of the page). Mario has learned (and now teaches) the unity of personal body and body politic for Haiti, but learned this lesson from a different "motherland" (Cuba). This lateral shift shows that while Casseus is intensely nationalistic in his cultural work, he nonetheless sees kinship with the other islands (Harlem, in contrast, is always referred to as a place of "amis," friends).

There is also a double resonance to "mama" here, as Mario may be referring not only to Haiti, but also to Africa itself. Indeed, he apostrophizes Africa as he heads towards the final confrontation: "Africa! Primitive continent where your skin reigns, an infinite desert over which the black loas keep watch, it is in you, and only in you, that the secret of eternal revolution is placed."[61] As central as Africa is to Casseus's negritude, he does not advocate for a return to Africa or flight to another Zion (such as Harlem), but suggests the portability of Africa's cultural resources throughout the black diaspora. Although he has never been to Africa, Mario can draw upon its "secret," which he accesses through drum and chant from the fellow Afro-Caribbean culture of Cuba. The closing image of the novel defends the "body of mother Haiti" by attacking the U.S. body. The narrator describes the dead body of Cap, which has been left in front of the statue of Dessalines that the Marines had defiled: "The flame glowed, the clouds brilliant, above the grimacing face of Cap where the knife was pushed into his carotid artery all the way up to the handle."[62]

In contrast to this intensely symbolic blow to the U.S. military and empire, *Le bête du Musseau* [*The Beast of the Haitian Hills*] (1946), by Philippe Thoby-Marcelin and his brother Pierre Marcelin, makes no reference to the American presence from the previous decades, and very little to the urban, native elite at all. As the brothers write in their introduction about the initially harsh response to their work: "Our great sin was that we had presented the life of peasants at grips with poverty and religious taboos, instead of idealizing them or vindicating the upper class."[63] The brothers Marcelin do reveal a cultural crosscurrent in the introduction by acknowledging a debt to Seabrook, whose attention to voodoo gave them a source of inspiration to break from representation of the upper classes: "It was Seabrook's work which changed my attitude by revealing to me that the *Vodoun* cult constituted a rich mine of material in which humor and fantasy blended with pathos and poetry, and by showing me the excellent use I could make of it in the literary field. . . . It was at this point that I felt compelled to 'go down' among the people, in order to see their life close up, to learn their language and find out their way of thinking" (xv).

Jacques Roumain's *Gouveneurs de la Rosée* [*Masters of the Dew*] (1944) did not draw any avowed inspiration from U.S. writers, but Roumain's "literary access," as Richard Brodhead would term it,[64] to the Anglophone world was brokered through Langston Hughes, who translated the novel with Mercer Cook in 1947. Roumain's novel refocused the Haitian literary gaze on the peasant class in a manner similar to that of the novels of the brothers Marcelin, but with a leftist vision of uplift through solidarity. Roumain offers little direct representation of elite Haitian life, but uses it as a point of reference against which his rural characters must struggle. As the narrator relates, "The high-class people in the city derisively called these peasants 'barefoot Negroes, barefooted vagabonds, big-toed Negroes.' (They are too poor to buy shoes.) But never mind and to hell with them! Some day we will take our big flat feet out of the soil and plant them on their behinds."[65] As if in celebration of this principle, Roumain trains his focus on the rural, making extensive use of dialect, folksongs, and attention to the family struggles of peasants to offer a validation of the agricultural class. Even with this rural focus, Roumain shows a vision distinct from that of Casseus and Thoby-Marcelin in his leftist distrust of folk spirituality: "The peasants forgot their troubles. Dancing and drinking anesthetized them—swept away their shipwrecked souls to drown in those regions of unreality and danger where the fierce forces of the African gods lay in wait" (78). With his sense of ritual as "anesthetizing," Roumain almost echoes Marx's critique of religion as an "opiate of the masses."

Roumain explores how distinctions of color, caste, and family lineage obscure the possibility of unity needed to move the nation forward. The plot of the novel centers around the struggle of Manuel (whose very name bespeaks the power of hands and manual labor), newly returned from Cuba like Casseus's Mario, to integrate back into his village and help its people find water for their farms, the basis of their livelihood. Perhaps in keeping with Roumain's concerns about spirituality as a nonprogressive force, Manuel does not feel connected to voodoo: regarding the spirits that his mother consults, he says, "I haven't heard them for a long time, mama" (55).

What Manuel has heard is the call for racial and class solidarity. As for Mario in *Viejo,* his militant stance is catalyzed by his time in Cuba. Manuel speaks to his comrades about the power he felt as a striking worker there: "Being mad's a great power. When we went on strike, each man stood in line, armed to the teeth with being mad—like a gun. To get mad, that's your right, your justice!" (38). As in *Viejo,* Cuba also provides a gateway into negritude through its music. Describing his commitment to the drum (though not necessarily to voodoo), Manuel tells his true love, Anna, "I danced and sang to my heart's content. I'm Negro, no? And I enjoyed myself like a real Negro. When the drums beat, I feel it in the pit of my stomach. I feel an itch in my loins and an electric current in my legs, and I've got to join the dance." Anna appears to perceive this idea of essential racial authenticity—that she should strive to be "real negro"—as foreign and asks, "Was it in the country of Cuba that you got those ideas?" (38).

Anna is relatively receptive to Manuel's visions, but almost all of his "ideas" for class unity are initially obstructed by a history of family divisions arising from unequal allotments of land. The consequences of this history connect the personal to the political in a manner that is again reminiscent of *Viejo.* Anna's family is a rival of Manuel's, so theirs is a star-crossed love that cannot be realized, although Manuel vows, "I'll wait for you, Anna" (83). Manuel's quest for water, then, is not simply to provide sustenance for the region's agriculture, but also to erase the material inequalities that foster divisions within the village: "It was his mission and his duty. Those Fonds Rouge peasants needed that water to bring about friendship between brothers again and to make life over as it ought to be—an act of good will between men, by want and fate made equals" (107). Manuel tells his mother, Delira, "Well mama, I tell you, just between us, the day isn't far off when there'll be neither 'those others' nor 'ourselves,' but just good peasants gathered together for the great *coumbite* of the water" (126). Roumain's novel finishes with a gesture of violence and renewal like that in Casseus, but with a sense that the stakes of national struggle lie within the village, rather than against the outside world. Manuel is brained to death by family rivals almost immediately after his engagement to Anna and his discovery of the water in the hills. In the process of burying him, however, the village finds the water source, and Anna feels a stirring in her belly: "'No, he isn't dead.' She took the old woman's hand and pressed it gently against her belly where the new life was stirring" (188). Roumain's concluding image suggests autonomous renewal from within Haiti, as the water and pregnancy will not only revivify Manuel's family, but also secure the future of his village and nation.

3 Expanding "Our America"

Caribbean Vistas in U.S. Modernism

DURING THE 1920s, many white U.S. modernists, including Hart Crane, William Faulkner, Eugene O'Neill, Wallace Stevens, and William Carlos Williams, gave significant attention to the Caribbean. In contrast to the U.S. literature about Haiti discussed in the previous chapter, most of these writings do not offer direct encounters with the islands themselves, but reveal the symbolic importance of the Caribbean to their authors. In spite of their projective nature, the imaginative visions embedded in these works are worth examining because these texts provided powerful alternative visions of New World history, especially in contrast to the contemporary nativist claims that the United States was, at its core, an Anglo-Saxon nation.

The Caribbean proved a rich space for diverse and even contradictory imaginative projections. In some cases, modernists used the Caribbean as a tragic locus, as in Faulkner's positioning of the Caribbean as the cursed fulcrum between Africa and the New World slave trade in *Absalom, Absalom!* or Eugene O'Neill's use of a Caribbean island as a chronotopic[1] setting for African and African American history in *The Emperor Jones*. More commonly, modernist writers looked to the Caribbean to reclaim a lost dimension of New World history and a multicultural vision of art and literature in the American hemisphere. Crane's long poem *The Bridge,* Williams's set of imaginative essays *In the American Grain,* and Waldo Frank's manifesto *America Hispana* all reach towards multi-ethnic paradigms of European, African, and indigenous intermixture, with the Caribbean serving as the crucible of American identity. Wallace Stevens uses the Caribbean as a New World sublime: he turns to the region as an epistemological resource for imaginative renewal, whether in shorter pieces like "O Florida, Venereal Soil" or in his epistemological mock-epic "The Comedian as the Letter C."

Despite their complicity in North American essentialist assumptions about the islands (Frank and Crane, in particular, use the region as a source of exotic renewal or cultural transfusion), these refractions of American identity through the Caribbean represent an innovation in their period. Indeed, these writers' Caribbean vistas posed great challenges to the Eurocentric models of American identity circulating in the 1920s and 1930s, evident in both monoculturalists like Madison Grant and Lothrop Stoddard and in multiculturalists like Randolph Bourne. As politically distinct as Bourne was from nativist theorists like Grant and Stoddard, they all shared a common faith in the necessity for ethnic cultures to remain true to their roots. In the case of the nativists, this ideal had explicitly hierarchical implications, as they argued for the need for immigration restrictions (e.g., the Alien and Sedition Acts) to stem "the rising tide of color" (the title of Stoddard's study) that threatened the purity and supremacy of white culture in the United States. Bourne, in contrast, perceived immigrant cultures as sources of cultural renewal and invigoration for the nation—as long as they remained true to their traditions.[2] What was notably lacking in this debate, even in Bourne's famous "Trans-National America," was the sense that cultural intermixture—whether *mestizaje, mulatez,* creolization, or other overlapping cultural identifications—could be productive, or that U.S. cultural identity may have had hidden, hybrid dimensions in its past. In contrast to Bourne and his opponents, Frank, Williams, Crane, and Stevens revisit the Caribbean for a recovery of lost sources of American identity and for a transformation of identity—usually as a remedy to the Anglo-Saxon Puritan traditions that have dominated U.S. visions of its national history.

Williams, Crane, and Stevens focus their attention most powerfully on the region as a chronotopic space of "discovery" by revisiting the arrival of Columbus in the Caribbean to reimagine the first encounter for their own artistic aims. Each of these modernists' "rediscovery" provides not only fresh visions of seminal cultural figures encountering the "New" World, but also offers new implications for understanding the history and future of the American hemisphere. Even in the midst of their optimistic renovations, this moment of first contact is nonetheless an object of contest among these authors, as they revisit Columbus and the Caribbean for different purposes. At the same time, they are alike in using the Caribbean primarily as a vehicle for poetic exploration or a screen for imaginative projection, rather than an end-in-itself.

Reinvigorating America: Waldo Frank and the Caribbean as Cultural Resource

Waldo Frank, essayist, critic, and confidant of many modernists, articulated the most direct link to Caribbean sources, as his books *Our America* (1919) and *America Hispana* (1931) draw direct inspiration (including the title of the former) from the works of José Martí. *Our America* is less overtly concerned with the Caribbean itself and more influenced by Martí's redemptive vision of a non-Anglo counterculture in the hemisphere. *America Hispana,* based upon Frank's travels through the Caribbean and Latin America, more directly engages with questions of hemispheric solidarity in the New World, and Martí, along with Bolívar, emerges as a central figure in Frank's vision. Lamenting the "ordeal of Cuba" under U.S. hegemony, Frank invokes Martí to call for his project of hemispheric integration to be brought to fruition: "The poet finds that this Cuban who creates his song [i.e., Martí] is a citizen of the unborn New World; and the image in his mystic eye makes him a man of action. . . . Martí escapes from his Cuban prison, and lives in Mexico, Guatemala, Philadelphia, New York."[3] Frank's metaphor of the New World as yet "unborn" epitomizes his visionary desire to help realize the unfulfilled potential of intercultural American connection, as well as his sense that there is somehow a natural process of cross-cultural fertilization that has already occurred in the Americas. Like Martí, he is concerned with contrasting the cultural legacies of North and South America, and he seems equally as distrustful as is Martí of the Anglo-Saxon legacy in the United States:

> But in the north lived a folk whose state of mind made them masters of the tool—destined masters of the age to come, when the *instrument* would be the primal need of the new world's cohering body. A simpler folk, hence more forcibly expansive. A folk that had not rendered its humanity complex by intermarrying with the Indian and the Negro. . . . The folk who look on earth itself and life itself as upon the simplicity of tools made for their personal end will be the best toolmakers. Whether they be the best wielders of tools they make is a deeper question. (10–11, emphasis in original)

Echoing the sentiments of Martí, Sylvain, and Firmin, Frank recognizes the technical prowess and effective force of the United States, but shows concern for the lack of wisdom and finesse with which it might be applied. In almost a moment of reverse anthropology, Frank treats the ostensibly well-developed and powerful North America as a culture of simple and primitive toolmakers—a powerful gesture in a cultural context when European and U.S. anthropologists like Melville Herskovits, Franz Boas, and Lucien Lévy-Brüehl were commencing in earnest their studies of the "primitive mind" outside the West. Indeed, at other times, perhaps invoking Upton Sinclair, Frank describes the United States as "the jungle" (346), relocating the sense of tropic danger and barbarism to the U.S. rather than the Caribbean and Latin America.

Although Frank's *America Hispana* embraces Mexico and South America, the Caribbean plays a singular role in his hemispheric vision, and he clearly aims to transform Americans' sense of what that space signifies. According to Frank, the Caribbean and the Gulf of Mexico should be united: "That Spain did not feel the unity of this water, giving it two names, is symbolic of her failure to find a form for her unitary will" (279). Rightly understood, this greater Caribbean should form the "central sea" (203) and "*Mare Internum*" (280) for the Americas. In addition, insofar as it connects to the Panama Canal, the Caribbean also forms part of a bridge between East and West: "the relic juncture of two legendary worlds that bound Iberia to Cathay" (4). Although Frank's vision sounds like an annexationist plan on new terms—this time cultural and aesthetic rather than political and economic—he takes pains to distinguish his vision of American unity from the imperial designs inhering in both the Spanish-American War and the occupation of Haiti. Notably, he sees the canal itself, particularly in the U.S. custody of the canal zone, as a failure of inter-American integration: "The Canal of Roosevelt is not the Canal of Bolívar. The body it aims to create is not the true and integral America of Bolívar" (21). More provocatively, Frank argues that the canal is not only "alien from America Hispana. It is alien to the great tradition of the United States" (21). With such gestures Frank evokes a sense of American Jeremiad and echoes the disappointed hopes of Firmin and Martí that the United States would temper its expansionist aims with respect for others' revolutions and struggles for sovereignty in the New World.

Unlike Martí, however, Frank is optimistic for the future relationship between the United States and the American hemisphere, hoping that it can be transformed by a revolution in arts and letters. For Frank, it should be the task for a new generation of artists both in the United States and America Hispana to "send a music of brotherhood across the waters" (282). Frank recognizes that the United States has indeed established a large presence in America Hispana and has had opportunities for cultural contact, but argues that it has failed to learn from these other traditions in its own hemisphere. Critiquing the stereotypical figure of the U.S. businessman abroad in Latin America, Frank writes, "He does not, like the Roman, absorb the deities of his liegemen; he tramples on them blindly. For his gods have retained one trait of the Puritan Jehovah: they are jealous" (281). Frank's respect for the Roman tradition runs parallel to Marti's validation of Latin culture in the Americas, but he hybridizes his anti-imperialism with the growing critique of Puritanism that emerged in U.S. modernist circles in the 1920s and 1930s.

Frank's vision departs markedly from Martí's in his optimistic faith that there could be a complementary relationship between the cultures of the Americas. By the end of his career, Martí was convinced that internal conflict would doom the United States, and he did not believe that a fruitful cultural intermixture could develop between the U.S. and *nuestra America.* Like Emerson or Adams, Frank was convinced of the expanding force of the United States as a world power, but feared that basic cultural failures had yet to be remedied: "We must hence conclude that the bases of life as it has been built in the United States are inadequate for the creating of whole human beings" (330). In turn, Frank argues that the cultures of America Hispana, although possessed of a "rich group life," have yet to achieve effective force on the world stage; the citizen of America Hispana "longs greatly for actualization of his ideals" (336). Frank envisions an "integration" (368) and marriage of cultures between North and South America, grounded in a "confederation of the central sea" (363) to solve the mutual needs of each region: "The problem in the United States is to free its impulse towards a fresh creative beginning: in America Hispana, it is to find the means of fulfillment. The problem in the North is one of religion—where the South folk are strong: the problem of the South is one of discipline, technique, and method, where the North is strong" (341). By the end of *America Hispana,* Frank articulates a strong sense of Manifest Destiny for all of the Americas, couched in language that evokes older notions of race while simultaneously aiming to transcend that vocabulary: "For the high promise of America Hispana, in essence, is not the promise of vastly potential races, not the promise of profound traditions, not the need of the Atlantic peoples for just such spiritual redemption as America Hispana seems by its genius capable of bringing: it is the simple challenge to men and to young nations to make of their lives an incarnate quest of the Truth" (371–72).

If Frank's visionary spirit of cultural renewal seems overly optimistic, even naïve, to the contemporary reader, it is worth placing his vision in the cultural context of North American discussions of race, nation, and culture in order to appreciate the boldness of his vision. Frank was by no means unique in seeking a modernist break from U.S. convention, but he found resources within the hemisphere, rather than in the East or the West, while aspiring for an alternative to the angst and weltschmerz of the Lost Generation. Frank, along with Crane, Williams, and Stevens, turned away from a dialectical engagement (whether hostile or embracing) with European traditions to seek other sources of American identity. In contrast to Bourne's "Trans-National America," Frank's Caribbean vista suggested that individuated cultural traditions would not be discrete injections of new cultural capital, but a crucible of a new inter-American identity that fused multiple global traditions (northern and southern European, African, and Indian) into "a new man, a New American" the likes of which Crèvecoeur could never have conceived.

Caribbean Counterpoints in Wallace Stevens's Re-vision of America

Wallace Stevens's first collection of poetry, *Harmonium* (1923), often turns to the Caribbean in search of a "new man" or "new American," especially for the sake of developing a new American artist. Stevens frequently uses spaces in the Caribbean basin—Key West, Cuba, the Yucatan, and the Caribbean Sea itself—as loci for his investigations of nature, fertility, and the poetic imagination. These Caribbean-inflected poems not only incorporate Caribbean references, but use the space as a vehicle for contrast with European and U.S. cultural traditions. Stevens's first poem that addresses Key West, "O Florida, Venereal Soil," begins with a familiar colonial stance: a sense of horror at the multicultural space on the Key, its Cuban, Mexican, and African American mix described as composing the "dreadful sundry of this world" (47). In this context the title's use of the word *venereal* references a sense of contamination or disease, but the second half of the poem seems to return the word to another etymological resonance: sexuality and generation. The poem eroticizes the natural scenery—"Lascivious . . . as the wind"—and concludes with an apostrophic appreciation of Florida as an exotic woman: a "Donna, donna, dark,/Stooping in indigo gown" with "A hand that bears a thick-leaved fruit" (48).

The erotic conjunction of fruit and femininity inhabits "Floral Decorations for Bananas," which presents a comparative still life of two possible fruit settings for a gentleman's table. With a satiric tone, the poem expresses an almost Popeian horror at the arrangement of bananas, suggesting instead that the gentleman offer his lady guests plums in an antique bowl—a respectable, European fruit in a traditional setting. The speaker then contrasts the primness of the plums and the ladies with an imagined scene of primitivism and sexual excess, declaring that, with the bananas at the table, the appearance of the women will be transformed, as the eye is drawn to their "shanks" and "slatted eyes." In the speaker's flight of fancy, the tropical fruit liberates the women from a respectable, boring party into an embrace of their embodied sexuality. In a striking close, the speaker exhorts the host to "deck the bananas in leaves/Plucked from the Carib trees" (54). Beyond showing appreciation for the Caribbean origin of the bananas, the speaker's injunction, couched in the imperative mood, argues that one should celebrate, not minimize, the tropicality of bananas. Rather than trying to take the "best" of the plant—just the fruit—one should bring the jungle ("the leaves") to the table and appreciate the wildness of the banana tree.

A frankly sexual appreciation for the tropical Caribbean is by no means unique to Stevens; but it is striking in its context, as there is no fear of the jungle as a symbol of degeneration or of barbarism, but rather a playful embrace of it. As sensual as his descriptions often are, Stevens's Caribbean explorations have more abstract resonances as well. In "Nomad Exquisite," the speaker celebrates the rich natural environment of Florida, but he is ultimately most interested in how the tropical setting will transform his art. Using an anaphoric structure of comparisons that echoes the epic simile, the speaker compares his own growth as an artist to the flourishing flora and fauna, concluding, "So, in me, come flinging/Forms, flames, and the flakes of flames" (95). The landscape here is portrayed as a fertile and inspiring muse, and it has transformed the sound of the poem itself: the closing alliteration gestures back to the earliest forms of English epic poetry, suggesting, perhaps, that this primal scene has renewed the vigor of the poet and his words.

Such conjunction of earthy and artistic appreciation for the Caribbean tropics is central to "The Comedian as the Letter C." Stevens's most substantive engagement with the Caribbean, this poem is essentially a reimagining of the discovery and colonization of the New World. In this poem (whose title puns upon the "sea"), the title figure is not precisely Columbus in any historical sense (though his name echoes "Christopher"), but a Columbus-like explorer voyaging from the Old World (Bordeaux) to the new. Crispin's journeys extend beyond those of Columbus, forming a voyage that unites the Caribbean basin to the North American coast, ranging from the Yucatan, to Havana, to the Carolinas. Crispin also differs from Columbus in being primarily "an introspective voyager."[4] Although there is no direct conquest discussed in the poem, Stevens does address questions of colonization, particularly through Crispin's plans to develop a new art in the New World. Beyond the specific physical journey, the poem (like most of Stevens's works) is most concerned with mapping mind's interaction with matter: how the human imagination grasps, shapes, and is dialectically shaped by the world.

As the title suggests, the idea of the "comedian" is central to Stevens's vision. Perhaps the central revision effected by Stevens is his conversion of the explorer into a comic figure—an oblique shift that moves him out of the polar oppositions central to historical debates about the nature of the discovery/conquest/encounter. Crispin is described as neither a visionary hero nor a conquering villain, but as something smaller and less consequential, a "knave," a "skinny sailor," a "merest miniscule in the gales" (28, 29). One of the prime inadequacies of Stevens's Crispin is that his perception is so dependent upon preconception, which affects his very experience of the passage to the Caribbean itself. The first section of the poem, entitled "The World without Imagination," describes the phenomenological challenges faced by the explorer because of his European weltanschauung. At sea, Crispin finds himself "In a starker, barer world, in which the sun/Was not the sun because it never shone/With bland complaisance on pale parasols,/Beetled, in chapels, on the chaste bouquets" (29). Crispin's inability to grasp the fullness of the sun provides an apt figuration of the limits of a colonizing imagination: he can only apprehend this elemental force according to a confined cultural map of protective feminine accessories (parasols) and restrictive religious spaces ("beetled" chapels). When removed from the social and religious contexts from Europe (promenades and chapels), the sun does not seem intelligible anymore for the voyager. Although Crispin and the Europeans will later succeed in imposing their "map" on New World peoples and social arrangements, Crispin cannot impose on the sea. In contrast to the ordering imagination Stevens famously celebrates in "The Idea of Order at Key West," the sea in "The Comedian as the Letter C" impinges on Crispin and *dis*orders his imagination:

The sea
Severs not only lands but also selves.
Here was no help before reality.
Crispin beheld and Crispin was made new.
The imagination, here, could not evade,

In poems of plums, the strict austerity
Of one vast, subjugating, final tone. (30)

Before even arriving in the New World, Crispin has already been subdued by the starkness of the sea and sky.

Although the sea forms a sublime realm in the poem that is beyond Crispin's poetry, he is able to commence an imaginative struggle to grasp the New World once he reaches land, San Salvador first, then the succeeding islands. Having landed, Crispin embarks upon a different voyage, that of the artistic imagination. In the New World, he tries to forge new poetry, "an aesthetic tough, diverse, untamed,/Incredible to prudes" (31). This poetic mission reveals that Crispin has started to overcome the perspective he brought with him from Europe, which hindered his imaginative potential and impeded his view of the sun. Indeed, Crispin seems destined to become Stevens's ideal vision of an exceptionalist, Emersonian poet: an author of new poetry for a new world. Like the ephebe in "Notes Towards a Supreme Fiction," Crispin undergoes poetic training, and he develops a new aesthetic from his Caribbean vistas: he finds "A new reality in parrot-squawks" (32), sees "how much . . . he never saw at all," and finds in the "essential prose" of the landscape he is exploring, "the one/Discovery still possible to make" (36).

This discovery, for Stevens's Crispin, develops into "The Idea of a Colony"—the title of the fourth section of the poem. The details of Crispin's poetic/political vision are both banal and radical, exotic and utopic. They are grounded in both tropical stereotypes—banjos, mescal, melons, peaches, and other iconic images one might find in a resort brochure—and in Stevens's own aesthetic commitment to valuing earthly delights as opposed to the chaste restrictions of Western religion and epistemology. Stevens presents Crispin's vision as an imperial imposition, as the voyager views his plan as superior to that of the natives. The poet writes to himself, "The natives of the rain are rainy men" (37), and "On what strange froth does the gross Indian dote" (38). Crispin, in contrast, will forge his poetry from the "ding an sich" (29) foreign to the Europeans and taken for granted by the natives, and "make a new intelligence prevail" (37). Less abstractly, Crispin "Projected a colony that should extend/To the Dusk of a whistling south below the south,/A comprehensive island hemisphere" (38). Based on his precept that "his soil is man's intelligence" (36), Crispin imagines an autochthonous poetry emerging for and from each American region, without regard to European forms, particularly those of Christianity:

The man in Georgia waking among pines
Should be pine-spokesman. The responsive man,
Planting his pristine cores in Florida,
Should prick thereof, not on the psaltery,
But on the banjo's categorical gut. (38)

Farther south, Crispin extends his call to "Sepulchral señors . . . [who]/ Should make the intricate Sierra scan" and "dark Brazilians in their cafés . . . [who]/Should scrawl a vigilant anthology" (38).

Crispin's observations pass without explicit comment, but his vision is larded with irony by Stevens, as "the idea of a colony" bears the marks of hubris already ridiculed earlier in the poem through, for example, Crispin's putative "preceptorship" (27) of the sea. Within the overall structure of the poem, it is revealed that pride goeth before a (banal) fall, and the remainder of the poem depicts Crispin's gradual failure to realize his grand designs.

In stark contrast to "the idea of a colony," the subsequent section of "The Comedian as the Letter C" is titled "A Nice Shady Home." Ideational expansion has been trumped by more worldly designs: "his emprize to that idea soon sped./Crispin dwelt in the land and dwelling there/Slid from his continent by slow recess/To things within his actual eye" (40). Surprisingly, physical colonization is rendered as reductive, rather than expansive, as both Crispin's mind and his "colony" have shrunken: "day by day, now this thing and that/Confined him" (40). Instead of an archetypal conquering hero (or villain), Crispin becomes a domesticated bourgeois, lulled into passivity by the fruits of the New World. Beautifully and humorously rephrasing Whitman, Stevens renders Crispin as helpless and nonplussed: "Effective colonizer sharply stopped/In the door-yard by his own capacious bloom" (44). Crispin learns that "The world, a turnip once so readily plucked,/Sacked up and carried overseas," when brought to the Americas, came "reproduced in purple, family font,/The same insoluble lump" (45). Instead of producing a new blossom or developing a new text, Crispin has replicated an old domestic space in a new land, with such regularity that the old way can be understood as a standardized typeface—a disappointing decline from his aspirations to a new poetry.

It obviously stands as a substantial revision of Caribbean and New World history to argue that the great colony envisioned never occurred, and one might balk at the insensitivity here to the displacement and extermination of native peoples, but Stevens is nonetheless radical in positing that European colonization failed as an idea or ideal. If the goal was to create a new exceptionalist space, whether a "City upon a Hill" or "Brave New World," "The Comedian as the Letter C" suggests that those designs have failed to achieve their potential. Although one might chafe at treating the question of colonization as such an abstract issue, it is crucial to remember that colonialism has often been justified as an ideal. One might recall Marlowe's claim in *Heart of Darkness* that colonialism "is not a pretty thing when you look into it too much. What redeems it is the idea only. An idea at the back of it; not a sentimental pretence but an idea; and an unselfish belief in the idea—something you can set up, and bow down before and offer a sacrifice to."[5] Stevens reveals that the idea "at the back of it" in Crispin's case is comic and unrealized.

One might further ask why Stevens chooses to reimagine a Columbus figure as the fantasizing bourgeois Crispin. A few lines from "An Examination of the Hero in a Time of War" may offer a glimmer of explanation. In that later poem, Stevens would write of the figure of the hero, "Devise. Make him of mud,/For every day" (275). According to this dictum, Stevens desires heroes made of earthly substance who bear a more intelligible relation to our own lives. In this version of the Discovery and the Caribbean, Stevens may have found an apt epitome for what he sees as the limitations of the U.S. perspective in the New World. Thus Stevens looked back into history and "devised" an explorer that would account for the limitations he observed in the twentieth-century United States. Within the realm of material comforts, Crispin foretells the passive, often dreaming but never fulfilled life of middle- to upper-class success. As a poet, Crispin has replicated European forms and failed to declare his own intellectual and cultural independence.

Even as the story of Crispin represents a falling short of an epistemological revolution, it is clear that Stevens's rendering of the Caribbean attributes a regenerative power for the imagination to the region, although it has not yet been realized. Much as Martí and Frank posited the Caribbean as the *mare internum* of the American hemisphere, Stevens uses it as the center of Crispin's imaginative vision. Crispin understands the Caribbean as a complement to balance North America: "An up and down between two elements,/A fluctuating between sun and moon," "Crispin knew/It was a flourishing tropic he required/For his refreshment, an abundant zone" (35). More than simply providing a hemispheric balance, the basin for Stevens possesses an ontological and epistemological force: "Here was the veritable ding an sich, at last," he writes (29); while the storms at Yucatan are "the span/Of force, the quintessential fact" (33). In this respect, Stevens effectively converts North America ("America was always north to him" [34]) into the margin, while treating the Caribbean tropics as the (imaginative) center. The logic of that centering is not merely a product of geography, but of Stevens's situating the Caribbean scenes in the poem as the locus of foundational forces that seem unavailable to Crispin elsewhere:

> elemental potencies and pangs,
> And beautiful barenesses as yet unseen,
> Making the most of savagery of palms,
> Of moonlight on the thick, cadaverous bloom
> That yuccas breed, and of panthers tread. (31)

The range of imagery in these lines—generation and death, abundance and starkness, beauty and danger—suggests that the tropical Caribbean offers the potential for the poetic imagination to reconnect with the natural patterns that have been ignored in a European phenomenology limited by social and religious constructions. Stevens posits later in *Harmonium,* in "Sunday Morning," that "death is the mother of beauty" (69), and his Caribbean scenes show a landscape with a fertile mix of abundance and decay to inspire such beauty.

Crucially, although Crispin's "idea" appears to have failed and Crispin is rendered with sympathetic irony, Stevens's poetry leaves the intense and wondrous renderings of the Caribbean region intact and unironized, suggesting that the potential for growth and regeneration is still there. Some aspects of "The Comedian as the Letter C," along with others of Stevens's poems, seem to call for a "re-encountering" or "rediscovery" of the Caribbean in order to reclaim lost potential and to transform both America and its literature. Indeed, the close of "Comedian"—"So may the relation of each man be clipped" (46)—expands the idiosyncratic Crispin into a representative figure of the poet-as-explorer, perhaps with the imperative that others (such as Stevens) must experiment with such an American reinvigoration, and that even if one fails as Crispin did, it is nonetheless a worthy aim.

Vitality and Vengeance: William Carlos Williams's Representation of the Caribbean in *In the American Grain*

William Carlos Williams's *In the American Grain* (1925) also reimagines a scene of the Discovery and its failures, but with an eye towards much more concrete issues of politics and war, grounded in Columbus's first encounter. Williams's entire text, as Vera Kutzinski notes, aims to recapture a more cosmopolitan sense of American hemispheric history, with due recognition for the blood and toil of the indigenous and non-Anglo peoples.[6] Williams devotes four of the first five chapters of *In the American Grain* to Caribbean encounters, as he examines, in succession, Columbus, Cortés, Ponce de León, and de Soto. For reasons both historical and symbolic, Williams situates Cuba in each of these chapters as the gateway to the New World. His first Caribbean chapter, "The Discovery of the Indies," examines the founding of that gateway, intertwining excerpts of Columbus's letters, actual and embellished, with Williams's own prose descriptions of the Discovery and its implications. Williams does not wholly demonize Columbus, but he does turn him into something much more complex than a celebrated hero. From the first paragraphs that introduce the landing at San Salvador, we learn of the Discovery as a history of failures and violations. The New World was

> marked with its own dark life which goes on to an immaculate fulfillment in which we have no part [i.e., it did not need invasion or "redemption" by Europeans]. But now, with the maritime successes of that period, the western land could not guard its seclusion longer; a predestined and bitter fruit existing, perversely, before the white flower of its birth, it was laid bare by the miraculous first voyage. For it is as the achievement of a flower, pure, white, waxlike and fragrant, that Columbus's infatuated course must be depicted, especially when compared with the arid and poisonous apple which was later by him to be proved.[7]

Williams expresses the Discovery in explicitly lapsarian terms, while nonetheless preserving some of the initial idealism evident in Stevens's vision. Much as Stevens's Crispin held "the idea of a colony," Columbus's initial goal is represented almost as a platonic ideal, "pure, white, waxlike." In its descent from the ideal, however, Williams's vision of Columbus's fault reverses the sexual dichotomy effected by Stevens. While Stevens's Crispin sees in the Indies an antidote to the "prudish" and "beetled" customs of Europe, Williams locates an aboriginal purity that is violated.

Columbus's coming is clearly meant to evoke a sense of rape and ravishment, with the land "laid bare," and the violation is instantaneous upon his arrival ("No more had Columbus landed, the flower once ravished" [7]). Williams does not delineate the atrocities of conquest in this chapter (as he would later in the book in his revisitation of Cortés and the Aztecs); it seems that the very act of colonial landing produces the sin. In keeping with the Miltonic sense of "fall" and "bitter fruit," Columbus is destined to be punished for his violation. Although initially successful upon returning to Spain, he seems possessed by a lust to return: "His triumph was acclaimed, his captives were paraded in Madrid, his gold was witnessed, his birds, monkeys, and native implements were admired. This over, immediately the urge was on him once more" (9). The bulk of "The Discovery of the Indies" focuses on the political fallout and unfulfilled promise of Columbus's successive voyages. In the wake of his encounter with the Indies, Columbus sees "before him the illusive bright future of a great empire" and he fantasizes that "henceforth I shall be called Don, and should be Chief Admiral of the Open Sea, perpetual Viceroy and Governor of all the islands and continents that I should discover" (9–10). These promises go unfulfilled, however. Williams's Columbus proves not to be the self-sufficient hero that he imagines himself to be, but rather a pawn in the larger game of European expansion. Rivals in Spain hinder his projects and prevent him from gaining the favor of the court. He is accused of and investigated for treasonous collusion with Portugal. Williams thus writes of Columbus that "America found in Columbus its first victim" (10). By removing Columbus from the realm of mythical idealism and placing him in the context of global power politics, Williams reconstructs a vision of the Discovery that speaks to the history of the Americas that followed, especially as detailed by writers like Martí, Firmin, and Sylvain. The network of intrigues, plots, and betrayals surrounding Columbus forms an apt prediction of what is to come in the hemisphere: colonial struggles, Manifest Destiny, the Monroe Doctrine, fights for independence, the Spanish-American War, and the occupation of Haiti.

At the same time, Williams is invested in the power of the poetic imagination to reset the course of history, and "The Discovery of the Indies" concludes with a new beginning, a reimagined version of Columbus's own journal that emphasizes the beauty of the people, flora, and fauna of the New World, rather than the prospects for colonization. Williams accomplishes this goal not primarily by inserting new language into Columbus's journal, but by judicious pruning and rearranging. In the original, Columbus's assessment of Hispaniola emerges over many days. Williams, in contrast, combines Columbus's multiple entries into one entry dated October 12, 1492, showing his intention to renovate the moment of discovery itself. Columbus's journal mixes geographic and ethnographic description with calculations regarding conversion, conquest, and economic opportunities, such as "these appear to me a more domestic and tractable people," or "they do not know any religion, and I believe they could easily be converted to Christianity."[8] Williams's version of the journal deletes all such references to dominion and control, while retaining Columbus's own descriptions of the natives, their crafts, and the natural world: "youths, well made with very handsome bodies and very good countenances"; "canoes, made out of the trunk of a tree, all in one piece, and wonderfully worked"; "bright green trees"; and "fish so unlike ours that it is wonderful" (25–26).

Williams also foregrounds Columbus's observation that the natives, although painted black, white, and red "are themselves neither black nor white" (25). The fact that Columbus perceives red, white, and black as merely paints upon the natives, who have no essential color themselves, takes on special force in the context of Williams's multiracial emphasis in *In the American Grain.* Columbus's own words, repositioned in a new context, may offer a subtle implication to Williams's readers to transform their own racialized vision away from the binary paradigms governing U.S. discourse on race and citizenship. Overall, Williams's revision and revisitation of Columbus's journal foregrounds the intelligence, craft, and skill of the natives, who emerge not as tractable subjects for conversion or conquest, but as wonders in their own right. This catalog emphasizing the beautiful strangeness of the islands is similar to those of Stevens and Crane, but Williams's staging of the scene (and his placement of it in the larger volume) inflects this reimagined moment with particular force. The fact that Williams can offer this re-presentation using the colonizer's own (albeit judiciously edited) words, gives an even more tragic inflection to the lapsarian nature of the original "discovery," as it suggests that Columbus had the vocabulary and the potential to view the Caribbean and the New World through a language of love rather than conquest, but failed to do so. By concluding his narration of Columbus with a re-vision of the moment of encounter under different terms (of awe and wonder rather than conquest), Williams posits an alternate way for European-Americans (then and now) to approach the hemisphere, imaginatively revirginating the Discovery.

If this moment of renewed and improved Discovery seems highly Romantic, it is dialectically balanced in "The Discovery of the Indies" with Williams's antipodal investigation of the harsh politics surrounding Columbus's voyages and his downfall: anti-Romantic details that have been edited out of the historical record of celebration and expansion. Moreover, Williams counterpoints his "improved" version of Columbus's encounter with an elliptical conclusion and a shocking chapter for juxtaposition. "The Discovery of the Indies" concludes with a strong sense of unfulfilled potential that withholds crucial information from the reader:

"During that time I walked among the trees which was the most beautiful thing which I had ever seen . . ." (26; ellipses in original). In Columbus's original journal, this sentence leads into a description of a tropical forest, but Williams leaves his version of the sentence incomplete and closes the chapter with a Latin prayer to Mary. The abrupt end of the observation prevents readers from ever receiving a full description of what that beauty is, which puts an onus on readers to realize that scene for themselves.

More harshly, Williams effects a substantial contrast by moving from Columbus's newly retooled appreciation for the Caribbean to a chapter demonstrating that Europeans had not learned from Columbus's errors, "The Destruction of Tenochtitlan." Indeed, this chapter suggests that Cortés's conquest of the Aztecs is part and parcel of a cycle of violence and revenge emerging from the Discovery: "Upon the orchidean beauty of the new world the old rushed inevitably to revenge itself after the Italian's return" (27). Williams also makes clear that colonization was internally compromised from the start by personal rivalries among the Spanish, that there was no pristine moment of Spanish ascendancy. At the start of his renarration of Cortés, for example, Williams notes that, "Velasquez, the Cuban Governor who sent him out, traitorously attacked him from the rear a week afterward" (28). While this ambush is a historical fact, not an imaginative addition, the author's choice to foreground this relatively obscure detail in the first paragraph of "The Destruction of Tenochtitlan" reveals his shaping hand. Williams illustrates the fact that the conquistadors' enterprise, beyond its murderous impact upon the New World, was fraught with fratricidal divisions from the outset.

The multiple lapsarian moments in Williams's first two Caribbean chapters in *In the American Grain* suggest that he intended to reveal the untapped potential of both what could have been and what might still be in Europeans' encounter with the New World as refracted through the Caribbean. In tracing the histories of Hernando de Soto and Juan Ponce de León, Williams establishes even more direct challenges to the efficacy of Euro-American hegemony. These chapters suggest that in spite of the apparently successful centuries of conquest and domination since Columbus, Europeans have been seduced or subdued by New World myths of plenty (e.g., El Dorado) and revitalization (e.g., the Fountain of Youth), and thus are doomed to repeat the mistakes of the original colonizers until they break free from these paradigms. In the case of de Soto, Williams constructs a figurative dialogue between the New World "she" and de Soto, commencing with his arrival at Cuba, extending to Florida, and tracing his travels out West in search of El Dorado. While the scope of this chapter extends beyond the Caribbean, that basin (Cuba, then Florida, then beyond) constitutes a lure that draws him into a fatal pursuit: "You will not dare to cease following me—at Apalachi, at Cutifachiqui, at Mabilla, turning from the sea, facing inland. And in the end, you shall receive of me, nothing—save one long caress as of a great river passing forever upon your sweet corse" (45). Indeed, at the end of de Soto's chapter, his death is ignominious, hidden ("lest the Indians might venture on an attack when they should learn that he whom they feared was no longer opposed to them"), and only celebrated in the sense that his rivals wanted him gone ("some were glad" [58]). Beyond the almost Wagnerian *liebestod* between the explorer and the New World, Williams imagines the latter not only seducing de Soto, but transforming and vanquishing him. Referring to him as "my Indian," she draws a sweet sense of victory at the prospect of de Soto's transformation: "And if, to survive, you yourself in the end turned native, this victory is sweetest of all" (51). This change is likely viewed by Williams's fictionalized de Soto as degeneration, but in the broader modernist context of Stevens, Crane, and Frank, the need to somehow "turn native" in the face of what has been lost in the Americas seems a powerful imaginative antidote for recovering a renovated sense of self and nation.

The chapter surrounding Ponce de León is more explicitly Caribbean in focus than de Soto's, and encompasses a parable of hubristic expansion (and later, contraction) with even more direct resonances for a U.S. audience in the 1920s. With one of the most confrontational narrative voices in the collection, the narrator of this chapter, entitled "The Fountain of Eternal Youth," reimagines a military confrontation between Ponce de León and the Carib Indians in the historical present tense, with an imaginative, chronotopic collapse of history between the twentieth and the sixteenth centuries: "Fierce and implacable we kill them [the Caribs] but their souls dominate us. Our men, our blood, but their spirit is master. It enters us, it defeats us, it imposes itself. We are moderns—madmen at Paris—all lacking in a ground sense of cleanliness. It is the Caribs leaping out, facing the arquebuses, thinking it thunder, looking up at the sky: No rain! No clouds! Then the second volley" (40). Rather than simply pitying the Caribs as victims of European warcraft, Williams identifies with the indigenous spirit of the people and imaginatively surrenders to it: "Their souls dominate us." After the Spaniards have fired their guns and released their hounds, Williams finishes the battle scene between Ponce de León's men and the Caribs with a daunting image of bravery and defiance:

> Listen to this. The Indian swam out, the Spaniards in the boat turned back for the beast. The dog was steadily gaining on his victim. But, O Soul of the New World, the man had his bow and arrow with him as he saw. Tell that to Wilson. He stopped, turned, raised his body half out of the water, treading it, and put a bolt in the damned hound's throat—whom sharks swallowed. Then to shore, not forgetting—leaping to safety—to turn and spit back the swallowed chainshot, a derisive yell at the Christians. (41)

This spectacular scene is rife with metaphoric implications, both for the original "conquest" and for Williams's historical context. The indomitable Carib, at home on land and sea, treading water in a liminal space as he fends off an invasion, seems a perfect emblem of not only military resistance but utter rejection of European domination. Here, truly, is a figure of American self-reliance. The hound is slain and consumed, the chainshot spat out, and the Christians mocked for their failure. The narrator's injunction—"listen to this"—suggests not only his awareness that he is introducing a spectacular anecdote, but that he is going to provide a lesson. The anachronistic order to "tell that to Wilson" indirectly engages (and implicitly faults) the U.S. president for his intervention in the Caribbean (i.e., the Haitian occupation). In so doing, the narrator suggests continuities between these violent confrontations, past and present, with a reminder that the history of the Caribbean shows a fierce resistance to invasion.

Besides providing a cautionary example against imperial expansion, Williams's battle scene between the Spanish and the Caribs emerges as a source of inspiration for the narrator in his own right, as he extends an imaginative identification back to this conflicted moment: "If men inherit souls this is the color of mine. We are, too, the others. Think of them! The main islands were thickly populated with peaceful folk when the Christ-over found them. But the orgy of blood which followed, no man has written. We are the slaughterers. It is the tortured soul of our world" (41). Williams's speaker envisions a transmigration of souls such that the indigenous has passed into the European, attempting to establish an imagined unity between the conqueror and the conquered. Williams also reclaims a counterhistory in this passage with the injunction "Think of them!" and the call to remember "the orgy of blood" of which "no man has written." With respect to American identity, Williams collapses distinctions between past and present, European and indigenous, even at the level of grammar and pronoun reference. By the end of the passage it is not quite clear with which soul "we" should identify, because "we are, too, the others" and "we are the slaughterers." What is the "it" that is the "tortured soul of our world?" Given the range of commands in this passage, it seems most likely that Williams's narrator intends the "soul" to encapsulate the conflicted scene itself. To the extent that American nations (and national identities) are both descended from and opposed to Europe, this scene forms an apt mirror of the convergences and conflicts in American identity. Later in *In the American Grain,* Williams revisits the indomitable George Washington standing against the British ("Resistance was, I believe, his code" [141]), and the Carib seems, in retrospect, to be his forbearer. More pointedly, in recent history the United States had found itself on both sides of the Carib-European divide in the Spanish-American War: removing Cuba from Spanish dominion while also invading that same island to "defend" it.

For Williams's narrator, reckoning with the doubled identity of colonizer and colonized, while recovering the indigenous history that we have repressed, is essential for renovating American identity. If we do not do so, we run the risk of ending up like Ponce de León, who, like de Soto and Columbus in *In the American Grain,* has attempted to conquer the New World but falls into fatal alienation from it. In Williams's account, Ponce de León is victorious in the military conflict against the Caribs, but has lost everything else: his friends, his native mistress, and even his dog. More pointedly, he has lost his soul: "Men who do not know what lives are themselves dead. In the heart there are living Indians once slaughtered and defrauded" (42). Ponce de León's success is thus a Pyrrhic victory. In his lust for land, wealth, and dominion, Ponce de León has acquired an objectifying view of life (he does not "know what lives") that cuts him off from the people and the vitality of the New World. His conquests do not satisfy him; he feels "embittered and defeated" after enslaving the island and has only gold as his balm. The conquest took his youth, which he cannot regain. Failing to recognize that his malaise is the product of his colonial enterprise, Ponce de León pursues a miracle of rejuvenation, which drives him, like de Soto, to an ill-fated end. One of the enslaved Indian women tells Ponce de León of the Fountain of Youth, and it is this chimerical opportunity that proves most damning for him. The narrator comments, "Picture to yourself the significance of that—as revenge, as irony, as the trail of departing loveliness, *fata morgana.* Yet the real, the thing destroyed [i.e., the New World] turning back with a smile" (43). The short chapter ends with Ponce de León's death in Florida: "This time the Yamasses put an arrow into his thigh at the first landing—and let out his fountain. They flocked to the beach, jeered him as he was lifted to the shoulders of his men and carried away. Dead" (44). The ironic inversions here are clear: Ponce de León finds death, not life, in Florida; he becomes the fountain himself; his mocked end is in ignominious parallel to the triumphant Carib at the start of the chapter.

The fate of Ponce de León, particularly in the context of the exhortation to Wilson, adds another layer of anti-imperial caution. To the extent that pro-expansionists and annexationists such as Roosevelt had advocated for interventions in the Caribbean to find a new frontier to test the nation's mettle, the Caribbean emerged as a fountain of youth for the United States. By revisiting Ponce de León's "second landing" in Florida, Williams may have been suggesting that U.S. interventions in the region (such as those into Cuba and Haiti) ran the risk of being similarly fruitless and deadly quests. More importantly for Williams as an artist, such literal territorial expansion would impoverish and forestall the metaphoric recovery of the New World embodied in the defiant Carib, who so firmly resisted European domination.

Uniting the four Caribbean encounters in Williams, readers are confronted by a series of imagined second chances for recolonizing the hemisphere (either literally or figuratively), and it is left to readers, particularly those of European descent, to ask if they want to repeat the cycle of slaughter and vengeance between the Old and the New, or to reconsider that history to build a new image of America that takes into account the suppressed Caribbean "other." In this light, the true "fountain of youth" in *In the American Grain* emerges from a commitment to build the future of American culture and identity not on "pure" European sources (as Stoddard and Grant argued), but on a recovery of the forgotten cultures and peoples in the American hemisphere.

A "Bridge" to a Different Shore: Hart Crane's Caribbean Poems

Williams's and Stevens's accounts of the Discovery in the New World both point out the failures of colonization, with an implication that a lost opportunity could be imaginatively recovered. Crane effects an even more striking refiguration of Columbus. Whereas Williams and Stevens expose or play upon selected historical elements of Columbus, Crane constructs a new myth entirely. His treatment of Columbus in "Ave Maria" forms the first section of his larger masterpiece *The Bridge* (1930). Crane frames Columbus as a mad prophet, an "exile in the streets" of Europe. As Columbus approaches the shore of San Salvador, he says to himself, "For I have seen now what no perjured breath/Of clown nor sage can riddle or gainsay."[9] By making the gainsayers range from clown to sage, Crane suggests that Columbus is opposed by the full range of conventional and erudite opinion in European society. The image of Columbus as an unbelieved visionary is a familiar one, but Crane takes his visionary spirit to a new level and renders Columbus more alienated than either Williams or Stevens do.

In "Ave Maria," Columbus offers an invocation, in which he calls upon Luis de San Angel and Madre María [Mother Mary] for aid in his quest. It is also Crane's invocation to Columbus, as Crane reaches back to find the first source of the energy he will trace in the rest of *The Bridge.* The poem builds towards a frenetic close, finishing with a figuration that combines Christian imagery with erotic promise:

still one shore beyond desire!
The sea's green crying towers a-sway, Beyond
And kingdoms
naked in the
trembling heart—
Te Deum Laudamus
O Thou Hand of Fire. (51–52)

The ravishment that Crane expects in this vision is not the political and military rape that Williams depicts in *In the American Grain,* but a holy coupling of worlds that will bear new fruit.

Crane thus converts the moment of Columbus's arrival into a sacred union between the New World and the Old. This choice is audacious: Columbus was in no way a good partner for the "naked kingdoms" of the New World. But Crane is not interested in representing history as it was—it is more accurate to say that he is representing history as he would have liked it to have been (as Williams reimagined Columbus's moment of discovery). Crane's mythmaking gaze is characteristic of the arc of the larger poem. In the concluding lines to the title poem, "To Brooklyn Bridge," he addresses the structure and intones, "Unto us lowliest sometime sweep, descend / And of the curveship lend a myth to God" (46). This last statement, for all its religious connotations, reverses traditional assumptions about God and the world. God needs to borrow a "myth," and Crane, paradoxically, prays for God to be supported by the bridge. More broadly, in *The Bridge* as a whole, Crane positions himself as constructing new myths for the Americas, and his revisitation of Columbus's arrival thus functions as the anchor for what is to come.

Crane moves away from Columbus in *The Bridge* following "Ave Maria," but he returns to Caribbean scenes in a variety of subsequent poems. Indeed, arguably his last planned collection, "Key West: An Island Sheaf," is centered in the Caribbean and uses the setting to great effect. As a matter of textual provenance, the poems in "Key West" are technically uncollected, as they were not published during Crane's brief lifetime, but they do provide a window into how Crane perceived America's tropical Caribbean as a source of poetic regeneration and inspiration. Although the grouping is relatively small (eighteen poems), the scope of expression and technique in "Key West" is quite extensive. Formally, the poems encompass free verse, broken sonnets, quatrains, ballads, prose poems, and monologues. In terms of tone and subject matter, the poems range from erotic appreciations of the tropical setting, to explicitly political critiques of U.S. imperialism ("Imperator Victus"), to set-pieces depicting island scenes ("The Mango Tree)," to romantic invocations.

An invocation with the Whitmanesque title of "O Carib Isle!" begins the sheaf. Like Stevens, Crane is fascinated by the dual processes of generation and death, eros and thanatos, unfolding within the islands. The sense of exclamation embedded in "O Carib Isle!" however, shows Crane's appreciation for this setting as a site of holy mystery rather than as a source of intellectual inspiration. The first stanza sets in motion twinned forces by presenting a paradoxical scene of life-in-death: wildlife crawling in a calm island cemetery—"The tarantula rattling at the lily's foot/Across the feet of the dead" (156). The exchange between life and death continues towards the center of the poem, as the speaker contrasts the measured plots of the graves around him with the unfolding abundance of plant life: "Tree names, flower names/Deliberate, gainsay death's brittle crypt" (156). The role of the speaker in evoking life as a counter to death, the need to name, as well as the abundant plants in contrast to the (presumably nameless) dead suggests almost a secular *logos* or a poetic epistemology similar to that of Stevens's "The Idea of Order at Key West," wherein the ordering imagination vivifies a natural scene.

The second half of the poem takes a more questioning turn, and Crane's speaker finds himself confronted by a crucial absence on the island, the lack of human authority, along with a sense of decay: "But where is the Captain of this doubloon isle/Without a turnstile?" The speaker's observation that there is a lack of either military authority ("Captain") or controlling gate ("turnstile") suggests that the island is a New World sublime: a place beyond the reach of human governance. While this was conspicuously not the case for the actual political sphere of the Caribbean, the evacuation of human authority in "O Carib Isle!" seems crucial for Crane's use of the island as a poetic and spiritual site. Rather than any specific historical or human connection in the island, Crane seeks a transcendent link to natural forces beyond the limitations of contemporary society and history. The poem closes with a sense that the poet has been equipped with a dangerous and subversive new voice through his contemplation of the play of life and death on the island: "You have given me the shell, Satan,—carbonic amulet/Sere of the sun exploded in the sea" (157). This closing image of a Satanic gift may reflect the poet's own recognition of the unorthodox and un-Christian metaphysics of "O Carib Isle!" At the surface, this poem echoes traditional notions of life or transcendence overcoming death, but it does so not via Christian redemption, but through either the logos of the poet or the animistic power of regenerating natural cycles. In addition, the observation that the pilgrim cannot be bound to earth suggests a Promethean urge to break away from conventional strictures—all themes that resonate elsewhere in Crane's poetry, but are registered here as an elemental, primal struggle.

In keeping with Crane's interest in contemplating and upending religious traditions, the succeeding poem in the collection, "The Mermen," contemplates the fall of the Spanish Cross, with implications both for Christianity and empire: "The Cross alone has flown the wave./But since the Cross sank, much that's warped and cracked/Has followed in its name, has heaped its grave." Crane's sense that the Cross has fallen in the islands has a political dimension as well: it shows that the old U.S. expectation that it would "free" the Caribbean from the Spanish Cross has come to fruition. Much like Stevens in "Sunday Morning," Crane calls for a more human connection to spirituality, asking that the listener contemplate "This Cross, agleam still with a human Face!" (158).

Crane plays upon this image for satiric effect in his bizarre but effective "Imperator Victus," which uses odd dialect to reference gunboat diplomacy and U.S. hegemony in the region:

Big guns again
No speakee well
But plain.

Again, again—
And they shall tell
The Spanish Main

The Dollar from the Cross (166)

One might recall Antonio Benítez-Rojo's model of the repeating "plantation machine" and see its echoes in Crane's observation of the "big guns" speaking "again, again" in the Caribbean.[10] Crane's depiction of the symbolic triumph here ("the Dollar from the Cross") is also telling, as he parodically sacralizes the image of U.S. currency as equivalent to the most ancient Christian emblem. In so doing, he evokes the truism that the U.S. worships "the almighty dollar," while also foregrounding the hubris and avarice at the heart of U.S. neocolonialism in the region.

Although they include gestures towards contemporary politics, Crane is more concerned in these Key West poems with the personal and the artistic, even as the role of the islands remains central. Indeed, late in the collection, Crane's speaker will attest that he has been tempered and strengthened by exposure to the extremes of the islands, from heat and hurricanes to tropic death and lushness. In "Key West," which carries forward the self-inquiring spirit of "O Carib Isle!" the speaker declares that his time in the islands has prepared him for a transition, whether to "heaven or hades," with another twist on biblical imagery of body and belonging: "Here has my salient faith annealed me./Out of the valley, past the ample crib/To skies impartial, that do not disown me" (171). The poet's descriptions of what he will be leaving well speak to why the islands are his point of embarkation. He reflects on cold urban landscapes composed of "apish nightmares" and "steel-strung stone," in contrast with Key West, where there is "water, and a little wind . . ." This description clearly shows that Key West is not a wasteland, but the poem does not evoke the elemental textures of life and death that animate "O Carib Isle!" Indeed, "Key West" closes with a sense of diminution that suggests that the poet may foresee a limit to tropical regeneration: "There is no breath of friends and no more shore/Where gold has not been sold and conscience tinned." The first line portends a permanent loneliness and a fear of exhausted possibilities, "no more shore." The last evokes an image of human connection being reduced to commerce and the human self to commodity. In this context, Key West provides a "last stand" for the poet to contemplate the sky and the infinite, away from the steel, stone, tin, and gold that are circumscribing human life. Across the scope of "Key West: an Island Sheaf," one can say that Crane uses the Caribbean setting to provide both *memento mori* and *memento vivi* that illustrate propositions counter to the normative, puritanical traditions that he saw as central obstacles to his life and art in the United States.

(Dis)locating the Caribbean in Eugene O'Neill and William Faulkner

The search for renewal in the Caribbean by modernist poets contrasts starkly with the uses to which the region was put by William Faulkner and Eugene O'Neill. These two writers each made an "intervention" into Haiti or a Haiti-like island, but used the space primarily for tragic ends. O'Neill's *The Emperor Jones* premiered in 1920, and Haiti is referenced ironically in the opening notes on the setting: "The action of the play takes place on an island in the West Indies as yet not self-determined by White Marines."[11] This description distances the setting of the play from Haiti, as there is not yet a Marine presence there, even as the oxymoronic description "self-determined by White Marines" makes the play topical by hinting at the hypocrisy of the U.S. intervention. In the play, an island much like Haiti emerges as a failed ground of conquest and expansion for the African American Jones, whose life emerges as a microcosm of the black diaspora. In this respect, the island is a screen for O'Neill's projective experiment: the play has essentially nothing to say about the Caribbean islands, their cultures, or their peoples on their own terms. Rather, the island provides the setting for a story that, while set in a foreign space, is still U.S.-centric, premised on the escape of an African American fugitive from the no-man's-land of American racial politics to a black island of his own. As Jones declares to his truckling assistant, Smithers, "From stowaway to Emperor in two years!" (190).

The Emperor Jones follows a clear and classical tragic arc, as the once great, now corrupt emperor is deserted by his subjects, flees into the forest, and finds death at the hands of the native islanders. Critics have skirmished over whether or not O'Neill is engaged in dangerous racial comedy (particularly in the context of the dialectical connections to the minstrel tradition) at the expense of his protagonist. Indeed, the choice to situate Jones as the head of failed revolution ("Den de revolution is at de post" [196], he tells Smithers) invites the question of whether or not O'Neill is mocking revolutionary concepts of self-determination. Those macrocosmic political issues drop away entirely, however, as the play delves more deeply into the realm of myth, tracing an allegorical, chronotopic journey "back to Africa" that is completed inside Jones's (un)consciousness. Fleeing from the palace into the forest, Jones confronts a host of images from a past that seems not only personal but racial: "little formless fears," a murdered Pullman porter named Jeff, a southern chain gang, an auction block, a slave ship, and then the Congo itself. As richly suggestive as the play's setting is, evoking both contemporary geopolitics and historical American desires for the islands, the unnamed island is essentially unimportant in itself for the play, except as a symbolic waypoint between the United States and Africa.

Almost every aspect of Jones's rise and fall gains meaning not from reference to a Caribbean context, but from a connection back to the United States and, later, to Africa. For example, when Jones lectures Smithers about "big stealin'" versus "little stealin'"—namely, that it is easier to steal from a country than from a person—he refers to his time as a Pullman porter: "If dey's one thing I learns in ten years on de Pullman ca's listenin' to de white quality talk, it's dat same fact" (191). Similarly, Jones appears to have used his rough-and-tumble past (or perhaps a fiction of it) in the U.S. to authenticate his right to rule and to intimidate the islanders. As Smithers notes, "I was only thinkin' o' the bloody lies you told the blacks 'ere about killin' white men in the States" (194). When Jones needs to comfort himself in the face of haunting spirits, he declares, "Doesn't you know dey's got to do wid a man was a member in good standin' o' de Baptist Church? Sho' I was dat when I was porter on de Pullmans, befo' I got into my little trouble. Let dem try deir heathen tricks" (200). He further reassures himself, "I tells you I'se safe's 'f I was in New York City" (201). When confronted by a vision of a southern chain gang, he draws a distinction between U.S. blacks and the "primitive" islanders: "Is you civilized, or is you like dese ign'rent black niggers heah?" (211).

When Jones does achieve a symbolic breakthrough in his unconsciousness, it is a reverie that references essentially a range of exoticist clichés: a witch doctor, the Congo, and a crocodile. Setting aside the obvious problem of a white playwright conjuring up an image of "essential" racial identity by use of stock figures from popular fiction and film, there seems to be a flaw in the backward moving logic of unconscious psychodrama within Jones: namely, how does the island fit into this symbolic pattern? If one examines closely the reversal of the middle passage trajectory, from Pullman (in the U.S. North), to chain gang (in the South), to auction block (at the U.S. coast), to slave ship (in the Atlantic), to the tribal scene (in the Congo), there is an enormous lacuna with respect to the Caribbean island on which the play takes place. One might argue that more of the dramatic action, at least as staged imaginatively in Jones's fears, takes place in a recollected United States than within the island setting evoked at the start of the play. That O'Neill sets a play on a Caribbean island and then subsequently avoids almost any specific reference to it well speaks to the paradoxically invisible role the Caribbean plays as the setting for *The Emperor Jones.*

If O'Neill regards the Caribbean as a place of devolution—the site where Jones's chronotopic return to Africa occurs—Faulkner shows a much more ambivalent approach towards the region. His writings touching on the Caribbean are relatively few, confined to a five-year period (1931–36), and include a couple of stories, a few crucial sections of *Absalom, Absalom!* and portions of an adapted screenplay. Scholars have rightly focused attention on these pieces, however, as they form a crucial keystone in the vision of New World history that develops across his work. These Caribbean vistas, however compact, also bear examining because they reveal Faulkner's placement of an intense symbolic weight on the region. Faulkner seems conflicted in his regard for the Caribbean itself within this relatively small body of work, which suggests its significance to him as an "other" that he found difficult to grasp.

Faulkner's first works set in the Caribbean are the stories "Black Music" (1934) and "Carcassonne" (1931), which he locates in the U.S. neocolonial space of Rincon, Puerto Rico, an oil town. Although these stories are slight, Faulkner chose "Carcassonne" as the final story in his *Collected Stories* (1950). As M. E. Bradford notes, Faulkner was insistent in his letters to Malcolm Cowley that it be the closing note for the collection—"set for one pitch, contrapuntal in integration, toward one end, one finale"—which suggests that this story encompassed something vital that he wished to accentuate.[12] In considering "Carcassonne" and "Black Music," one finds a range of familiar and unfamiliar tropes from literatures of the tropics and colonization. The central character in each story, Walter Midgleston, lives as a drunken mendicant and storyteller, a character who would be at home in a B. Traven novel like *The Treasure of the Sierra Madre* (1927). In contrast to conventional expectations of moral decline in the tropics, Midgleston's decline appears to have happened already, back in the United States. In a dialogue with the narrator that forecasts some of the storytelling rhythms of *Absalom, Absalom!* Midgleston discloses a personal history, in muddied anecdotes and newspaper articles, that reveals a spectacular incident of gothic excess. Traveling to the Virginia woods to show architecture plans to his firm's client, the New York socialite Mrs. Van Dyming, Midgleston becomes drunk on the way, perceives himself as a faun, and chases Van Dyming through the woods in a bout of attempted rape and/or murder, thus creating a scandal and a legend regarding a mysterious half-naked madman in the countryside. Midgleston's history of momentary excess and flight from respectability in "Black Music" embodies an almost Hawthornian sensibility of guilt, in which the true darkness and the "imp of the perverse" comes from within, not without. In this context, it is crucial to note that in Rincon, in contrast to dominant expectations of sexualization, excess, and Caribbean exoticism, Midgleston is precisely the opposite: asexual, nonlibidinous, and utterly spent. He spends his days begging from tourists and locals alike, and sleeps each night on a tarpaper roll in the garret of a tavern.

Given that Rincon is simply a framing spot for a narrative primarily focused on Virginia, one might ask whether or not the Caribbean context is relevant at all to the story. However, small details in both "Black Music" and "Carcassonne" suggest that Faulkner is interested in the role that the island plays as a non-national neocolonial space for U.S. citizens. In each story Faulkner makes profuse mention of either the Standard Oil Company or the Universal Oil Company, which appears to be in total control of the town. Although it would be an overstatement to read Faulkner's portrait of "big oil" as somehow a critique of neocolonialism, it is striking how Rincon appears to be a dark wasteland under the capitalist dominion of the oil company. As Midgleston heads to his tarpaper bed, he reflects on the town, "Beneath him Rincon followed its fatal, secret, nightly pursuits, where upon the rich and inert darkness of the streets lighted windows and doors lay like oily strokes of broad and overladen brushes."[13] The paradoxical construction "rich and inert" reflects both the economic productivity of the town and the apparent passivity of its occupants, who appear to be "owned" by the company: "But the Standard Oil Company, who owned the garret and the roofing paper, owned the darkness too; it was Mrs Widdrington's, the Standard Oil Company's wife's, darkness he was using to sleep in" (897). The fact that the oil company has come to own the darkness itself suggests an evacuation of potency and meaning from even the elements of nature (darkness is always symbolically rich in Faulkner). In addition, Midgleston and his habitat in this passage are utterly feminized, as they are subordinated not merely to the company, but to the owner's wife.

Indeed, much of the force of "Carcassonne" emerges from a contrapuntal development between Midgleston's visions of Tennysonian heroism and his slow, meaningless death in the unheroic and apparently banal "company town" of Rincon. Much like Eliot's J. Alfred Prufrock (or Edwin Arlington Robinson's Miniver Cheevy), Midgleston contemplates fantasies of heroic action that will never reach fruition: "'I would like to perform something,' he said, shaping his lips soundlessly in the darkness, and the galloping horse filled his mind again with soundless thunder. . . . *I want to perform something bold and tragical and austere*" (898–99; emphasis in original). The contrast between sound and silence, passivity and boldness, becomes all the more potent when one considers that the United States obtained Puerto Rico via the Spanish-American War, which, particularly in the vision of Theodore Roosevelt and his own cavalry of "Rough Riders," was seen as a means to reinvigorate U.S. masculinity and colonial opportunity. In these stories, U.S. colonization of the Caribbean has produced not a bang, but a whimper, as personal heroism and action have devolved into economic capitalization and corporatization.

In contrast to the exhausted destiny of Midgleston in Puerto Rico, the Caribbean in *Absalom, Absalom!* (1936) provides another character from Virginia, Thomas Sutpen, with a place to seize his own personal destiny. Much as it did for Emperor Jones, Haiti serves as a proving ground (and arguably, the root of a tragic fall) for a lowborn U.S. man, this time a poor white rather than an African American. Faulkner's intensely rewritten drafts of the Haitian passages in Sutpen's history in *Absalom, Absalom!* show him struggling to locate an ur-scene of defiance and betrayal that could encapsulate the Black Atlantic interconnections between North America, Africa, and the Caribbean. For Faulkner, these interconnections are especially conflicted, as the Caribbean (particularly the Latin Caribbean) resonates both as a register of difference and as an uncanny double for the South. In recent years, with the rise of globally directed American studies, many excellent critics—including Édouard Glissant, Vera Kutzinski, and John T. Matthews—have directed substantial attention to unraveling the role that the Caribbean, and the Black Atlantic more generally, plays in Faulkner's work. Such scholarship usually argues that Faulkner offers a critique of hemispheric imperialism in the islands (both European and American) comparable to his searing examination of racial politics within his home region of Mississippi. Maritza Stanchich finds that "Faulkner's portrayal of Haiti . . . solidly links the curse of Southern slavery with the curse of American imperialism."[14] Matthews argues that the Haitian connection in *Absalom, Absalom!* "signals a persistence of historical knowledge that survives even the effort to shut one's eyes to it."[15] While I agree that Faulkner's Caribbean and Atlantic glances do "recall," in Matthews word, hemispheric connections that are often ignored, I assert that Faulkner's vision of the Caribbean and Africa simultaneously evades such specific "historical knowledge," in favor of a mythic projection of guilt that is symbolically rich but historically impoverished. I draw upon archival findings from the manuscript history of *Absalom, Absalom!* and the screenplay *The Last Slaver* (1936) to illuminate how Faulkner's handling of the Caribbean and the Black Atlantic both recalls and obscures these regions.

In *Absalom, Absalom!* the Caribbean is both overdetermined and underrepresented at the same time. The dangerous and fertile Caribbean is both Sutpen's mentor and his nemesis, a source of wealth and a source of contamination: there he learns the slave trade and passes into manhood, and there he fathers the (possibly) mulatto son who will later ruin his plans for a southern dynasty. At the same time, the Caribbean past within the text is disembodied, abstract, and unvoiced. Not a single unmediated word is transmitted from those episodes; rather, their history descends through many layers of Compson family narrators.[16] The attenuated origin of the West Indian story should caution readers against treating these passages as Faulkner's attempt to evoke a reliable historical portrait of that regional connection. Similarly, critics should resist the temptation to use Sutpen as a figure intended to represent the South as a whole. Although Stanchich and Matthews situate Sutpen's Haitian past as emblematic of the conflicted relationship between the United States and the Caribbean,[17] Sutpen is presented as an outsider and arriviste in *Absalom, Absalom!* Using a marginal white figure like Sutpen to establish a West Indies connection confirms a connection between the wealth of the United States and that region, while evading the direct historical juxtaposition of Caribbean and southern slavery that might result from comparing a Haitian plantation to that of Faulkner's first families of Yoknapatawpha, such as the Compsons or the Stevenses.

At first glance, there may seem to be a distinct tension here between Faulkner's use of Haiti both as an overdetermined proving ground and as an underrepresented, or even unrepresentable, other, but these two qualities are actually complementary. It is precisely because the region is not locatable as a historical space within the novel (indeed, it is a historical impossibility—Sutpen could not have been working on a plantation in Haiti at that time, as slavery had been outlawed in the Haitian Constitution of 1804[18]) that it can serve as such a capacious symbolic reserve. Faulkner's process of revision surrounding the novel's Caribbean passages confirms a design to use the region as a kind of New World unconscious, a place that is resonant but unvoiced. His revisions of the West Indies section form a set of precise subtractions that make the region and

Sutpen's time there more shadowy and underrepresented. One might say that Faulkner revised not for clarity in his handling of the Caribbean, but for carefully orchestrated obscurity.

Most of these revisions center on the "siege" scene: Sutpen is barricaded in the sugar planter's house, and he performs the vigorous defense of the family that earns him his fortune, his bride, and, perhaps, his curse. In the original manuscript, Faulkner treats the actions of the black Haitians as a political revolt. For example, when Sutpen shoots his musket, in the original he does so "into the Haitian darkness where the insurrecting niggers crept and hid and howled and sang."[19] The manuscript shows that Faulkner crossed out that passage, and, in the first published version of *Absalom, Absalom!* all mention of "insurrection" disappears. Sutpen simply "fired through the windows" and there is no mention of the Haitians outside or their sounds.[20] In a similar vein, the period of waiting is described in the original as a war scene: "during the 7 or 8 nights while they were besieged" (257). In the published version, it is rendered as "the seven or eight nights while they huddled in the dark" (249). The effect of these subtle changes is to remove the conflict between the planter and his slaves from the realm of a political insurgency to a primal confrontation between Sutpen and an impersonal, disembodied "darkness" outside the house.

The sense of historical guilt located in Haiti is also depersonalized by Faulkner's revisions. In a bravura section that touches on displacement and the Middle Passage, Faulkner wrote in his original manuscript of "that land, earth, which would require 10,000 years of equatorial heritage to bear it—a little island which was not even the halfway point between the jungle they came from and the civilization they were doomed for, which the black blood, the black arms, and hands and bones and thinking and remembering and hopes and desires. . . ." (258). This passage was crossed out in the manuscript by Faulkner, but it is restored in almost exactly the same form in the final version of the novel, except that the arms and hands have disappeared in favor of "the black blood, the black bones, and flesh," and the island is reframed as "the halfway point" between jungle and civilization (250). In neither version is the black body embraced as a whole entity, but in the second it is not even differentiated into limbs (arms and hands, which have the power to act), but into raw tissues—blood, bone, and flesh. These revisions depoliticize Haiti, paradoxically, even as they locate it as an original site of historical guilt. The descriptions of the Haitians render them as entirely abject victims, without agency or voice. Faulkner represents the island as a "theater for violence" (250) in this section of the novel, but, in theatrical terms, the blacks have no roles. Such passages, particularly in their revised versions, show Faulkner to be offering a paradoxically ahistorical anti-imperialist critique, one that is as evasive as it condemning. The stereotyped abstraction (jungle versus civilization) and the misleading symbolic resonance of Haiti as a "halfway" point between Africa and America serve to position the Caribbean and the Middle Passage not in the realm of recovered history but in that of transcendent myth, where responsibility is abstracted rather than historicized. The hyperbolic time frame ("10,000 years") escalates the scope and resonance of the slave trade so that it becomes an epic enormity outside of modern history, rather than a specific economic and political system with recent connections to the hemisphere's development. Especially given Sutpen's role as an outsider within Yoknapatawpha County, the Haitian passages seem less an apotheosis of the southern system, or a chronotope of hemispheric imperial exchanges, and more a screen for evoking a system of slavery that is fecund, primal, and dangerous, but reassuringly distinct from the "civilization" of the United States.[21]

Faulkner evokes and evades the Black Atlantic even more powerfully in one of his most unusual film projects, *The Last Slaver,*[22] which he helped write in 1936, the same year that *Absalom, Absalom!* was published. *The Last Slaver* forms a fine parallel to *Absalom, Absalom!* and it provides scholars with the only Faulknerian enterprise that depicts African scenes and the Middle Passage itself. In addition, this melodrama, especially in its early drafts, offers perhaps Faulkner's most powerful vision of slavery as a *national* institution in his body of work. Much as the story of Sutpen is the product of multiple narrators, *The Last Slaver* has a similarly tortuous narrative history. The screenplay's origin is traceable to an obscure novel from 1933 by George S. King. Faulkner was brought in by Daryl Zanuck, founder of Fox Pictures, to adapt the screenplay, with help from Sam Hellman and Gladys Lehman. King's novel *The Last Slaver* is based on a historical episode in which a member of a New York yacht club converted a pleasure/racing yacht for the purpose of slave running in disguise. King builds a maritime adventure novel out of this episode, with a geographic range from North America, to Africa, to the Caribbean, and eventually to London. The primary dramatic tension in the novel arises from the fact that the third mate, Kane, is a Yankee sailor of "old revolutionary stock" but is tricked into serving on the *Wanderer,* a slave ship.[23] The ship is captained by the superficially charismatic but ultimately dissipated and tyrannical Pierre LaRoche, a native of New Orleans, who works for the shadowy African Trading Company.

The bulk of the plot stays above deck and at sea, where Kane struggles, along with a large and loyal African cook, Kalva, and a right-minded group of Anglo-Saxon European sailors, to defeat LaRoche and his Latin partisans. King includes infrequent but detailed scenes of the slave trade—the irons, the purchasing, visits to the slave fort at the Congo, and a trip into belly of the ship, where the slaves are held. By the end of the novel, Kane, in contrast with his biblical namesake, acts as his black brothers' keeper, and repatriates the slaves to the Congo with the help of the British navy. The denouement of the novel is essentially a sunny revision of *Heart of Darkness*. Kane and his British allies overthrow the Portuguese slave fort and, in gratitude, the Africans lead them to a cache of ivory upriver, bearing them on royal litters most of the way. At the end, Kane sails in triumph back to London, with the *Wanderer* now his ship, a load of ivory in the hold, and an English lord's daughter as his intended.

Faulkner's two screenplay adaptations of the novel are essentially wholesale rewritings. In terms of overall focus, Faulkner and his co-writers kept *The Last Slaver* largely a melodramatic sea tale of love, mutiny, and smuggling. A key difference from the novel, however, is the underrepresentation of the Africans themselves. While Kalva in the novel is essentially a stock character—the simple, loyal African—he has a large speaking role and figures significantly in the revolt on board, even saving the life of the hero, Kane. In Faulkner's screenplay version, by contrast, there is only one speaking part for a black actor; a "negro boy" delivers a letter to the mate and tells him, "White man gimme this to give you."[24] Furthermore, the slaves themselves are reduced to a mere backdrop for the action: they are seen only when being loaded or unloaded into the ship. In this respect, the role of the slaves is parallel to that of the Haitians in *Absalom, Absalom!*—a source of horror and victimhood in the background, with white masculine struggle in the foreground. An even greater change is that the slaver captain (renamed Lovett) becomes the primary character in Faulkner's adaptation, rather than the Yankee sailor (renamed Duncan in the first two screenplays). Captain Lovett bears more than a passing resemblance to Thomas Sutpen. He is strong, charismatic, and straightforward, but rough around the edges. Nevertheless, he is represented as basically a decent man trapped in a system, with perhaps a dose of the "innocence" attributed to Sutpen by Mr. Compson. In both versions, he explains to Nancy, his wife, that he got into the business as a boy and found it was "too late" to get out:

> I went into when I was a boy. All it meant to me then was excitement. Boys have no sense. Then it was just my life—like farming is somebody else's life. I never thought any more of it than that—and then I was older, before I knew it, and I met you. That told me what I—what I was—and what I was doing. I knew then that I was dirty . . . filthy . . . I was ashamed. But I loved you so much—that I thought I could escape from it, so you'd never know—and that's what I tried to do. But it was too late . . .[25]

After falling in love with and marrying Nancy, Lovett tries to end his career as a slaver. He surprises the crew with Nancy and indicates that he is going to Jamaica to retire as a sugar planter with his wife. The crew, led by the violent first mate, Thompson, mutinies, and forces Lovett back to Africa for another slave run. After taking on a load of slaves, Duncan steers the ship to a safe colonial port, and the screenplay reaches its dramatic climax. Duncan spirits Nancy away on a boat while Lovett unchains the Africans and has a final gunfight with Thompson. Lovett finishes as a tragic hero who has finally done the right thing, but must die for his sins. Each version ends with the ship exploding after a lantern fire reaches the powder magazine. Lovett's ship and legacy, the *Wanderer,* meets the same spectacular end as Sutpen's home.

This romantic handling of a slave captain may be galling to contemporary readers, but nevertheless there are complexities of politics and plot that hint at a more challenging understanding of the history of the slave trade, and a broader sense of the Black Atlantic, than in *Absalom, Absalom!* While King's novel basically follows the historical routes of the nineteenth-century slave trade, Faulkner makes some key revisions. First, he eliminates the West Indies altogether, except as a hoped-for place of retirement for Lovett. In doing so, he sidesteps both the geography of the novel and much of the history of the trade routes themselves. Why would Faulkner make this choice, especially given his interest in the Caribbean in portions of *Absalom, Absalom!* published that same year? Faulkner's revision of the plot within *The Last Slaver* shows a design to depict an enlarged geography of the slave trade in North America, in effect expanding the vision of a Black Atlantic that he touched on in the Haitian passages in *Absalom, Absalom!* Both screenplay versions begin with a launching not in New York City but in Salem, Massachusetts. A young girl, explicitly Nancy in the second version, christens the yacht, but as soon as she breaks the champagne on it and it launches into the water, it crushes a sailor. An old sea salt watching the scene proclaims it is "launched in blood!" "She's evil. She's begun evil and she'll end evil"

(24 September 1936, 4–5). The ship passes to Captain Lovett at an auction, where he is the sole bidder, as mishaps have given it a reputation as a cursed ship. In both screenplays, the *Wanderer* will never go farther South in the U.S. than Virginia. In choosing to stay so close to the North and the mid-Atlantic, Faulkner relocates the focus of slave trade away from the deep South and the Caribbean towards the heart of the eastern seaboard. In giving the ship a Massachusetts origin, he also creates a symbolic connection that unites the slave trade with the cradle of liberty. One might call this sectionalist evasion, but in this revision Faulkner achieves a Hawthornian evocation of the deep, guilty dependence that *all* of the United States had on slavery for its wealth and development.

Indeed, in the first version of the screenplay Faulkner creates a symbolic and polemical reminder that the entire United States, not just the Deep South, was involved in the slave economy. When Lovett purchases the ship, it most recently was owned by someone from the "Potomac Yacht Club," the premier boating club in Washington, D.C., to which the admiral of the U.S. Navy himself belongs. Lovett keeps the Potomac's insignia and uses its elite provenance as a disguise: no one will pull over a ship thought to belong to the club, even navy cruisers, as the captains fear offending the admiral and the Washington elite. As Lovett brags to his mate, "With this yacht and that pennant up there, I've practically got a license from the government to import slaves" (19). Although this is a rather flimsy plot device (which may be why it was eliminated in the second version), it evokes the sense of national complicity, even as the Webster-Ashburton Treaty of 1842 mandated that Britain and the United States patrol to eliminate slave ships. By placing a slave ship in the heart of the nation—at its very capital—Faulkner suggests the inextricable connections between the nation and the illicit trade.

Faulkner's depiction of U.S. enforcement of the treaty in the first draft is deeply cynical. When the exploits of the slaver come to light, the British ambassador confronts the secretary of state: "To put it bluntly, Mr. Secretary, our English government simply cannot understand how this running of African slaves can continue in the face of our treaty to fight it with both our navies." The American secretary "suavely" offers a lukewarm reply: "You may rest assured, sir, that the matter will not be allowed to pass without the fullest inquiry" (8). This same exchange is then parroted down the bureaucratic chain of command: to the secretary of war, to a Navy admiral, to a commodore, to his lieutenants. The effect of this repetition (the dialogue repeats exactly) is to suggest a rote exchange of official pronouncements, with the promises ultimately hollow. In the first version, an idealistic young lieutenant, Tom Duncan, suspects that the *Wanderer* is a slaver, and speaks with the Secretary of War about his suspicions, but he is promptly fired for his allegations: "Are you implying that a member of the Potomac Yacht Club is running slaves?" (54). After his discharge, Duncan goes to work in a tavern, where he ends up being recruiting by Thompson, to serve, unwittingly, on the very ship he had almost caught.

Producers Zanuck and Johnson were not enthusiastic about these governmental scenes, and they were all excised in the second version of the script. There is no focus on the navy's failure to catch the slaver, and Duncan is rewritten as a disgraced British seaman who signs on in Africa when the *Wanderer* is taking in slaves during its first voyage. The screenplay offers a series of Senate speeches, where senators from Massachusetts and Georgia alike deplore the slave trade, culminating in a senator shouting, "Slaving ships must be driven from the sea!" which is met with "applause from the galleries and the floor" in great "waves." (12). To enhance the melodramatic effect of discovering that her husband is a slaver later in the film, Faulkner has Nancy in the gallery, watching these speeches about the slave trade. The need to emphasize an American commitment to ending the trade appears to have been very strong, because in the second version, justice emerges not from a final confrontation near the British naval base of St. Helena, but at a fictitious American antislavery outpost in the Atlantic named Maricoba.

The elimination of the cynical political backdrop effectively reduced the sense of national complicity at the level of official government, but Faulkner and his cowriters tweaked some details in the second version to locate another kind of responsibility—uncanny and personal—centered in the role of Nancy. As previously mentioned, in the second version the fatal christening of the ship, named "Silver Queen," was accomplished by Nancy as a young girl, so that she, from the start, has figurative blood on her hands and a direct connection to this ship, although she does not realize it until much later in the screenplay. When Nancy confides to Lovett her traumatic memory of the episode, which gives her a fear of sailing, she relates, "It was awful! But now that I'm with you, darling, nothing matters—I'm going to love the Wanderer because it's yours" (73). Lovett replies to her with a line that will soon take on a chilling resonance: "Ours, sweetheart. Let's never say 'yours' or 'mine'—always 'ours.'" In the second version, Nancy makes a shocking discovery (for her) that proves Lovett's claim of their shared ownership, although with a different connotation. Right after Lovett confesses his occupation to her, she flees him and "goes to a porthole for air," where she discovers that "engraved in the copper are the words: SILVER QUEEN." The stage directions read: "Her eyes widen in horror. This is the yacht she christened as a little girl—the yacht that was launched in blood" (100). This discovery of her personal tie to the ship, combined with the revelation of her husband's profession as a slaver, links her intimately, in both girlhood and womanhood, to the destiny of the slave ship. The honeymoon cruise, launched with the blessings of the domestic union and personal renewal, becomes a site of contamination by illicit commerce and guilt.

Nancy later makes a surprising discovery on the African shore that establishes a more personal, embodied link to the slave trade. In both screenplays, shortly after they embark, Lovett offers her "his dowry"—a casket of jewelry. Nancy rifles through the jewelry, finds the "loveliest bracelet," puts it on, and exclaims, "It's so exciting it's, it's sinful" (24 September 1936, 79). When the ship reaches Africa, Nancy discovers the origin of the bracelet, and it provides a horrific scene of gothic revelation—perhaps the most worthily Faulknerian scene in the screenplay. As the *Wanderer* takes on its last load of slaves, Nancy watches. A scene without dialogue ensues, with the following stage directions: "Approaching her are several female slaves. As they draw nearer, Nancy's eyes are caught by the bracelet on a woman's arm. She gasps. It is a duplicate of the one on her own arm. Wresting the bracelet from her arm, she throws it into the sea, and then runs from the deck, unable to bear the sight of it any more" (24 September 1936, 109). Nancy's bracelet forges a connection between her and the African woman, and it bespeaks doubling, theft, and contamination simultaneously. This bracelet was "the loveliest of all"—chosen by Nancy as her prize—but it is now linked to this abject woman. Was Nancy's bracelet the matching twin, and was it stolen as part of the trade? Was the bracelet given to the female in exchange for some kind of favor or as compensation? Is it a mark of ownership or betrothal? The precise origin of the bracelet is never revealed, but Nancy has now seen the roots of the wealth she admired and the jewelry she prized, and her sensation of "sin" has been confirmed. Nancy may also feel that, with the parallel bracelet, she too has been "enslaved"—either by Lovett or by the trade itself, which has provided the jewelry she loves. Thus, much that she has valued—beauty, wealth, her husband—is revealed to be an outgrowth of injustice, of victimhood, and of Africa itself, much as the West Indies is the foundation of Sutpen's wealth in *Absalom, Absalom!* It may also horrify Nancy that the jewelry itself has been on the arms of this woman, and she has been rendered impure by its touch, much as Rosa

Coldfield is shocked by Clytie's touch in *Absalom, Absalom!* If Faulkner reddens Nancy's hand at the ship's christening, he blackens her arm in this scene with the bracelet.

Faulkner's handling of Nancy as a vessel of guilt and responsibility brings back the questions of abstraction and historicity that arise from the West Indian sections of *Absalom, Absalom!* Even as both drafts of *The Last Slaver*—especially the first one—evoke a more complex geography of the slave trade than anything else in Faulkner's work, that historical/political recovery is revised for an elemental plot of personal, biblical sin. While the first version implicitly critiques the operations of power within the U.S. government for enabling or tolerating the trade, the second takes pains to show that the "system works," even inventing an American naval base to bring the career of the *Wanderer* to a close. Relocating the guilt plot into the hands and arms of Nancy is symbolically powerful, but functions largely as myth rather than history. In giving her a melodramatic connection to the ship, Faulkner links the personal to the political, as it were, but this connection vitiates the political history of the trade in an almost irrational way: in what way is Nancy's christening really a causal link to what ensues? Perhaps Faulkner aims to suggest that even "innocent" women are enablers of slavery, but it seems odd, perhaps even misogynistic, to devote so many scenes to painting Nancy as the wellspring of guilt, when Lovett has plied the trade his entire life.

Faulkner's choice to favor the symbolic over the historical in his vision of the hemisphere is all the more striking given the ferocious intensity with which he revisits U.S. southern history and origins elsewhere in *Absalom, Absalom! Go Down, Moses!* and the Snopes trilogy. Why would an author so committed to chronicling the most problematic sides of his own regional history, including questions of race, power, and racial violence, avoid a comparably illuminating historical vision when turning to the Caribbean and the Middle Passage? Shreve McCannon's prophecies about miscegenation at the end of *Absalom, Absalom!* may provide a clue: "I think that in time the Jim Bonds are going to conquer the Western hemisphere. Of course it wont quite be in our time and of course as they spread toward the poles they will bleach out again like the rabbits and the birds do, so they wont show up so sharp against the snow. But it will still be Jim Bond; and so in a few thousand years, I who regard you will also have sprung from the loins of African kings" (378). Shreve offers a vision of racial apocalypse, with mixed-descent characters like Jim Bond supplanting the West and lines of blackness and whiteness blurring beyond recognition. In this light (or dark), Faulkner's insistent revisions in *Absalom, Absalom!* and *The Last Slaver* may have been aimed at countering or repressing the fearsome prediction of an expanding Black Atlantic. Indeed, most of Faulkner's revisions to these texts had the effect of reducing the stature of black voices, black bodies, and black power. Faulkner edited out the hints of insurrection and embodiment within the West Indian scenes in *Absalom, Absalom!* effectively reducing the Haitians from a revolutionary force of blackness to eternal victimhood and powerlessness. In *The Last Slaver,* Faulkner and his cowriters eliminated black agency and voice altogether, in some ways taking a step back from King's vision of Africans, which was hardly progressive. Although *Absalom, Absalom!* and *The Last Slaver* each probe the darkest origins of slavery, neither is really concerned with the Haitians or Africans as people, or even bodies, but as the raw material of sin and guilt in the New World. Faulkner's hemispheric vision shows a deep awareness of the origins of the Black Atlantic, but also a fear of it, as evidenced in his tendency to repress black agency or to treat it as a source of contamination. In this respect, Faulkner may evoke an image of the Black Atlantic not in order to recognize a specific history so much as to exorcise it.

4 Nationalizing Blackness in the New Negro Renaissance

WEST INDIAN expatriates were essential architects of the New Negro movement. Claude McKay, W. A. Domingo, J. A. Rogers (each from Jamaica), Eric Walrond (from Guiana by way of Panama), and Arthur Schomburg (from Puerto Rico) immigrated to the United States in the early part of the twentieth century. All of them made vital contributions to the New Negro Renaissance with their poetry, fiction, and essays; all of them worked closely with the Urban League and the NAACP; all were represented in Alain Locke's seminal anthology *The New Negro* (1925). McKay's defiant poem "If We Must Die" became the anthem of a generation of progressive black and white writers during the jazz age.[1] There were also significant West Indian leaders and intellectuals in Harlem who, while not identified with New Negro circles by current scholars, provided alternative models of black uplift; these include Marcus Garvey (from Jamaica) and Hubert Harrison (from St. Croix). Significant Caribbean-U.S. exchanges also occurred outside of Harlem, particularly at Fisk and Howard Universities, where, for example, George Padmore (from Trinidad) was educated and began his career as an international revolutionary.

The black West Indian community was rarely recognized for its contributions in the United States, though it was occasionally a subject of discussion in the African American press in Harlem. The Caribbean origin of authors whose works were deemed desirable (particularly McKay in his early career) was rarely acknowledged by African American intellectuals and white publishers, who effectively "nationalized" them by treating them as U.S. writers. In many cases, the subject of West Indian ancestry arose only when an author's works were deemed threatening (as in the case of Garvey's platform), and then the island ancestry was cited as evidence of the author's limitations and lack of authority on domestic matters in the United States. In this chapter the idea of the "purloined islands" takes on particular relevance, as I demonstrate that the contributions of Caribbean writers were incorporated by U.S. New Negro leaders into the movement without due credit to their West Indian colleagues. Indeed, this pattern of appropriating and erasing West Indian sources was hauntingly parallel to the way in which Carl Van Vechten[2] and other white authors borrowed from African American culture and used that cultural capital to secure a place for themselves in the U.S. literary field.[3] In this respect, the experience of West Indian artists during the New Negro Renaissance may trace another pattern of "love and theft"[4] in U.S. cultural history.

At first glance, it is surprising that there would be a critical void regarding the Caribbean role within the New Negro Renaissance, given the multinational group of West Indians that played central roles in the movement: one might rightly say that their contributions, in this light, are hidden in plain sight, like Poe's purloined letter. Many African Americans associated with that period spent crucial formative years within the Caribbean region, notably James Weldon Johnson and Langston Hughes. When one considers that key authors of the period were frequently engaged in discussion of black cultural and political figures from the Caribbean, such as the entertainer Bert Williams or the entrepreneur and militant leader Marcus Garvey, then it becomes quite easy, at a glance, to see Harlem in substantive dialogue with the islands at the height of the renaissance. As Heather Hathaway notes, "The impact of Caribbeaners on black life in Harlem during the first wave of immigration was profound."[5] David Levering Lewis has demonstrated that, in addition to their literary contributions, black West Indians profoundly improved the political and economic landscape for African Americans in Harlem and New York in general. Lewis examines how West Indians served not only as the "shock troops" (in W. A. Domingo's words) for much of the class-based activism of the time, but were a primary source of black financing for the renaissance. Casper Holstein (from St. Croix), for example, is credited with inventing the numbers racket in Harlem, but he was far more than a conventional gangster. According to Lewis, by 1926 he was a millionaire, and he and fellow West Indian P. M. H. Savory served as unofficial bankers to much of the Harlem community.[6] Indeed, it was a $1000 contribution from Holstein that funded the first round of *Opportunity* literary awards in 1926. I aim to show in this chapter that the wide range of West Indian participation in Harlem's literary and intellectual life well justifies Hubert Harrison's claim that "almost every important development originating in Negro Harlem . . . has either been fathered by West Indians or can count them among its originators."[7]

I argued in my first chapter that critics have sometimes mistakenly located the New Negro Renaissance as the point of origin for pan-Africanism, when it is more fairly understood as part of a continuum of ideological development that began in the later nineteenth century, with deep roots in the Caribbean. Although many U.S. New Negro writers sought to articulate a global vision of black uplift, they frequently overlooked the Caribbean, which was an especially striking omission to make when West Indian writers, past and present, were often key advocates of such an internationalist vision. Beyond specific conceptual and artistic contributions, the Caribbean played a structural and symbolic role in works by many African American contributors to the renaissance. Arna Bontemps and Langston Hughes each toured the Caribbean and gathered source material that expanded the vision of their novels and poems. Zora Neale Hurston and Richard Wright each visited Haiti and completed ethnographic writings that situated the region as the naïve "double" in need of salvation by U.S. leadership.

The multinational dimensions of the renaissance, however, have generally been ignored by most U.S. literary scholars. Heather Hathaway, Carl Pederson, and Louis Parascandola have given valuable critical attention to Caribbean authors in the Harlem Renaissance (especially to Eric Walrond and Claude McKay) but without a thorough investigation of the dynamic and sometimes fraught interactions between these authors and their U.S. colleagues. Pederson aims to reposition Walrond and McKay as "part of a postcolonial Caribbean tradition,"[8] but essentially leaves the renaissance untouched as a U.S.-centric enterprise, not considering the effect that that postcolonial tradition had in shaping the renaissance itself. Hathaway's investigation of McKay more broadly considers the relations between the Caribbean and African American communities in Harlem, but aims for a politics of integration and "reconciliation" and thus does not address the conflicts of ownership and appropriation that emerged between U.S. intellectuals and West Indian writers during the renaissance (84–85).

Surprisingly, the landmark, classic studies of the Harlem Renaissance have offered the least attention to West Indian cultural contributions. Houston A. Baker Jr.'s potent theoretical account of black aesthetics and political transformations before and after the renaissance, *Modernism and the Harlem Renaissance,* treats the movement with a strongly nationalist U.S.-centric bent, grouping McKay, Bert Williams, and Garvey with

African American artists, with no reference to their Caribbean ancestry. Baker overlooks the West Indian presence within the renaissance even as he explains its cultural moment by borrowing from Caribbean models, such as "maroonage"[9] (a term describing creole slave communities that formed in Jamaica and Florida when fugitives mingled with Indians to resist whites) and the Caliban myth reappropriated by Césaire and George Lamming (53–56). Ann Douglas's *Terrible Honesty: Mongrel Manhattan in the 1920s* privileges only one kind of "mongrelism": interactions between white and black culture. When Douglas turns her attention to the history of immigrants in New York during the period, she focuses on alliances and conflicts between European immigrants and Harlem blacks. Throughout her discussion, Douglass uses the word "immigrant" synonymously with "white European immigrant," ignoring black West Indian immigrants altogether.[10] Even scholars who have investigated the multiple facets of black identity within the New Negro movement have largely ignored the role of West Indians. J. Martin Favor, for example, skillfully investigates the complexities of African American identity as constructed or reconstructed during the New Negro Renaissance, but confines his scope to U.S. black identity.[11] Favor persuasively argues that the urban, educated African American class during that period represented the southern African American "folk" so as to legitimatize their own elite subject position in the North, while still garnering personal authenticity from the South. Favor persuasively demonstrates the ways that the southern African American folk culture was condescended to, appropriated, or essentialized by such gestures. A parallel phenomenon emerged in the approach to black West Indians by U.S. New Negro writers, many of whom depended upon substantial dialogue with their Caribbean brethren, while simultaneously erasing their debts to West Indians or condescending to them as a peasant class in need of civilization.

Du Bois and the "Limits" of the West Indies

An unsigned editorial published in the *Crisis* early in the New Negro Renaissance (1920), attributed to W. E. B. Du Bois, neatly encapsulates the mixed regard for West Indians from the African American mainstream. Entitled "The Rise of the West Indian," the opinion piece called attention to the West Indian presence in New York City, citing data suggesting that there were now one hundred thousand "foreign-born Negroes" in the city, primarily from the Caribbean islands. The author clearly admires the West Indian population in New York, even though he regards it as a "country cousin" in need of guidance. Describing the immigrants as a "mass of peasants," the author describes the political potential of their community in rather mixed terms:

> The movement is yet inchoate and indefinite, but it is tremendously human, piteously sincere, and built in the souls of a hardworking, thrifty, independent people, who, while long deprived of higher training, have nevertheless very few illiterates or criminals. It is not beyond possibility that this new Ethiopia of the Isles may yet stretch out hands of helpfulness to the 12 million black men of America.[12]

A puzzling mixture of admiration and condescension is present throughout this passage. The closing speculation, while poetically yearning for a partnership with this "new Ethiopia," is explicitly U.S.-centric in the expectation that the United States is the proper object of concern, to which the West Indian "hands" should stretch. More subtly, Du Bois's citation of "12 million black men of America," in comparison to the unnumbered West Indian population, seems intended to remind readers that the United States is the true center for black energy. The opening comments are even more problematic. Would the editors of the *Crisis* have been comfortable with the *New Republic* characterizing African Americans as "piteously sincere"? Perhaps most noteworthy is the bathetic, if not intentionally backhanded, compliment that West Indians have "few illiterates or criminals." The insistent viewing of West Indians as "deprived" peasants, in spite of their multiple and sophisticated contributions to Harlem, would characterize the (relatively) small portion of New Negro discourse that addressed the Caribbean.

Du Bois's own attention to this "new Ethopia of the Isles" would quickly wane. Much as he seemed to "forget" the first Pan-African Conference for most of his career, Du Bois, over time, commented less and less on the Caribbean in his own writing, eventually marginalizing the West Indies in studies that purported to reckon globally with African diasporic cultures. For example, in Du Bois's first survey of black history in a global context, entitled *The Negro* (1915), he closes with a sense of future partnership between the West Indies and the United States for mutual black uplift: "The most significant centers of this new thinking [pan-Africanism] are, perhaps naturally, outside Africa and in America: in the United States and in the West Indies."[13] In the expanded version of this historical survey, *Black Folk Then and Now* (1939), Du Bois does not give any credit to the West Indies for the role it played in fostering pan-Africanism, as he did in his 1915 study. Rather than perceiving West Indians as partners or colleagues in this study, he pities them as simple and misguided brethren: they are "distracted by petty internal jealousies and provincialism. . . . The people are European in speech and outlook, but largely African in their unconscious memories and survivals; and still so filled with a naïve joy and exhilaration."[14] The closing chapter of *Black Folk Then and Now* examines black political trends almost everywhere throughout the world, but mentions the Caribbean only once, citing the black West Indies as a "new world Africa" in need of development and leadership (262), presumably from African Americans.

Du Bois's diminishing regard for the West Indian community may have been due in part to the hostility that evolved between him and Marcus Garvey over the 1920s. At the same time, there were significant points of continuity and contact between the two leaders early in the decade, and it is worth considering what Garvey had in common with other New Negro intellectuals before their rhetoric became so mutually divisive later in the 1920s. Garvey notes in his autobiographical writing that his own program for racial uplift was kindled by reading the works of U.S. African American leaders, notably Booker T. Washington: "I read 'Up from Slavery' and then my doom—if I may so call it—of being a race leader dawned upon me."[15] When Garvey set sail for the United States in 1916, he had previously exchanged correspondence with Washington and was planning to meet with him, but the elder statesman of Tuskegee had died late the previous year.

Perhaps because of the trenchant and litigious tone of his later writings (which primarily aimed to refute the mail fraud charges that led to his arrest and deportation), recent scholars have tended to ignore Garvey's contributions to New Negro discourse in the 1920s. Although Garvey's writings emerged episodically in *Negro World* (the chief journal for the Universal Negro Improvement Association), they form a coherent argument about the future of global African cultures. They were widely read at the time and sufficiently in demand that they were quickly collected into *The Philosophy and Opinions of Marcus Garvey* and published in 1923. Garvey's first volume effectively bridges prior pan-Africanist ideologies in Caribbean discourse and domestic concerns for the status of African Americans in the United States. To be sure, Garvey's commitment to racial purity—"we believe in the racial purity of both the Negro and white races" (86)—was a reactionary position ripe for criticism, and certainly dissonant with the programs of the NAACP. Garvey's solutions to the "problem of the color line"—advocating emigration to Africa and, later, establishing a coalition with the Ku Klux Klan—were equally problematic. Those limitations notwithstanding, Garvey's early analysis of the problems faced by diasporic Africans was highly nuanced, multifaceted, and comparable to the writings of his Harlem Renaissance coevals like Du Bois, Locke, and Johnson. Although Garvey later cut off all ties with the U.S. leaders of the NAACP and Urban League (especially after Du Bois's articles on Garvey in the *Crisis* in 1921), he initially positioned his struggle within the general vocabulary of uplift of the time, writing of the "awakened spirit of the New Negro . . . [who] is demanding a place in the affairs of men" (56).

At the same time, Garvey was aware of the peculiar position he occupied as an immigrant entering in domestic discourse on race: "My enemies in America have done much to hold me up to public contempt and ridicule, but have failed. They believe that the only resort is to stir up national prejudice against me, in that I was not born within the borders of the United States of America" (36). Garvey responded to this "national prejudice" with a bracing cosmopolitanism, noting that "great ideals know no nationality" and stating that "I know no national boundary where the Negro is concerned. The whole world is my province until Africa is free" (37). In a similar vein, Garvey effectively catalogued the problems facing African-descended peoples to make the case for global resistance to white domination and imperialism. For example, in a document entitled "Declaration of the Rights of the Negro Peoples of the World" (1920), Garvey and the UNIA offered a manifesto in defense of black peoples throughout the world. This document began with the general proposition that "nowhere in the world, with few exceptions, are black men accorded equal treatment with white men . . . but, on the contrary, are discriminated against and denied the common rights due to human beings for no other reason than their race and color" (135). As it continues, the declaration offers a comprehensive catalog of oppressive systems faced by black peoples throughout the world: Jim Crow and lynching in the United States, imperial dominion over Africa, educational restrictions in the United States and Europe, and covert discrimination within the West Indies.

David Levering Lewis credits Garvey for creating a unifying, inspirational model that transcended the class and racial barriers explicitly or implicitly upheld by Du Bois's "Talented Tenth":

> Marcus Mosiah Garvey's message was truly extraordinary. Afro-Americans who, with rare exception, cringed or laughed at the mention of African heritage, whose incidental thoughts about the "Dark Continent" came on occasional Sundays with the passing of the missions collection plate, heard from Garvey that European imperialism was fading away, that there was an interlocked

> destiny among people of color. . . . "Africa," Marcus Garvey shouted—"Africa for the Africans!" It was electrifying; since the similar slogans of Martin R. Delany on the eve of the Civil War and Bishop Henry McNeal Turner two decades after the Civil War, almost nothing of the kind had been heard in America. (35)

Garvey enhanced his globalized perspective by carefully inserting himself into a U.S. discourse of resistance and justice. Besides citing Booker T. Washington as his inspiration, Garvey defends his so-called radicalism by citing it as a patriotic tradition in the United States: "George Washington was dubbed a radical when he took up his sword to fight his way to liberty in America one hundred and forty years ago" (18). Within his "Declaration," he adapts the language of the U.S. Declaration of Independence—"whereas all men are created equal and entitled to the rights of life, liberty, and the pursuit of happiness" (136)—as precedent for his claims for justice. More pointedly, Garvey cites examples from U.S. history both to offer a cautionary tale about imperialism and to make a claim for what the United States, in particular, owes to Africans and their descendants: "If we in the Western World take no interest in the higher development of the African natives, it will mean that in another hundred years historians and writers will tell us that the black man once inhabited Africa, just as the North American Indian once inhabited America" (60). In establishing a commonality between the imperial practices of the United States at home and Europe abroad, Garvey echoes Martí's discourse from the previous century. In observing the treatment of Native Americans in the United States as a possible parallel for the future of Africans, he cites a fearsome exemplum that was little noted by other New Negro writers at the time. Anticipating subsequent debates about debts and reparations owed to African Americans, Garvey argues for the centrality of black labor in enriching and protecting the United States, and hence claims a share for his people in return: "Good and dear America that has succored us for three hundred years knows our story. We have watered her vegetation with our tears for two hundred and fifty years. We have built her cities and laid the foundation of her imperialism with the mortar of our blood and bones for three centuries, and now we cry to her for help. Help us, America, as we helped you" (121). While Garvey did not pursue this political history in a rigorously documented academic direction, his claims presage the arguments of subsequent African American polemical histories, such as Du Bois's in *Black Reconstruction in America* (1935), which analyzed the substantive role that African

Americans had played in the cultural, political, and economic development of the United States. In this light, Garvey's combining domestic and international analysis of the status of African-descended cultures forms an important waypoint between the discourse of the first Pan-African Conference and the global analyses of racism and capitalism that would later emerge in the 1930s and 1940s.

Beyond philosophical and conceptual connections, Garvey and Du Bois shared, at least early on, a respectful relationship with warm intentions, though missed connections. A month after arriving in New York in 1916, Garvey arranged his first public lecture and wrote to Du Bois to invite him to serve as chair of this first meeting of the U.S. branch of the Universal Negro Improvement Association.[16] Du Bois was out of town at the time, so he could not participate, but in subsequent years the two men would exchange correspondence and even seek coalitions with the other. With his skillful populist verve, Garvey planned for the UNIA to host a popular election to determine "the accredited spokesman for the American Negro people," and he personally wrote to Du Bois to ask him to stand for election: "You are hereby asked to be good enough to allow us to place your name in nomination for the post."[17] Du Bois politely demurred, but he took advantage of the contact to ask for further information about the UNIA, acknowledging that it was a growing movement of interest to many readers of the *Crisis:* "For some time *The Crisis* has been in receipt of inquiries concerning you and your organization. To these we have simply answered that we had no reliable information at hand. It seems, however, increasingly important as your movement grows that we should present to our readers a critical estimate of it."[18]

Du Bois's requests for information about the UNIA and Garvey's solicitations of Du Bois for leadership positions show good faith attempts, initially, for cooperation between Du Bois's and Garvey's organizations. As Garvey's popularity grew and the attendant scandals regarding Black Star, Liberia, and the Klan developed, Du Bois's estimation changed considerably, and he was not alone in this assessment. W. A. Domingo, a Jamaican emigré and former loyalist of Garvey's, published critiques of him in the *Messenger* in 1922. Domingo subsequently contacted Du Bois to share their mutual opinions about the UNIA and Garvey. Du Bois wrote back to him and commented that "his [Garvey's] propaganda for the most part is absolutely wrong and to some extent criminal," but he also expressed a firm belief that they should avoid an ad hominem approach in responding to him: "In the attack on Garvey, the object should be the opinions of the man and not the man himself or his birthplace." Du Bois expressed to Domingo his sense of shared solidarity with the West Indians and confided that he did not want a division between the West Indian and African American communities to emerge on the basis on their critiques of Garvey: "American Negroes, to a much larger extent than they realize, are not only blood relatives to the West Indians but under deep obligations to them for many things. For instance without the Haitian Revolt, there would have been no emancipation in America as early as 1863. I, myself, am of West Indian descent and am proud of the fact."[19]

Du Bois's private acknowledgment to Domingo of the debts owed to West Indians by African Americans, as well as avowal of kinship to the islands, is a moving statement, but stands in notable contrast to his published commentary in that regard. In none of his publications during the New Negro Renaissance period, particularly political assessments of the future of the race, did he cite such West Indian–U.S. connections and profess his admiration. Indeed, although he wrote to Domingo that Garvey's "birthplace" should not be the object of attack, his later writings that year on Garvey would effectively reduce Garvey to a narrow product of his island background.

Du Bois examined Garvey in a series of articles in the *Crisis* between 1920 and 1923,[20] and he collected these articles into a more well-developed examination published as "Back to Africa" in *Century Magazine* in 1923. The article commenced with some assessments that seemed very much ad hominem, but swiftly shifted towards a broader attack that one might term *ad islas,* insofar as he aimed to delegitimize the political value of the West Indian community itself—all of which seems entirely opposed to the private comments he confided to Domingo earlier that year. Written in the wake of a national investigation into the corruption of Garvey's Black Star shipping corporation and the collapse of the Universal Negro Improvement Association, Du Bois's article examined the rise and fall of Garvey in retrospect. Du Bois reveals his thesis by implication from the start of his essay, as he describes Garvey in his military finery "knighting" his followers—a scene such that "a casual observer might have mistaken it for the dress-rehearsal of a new comic opera."[21] The article takes a more serious tone as it traces Garvey's roots in Jamaica, and Du Bois deploys his sociological acumen to describe the problem of colorism in the West Indies as the white and mulatto elites, in tandem, hold the black underclass in subjugation. Thus, for Du Bois, "There must naturally arise a more or less insistent demand among the black peasants for self-expression and for an exposition of their grievances by one of their own group. Such leaders have indeed arisen from time to time. Marcus Garvey was one" (267).

After crediting Garvey for his commitment to the "removal of injustice" and his ability "to express himself in grammatical and forceful English" (267) (a backhanded compliment in itself), Du Bois's assessment soon turns negative. Du Bois faults Garvey, at first, largely on the basis of his person rather than of his philosophy, denouncing him as vain, egotistical, jealous, and impatient. As the article continues, Du Bois attributes Garvey's deficiencies to his "peasant roots": "Garvey had not a thorough education and a very hazy idea of the technic [sic] of civilization. . . . He had the common weakness of untrained devotees that no dependence could be put upon his statements of fact. Not that he was a conscious liar, but dream, fact, fancy, wish were so blurred in his thinking that neither he himself nor his hearers could clearly or easily extricate them" (267).

Given Du Bois's faith in the "Talented Tenth," such condescension is predictable. Perhaps more surprisingly, Du Bois's diminution of Garvey as an individual quickly extends to the Caribbean itself. After offering a timeline of Garvey's troubles, ranging from his misguided purchase of the decrepit steamer *Yarmouth* to his failed attempt to relocate the UNIA to Liberia, Du Bois returns to the task of explaining the root causes of Garvey's limitations, which he attributes to the islands themselves: "Being an islander, and born in a little realm where half a day's journey takes one from ocean to ocean, the world always seemed small to him, and it was perhaps excusable for this black peasant of Jamaica to think of Africa as a similar, but slightly larger, island, which could easily be taken possession of" (270). As his essay develops, Du Bois continues to make a political/geographical association between the limitations of the islands and the parochialism of Garvey's ideology. Garvey thus becomes a quintessential representative of faults that were not merely his own, but representative of his class, region, and culture.

Du Bois immediately juxtaposes the excesses of Garvey and his followers (who were not exclusively West Indian, though Du Bois represents them as so) with the contrasting efficacy of Du Bois's own North American brethren: "When the rank and file of ignorant West-Indian negroes were going wild over Garvey, the American Negroes sat cool and calm, and were neither betrayed into wild and unjust attacks upon Garvey nor into uncritical acceptance" (273). Du Bois effects a skillful triangulation for his own political position. If Garvey represents an extreme of militancy, and Booker T. Washington an extreme of "cooperation and consent" (274), Du Bois, in contrast, represents a balanced path of educated resistance, one anchored in "the technic of civilization." Moreover, by the end of

"Back to Africa," Du Bois positions his "middle way" as possessed of the most popular support: "It is no ordinary tribute to American Negro poise and common sense, and ability to choose and reject leadership, that neither of these programs [Washington's or Garvey's] has been able to hold them" (274). Across Du Bois's articles about Garvey, the assessment of the legacy of his rival gradually transforms into a legitimation of the exclusive role of African Americans as the cultural and political vanguard of the New Negro.

It was not only "American Negroes," however, who ultimately rejected Garvey. Claude McKay criticized Garvey on a basis that contrasted with Du Bois's assessment: not for his peasant-like simplicity, but rather for the fact "that Garvey's political ideas should be so curiously bourgeois-obsolete and fantastically utopian."[22] McKay would later level similar charges of "bourgeois" leanings at Du Bois, and some of Garvey's other West Indian critics pointed to Du Bois as an opposing extreme from Garvey that African Americans and West Indians should avoid. Eric Walrond, for example, concludes his examination of Garvey, in which he criticizes Garvey for "incompetency, dishonesty, mismanagement, fraud," and for "creat[ing] a fairy dream world" for his followers, with an equally pointed attack on Du Bois. While praising Du Bois as "undoubtedly the most brilliant Negro in the United States today," Walrond portrays him as essentially an "intellectual" so wedded to his academic perspective as to be irrelevant to blacks from less elite classes: "Proud, haughty, an incurable snob, he is probably the most unfit man temperamentally for the craft of leadership. . . . He has no sympathy for the black masses. He is incapable of comprehending their dreams and aspirations."[23] Whether or not one agrees that Du Bois's career either proved or disproved Walrond's assessment of his leadership, it is vital to note that, even from the vantage point of West Indians who critiqued Garvey, Du Bois did not represent a palatable alternative, and was "other" to them in a way that parallels Du Bois's description of Garvey as too far outside the mainstream of political life.

In the wake of Garvey's conviction for mail fraud, pardon (from Calvin Coolidge), and deportation, Du Bois and the *Crisis* received a number of hostile letters blaming the NAACP for Garvey's fall, alleging, for example, that the NAACP had turned over evidence to the federal government or influenced judges against him. As critical as Du Bois was in his final articles in 1923, there is no evidence to support such claims. Indeed, as his prior correspondence revealed, Du Bois needed documentation and evidence from the UNIA so that he could write about them; it is not clear from correspondence if Garvey ever furnished such information. Perhaps recognizing the fraught nature of the situation, given the large body of support for the UNIA in Harlem, Du Bois responded with careful poise and equanimity, even as he clearly denied the accusations. Writing to his most prominent correspondent on the subject, P. B. Young, editor of the *Norfolk Journal and Guide,* Du Bois stated, "It is absolutely untrue that the NAACP is a rival organization to the UNIA or instigated the charges against Garvey. The charges of misusing funds originated with the prosecuting attorney of New York City before the *Crisis* had even mentioned Garvey and before the NAACP had known anything of his activities."[24]

Reflecting back on the 1920s in his autobiography, Du Bois does acknowledge the popular role of Garveyism in that era, even as he expresses his continued distaste for it: "The Pan-African congresses which I called in 1919, 1921, and 1923 were chiefly memorable for the excitement and opposition which they caused among the colonial imperialists. Scarcely a prominent newspaper in Europe but used them as a text of warning, and persisted in coupling them with the demagogic 'Garvey movement,' then in its prime, as a warning for colonial governments to clamp down on colonial unrest."[25] I have already discussed Du Bois's tendency to monopolize the term pan-African, so I will point out only briefly that in his recollection of the heyday of these congresses, he makes no mention of either the roots of these gatherings in the Pan-African Conference of 1900, nor of West Indian co-coordinators of the congresses such as George Padmore (in contrast, Padmore himself was quite generous in his own writings in acknowledging Du Bois's leadership at the Pan-African Congresses[26]). What is clear from this recollection is that the mainstream European media, even as recalled by Du Bois, linked Garveyism and Du Bois's pan-Africanism. Du Bois's careful choice of words—"persisted in coupling them with the demagogic 'Garvey movement'"—reveals his dislike of this linkage, but also shows (perhaps) a grudging recognition that the combined force of their platforms drew greater alarm and notice from the colonial power structure.

More revealing than the individual criticism of Garvey by Du Bois, however, is the symbolic role that the leader comes to occupy in the writings of Du Bois and other architects of the renaissance. From the Garveyesque terrorist Perigua in Du Bois's *Dark Princess* (1928) to the Caribbean "revolutionaries" in James Weldon Johnson's "Down by the Carib Sea," the politicized West Indian became a stock character in New Negro discourse. One might argue that this was merely a satiric outgrowth of competition for authority and that Garvey, not the Caribbean, was the target of such depictions, but the absence of any competing respectful representations from key Harlem Renaissance writers suggests that many were all too comfortable letting Garveyesque caricatures stand in as representatives of the islands. Doing so had not only the effect of delegitimizing a competing source of political and cultural authority, but also of putting the islands "in their place," as the peasant cousins in need of salvation from their North American cultural "betters."

Five years after publishing his retrospective assessment of Garvey, Du Bois published *Dark Princess,* in which a Garveyesque character plays an important role as a foil to the protagonist, Matthew Towns. The novel weaves together the story of Towns's coming-of-age and increasing political awareness with a global plot of postcolonial activism sponsored by the titular Princess Kautilya of Tibet against "the white leviathan."[27] After a medical education curtailed by racism, Towns travels to Europe, where he meets Princess Kautilya and agrees to carry a message back to the United States to a community leader in Harlem, Michael Perigua, with the ultimate task of reporting to her on this figure's political potential. After returning to the United States, Towns commences work as a Pullman porter and upon arriving in Manhattan, he visits Perigua's headquarters. Perigua is so impressed by Towns that he appoints him to serve as an inspector in his organization to report upon the organizing potential in the communities he visits on his north-south train line.

Perigua's national background is left unspecified, but he seems to come from a Caribbean island, although it is not clear which one. He is fluent in French and Spanish, and one of his first grievances is that an Englishman seduced his wife (44). Beyond these elements of his background, Perigua is Garveyesque in his agenda, and has his political base in a cult of personality in the West Indian community. When Towns first meets Perigua, he find the leader's supporters chanting his name: "'Perigua—Perigua forever!' And a song with some indistinguishable rhyme on 'Perigua forever' began to roll until he stopped it with an impatient shout and a gesture" (34). This sense of repetitive, populist support—from a group whose voice cannot even produce a distinguishable rhyme—echoes Du Bois's critiques of the West Indian community in his articles on Garvey. Perigua himself seems a more educated version of Garvey, but with even greater inclinations towards violence. Towns first analyzes him thus: "Matthew had at first thought him an egotistical fool. He next put him down as an ignorant fanatic—but he was not ignorant. He was well read, spoke French and Spanish, read German, and knew the politics of the civilized world and current events surprisingly well. Was he insane? In no ordinary sense of the word; wild, irresponsible, impulsive, but with brain and nerves that worked clearly and promptly" (35). In this passage it is as if Du Bois were imagining a more politically sophisticated and dangerous version of the Jamaican-born leader. Like Garvey, Perigua plans his struggle along essentialist racial lines, but with a desire for a violent fight against racism in the United States rather than a liberatory return to Africa. "Terrorism, revenge, is our program," he confides to Towns (36). Towns is both fascinated by and frightened of Perigua's energetic plans, and he reports to Kautilya with an assessment uncannily similar to what Du Bois had been writing about Garvey and the West Indian community from 1920 to 1923:

> These classes have no common program, save complaint, protest, and inner bickering; and only in the small class of immigrant West Indian has this complaint reached the stage that even contemplates violence. Perigua is a man of intelligence and fire—of a certain honesty and force; but he is not to be trusted as a leader. His organization is a loose mob of incoherent elements united only by anger and poverty. . . . Perigua and those whom he represents have a grievance and a remedy, but he will never accomplish anything systematic. Do not think of contributing to his organization. (44)

In spite of Towns's dismissal of Perigua's potential, the young man is drawn by the leader into a plot of domestic terrorism, and they plan to bomb a train loaded with Klansmen in retaliation for the lynching of a fellow Pullman Porter, Towns's friend Jimmie. This operation fails when Towns learns that the Princess is on the train and forces it to stop in time; Perigua is then found dead, and his political program expires shortly thereafter. Subsequently, the West Indian community disappears entirely from view in the novel—a surprising twist for a text whose political aim is (to quote the Princess) to show that "Pan-Africa belongs logically with Pan-Asia" (14). Indeed, Perigua and his West Indian militancy seem to function merely as a cipher to be rejected in the personal and political plot of *Dark Princess.* Much as Du Bois cited Garvey's excesses in 1923 to bolster the position of the Northern African American elite, Perigua's violence and hubris serves to cast the political aspirations of Towns and Kautilya as the legitimate and rational path for political change. Whether in his writings about Garvey or his interpretation of the West Indian community in general, Du Bois seemed unable to envision a black West Indian as a genuine leader or intellectual—a surprising lack given that Du Bois collaborated early in his career with great thinkers from the Caribbean like Williams, Sylvain, and Firmin.

Hubert Harrison's Triangulation between Garvey and Du Bois

As important as it is to consider the Garvey–Du Bois exchanges during the New Negro Renaissance, one must be careful not to let that debate occlude other vital discussions during the period. Indeed, Hubert Harrison, one of the most important but often neglected contributors to the philosophical underpinnings of the New Negro Renaissance, has been thoroughly displaced by recurrent focus on Garvey and Du Bois as the signal opposites defining the field of New Negro discourse. Because of the dedicated scholarship of Jeffrey B. Perry, both a thorough biography and a reader of Harrison's works are now available, and they reveal a powerful political voice pursuing a path different from either of those leaders.[28] Harrison makes for an especially rich comparison with both Garvey and Du Bois because he was in dialogue with both (and briefly worked for Garvey). Moreover, much as Du Bois triangulated a position for himself and the NAACP as the "middle way" between Garvey and Washington, Harrison positioned himself as an alternative to Garvey and Du Bois.

Harrison was born in St. Croix, Virgin Islands, in 1883, when it was still in possession of Denmark, and moved to the United States at the turn of the century. In New York, he participated in a wide range of progressive and leftist movements, though he later distanced himself from socialist movements because he, like many New Negro intellectuals, found them insufficiently attuned to questions of race, both domestically and globally. Early in his career, Harrison published articles in a wide range of venues, from the *New York Times,* to the *International Socialist Review,* to the *Colored American Review,* to the *Pittsburgh Courier,* and he later grew to assume substantial responsibilities as an editor and publisher as well. He worked as an assistant editor to the *Masses* (1911), founded the *Voice* (1917), and served as editor of *New Negro* magazine (1917) and of Garvey's *Negro World* in its most productive years (1920–22), during which Harrison also contributed numerous articles. Harrison was one of Garvey's earliest friends in the United States and introduced him to the Harlem political and cultural scene when the latter arrived in New York. Although Harrison fell out with Garvey, he did not realign himself with other Harlem intellectuals such as Du Bois or Johnson, but sought instead to establish his own distinct progressive voice.

Harrison's writings are particularly noteworthy for their prescient focus (well in advance of 1919, the date traditionally assigned to the start of the New Negro Renaissance) on questions of race, blackness, and justice from both a domestic and an international perspective, with a sophisticated sense of their interconnection. He wrote on a wide range of subjects—socialism, pan-Africanism, domestic civil rights, the contributions of and challenges faced by West Indian immigrants to the United States, the international rights of colonized peoples—while also publishing a wide range of literary criticism, drama, and music reviews. In many respects, his writings might be the best exemplar of the pan-Africanist approach espoused in the Pan-African Conference of 1900 and the Pan-African Congress of 1919. Harrison was particularly astute in thinking about the intersection of international geopolitics with domestic concerns—especially the dichotomy between the promotion of freedom by the United States overseas (as in Wilson's ideals) and the suppression of such struggles at home. Harrison did not shy away from arguing that African Americans ought to withhold their contributions to the United States' global efforts (such as World War I), lest the "patriotic" path of pulling together make African Americans the dupes of white U.S. and European elites. This position sharply divided him from NAACP leaders like Du Bois and Johnson, who argued for cooperation and accommodation with the United States, with the hope of eventual restitution in the form of social justice.

One of Harrison's earliest pieces, "The Black Man's Burden," well encapsulates his analytic framework and rhetorical skills, while anticipating his later journalism at the height of the renaissance. The title, of course, rephrases Kipling's poem, but with multiple resonances. Harrison examines not only what black peoples must bear from white colonialism, but also the responsibility of blacks to advance world justice because whites cannot be relied upon to do so. He skillfully uses the United States an example for this "burden," noting that "in a republic all the adult male natives are at least citizens. If in a given community some are citizens and some are subjects, then your community is not a republic" (64). Harrison confronts his readers, white and black, with the bold claim that the United States is not even possessed of the representative government it claims for itself. In the context of the title, it is thus the "burden" of black peoples to ensure that the United States expands its citizenship to become a true republic. Amplifying this point, Harrison observes that African Americans in the South are effectively "political serfs" and that sharecropping is a system of de facto slavery: "Peonage is slavery unsanctioned by law. . . . Any one who disputes this may look to modern Mexico for proofs" (65). Harrison's citation of Mexico for comparison to the agriculture of the U.S. South is a particularly resonant choice. To suggest that the United States, in its political and economic oppression of African Americans, was comparable to Mexico was to make an unflattering linkage of the highest order. In contrast to traditional U.S. representations of the nation as an avatar of New World "liberation" against Spanish/Latin "tyranny," Harrison collapses a polar opposition by which many U.S. politicians legitimated American expansionism.

Much earlier than Du Bois and others in the New Negro movement, Harrison discussed in detail the complex interconnections between the domestic problems of African Americans and broader oppressive structures of colonialism and imperialism practiced by Europe and the United States. Harrison was especially committed to reminding U.S. readers of their nation's participation in imperial expansion because he found that "most Americans who are able to see this process more or less clearly in the case of other nations are unable to see the process implicit and explicit in the career of their own" (239). In order to combat this blindness, Harrison's analyses of imperialism often put the United States in a challenging context for comparison with powers from which it would prefer to distance itself. For example, in an essay entitled "Our Larger Duty," he positions the United States alongside Belgium, widely regarded as the most brutal colonial power in Africa:

> It [the white race] is on top by virtue of its control of the physical force of the world—ships, soldiers, guns, money, and other resources. By virtue of this control England rules and robs India, Egypt, Africa, and the West Indies; by virtue of this control we of the United States can tell Haytians, Hawaiians, Filipinos, and Virgin Islanders how much they shall get for their labors and what shall be done in their lands; by virtue of this control Belgians can still say to the Congolese whether they shall have their hands hacked off or their eyes gouged out. (99)

In this passage Harrison describes a continuum of exploitation, positioning the United States squarely in its center, and he orchestrates the description to sobering effect. Rather than positioning Belgium's horrific violence against the Congolese as an exceptional abuse distinct from English or U.S. imperialism, Harrison uses an anaphoric litany (predicated on "by virtue of this control") to put these abuses in strict parallel, suggesting that desecration of the body is a corollary consequence of the "physical force" underwriting white power throughout the world. Harrison's catalog reminds readers of the imperial dimensions to U.S. power and does so at a most unwelcome moment, in 1919, as the Paris Peace Conference was in progress and the United States and Europe were optimistic they could secure a peaceful world order out of the ruin of World War I.

The subject of World War I, and the question of if and how African Americans should join in that struggle, provided perhaps the greatest division between Harrison and the NAACP establishment led by Du Bois and Johnson, each of whom had close ties to the U.S. government under a variety of auspices. Indeed, Harrison frequently termed Du Bois and his brethren "the subsidized Sixth" (111), which is not merely an ironic reference to the "Talented Tenth," but a reminder that the NAACP and the Talented Tenth depended, in part, on support from white establishment sources (such as white philanthropists like Joel Spingarn or white patrons like Carl Van Vechten) that could compromise or restrict the degree of change effected by the organization. Unlike Garvey, Harrison couched his argument not in the terms of racial authenticity but in a pragmatic analysis of competing institutional and bureaucratic allegiances. For example, in his most thorough critique of Du Bois's leadership, entitled "The Descent of Du Bois," Harrison criticized the former for the personal and philosophical compromises embedded in his support of World War I. Du Bois articulated this support in an influential editorial in the *Crisis* in 1918 in which he recommended that African Americans "forget our special grievances and close our ranks, shoulder to shoulder with our white fellow-citizens and the allied nations that are fighting for democracy." As Perry notes, a scandal emerged among the New Negro intelligentsia when it was discovered that Du Bois published this article while being considered for a position as captain of military intelligence within the War Department.[29] Although there is no clear-cut evidence that this editorial was written at the War Department's request, this situation created the appearance of a quid pro quo, with the implication that Du Bois had offered propaganda for the sake of securing a personal position. Harrison's commentary on the scandal is far more tempered than the vitriolic language of the Garvey–Du Bois debates, and he focuses much more on the political implications of Du Bois's support for the war, rather than the personal scandal of his failed attempt to secure a military position. Acknowledging that Du Bois's "former services to his race have been undoubtedly of a high and courageous sort," Harrison reminded readers that the "special grievances" that Du Bois asked be set aside were urgent matters of basic civil human rights: a call to end "lynching, segregration, and disenfranchisement" (171). As in "The Black Man's Burden," Harrison concluded that there could not and should not be a schism between the fight for freedom abroad and the fight for freedom at home, countering that: "Instead of the war for democracy making these things [the grievances] less necessary, it makes them more so" (171).

Harrison continued this argument later that year as the war came to a close, prophesying that the decision by Du Bois and other New Negro leaders to support the war would reveal them to be dupes of the Wilson administration. In Harrison's astute political calculations, the reorganization of Europe and its colonies after the war meant that there would be no attention given to questions of racial justice, as the victors would be concerned with dividing the spoils and punishing Germany and Turkey. Moreover, the fact that the United States received free and open support from African Americans—with no concessions or securities guaranteed or even promised in advance of that support—meant that there would be no onus on the Wilson administration to improve their lot in the U.S. According to Harrison, "Now that they have helped to win the war against Germany, the Negro people in the United States feel the absurdity of the situation in which they find themselves. . . . They have done all this to make the world 'safe for democracy' even while in sixteen States of the south in which nine tenths of them reside, they have no voice in their government" (209). Moreover, sadly and ironically, the fact that the United States provided the deus ex machina to end the war (with the help of African Americans) meant that there would be no impetus for international pressure from allies like England and France, as they were in debt to the U.S. for their assistance: "And since it was only by the military aid of the United States that the Allies were able to win the war, why should our people be stupid enough to think that the allied nations will aim a slap in the face of the United States (even if such things were customary) by attempting to interfere in her domestic arrangements and institutions" (209). The outcomes of the Paris Peace Conference, concluded by the end of 1919, proved Harrison's predictions correct. Indeed, the victors' division of most of Asia, Africa, and the Middle East into colonial protectorates guaranteed that colonial hegemony would increase after the war's resolution. In the years following the Peace Conference many New Negro leaders who had supported the war, including Du Bois, would denounce the colonial expansion after the conference. Harrison, who could not resist reminding his readers that he had predicted such an outcome, pointed to the aftermath of the Peace Conference to illuminate the failures of moderate New Negro leadership under Du Bois in an article polemically titled "When the Blind Lead." Harrison argued that the division of colonial spoils were "the necessary consequences of the Allies' success. . . . Was Du Bois so blind that he couldn't see them? In 1918 the lynchings were still going on while Dr. Du Bois was solemnly advising us to 'forget our grievances'" (173).

Harrison's belief in the primacy of the struggle for domestic racial justice (i.e., focusing on those grievances rather than those of Europe) should not be confused with a narrow parochialism or isolationism. Rather, he argued for a strategic awareness of how African Americans could most effectively use their political and economic influence to leverage improvements for black peoples both in the United States and abroad. For Harrison, the relationship between black West Indians and African Americans was a particularly promising avenue for cooperation, as each group had a benefit to contribute to the other's political and social advancement. Harrison noted that African Americans, in spite of the tyrannies imposed upon them in the U.S. South, had a freedom to organize and militate that was denied to black West Indians under either British dominion or U.S. occupation: "Agitation and propaganda which have been outlawed in Hayti, the Virgin Islands, and the British West Indies can still be carried on in the Northern states of the union. . . . They could, at any rate, bring effective pressure to bear against the horrifying brutalities which black people are now compelled to endure from the 'cracker' in the Caribbean" (156). In a succession of articles Harrison called for African American activism on behalf of the Caribbean, skillfully modulating his rhetoric to place the struggles of black West Indians in a context that would draw the concern of a wide-ranging U.S. audience. Comparing Haiti to an "American Ireland," he commented that "the people of Hayti are being shot, sabred and bombed, while resisting an illegal invasion of their homes" (235). Besides citing the Irish call for independence that had growing support in the United States, Harrison's description of Haitian unrest as "resisting an illegal invasion of their homes" echoes discourse of the Bill of Rights in the U.S. Constitution. Harrison continued this rhetorical tack in subsequent articles, arguing that activism on behalf of Haiti was necessary to combat the narrow sectional and financial interests that had dictated the invasion. Reminding readers that Congress, not the Navy, has the right to declare war, Harrison attributed the occupation of Haiti to the "'cracker' statesmanship of the South," which had effected the occupation "without one word of protest from that defunct department, the Congress of the United States!" (237). Harrison thus positions the occupation as a threat to the sovereignty not only of Haiti but of the United States itself. In this regard, African American activism on behalf of the West Indies would not only benefit the peoples of those islands, but would restore a healthy balance of powers to the U.S. republic itself.

Reciprocally, for Harrison, West Indian immigrants had much to contribute to the political and economic future of African Americans and of the United States itself. In an article on West Indian immigration published in the *Pittsburgh Courier,* Harrison offered a catalog of notable Americans of West Indian descent, past and present, including John Brown Russwurm (publisher of the first African American periodical, *Freedom's Journal*), Denmark Vessey (leader of a slave revolt in Charleston), and Casper Holstein (Harlem businessman and arts patron), as well as founding father Alexander Hamilton (who was born on Nevis and raised on St. Croix). In terms of domestic racial politics, Harrison acknowledged that there had sometimes been initial "problems in adjustment" as black West Indians settled into African American neighborhoods, but that cooperative relationships developed between the communities: "The West Indian Negro has often played a great part in the drama of Negro development in America" (251). He noted that the first generation of West Indian immigrants were "students and scholars seeking wider fields of usefulness," thus bringing to the United States men who were "paragon[s] of intelligence . . . of birth and breeding" (251). For Harrison, West Indians of lower and middle classes—"tradesmen and skilled workers"—played a valuable role by "thrusting themselves forward into better positions and breaking the trail for Negro-Americans to follow" (251). In contrast to Du Bois's sense that the West Indian was a peasant who needed civilizing from his U.S. brethren, Harrison projected a more reciprocal and optimistic vision of the relationship between the communities: "When the years bring their harvest it will be found that the mingling of the West Indian with American Negro has been highly beneficial to Harlem—and to American at large" (253).

Rum and Revolution: James Weldon Johnson's Tropical Comedy in "Down by the Carib Sea"

Harrison's writings reveal that the political possibilities offered by West Indian intellectuals transcended Garveyism and the limited roles assigned to the Caribbean by New Negro leaders like Du Bois. Besides assumptions about their lack of "civilization" and "simple" militancy, West Indians faced another set of stereotypes: that life in the Caribbean was a permanent vacation of "easy" living. Even James Weldon Johnson, who had family roots in the Bahamas and was a notable advocate for Haiti, falls into these comic stereotypes when turning to the Caribbean in his poetry. Like Stevens and Crane, Johnson composed a long Caribbean-inflected poem, "Down by the Carib Sea," but he did so for the lightest of comic purposes, at the expense of island cultures. The poem begins reverently at first, with an invocatory appreciation of "Sol, sol, mighty lord of the tropic zone."[30] From thereon, however, the poem relies upon the usual tropical stereotypes—tobacco, alcohol, revolutions, lassitude, and exotic women. This narrow range of representation is evident in the titles of the poem's subsections: "Los Cigarrillos," "Teestay" [a Nicaraguan brandy], "The Lottery Girl," and "The Dancing Girl." "Los Cigarrillos" begins with languor—"we dream away/Both the night and day"—and passes through revolutions and towards a lazy smoke:

> Tropical constitutions
> Call for occasional revolutions
> But after that's through,
> Why there's nothing to do
> But smoke—smoke;
> For life in the tropics is only a joke,
> So we pass it in dreams, and we pass it in smoke. (47)

At the risk of stating the obvious, life in the tropics is *not* a joke, and revolution there (as one would think Johnson knew well) is a serious matter indeed.

Less politically charged, but similarly exotic, observations characterize the other sections of the poem, which celebrate the local brandy ("*Teestay,* a drink with a history,/A delicious, delectable mystery") and the local women ("Oh, limpid-eyed girl,/I would take every chance,/If only the prize/Were a love-flashing glance/From your fathomless eyes" [49]). "The Dancing Girl" continues in a similar vein, celebrating the "dusky-haired *señorita* . . ./. . . And her scarlet-red mouth/Like a rose of the south" (50). These clichéd images of tropical beauty in simplistic meter would seem more at home in a Broadway musical than in the works of a New Negro poet reflecting on his West Indian kin. More problematically, this poem reduces the islands to objectified, luxurious commodities (tobacco, tiste, and beautiful women) and ridiculous politics ("occasional revolutions"). One might like to argue that Johnson is producing an ironic pastiche or satirizing the tropical tropes, but there are no alternate voices or contrasting points of view to justify such claims to irony, either within this poem or in his other poetry on the region. Nor does this poem, though lightly touched by vernacular Spanish and turns of phrase, show any of the folkloristic reverence of Johnson's U.S. dialect poems or the majestic, complex cadences of the sermons in *God's Trombones*. Indeed, "Down by the Carib Sea" is so univocal and unequivocal in its deployment of U.S. clichés about the Caribbean that it is hard to read the poem as anything but Johnson's participation in a broader tradition of U.S. condescension towards the Caribbean.

Where Is the West Indian in the New Negro and *The New Negro*?

The Caribbean literary community in Harlem seemed aware of the possibility that it was not being accorded due respect by New Negro leadership, and several authors, in the spirit of Harrison, continued to point out the contributions and potential of West Indians to combat the stereotypical associations ascribed to the islands. Eric Walrond, in "The New Negro Faces America" (1923), argued that in contrast to representations of West Indians as "a mass of peasants," "On the whole the West Indian is intelligent. He is an indefatigable student. When the epic of the negro in America is written, it will show the West Indian as the stokesman in the furnace of negro ideals."[31] In a series of essays in the *Messenger,* J. A. Rogers commented extensively on the political potential of West Indians, either in their resistance to U.S. annexation of the islands or in their distrust of false promises of racial justice from the United States: "They see that even a newly landed immigrant, who is white, is accorded privileges that are withheld from Negro America. . . . Consequently, they are inclined to look down on the value of American citizenship." For Rogers, from that very skepticism, however, comes a militant resistance that extends beyond traditional party lines and provides another front for combating Jim Crow: "The destiny of the West Indian Negro and the American brother, as is also that of the white American, appears to be firmly linked. To the far-visioned and humane it will seem no different whether the battle against color hate and injustice be fought in the West Indies or in the United States."[32] These comments from Walrond and Rogers reveal their consciousness of the expatriate West Indian community's political power and potential, as well as their intertwined connections to African American movements for uplift and civil rights.

In contrast to Walrond's and Rogers's high degree of self-awareness of West Indian potential, Alain Locke's seminal anthology from the renaissance, *The New Negro* (1925), turns a blind eye to the Caribbean while simultaneously benefiting from the works of West Indian writers. Arthur Schomburg, Claude McKay, Eric Walrond, J. A. Rogers, and W. A. Domingo all contributed substantively to *The New Negro,* and ideas rooted in the Caribbean, like pan-Africanism, circulate extensively in the anthology. McKay's poetry, in particular, is cited as the quintessential embodiment of the defiant New Negro spirit, even as his West Indian roots are barely acknowledged by those who quote him. Charles Johnson, for example, who laments the "backward cultures" of the West Indies in his essay "The New Frontage on American Life," cites McKay's "If We Must Die" (a poem produced by someone from Jamaica, one of those "backward cultures") as evidence of the New Negro's spirit of militancy.[33] In spite of these contributions, the U.S. authors in *The New Negro* either overlook the Caribbean entirely or condescend to it as a land of peasants and Garveyism.

Alain Locke's foreword and introduction to *The New Negro* epitomize both the breadth and the limitations of the volume's vision of global blackness. His foreword strategically situates the emergence of the New Negro as part of the struggle for cultural and political independence occurring in many regions of the world: "As in India, in China, in Egypt, Ireland, Russia, Bohemia, Palestine, and Mexico, we are witnessing the resurgence of a people" (xvii). Similarly, in the title essay of the collection, Locke compares Harlem to other centers of cultural and political awakening: "Harlem has the same role to play for the New Negro as Dublin has had for the New Ireland or Prague for the New Czechoslovakia" (7). Locke's rhetoric in these passages is well chosen, as he juxtaposes the uplift projected within his anthology with causes celebres throughout the world. Given the geographic breadth of his claims, it is striking that Locke overlooks contemporary instances of resistance within the Caribbean, such as Haitian struggles against the U.S. occupation and the development of trade unions (and strikes) in Trinidad and British Guiana. These patterns offer even better support than events in Dublin or Prague for Locke's claim that the moment of black emergence has come. In omitting these strong parallels with his own movement, it is as if Locke wishes to claim for Harlem and his colleagues a New York monopoly on black uplift. When Locke does consider the cultural diversity of the black population in the United States, he focuses almost exclusively on internal geographies, such as the "shifting of the Negro population" north because of urban migration (5). Locke acknowledges the multiple branches of black peoples converging in Harlem, including Africans and West Indians (6), and he sees this convergence as productive of a "race welding" that will realize black potential as Harlem becomes the center of New Negro "Zionism" (14). In this respect, Locke is well aware of the cosmopolitan makeup of the renaissance, and he shows an interest in international affairs that anticipates the postcolonial movements later in the century.

At the same time, Locke's internationalist vision is unwittingly parochial in its unquestioned sense that it is the place of African Americans in the United States to edify and uplift their benighted black brethren throughout the world. Indeed, Locke is rather cautious on the subject of where "Zion" is in his model: is it Africa, or Harlem? The balance of his essay (as well as his scorn for Garvey) suggests the latter. Locke writes of the New Negro's "consciousness of acting as the advance-guard of the African peoples in their contact with Twentieth-Century civilization" as well as "the sense of a mission of rehabilitating the race in world esteem from that loss of prestige for which the fate and conditions of slavery have so largely been responsible" (14). It would perhaps be unfair to label Locke's designs as somehow culturally colonialist, but this missionary zeal does echo uncannily the language of uplift and burden that white Europeans have used to claim dominion over much of the world. Locke's vision of African Americans as the vanguard to liberate and civilize "pan-Africa" also elides the fact that the New Negro and pan-Africanist ideologies had significant roots in the work of diasporic Africans outside the United States. Paradoxically, in Locke's perception, it is the role of the U.S. "New Negro" to enlighten and awaken Africans and West Indians to an ideological perspective that those same peoples have helped to produce.

The failure to recognize Caribbean black cultural production is all the more striking in *The New Negro* given that many of the essayists aim to reconstruct African American historical, artistic, and musical traditions that have been overlooked by U.S. white culture. For example, Albert C. Barnes's "Negro Art and America," provides an apt overview of the unheralded contributions of African Americans to United States art and culture. He thus argues that what many in the U.S. have thought of as "American" should be appreciated, at least in part, as "Negro." Ironically, Barnes himself appropriates Caribbean writers like Claude McKay and terms them as "American Negroes," without giving attention to how their island roots have brought a new dimension to African American and American art (23).

Charles Johnson shows another elision of Caribbean tributaries to U.S. culture in his otherwise probing essay "The New Frontage on American Life." Johnson examines how patterns of migration have made U.S. cities in the north incubators of a new black identity, but maintains a strictly domestic focus. He traces patterns of migration from the South to the North, to industrial cities like Chicago, Pittsburgh, Cleveland, Hartford, and Detroit, while also giving due attention to eastward and westward migration from city to city (primarily with Chicago and New York as endpoints of this trajectory) (278–79). With each gesture towards this national landscape, Johnson shows almost a Whitmanesque appreciation for the cultural mixtures produced in each city by the influx of new African Americans encountering older European stocks. Yet Johnson gives no significant attention to how international migration has shaped black cultures in the United States. When Johnson does acknowledge the influx of foreign-born African-descended migrants, he does so in a belittling spirit. Speaking of immigrants from the West Indies, Johnson praises "their endowments of skill and strength" but speaks just as strongly of "their repressions and telltale marks of backward cultures" (294) that must be overcome and transmuted by Harlem.

James Weldon Johnson also cites Harlem as possessing a singular role, describing it as the "culture capital" (in a phrase that provides the title of his essay) for all Negroes worldwide: "The lure of it has reached down to every island of the Carib Sea and has penetrated even into Africa" (301). While Harlem was undoubtedly a crucible for new strains of black identity in the 1920s, it seems quite parochial, with a broad view of Black Atlantic history in mind, to privilege it as the global "lure" for all African-descended peoples. As innovative as Johnson and his U.S. colleagues in *The New Negro* may have been, such claims invoke one of the oldest American traditions, a nationalist exceptionalism, echoing Winthrop's "city on a hill" metaphor, with its grounding vision of a model Zion used as a beacon for the rest of the world. Significantly, this vision of Harlem-as-Zion was disputed by black immigrant writers during the New Negro Renaissance. Indeed, many West Indian immigrant authors, particularly Walrond and McKay, would eventually incorporate a critique of the limitations of Harlem, in spite of its "lure," into their fiction and poetry.

Towards the end of *The New Negro,* W. E. B. Du Bois envisions the future of global Negro activism in "The Negro Mind Reaches Out," but shows a surprising blindness towards the Caribbean. Repeating his prediction from *The Souls of Black Folk* that "the problem of the twentieth century is the problem of the color line," Du Bois surveys how race is intertwined with issues of colonialism and resistance to colonialism. Drawing upon his experience at the Third Pan-African Congress, Du Bois predicts the postcolonial struggles ahead: "With nearly every great European empire today walks its dark colonial shadow, while over all Europe there stretches the yellow shadow of Asia that lies across the world. One might indeed read the riddle of Europe by making its present plight a matter of colonial shadows, speculating on what might happen if Europe became suddenly shadowless." (306). Du Bois proceeds to narrate a history of resistance to colonialism throughout Europe's empire, focusing particularly on West Africa and the Congo. While his attention to the nascent resistance to Portugal, Belgium, France, and England within these regions is certainly correct, it is startling that he makes no mention of the turmoil within the West Indies, particularly given the history of Haiti and its founding of the first black republic in the New World.

Du Bois does make a passing reference to political agitation in the black West Indies, but his very grammar (mis)represents it as a new development: "Since the war not only has West Africa thus spoken but the colored West Indies have complained" (401). The revealing structure here is "not only . . . but"; Du Bois cites the Caribbean to illustrate that resistance is occurring *even* there, which proves, for him, the extent of colonial discontent. This representation of Caribbean political awakening as an unprecedented moment is an odd claim given the extensive history of militant struggle in the Caribbean and the activism at the Pan-African Conference of 1900, which Du Bois himself attended. Du Bois's failure to take the West Indies seriously as part of a global black struggle is also evident in his roll call of black populations at the end of the essay, where he summarizes all the world's locations of Africans and their descendants, but makes no mention of the Caribbean at all. He closes the essay with an assertion that is in the spirit of the rest of the volume, exhilarating and optimistic, but also curiously nationalist and parochial: "This hundred and fifty millions of people are gaining slowly an intelligent thoughtful leadership. The main seat of their leadership is today the United States" (411).

In contrast to Du Bois's confidence that black cultural uplift proceeds from the United States to the rest of the African world, W. A. Domingo, in "Gift of the Black Tropics," argues that Harlem has benefited substantially from the influx of black West Indians and that the New Negro is a hybrid, global concept. Domingo endorses the pluralist black vision presented by other New Negro writers, but perceives that identity as a product of multiple forces in tension: "Divided by tradition, culture, historical background and group perspective, these diverse peoples [in Harlem] are gradually hammered into a loose unit by the impersonal force of congested residential segregation" (306). Both Domingo's vision of the source of racial unity—born of the "impersonal force" of an urban racial divide—and his summary of that unity—"hammered into a loose unit"—speak of a stronger sense of social forces and social conflict, which anticipates the role he describes for West Indians in Harlem as his essay develops. Domingo cites the roles West Indians have played in the "colored" world of the United States, noting that a Jamaican, John Brown Russwurm, "was the first colored man to be graduated from an American college" and that Peter Ogden, also from Jamaica, founded the first organization of colored unity in New York, the "Odd-Fellow Lodge for Negroes" (344). Domingo comments upon the reception of West Indian contributions to African American life with an unusual passive-voice construction: "The part they have played in Negro progress is conceded to be important" (345). Domingo's grammar and choice of words in this sentence is revealing. The word "conceded," along with the obscurity of the implied subject (who is "conceding" the part?), suggests that this acknowledgement has been made grudgingly and that there has not been a sufficiently open embrace of West Indian contributions. The silence on the Caribbean elsewhere in *The New Negro,* even from globally-minded U.S. writers from whom one would expect such attention, suggests that Domingo's sense of neglect is not misplaced.

Domingo argues later in the essay that West Indians have played a special role in the fight for racial justice in the United States. He contends that the particular colonial experience West Indians brought to North America provided a catalyzing perspective that challenged the status quo of white and black Americans alike. With their skills as tradesmen, Domingo observes, they fought closed unions from the moment they entered America, and "in many cases [they] have been pioneers and shock troops to open a way for Negroes into new fields of employment" (345). He perceives the "trait of nonconformity" as a virtue of West Indians, and cites their lack of experience with American racial politics as a gift West Indians bring to the black body politic: "Forming a racial majority in their own countries and not being accustomed to discrimination expressly felt as racial, they rebel against 'the color line' as they find it in America" (347).

Domingo is particularly insistent on the political and economic radicalism of the West Indian classes in New York: "Unlike their American brothers, the islanders are free from those traditions that bind them to any party and, as a consequence, are independent to the point of being radical. Indeed, it is they who largely compose the few political and economic radicals in Harlem; without them the genuinely radical movement among New York Negroes would be unworthy of attention" (346). Domingo also notes that "the greatest black comedian of America, Bert Williams, was from the Bahamas" (346). This historical note is particularly important, as many other authors in the volume cite Williams as a quintessential artist embodying the Negro spirit, but treat him as purely African American, with no reference to his island past. Domingo closes with a more positive note of intraracial reciprocity: "Just as the West Indian has been a sort of leaven in the American loaf, so the American Negro is beginning to play a reciprocal role in the life of the foreign Negro communities" (348).

Domingo, like many other contributors to *The New Negro,* finds himself at odds with the most famous black West Indian in New York, Marcus Garvey, and is well aware of the shadow he casts on the image of islanders in America: "It has been asserted that the movements headed by the most advertised of all West Indians, absentee 'president' of the continent of Africa, represents the attempt of West Indian peasants to solve the American race problem. This is no more true than it would be to say that the editorial attitude of *The Crisis* during the war reflected the spirits of American Negroes respecting their grievances or that the late Booker T. Washington successfully delimited the educational aspirations of his people" (348). Domingo strikes a blow here not only at Garvey and Washington, but, more subtly, at the supposition that these celebrated leaders and organizations fully represent the constituencies for which they claim to advocate. In subtly opposing the politics of elite leadership, Domingo's essay forms one of the most radical statements in *The New Negro,* showing him to be one of the "shock troops" in the struggle for black uplift as well.

Claude McKay's Poetry, Harlem, and *The New Negro*

Claude McKay had significant poems included in *The New Negro,* although the choices Locke made in handling his works suggest a desire to rein in McKay's radicalism and keep him "in his place." Almost immediately after the publication of the anthology, McKay wrote to Locke to express concern that his work had been misrepresented in *The New Negro.* McKay was particularly upset that the title of his sonnet "The White House" had been changed to "White Houses," which altered the inflection of the poem. In a letter to Locke in August of 1926, McKay explains his frustration:

> I received a copy of *The New Negro* a few days ago. Many thanks to you and the Bonis. However, I am displeased about my representation in it. I remember writing to you that "White Houses" was *not* the title of the poem published under that title in the *Survey Graphic* [a journal also published by Locke]. In the *Liberator* it had appeared under the title "The White House." That is a symbolic title. When you change it to "White Houses," the poem immediately

> becomes cheap, flat, Afro-American propaganda. What does a man of creativity, a poet, care about entering a lot of uninteresting white houses? The whole symbolical import of my poem is lost under the title you have chosen to give it and allowed to remain after I had called your attention to it.[34]

"The White House" (I will use McKay's preferred title) opens with a defiant declaration laced with potential violence: "Your door is shut against my tightened face;/And I am sharp as steel with discontent." The speaker struggles not only with racial barriers in the United States (the shut door), but also with his need to control the violence (sharp as steel) born of that frustration. Thus the poem closes with a couplet stating that "I must keep my heart inviolate/Against the potent poison of your hate." The couplet effects a fruitful turn, as it switches the energy of the poem away from an external blow contemplated by the "chafing savage" towards an internal struggle to remain pure in an environment of injustice. In this context of purity set against violence and barriers against openness, Locke's change of title has obvious implications. While the poem does not directly reference Pennsylvania Avenue, the title "The White House" evokes the central seat of U.S. government that has, in effect, barred the door to racial equality and opportunity since Reconstruction. To change the title to "White Houses" is to reframe the political impact of the poem towards the speaker's personal yearning for entry into something much less symbolic, what McKay dryly summarizes in his letter to Locke as "a lot of uninteresting white houses."

In spite of the limitations of Locke's choices, the overall canon of McKay's poems produced in the 1920s showed McKay to be one of the most valuable (and retroactively "Americanized") of the West Indian writers, particularly in his attention to cultural traffic between the Caribbean and the United States. McKay's early poetry, written while in the U.S., shows nostalgia for the Jamaican landscape. Poems like "Flame-Heart," "The Sukee River," "To One Coming North," "North and South," "Home Thoughts," and "I Shall Return" all reveal his deep affection for his native soil, even in his chosen exile from it.

Many of McKay's poems also celebrate the energy of Harlem. Poems like "The City's Love" and "Dawn in New York" show his appreciation of the light and life of the cityscape, even as poems like "When Dawn Comes to the City" suggest that the speaker's heart tends towards other islands: "But I would be on the island of the sea,/In the heart of the island of the sea."[35] Many of McKay's poems simultaneously render the excitement of Harlem life while acknowledging its limitations. "The

Harlem Dancer," for example, begins with a celebration of the sexual vitality of the title figure: "Applauding youths laughed with young prostitutes/And watched her perfect, half-clothed body sway;/Her youth was like the sound of blended flutes" (61). It concludes, however, with a strong note of pathos as the speaker observes, "But looking at her falsely-smiling false,/I knew her self was not in that strange place" (61). One need not read the sense of "place" here as literally spatial or regional, but the sense of dislocation is clear: the dancer is both the center of attention and decentered at the same time. The speaker of "On Broadway" faces a similar conundrum. Noting the glamour and spectacle of the street—"Desire naked, linked with Passion/Goes strutting by in brazen fashion"—he seems mesmerized but desolate: "As in a dream I stand and gaze/At Broadway, shining Broadway—only/My heart, my heart is lonely" (67). These poems evoke a sense of simultaneous presence and absence in Harlem: that everything appears there in bold relief, even as nothing is quite rooted there and the speaker feels pulled elsewhere. The complex feeling of community and isolation in the city stands in marked contrast to Locke's and Du Bois's confidence in Harlem as a metropolitan Zion and a kind of synecdochic site for global blackness. McKay's sense of Harlem as both centralizing and alienating would become a characteristic feature of his gaze toward that urban center.

McKay's militant poems provided some of the most important contributions to Locke's and Du Bois's plans for cultural and political struggle, and they were strikingly innovative in their context. The poems of McKay's recent precursors, such as Paul Laurence Dunbar and James Weldon Johnson, were frequently engaged with questions of political and cultural identity for African Americans, but the concept of "America" itself was rarely questioned. Although Dunbar and Johnson critiqued lynchings and racism in their poems, they showed caution in expressing violence or rage within their texts, especially towards the nation. Even among his contemporaries, such as Countee Cullen and Langston Hughes, McKay in his poems stands out for his trenchant defense of black culture and calling to account of the United States for its injustice. For example, while Hughes's early poems express a sense of black historical and cultural continuity ("The Negro Speaks of Rivers") and a sense of integration as national destiny ("I, Too, Sing America"), McKay is willing to attack the image of the nation itself in "The Lynching," "The White House," and "Look Within," and even his earliest poems call out for explicit resistance. "If We Must Die" (which was not included in *The New Negro*), for example, famously closes with a defiant couplet: "Like men we'll face the murderous, cowardly pack, / Pressed to the wall, dying, but fighting back" (36). In some poems, he effectively juxtaposes his love and hate for the United States. "America" vividly captures this paradoxical combination:

> Although she feeds me bread of bitterness,
> And sinks into my throat her tiger's tooth,
> Stealing my breath of life, I will confess
> I love this cultured hell that tests my youth!

The image of the U.S.-as-tiger recurs in several of McKay's poems, and it produces at least two outstanding effects. First and most obviously, the "she" of America (usually linked with images such as Lady Liberty) is here recast as a predatory exploiter. Second, and perhaps more subtly, this tiger comparison effects a reverse exoticism. Rather than figuring the United States through a predatory national animal native to its own soil (e.g., an eagle, a wolf, a bear), McKay compares it to a tropical beast that, at least since Blake, has been identified with heat, savagery, and excess—the very metaphorical associations attached to McKay's own Caribbean in so many U.S. descriptions.

McKay's metaphoric "discovery" of tropical predation in the United States reveals the subtle cross-cultural work that emerges when he self-consciously marries a West Indian perspective with a U.S. subject. Surprisingly, it is on this subject that scholars have least reflected, even those seeking to restore a Caribbean perspective to U.S. readings of the author. For example, while Hathaway's excellent study of McKay examines his writings about Jamaica and Harlem in tandem to make a case for the "hybridity" of his diasporic identity (46), she skips over the key moments in his fiction and poetry when he engages in a comparative juxtaposition of the two spaces—the very spots where he effects cross-cultural comparison and self-consciously reckons with the pros and cons of that cultural contact. In "The Tropics in New York," one of the five poems selected for *The New Negro,* for example, the poet explores the paradoxical simultaneity (captured in the title) of experiencing two places at once. The poem begins with a description of beautiful tropical fruits available in a New York store:

> Bananas ripe and green, and ginger-root,
> Cocoa in pods and alligator pears,
> And tangerines and mangoes and grape fruit,
> Fit for the highest prize at parish fairs. (31)

This last line inflects the stanza with a sense of cosmopolitan promise, as these fruits are not inferior to those of the tropics, but "fit for the highest prize." At that moment in the poem, then, McKay's speaker seems to feel the resonance of the title in the most optimistic manner possible: the tropics *are* in New York, virtually, and the speaker can experience a sense of fulfilling simultaneity—the best of both places, as it were.

This sensation does not last long, however, as the fruits, in the second stanza, are "bringing memories," which transport the speaker back to the tropics. Ultimately, the poem finishes not merely with a "wave of longing," but a disavowal of the scene itself for the pain it causes: "hungry for the old, familiar ways,/I turned aside and bowed my head and wept" (31). As much as McKay's writing would embrace Harlem for its excitement and opportunity, poems such as this reveal that it could not fulfill the task (as many essayists in *The New Negro* seemed to believe) of fully encapsulating a virtual community of the black diaspora. Indeed, the very availability of the produce becomes a tantalizing torment in itself, as it both brings the speaker into proximity with the tropics and reminds him of his displacement from them.

In a similarly poignant vein, McKay links the tropics to New York in "Subway Wind." After focusing on New Yorkers striving to get free of the cramped tunnels, the poem turns to the wind itself, which it figures as imprisoned as well, a "captive wind that moans for fields and seas;/Seas cooling warm where native schooners drift" (75). The poem then imaginatively voyages back to the tropics, where "islands of lofty palm trees blooming white/. . . lend their perfume to the tropic sea,/Where fields lie idle in the dew-drenched night,/And the Trades float above them fresh and free." Beyond this poem's deft sweep from north to south and its aching lyricism, it accomplishes several comparisons that reverse typical expectations of what New York means in a "New Negro" context. Although expressing a desire for freedom fits into dominant poetic discourses of the time, the poem's location of that freedom does not. As admiring as McKay is of New York's vitality and life in other poems, in "Subway Wind" it is the tropics, not the urban metropole, that represents freedom. Even more boldly, in linking the wind itself to a yearning for tropical origins, McKay extends the scope of the poem from the personal meditation of "The Tropics in New York" towards a hint that even the natural forces of the city long to be elsewhere, perhaps with according implications for the human habitants (whose race is notably unnamed in this poem). In this respect, McKay renders New York itself as "other," not simply to West Indians, but to the wind itself: Locke's Zion becomes, in this poem, a city not so much of unified desire but of universal exilic yearning.

In Search of a Safe "Zone": Eric Walrond's Fiction and the United States

Like McKay's poems, Eric Walrond's fiction also represented a fruitful body of cross-cultural engagement between the United States and the Caribbean, but his work was not substantively embraced by Locke and other elite African American intellectuals (though one of his stories was reprinted in *The New Negro,* the inclusion of which I will discuss later). Walrond's early short fiction was published primarily in periodicals like *Negro World* and *Opportunity,* and, in spite of (or perhaps because of) his residing in New York at the time, his short pieces usually depict the United States as a space that his characters need to flee. In "I Am an American," for example, the narrator, a tourist in Cuba, is approached by a laborer who appears to recognize him as a countryman. Rather than sharing a moment of patriotic discourse, the laborer describes his preference for Cuba: "I left my home town in Georgia about eight years ago. . . . I tell you. I meet a lot of fellows and they try to get me on ships to work my way back to the United States, but the way I figure it out, I can't see it. I tell 'em nothing doing. Nothing doing. I ain't going to leave Habana. I am not going back to the States. You don't hear of any niggers getting lynched in Habana. Nor any black and white laws—laws for the white folks and laws for the black folks."[36] In "Vignettes of the Dusk," a character bearing a striking resemblance to Walrond himself considers the pros and cons of staying in America:

> In 1918 he came to America. That means he is still a foreigner. He is not a citizen—yet! But he is going to be. It is going to be the big adventure of his life. But wait—
>
> Sometimes he stops and thinks. He is a Negro. He is a foreign Negro. Every day he reads of lynchings in the South. He is besieged on all sides by vicious soul pricks. No, they'd say to him, you musn't go South; you won't like it down there. . . . "But I must go," he screams back at them. "I must! I can't be an American unless I am able to go South. I've got to go."[37]

Although this particular monologue remains unfinished (as is the case for each of the vignettes), it encapsulates an invaluable perspective on the United States from the point of view of blacks from the Caribbean: that while the United States (particularly New York) represents a land of economic opportunity beyond that available in the islands, a large part of the nation represents a kind of racist terror far beyond what they experienced at home. In interrogating the value of officially becoming "American," Walrond's speaker effectively calls into question the coherence of U.S. citizenship itself for black Americans: how can one truly be a full citizen of a nation if one's rights are variable within that national space? This idea would be further developed in C. L. R. James's *Mariners, Renegades, and Castaways,* in which James would argue that the United States itself was in a process of "becoming," as it had not yet developed a sense of citizenship commensurate with its exceptionalist claims for democratic potential.

Short sketches with polemical interruptions constitute most of Walrond's early fiction, but his writing quickly matured to produce some of the most challenging and sophisticated short stories of the New Negro Renaissance. His collection *Tropic Death* (1926) offered a unified set of thematically connected stories. Taking clear cues from Jean Toomer's *Cane* (1923),[38] the stories in the collection conjoin richly textured meditations on landscape, violence, and sexuality in the Caribbean with strong dialect and an emphasis on folk life. Unlike Toomer in *Cane,* Walrond does not embed poetry between his stories, nor is there as apparent a symbolic narrative arc, but the stories are clearly patterned to reflect upon serious issues faced in West Indians' lives. In terms of geographic scope, *Tropic Death* extends across a wide range of Caribbean spaces, encompassing Jamaica, Barbados, Panama, and British Guiana. Walrond's characters migrate extensively among those spaces, typically due to changing political and economic conditions. In contrast to the free and easy portraits in U.S. poems or travel literature about the Caribbean (such as Johnson's "Down by the Carib Sea"), the stories in *Tropic Death* examine, from varied angles, the high stakes of survival and power there. Indeed, Walrond's focus on death and violence in the region has a polemical aim, as in his literary criticism he complained that too often European and American authors had simply offered a "pretty Continentalized version" of the Caribbean in their writings.[39] In a manner that anticipates Richard Wright's *Uncle Tom's Children* (1938), *Tropic Death* provides an anatomy of deaths from varied perspectives, usually involving violent conflict. Animals, Englishmen, and black West Indians meet varied and almost always untimely ends in these stories. Death comes from a range of sources: from fellow blacks, to Spanish rivals from Cuba, to U.S. Marines, to natural forces beyond anyone's control.

While the violent plots in *Tropic Death* are often rooted in personal conflicts, they have rich political and cultural implications. Typically, it is the United States, not Britain, that looms as the colonial "other" faced by Walrond's characters. The narrator of "Drought," for example, uses the United States as a negative foil for considering sexual relationships between whites and blacks. The main character, Coggins, eyes a young black woman on a village road and comes to the (for him) unfortunate realization that she is already attached to a white man: "Grumblings. Pitch-black, to the 'washed-out' buckra she was more than a bringer of victuals. The buckra's girl. It wasn't Sepia, Georgia, but a backwoods village in Barbadoes. 'Didn't you bring me no molasses to put in the rain-water?' the buckra asked, and the girl, sucking in her mouth, brought an ungovernable eye back at him."[40] At first glance, this scene might seem a simple echo of sexualized racial domination in the United States, thus establishing an unfortunate likeness between the regions. But Walrond registers this scene as one of distinction between those spaces: "It wasn't Sepia, Georgia." If this were Georgia, Coggins could flirt with the girl once the "buckra" left, because although she might have been his servant, she would not likely have been (at least openly) his "girl." Here, Coggins is frustrated precisely because the girl is "more than" a servant to the white man, and she herself is rendered not as subservient but as "ungovernable." Unlike the sexual liaisons in Toomer's "Blood Burning Moon," for example, the sexuality here is open and playful, displayed in public with jokes about "molasses" in the "rainwater." Also unlike "Blood Burning Moon," there is no violent triangulation: Coggins simply plays a song, moves on, and there is no upshot whatsoever from the relationship Coggins witnesses. The very uneventfulness of this meeting is significant.

To be sure, Walrond's islands in *Tropic Death* are no multiracial utopia, but there are distinctions between U.S. culture and island cultures, even those under British control, that contrast with the apparent consensus in *The New Negro* that the United States should be the unquestioned Zion for global blackness. At times, for example, Walrond's characters assert their "Britishness" as means of countering U.S. claims to power. In "Panama Gold," for example, a former canal worker, Poyer, relates to his friends at a Barbadian village store how he exacted payment from the United States for an injury that destroyed his foot: "I mek dem pay me! Deeds I dids! Says to dem, 'pay me or be Christ, you'll stan' de consequences!' 'Pay me,' I says, 'or I'll sick de British bulldog on all yo' Omericans!' . . . I let dem understand enough dat I wuz a Englishmen and not a bleddy American nigger! A' Englishman—big distinction in dat, Bruing! An' dat dey couldn't do as dey bleddy well please wi' a subject o' de King!" (43). Walrond likely intends this passage to be read with some irony at Poyer's expense, as the speaker overestimates the intervention likely to come from the "British bulldog": "Man, I wuz ready to sick Nelson heself 'pon dem. At a moment's notice, me an de council wuz gettin' ready fo' ramsack de Isthmus and shoot up de whole blasted locks!" (42). While Poyer's claims to "Britishness" may seem naïve in the context of race relations in the colonies (indeed, George Lamming would later critique Barbados's self-conception as "Little England"), it is clear that it provides an oppositional identity that distinguishes Poyer from both U.S.-born blacks and from the United States itself.

Less ironically, small moments of conflict in *Tropic Death* reveal an axis of opposition between the United States and the islands that is shared by both whites and blacks. In one story, a drunken white Englishman and a white American who are competing for the attention of a woman insult each other on explicitly national terms. The Englishman calls the other man "yo' gawd dam American," while the American insults his rival as "a goddam lime juicer" (an epithet like "limey") (94). In "The Yellow One," with an entirely different class and racial setting, the violent conflict arises from the jealousy of an African American from Florida named Hubigon towards a handsome mixed-race Cuban, oddly nicknamed "Porto Rico": "A son of the Florida Gulf, he [Hubigon] hated 'Porto Rico' for reasons planted deep in the Latin's past. He envied him the gentle texture of his hair" (60). Hubigon later instigates a fight with Porto Rico, and although neither is killed, death still appears to be in the air: "In the scuffle the woman collapsed, fell under the feet of the milling crew" (66). This woman, a mother with a baby, may not be dead, but she is led off to a surgeon and a baby is left behind, "now on its third hunger nap" (66). The story's shift to the mother and the abandoned (and possibly orphaned) child reveals the collateral cost from the men's struggle. While Walrond is not unique in noting intraracial rivalry along "colorist" lines (hence the title "The Yellow One"), it is significant that he chooses to align this rivalry also along national lines, with the representative of the United States as the "other," the jealous aggressor against the islands.

Indeed, Walrond recurrently portrays the United States as a neocolonial aggressor far more dangerous than the original colonizers from Europe. In the collection's most politically charged story, aptly titled "Subjection," the main character, Ballet, faces an escalating range of threats from a U.S. marine in the Canal Zone. At the outset of the story, Ballet intervenes to stop the marine from beating a young boy to death. He tells the marine, "Yo' coward, yo'—a big able man lik' yo' beatin' a lil' boy lik' dat. Why yo' don' hit me? Betcha yo' don' put down yo' gun an' fight me lik' yo' got any guts" (102). Although Ballet succeeds in saving the boy, he is threatened by the marine in return: "I'll git you yet . . . I'll fill you full of lead yet, you black bastard!" (102). This conflict reaches a climax at the end when the marine shoots Ballet in cold blood, but the implications for the struggle between Ballet and the marine extend far beyond the personal. As the plot develops after the initial confrontation, Walrond's story reveals how the blacks are, in the words of one woman, "under de heel o' de Buckra" (104). The story details how Ballet and his friends are essentially impressed into labor by marines:

> "Don't stand there, boys, getta move on! Jump in this boat—another one's coming—no time to waste—jump in there!"
>
> A marine lieutenant, pistol in hand, superintended the embarkment. A squad of khakied men paraded the strip of seashore. (110)

Although Ballet and his friends are not forced to provide free labor (there is some mention of pay, although it is never given in the story), they are clearly under white dominion: their work is supervised at gunpoint, the work site resembles a military camp, and working is not a matter of choice once the marines are present. This story not only anticipates subsequent exposés of conscripted labor at the hands of U.S. forces (notably, Richard Wright's "Down by the Riverside"), but suggests that the neocolonial intervention by the United States is, in effect, bringing its own version of neo-slavery to the region.[41] The U.S. Marines' account of Ballet's murder, as revealed at the end of the story, represents the violence as a matter of political necessity: "In the Canal Record, the Q.M. at Toro Point took occasion to extol the virtues of the Department which kept the number of casualties in the recent native labor uprising down to one" (112). There is no uprising in "Subjection," but this official account provides an exonerating cover story for the U.S. Marines. Walrond crafts that sentence, which closes "Subjection," with a richly disturbing sense of synchronicity. The official history of the "event" reaches both backwards and forwards. The language of "native uprising" clearly echoes colonial tropes (albeit mistakenly so, as most are migrants, not natives), and the word "labor" evokes the discourse of contemporary class struggle erupting in the United States in the 1920s. In this regard, the United States in this story represents a disturbing new kind of colonial superpower, as it combines the perspectives of U.S. racism, European colonial views, and the language of modern class warfare in its "subjection" of the island.

Written during the height of the U.S. occupation of Haiti, the stories in *Tropic Death* show just how radically Caribbean discourse on the United

States had changed since the turn of the century. Firmin, Thomas, and Martí (at first) situated the United States as an antipodal force to check the colonial powers of Europe, but in the works of McKay, Walrond, and Domingo, that balance had clearly shifted such that the U.S. was now the primary aggressor. Although Walrond registered that conflict vividly in several of his stories, his most charged prediction of the fate of U.S. intervention occurs in a highly symbolic register, in a story titled "The White Snake." The story centers around the struggle of a young woman, Seenie, to feed her child, Water Spout. Water Spout's health is clearly precarious, as registered in his weak body: "He had a scrawny neck. It had its base in a hollow-sounding delta. A stack of bluey veins, loosely tied in a clot of skin, connecting a hairless cocoanut to a brown, belegged pumpkin. The navel string, prematurely plucked, hung like a ripe yellow cashew" (130). It is striking that Walrond chooses to figure this weak boy with language redolent of fertility. His body echoes not only the shapes of some of the most important produce of the region (cashews, coconuts, and pumpkins) but fertile geography itself (a delta). Indeed, Water Spout's very name suggests renewal, life, and the most elemental of natural resources. In this light, Seenie's need to feed Water Spout—"she made sure of one eternal thing—Water Spout had to be fed. Feeding him was her one active passion" (131)—suggests her commitment not only to the future of her child, but to the Caribbean region itself, as registered in the geographical and agricultural potential figured upon his body. In parallel to the question of Water Spout's thriving, everyone in the story is waiting for rain to arrive to end a drought, much as the characters in Roumain's *Masters of the Dew* seek a new water source to reinvigorate their village. Also as in *Masters of the Dew,* this need for water and fertility is tied to national and cultural potential. With this charged (and perhaps neo-Edenic) symbolic structure, any threats to the health of Water Spout (such as, for example, a snake) take on an even more terrifying resonance. Walrond achieves a superb deferral in the story, however, by naming the snake in the title but only revealing it at the end. The revelation of the snake's presence is gothic and grotesque. As Seenie drifts to sleep, she feel confused because she hears Water Spout crying across the room but also feels a tugging at her breast that suggests he is nursing off her. She resolves the conflict by assuming that she is dreaming the cries while her baby is nursing: "Here—his cold head pegging at her armpit, here—tugging away at her very gizzard. She began to feel for him. A soft, cool, flat something met her hand" (143). Her suspicion grows as Water Spout apparently cries across the room and nurses at the same time: "Was he a dual being?" (143). She soon learns, however, that something else is nursing: "But suddenly, the head receded, slipped down into the gut of the straw. And on the other side of the room Water Spout gave an unmistakable yell" (143). Seenie then grabs Water Spout and flees her hut. It is not clear whether Seenie sees precisely what had been nursing upon her, but the reader learns of it later via a scene with a local policeman: "Some six hours later he returned, dragging on the coral road to the sea the fresh dead body of a bloaty milk-fed snake the sheen of a moon in May" (143).

Walrond clearly intends this scene of milk theft, with its echoes of rape, violation, and phallic predation, to shock the reader. What is striking, however, is that the violation occurs with such stealth. Seenie, as dedicated as she is to Water Spout, is mistakenly, for a time, giving her milk not only to another being but to another species, and a predator at that. In the context of Water Spout's possibly representing the future of her country (British Guiana), this may suggest the dangerous possibility of being tricked into diverting one's elemental nutrition away from the black child and towards the white invader. Significantly, however, it is not the mother and child who are the victims of "tropic death" in this story, but the snake itself, who is not killed by any human but destroyed, apparently, by its own voracious appetite. In this light, the tropics are figured as a self-regulating system, in which a predator who is too greedy can actually feed himself to death. This image not only skillfully links the snake to other "white" invaders (and I would argue primarily the white United States) who threaten to steal the produce and future of the region, but also foretells the invaders' "tropic death."

Given that so many of Walrond's stories explore, either symbolically or explicitly, the relationship between black West Indians and the United States, one might expect a story of that nature to be prized for its relevance and included in *The New Negro*. In spite of (or perhaps because of) the charged nature of the portrayal of the U.S. and U.S. characters in "Subjection," "The White Snake," and "The Yellow One," Locke kept those stories out of the anthology. The single story from *Tropic Death* that was anthologized in *The New Negro,* "Palm Porch," is a relatively conventional portrait of expected local color from the Caribbean. It focuses on a high-end saloon-house (the Palm Porch) owned by a decorous and cunning madam named Miss Buckner. The story relates the rivalries among the girls and their clients and focuses on varying degrees of exotic beauty and violent competition between the wide range of men (black and white) who visit the house. Like all of the stories in *Tropic Death,* it finishes with a death; in this case, that of a dissipated vice-consul who angrily competes with another man for the affection of the beautiful Anesta. Although the story is innovative in conjoining Victorian propriety with tropical dissipation—Miss Buckner and her charges are quite proper in carrying out their profession—it renders the Caribbean in the broad strokes of heat, rum, sex, and internecine violence that were typical visions assigned to the region. That Locke chose "Palm Porch" for *The New Negro* rather than another story by Walrond is revealing in itself, as almost every story published by the author had more direct engagement with connections between the Caribbean and the United States. The fact that Walrond generally portrayed the United States in his stories, whether represented by white marines or African Americans from Florida, as hostile to an independent Caribbean may have, to Locke's mind, run the risk of inflecting *The New Negro* with too radical a critique of U.S. imperialism, or of destabilizing the centrality of Harlem as a locus by suggesting alternative spaces for progressive black uplift.

A New "Opportunity" for Dialogue: Charles Johnson's Special West Indian Issue

A more reciprocal dialogue between the black West Indian and African American communities would emerge a year after the publication of *The New Negro* in a special issue of *Opportunity* in November 1926, edited by Charles Johnson and with the assistance of Eric Walrond. Although relatively modest in size and in political aims compared to *The New Negro,* it provided a venue for voicing key concerns unexamined in previous Harlem Renaissance discussions. In their introduction, the editors state that there is a need for this special issue because of the "questions and difficulties" that obtain between the two communities and that they seek to use this issue to promote "an essential friendship" in place of that distrust. The editors also recognize the asymmetry in the representation of black cultural life in African American journals: "The American Negro is constantly present in his newspapers and magazines; in this issue the West Indian speaks."[42]

The terms of that speech seem up for debate within that very issue, however. Waldo Frank's review of Walrond's *Tropic Death* (published that same year) argues that Walrond had adopted the wrong literary language and thus failed to fulfill his potential as a West Indian writer:

> Mr. Walrond, who, for all I know, may be a subject of the King *is* in his language an American. And I hereby claim him! Wherefore, having cavalierly made him my brother, I claim the right to scold him. I don't like your sophistication,

> brother Walrond. I wish you'd realize that you'll wield your noble youthful language better if you'll take it *easier.* Perhaps one of your ancestors was a Caribbean peasant. When he wielded the hoe or the knife, did he not grasp it loose in his brown hand? Do you likewise with your language.[43]

Beyond the sense of spontaneous ownership—"I hereby claim him!"—Frank's view of Walrond is ripe with essentialist condescension. This perspective shows the limitation of his valuing the Caribbean as an exotic cultural resource, as it confines Walrond to the expectation that he will reject European sophistication and be "authentic" to his perspective as a peasant. According to John Escobedo, the fact that Johnson was comfortable publishing such a reductive review shows that West Indian writers "had reason to be cautious with [their] literary venues" in the United States.[44] More broadly, Frank's commentary, along with Johnson's willingness to print it in a special issue aiming at rapprochement between West Indian and African American communities, shows that the New Negro establishment was still quite comfortable when the West Indian was kept in his "place," even by a member of the white literary establishment like Frank.

Fortunately, there were many other opportunities for the West Indians to speak on their own terms in that issue: poems from Claude McKay, a brief overview of the Caribbean by W. A. Domingo, a survey of recent West Indian composers and musicians by Arthur Schomburg, a history of the U.S. Virgin Islands by Casper Holstein (who also introduced the Casper Holstein Arts Prize in that same issue), a listing of "Some Prominent West Indians," and a small symposium on West Indian–American relations. This last dialogue was less substantive and proactive than one might have hoped for, however; it closes with a rather underwhelming declaration by Eugene Kinckle Jones, executive secretary of the Urban League: "I think that the best example of the possibility of cooperation between the American and West Indian Negro has been seen in the development of the American Tennis Organization, an organization which has become one of the greatest forces for good fellowship in the social world among Negroes in this country."[45] Other contributors are less sporting and more politically engaged, though the tenor of the issue is generally centrist. Domingo and Holstein treat the occupation of Haiti very much like the proverbial "elephant in the room," touching upon it only lightly. The question of the West Indies' political future, particularly vis-à-vis the competing influences of Britain and the United States, produces the most interesting discourse in the issue. Holstein's examination of the status of the U.S. Virgin Islands (his native island was St. Croix) seems, at first, to be building a case for self-rule and freedom from the United States. He begins his article by recounting the revolutionary history connected to the Virgin Islands, including Denmark Vesey's revolt in 1822 (which he started in Charleston) and the revolt of 1848 against the Danish Crown, which resulted in the abolition of slavery on those islands. In considering the present, however, Holstein speaks with a firm U.S. voice: "The argument that they [the Virgin Islands] are a liability to this country is beside the point. In the case of our own Virgin Islands their geographic position and consequent strategic importance led us to acquire them and these same considerations may in time bring the entire West Indian islands under our control."[46] With this strong language of possession ("our own Virgin Islands"), Holstein articulates a position of patriotic responsibility; while he does not necessarily embrace the prospect of "bring[ing] the entire West Indian islands under our control," he does not discount or criticize it either. Holstein does fault the United States for bringing a level of "race prejudice" to the Virgin Islands that was not there under Danish dominion. His primary concern, however, is not that the United States has control over the islands, but that it has not equitably developed the islands' economies or given Virgin Islanders the rights of U.S. citizens. Indeed, for Holstein, the solution is not to remove the U.S. presence, but to bring the Virgin Islanders closer to being "brothers" of the United States: "The former governor and the present incumbent have put in the colonial council by executive fiat white foreigners who owe allegiance to Britain and other European countries to administer Naval law and wield administrative and legislative authority over what should be American citizens in a colony belonging to the United States" (345). With this closing comment Holstein shrewdly depicts a convergence of interests between the United States and the islanders, suggesting that the current administration of the islands is not only failing to grant proper rights to the islanders, but allowing European interests to dominate what should be a U.S. sphere of influence.

W. A. Domingo is much less sanguine in the issue about the prospects of the United States developing equitable systems of government and production in the Caribbean. While he enumerates the failures of England to produce just development in the Caribbean, he reports that West Indians would not prefer alignment with (or worse, annexation by) the United States:

> Informed and influential West Indians bewail the failures of the British government . . . but there is little disposition on their part to welcome American

> control. They fear that under the hegemony of the United States they would be made to experience the social degradation to which Americans of color are subject. . . . West Indians, rightly or wrongly, regard their condition as superior to any that they would secure if controlled by the United States.[47]

Domingo's bracing criticism of U.S. hegemony and "social degradation" strikes a far more militant note than those other contributors to the issue, but as in his contributions to *The New Negro,* he is very much the exception that proves the rule of dominant discourse.

Perhaps recognizing the inflammatory potential of commentary like Domingo's, the editor counterpointed his article, on the same page, with poems that fostered a sense of reconciliation with the United States. Ironically, these two poems came from Claude McKay, whose work was generally quite militant in gaze, but Johnson selected two poems that had an opposite effect, especially in the context of Domingo's article. The first, entitled "My House," is abstracted from the specifics of American life compared to the vast majority of McKay's poems. Like much of McKay's work, it contemplates the struggles of being alien ("I know the dark delight of being strange"). As the poem moves towards its close, it resolves that tension not through any explicit or external struggle, but by affirming, aspirationally, the internally transformative power of the imagination:

> Then he may fall into a drunken sleep
> And wake up in his same house painted blue,
> Or white or green or red or brown or black—
> His house, his own, whatever be the hue.
> But things for him will not be what they seem
> To average men since he has dreamt his dream!

Of course, to deploy the language of "dream" in the context of the New Negro movement is to allude to all kinds of internal and external struggles, but this poem does so without calling to account anything specific within the United States and without avowing the militant stance typical in most of McKay's works.

The subsequent poem by McKay on that same page, "America in Retrospect," articulates an even more affirming vision of reconciliation. While the poem briefly figures the moral failures of the United States as a looming shadow, it quickly shifts to an evocation of forgiveness: "My thoughts of you [America] are memories of a child, / A healthy child that soon forgets its hurt; / Wistful, I feel no hatred deep and wild" The reserved narrative of this poem smoothes over rifts of distance, history, and pain—hardly a typical ending for McKay. In its overall effect, this poem offers U.S. readers the reassurance that McKay, though he had left the United States in body, still felt connected in spirit and had moved from hostility to acceptance, even as he recognizes the problems (the shadow) still afflicting the U.S.[48]

Is He Coming Home to Harlem? McKay and the New Negro Establishment

Given that by 1926 McKay had grown increasingly disenchanted with the domestic politics of the New Negro and of the United States more generally (indeed, he left the U.S. in 1922 to visit the Soviet Union at the height of his commitment to communism; he would not return until 1934), one might rightly ask why he would give consent for the publication of poems that offered such a strong sense of reconciliation with the U.S. The answer is simple: he did not. Johnson's use of McKay's poetry for that special issue, along with Locke and Du Bois's handling of McKay's and Walrond's work in *The New Negro,* quickly became a subject of concern for the authors, as they felt that their works were being used without appropriate permission and compensation. In November of 1926, Johnson, in his capacity as editor of *Opportunity,* wrote to McKay to inform him that he had used some of McKay's poems for the special Caribbean issue without permission:

> Our November issue of OPPORTUNITY is a Caribbean issue on which I have had the assistance of Eric Walrond in assembling. The liberty was taken in making use of three of your poems in this issue—DESOLATE, MY HOUSE, and AMERICA IN RETROSPECT. And although we are not in any position to pay for these contributions, I am attempting to secure for them, from sources outside the provision of our budget, some compensation.[49]

Johnson's letter well encapsulates the conundrum faced by many West Indian writers dependent on the sponsorship and patronage of the Harlem elite. On the one hand, it was an important intellectual acknowledgment of West Indian creative work that Johnson would devote a special issue to it. On the other, the letter also reveals the degree to which Johnson felt a sense of proprietary control over McKay's poems, so much so that he could select and publish them without consultation and without compensation. Johnson politely acknowledged what he was doing as a "liberty" and, perhaps sensing the forthcoming objections, offered an argument that this plan was ultimately in the best interest of McKay: "I am more than commonly interested in having American readers re-establish that keen and delightful direct contact with you through your verse, which your absence has broken. You were the first clear voice of this new school of Negro writers of whom we are now hearing so much, and whom this journal has bent its full efforts toward aiding."

The "absence" to which Johnson refers, of course, is McKay's time abroad, since he had left Harlem in 1922 to travel to Russia and then to France. A recurrent feature of McKay's correspondence with Harlem intellectuals following *The New Negro* was their admonishing him that he needed to return "home" to, in Johnson's word, "re-establish" himself in the movement. Indeed, the following spring, Du Bois would write to McKay in terms far less diplomatic than Johnson's: "Will you please tell me frankly why you do not return to the United States and to your literary work? Is it because the United States authorities refuse to visé your passport? If this is so, it is barely possible we may do something to help you. At any rate, I should like to know from you personally just what the difficulty is."[50] Rather than flattering McKay by alluding to the potency of his voice and the need for contributions, Du Bois writes in a strictly paternal, even disciplinary mode. McKay also struggled over control of his work with Du Bois, and complained that the latter had published poems without his permission in the *Crisis* in 1927.[51]

McKay later asked Johnson to return all of his poems to him, and Johnson did so, but explained that he had only the best motives and was attempting to keep McKay's career alive in the United States:

> The motive back of any reference that we have made you at all, has been that which I expressed to you in a letter more than a year ago—that we wanted simply to keep you warmly alive, thru a period when practically nothing was appearing from your pen in this country, and we were getting so many inquiries from your admirers who felt that your voice should be heard in that chorus of gifted young Negro artists which you undoubtedly began. . . . Under another cover, I am returning to you all of the manuscripts belonging to you which we have in the office.[52]

Although one might sympathize with Johnson's and Du Bois's desire to bring McKay "home to Harlem," it is striking how their correspondence shows both a sense of entitlement to McKay's work and a faith that they understood the proper shape of his career better than he did himself.

Lest one attribute these debates to simple clashes of personality, it should be noted that other writers from the Caribbean showed similar concerns. Hubert Harrison, in contemporary reviews in the 1920s, complained that Du Bois and other editors were "guardians of the gate" who sought to micromanage what would "count" as New Negro literature, while discounting other literary achievements that they did not perceive as part of their Harlem canon: "Each such discoverer thinks that the stream of Negro literary production bubbled up at the precise point that he discovered it" (353). Harrison also complained that anthologists like James Weldon Johnson selected poems that would not offend white audiences, effectively "emasculating" more radical authors (395). More recently, John Escobedo has documented Arthur Schomburg's later conflicts with the New Negro establishment in the 1930s, including his sense that Du Bois and Johnson had taken his historical research and philosophy for granted and without citation:

> First chance you have at a Library get hold of J. W. Johnson's *Black Manhattan,* [t]hen turn to the Preface and see for yourself the passive way this "great American" thanks his fellow man. It is a scream! I mean he thanks the collection and mentions my name for having collected play-bills, no personal reference of a man's thought. It is hell, how some men do things. But the good Lord has kept me this long for some purpose or other.[53]

Walrond specifically advised McKay against leaving his manuscripts in the hands of Harlem publishers while he traveled abroad:

> If I were you I'd cease sending them MSS until I've heard something about the money you were promised. I think, too while I'm on the subject, it is undoubtedly a foolhardy business to try to sell MSS from such a distance without an agent acting on your behalf. Everybody here is so selfishly doing marketing or performing for the market wares of his own that it is a waste of time to try to butt in anywhere. If I were you I wouldn't bite my tongue when I write Johnson: tell him you are up against it and ask him what about that money he promised you for the stuff he has used. Bombard him to death; he's sure to squirm under continuous fire. . . . "The New Negro" is going slowly to hell and is read by practically no one of consequence. I'd lift my eyes elsewhere if I wanted to see my stuff. Can't you try to get back to America? The world seems to have gone around a hundred times since you have been away.[54]

Perhaps influenced by Walrond's advice, in the spring of 1927, as a third edition of *The New Negro* was being prepared, McKay wrote to Locke alleging that the second edition included poems for which he had not given permission and for which he was not compensated. Locke wrote back with a tutorial on intellectual property and a firm sense that he knew the place of McKay's art:

> Poets are anthologized on publisher's permissions (as they legally hold the copyright) time in and time out. We were giving you, however, the courtesy of notice and request for cooperation. Personally there was no question in my mind—as you may remember giving me duplicate carbons of most of this material—(and more) and verbal carte blanche. . . . I think I have kept both the letter and the spirit of that—and am as dumb-struck by your attitude as you seem to be with mine. It is a simple enough proposition for the future—for I shall gladly respect your wishes to be left out and left alone. The movement suffers—but that is your prerogative. I hope you will find the abstract universal recognition you desire. My opinion is that your previous work and acceptance of racial representativeness and spokesmanship will follow you through life and posterity. . . . I note you say: "I am hoping that this time I shall not be so badly present as I was in your "New Negro." I hope you will think so after seeing the Pamphlet Poet's anthology. Certainly none of us, including myself, has anything but the highest respect and sincerest wishes for your art.[55]

While Locke is right in the abstract regarding permissions, his response does not get to the core of McKay's conundrum. Because most of his selections included in *The New Negro* had been published in journals sponsored by Locke and Du Bois, no real negotiation of rights had taken place. This was not so much a case of conflict of interest as of unusual opportunity for literary editors. In effect, early publishers of McKay and others had the chance to "double publish" the poems—first in the *Crisis* or *Opportunity* and then in anthologies they edited—all for one price. Although McKay had a famously prickly personality, one can understand his concern that, once he had been paid once for a poem, it could be readily anthologized and edited at will because the same editors were responsible for the periodical and the book. McKay was no doubt frustrated by the small royalty for the second edition (by Locke's calculations, $15), but he seemed even more frustrated by his lack of control of his works. Indeed, Locke's assurance that he would be well represented in the Pamphlet Poets anthology did not soothe him, as this was apparently McKay's first learning about the volume. As McKay complained to his friend Harold Jackman, "He [Locke] put poems in 'The New Negro' that I had discarded, changed the title of another, for political reasons he informed me when I protested and put me in his pamphlet series without even the courtesy of mailing me."[56]

Beyond the material questions of intellectual property, these letters show a recurrent concern for McKay's proper "place," whether geographic, political, or racial. McKay's recurrent travels obviously revealed his interests in exploring identity and politics globally, and in his private correspondence with Harold Jackman he confided his feeling that he did not readily fit into the "position" expected of him by Harlem intellectuals:

> I have always felt a certain hostility on the part of the Afro-American intellectuals toward me. I don't know why. Maybe it is because when I write, I express the things that they feel so deeply and yet are forced from social and economic reasons to dam up in themselves. Yet I think they might extend to me a certain racial indulgence as I am so far outside of their field. Somehow I am glad I am not in on any of the groups, so that I can see them all from a detached standpoint.[57]

McKay's belief that he was expressing something "dammed up" among Afro-Americans shows his own awareness of his class position with respect to the elite, and while his comments might indulge in a bit of self-exoticizing, his claims find support not only in the harsh reception of McKay's portraits of lower-class life, but also in the recurrent figuration of the islands by Du Bois and others as essentially a peasant culture. More pointedly, he confided to Jackman his feeling that he had been used by the movement: "But after all I have never been *in* with members of the Negro intelligentsia. Maybe they thought I was of use to them, an easy one, and if in trying to know me they found I was a hard case, all they had to do was to drop me hot, as they probably have done."[58]

In contrast to Du Bois's insistence that McKay's proper "place" was back in Harlem, McKay's two most important novels in the immediate wake of *The New Negro, Home to Harlem* (1928) and *Banjo* (1929), cast a skeptical eye on whether there was any appropriate "place" for artists like McKay. Although the title itself of *Home to Harlem* would suggest a cultural centering in the space, the city does not play a unifying role, overall, for the novel's characters, although it is a place of attraction and opportunity for many of them. As in McKay's poetry, the characters of *Home to Harlem* find a mixture of excitement and danger within the city. Most of the central characters in the novel are attracted to Harlem. As Jake returns from his postwar stint as a sailor, he exclaims, "Take me home to Harlem, Mister Ship! Take me home to the brown gals waiting for the brown boys that done shown their mettle over there."[59] For most of McKay's characters, however, Harlem functions not as a political or economic center, but as a carnival space, where blacks of all origins and professions commingle in an electric and often dangerous atmosphere of sex, music, gambling, drinking, and fighting. It was undoubtedly such a focus on vernacular "low" city life that earned it harsh reviews from Du Bois while creating a sensational success for McKay.

Harlem functions as a refuge at some points in McKay's novel, but primarily it functions as an escape from the domesticity of Miss Curdy and Susy, who aim to keep their men close and fear Harlem as "a bloody ungodly place where niggers nevah go to bed. All night running around speakeasies and cabarets, where bad, hell-bent nigger womens am giving up themselves to open sin" (79). On the international front, McKay pays careful attention to the complex West Indian presence in Harlem, and he does so with an apparent eye to reveal the narrow range of judgment trained upon them by African Americans. Although characters like Jake and Zeddy look down on the West Indians and refer to them as "monkey chasers" (97), McKay reveals the class complexity within the West Indian immigrant community. For example, a scene of "wild women" from the islands fighting and cursing in Caribbean-inflected dialectic is interrupted by another West Indian girl in a very proper "frock" who addresses them in the Queen's English: "It's a shame. Can't you act like decent English people?" (97). Such moments not only reveal the multiplicity of class and national identifications attached to the West Indian community, but also demonstrate the inadequacy of the narrow range of judgments applied to them by their African American brethren in the novel.

Indeed, as a corrective to these prevailing assumptions of Caribbean inferiority, McKay enriches the multivocal texture of the novel by introducing to Jake a highly cultivated Haitian immigrant, Ray, who is working as a waiter to support his studies. By rhyme, by origin (though he is Haitian, not Jamaican), and by intended profession (writer), Ray is clearly intended to echo McKay's experience as immigrant, although he is not a direct representative of the author (McKay later commented to a friend that "Ray is not altogether myself"[60]). Ray provides a rich counterpoint to Jake's perspective. Ray speaks in perfectly accented English and French (his dialogue is not rendered dialectically, like that of Jake, Zeddy, and most of the characters), and he has a thorough background in literature and history. After learning that Jake speaks a bit of French, Ray describes his Haitian origin and offers Jake a history lesson about the Haitian revolution: "For the first time he [Jake] heard the name Toussaint L'Ouverture, the black slave and leader of the Haytian slaves. Heard how he fought and conquered the slave-owners and then protected them; decreed laws for Hayti that held more of human wisdom and nobility than the Code Napoleon; defended his baby revolution against the Spanish and the English vultures; defeated Napoleon's expedition" (132). Perhaps the most important aspect of this passage is "for the first time," as McKay foregrounds the fact that this Caribbean history is little known, even to African Americans. Ray comments to Jake that "the world doesn't know how great Toussaint L'Ouverture really was" (133). C. L. R. James would take notable steps to correct this lacuna five years later, but it is significant that McKay already recognized the need to educate his audience on this important history, as even the historians and essayists in *The New Negro* had shied away from the subject. Ray's discourse on Haiti also allows McKay to interpolate a critique of the occupation. Ray explains that he is in the United States as a waiter because his university studies were cut short by the imprisonment of his father and the murder of his brother by U.S. marines: "Uncle Sam put me here. . . . Maybe you don't know that during the World War Uncle Sam grabbed Haiti" (138). Besides offering these specific lessons, Ray serves as an example for Jake, one that causes him to reconsider his previously condescending assumptions about foreign-born Africans: "Jake was very American in spirit and shared a little of that comfortable Yankee contempt for poor foreigners. And as an American Negro he looked askew at foreign niggers. Africa was jungle, and Africans bush niggers, cannibals. And West Indians were monkey-chasers. But now he felt like a boy who stands with the map of the world in colors before him, and feels the wonder of the world" (139). Although McKay's *Banjo* is rightly understood as his most cosmopolitan work, this passage reveals that even in a narrative ostensibly centered on Harlem, it is vital for McKay to gesture beyond the city to an international diasporic community that has not been fully recognized or appreciated in the United States. McKay's use of Ray, rather than an African American intellectual, as the educator who brings the "map of the world" to Jake suggests a polemical choice. With Ray's lessons to Jake, McKay confronts his U.S. readers—white and black alike—with a sense of their own parochial perspective, a view that is remedied and improved by the contribution of a West Indian intellectual, who can apprehend the United States through a lens that is less nationalistic and more international.

As privileged as Ray's perspective is within *Home to Harlem,* McKay reveals that he has something to learn from African Americans like Jake as well. Although Ray is polite enough not to reveal his judgments to Jake, he possesses an elite perspective of his own, which is ultimately mitigated and transformed by his encounters with Jake. After an evening of reminiscing about the natural beauty of Haiti, Ray reflects on his complex position in the world of color: "He remembered when little Hayti was floundering uncontrolled, how proud he was to be the son of a free nation. He used to feel condescending sorry for those poor African natives; superior to ten millions of suppressed Yankee 'coons.' Now he was just one of them and he hated them for being one of them" (155). As the novel develops, Jake introduces Ray into a wider range of African American life than he had experienced, thus changing and improving Ray's loathing at being "one of them." When Ray pays a visit with Jake to a high-class brothel in Philadelphia, he feels a "shock" and sense of familiarity at how this demimonde mimics spaces familiar to him: "It looked so much like a comfortable boarding-house where everybody was cheerful and nice coquettish girls in colorful frocks were doing the waiting" (190). Ray longs to fit in with everyone as well as Jake, to "fall naturally into its rhythm" (194). Although he does not fully connect to the girls there that he desires—"something was between them"—he does feel a sense of belonging through the music itself, which, though African American, somehow reconnects him to the tropics: "The notes were naked, acute, alert. Like black youth burning naked in the bush. Love in the deep heart of the jungle. . . . The sharp spring of a leopard from a leafy limb, the snarl of a jackal, green lizards in amorous play, the flight of a plumed bird, and the sudden laughter of mischievous monkeys in their green homes" (197). This moment of virtual community through music anticipates many of the crucial scenes in *Banjo,* and it suggests McKay's sense that there is a fruitful potential crosscurrent between the islands and Harlem, though it is unvoiced. Much as Ray succeeds in teaching Jake a lesson about politics and history via his discourse on Haiti, the discourse of the blues, produced by a U.S. player, has helped Ray feel a vital connection to the islands and, arguably, to Africa itself—connections that he had despised and feared earlier in the novel.

As *Home to Harlem* moves to a close, Ray contemplates settling in Harlem, but ultimately chooses not to. Instead, he leaves a literary love letter to Harlem, however, by telling a story to his friends about his early days in New York after his passage from Haiti. The importance of Harlem to Ray is reflected not only in the subject of the story—the complex domestic life of these "low" characters (in particular, Jericho, a pimp, and his lover/prostitute Rosalind) who helped him when he was in need, but also in McKay's narrative presentation. The story is a self-contained episode narrated in the first person as a distinct chapter entitled "He Also Loved," whose title refers to Jericho's love for Rosalind, such that he kills himself after her death from "the grippe." This chapter seems to mark the birth of Ray as an author, and I would also argue that it represents a transformation in his class consciousness. Perhaps quickened by his time in the "underworld" of black life with Jake, Ray is now prepared to reckon with and to recognize the virtue and value of lower-class situations that he had previously despised. The value of the time he spent with Jake seems to be reflected structurally, as it is only after his tutelage from Jake that he is willing and/or able to relate this story. Thus Jake has helped Ray take possession, retrospectively, of a seminal moment in his own experience—his arrival in the United States. In this light, one might argue that Ray does come "home to Harlem," at the end, but in a virtual manner through his art (much as, one might argue, McKay did in writing the text itself).

Ray's time with Jake and his friends causes him to feel a fear of Harlem by the end of the narrative, but for reasons almost entirely opposed to those articulated by other characters in the novel. Whereas characters like Susy and Miss Curdy object to Harlem for its licentiousness and threat to domesticity, Ray fears that it will be a threat to him precisely because of the possibility of domesticity. Given his education and experience, Ray feels that he cannot be like Jake and "hitch up for a short while and be irresponsible" (263). Ray and his new lover, Agatha, are "slaves of the civilized tradition" and thus he fears that if he goes to Harlem, it will be *home* for the final time, with a wife, occupation, and children to bind him: "Soon he would become one of the contented hogs in the pigpen of Harlem, getting ready to litter little black piggies" (263). Ray opts instead to get work on a freighter in order to see the world and broaden his perspective—a plot that will be followed up in *Banjo*. As he prepares to leave, he muses, "Going away from Harlem. . . . Harlem! How terribly Ray could hate it sometimes . . . [but] he had known happiness, too, in Harlem, joy that glowed gloriously upon him like the high-noon sunlight of his tropic island home" (267). The closing phrases of Ray's reflection offer an image of cross-cultural complementarity, connecting his emotional state in New York to the island sun through simile. Unlike other such moments in his poetry, as in "Subway Wind" or "The Tropics in New York," this image is one of balanced, simultaneous fulfillment, alluding to a moment when Ray seems to feel at home in both places. Ironically, however, Ray experiences this recollection liminally, as he is on the threshold of leaving, and, upon closer examination, the vehicle for the image here (the high-noon sunlight) is itself liminal and fleeting, suggesting the impossibility of resting in such a moment and hence, perhaps, the need to move on.

While Du Bois was writing to McKay to insist upon his return the United States, McKay was preparing the manuscript of *Banjo*, which would raise the stakes of globalism hinted at in *Home to Harlem* and would, arguably, offer the most cosmopolitan vision of diasporic black culture during the New Negro Renaissance. Appropriately subtitled "A Story Without a Plot," *Banjo* centers on a community of vagabonds, tramps, and travelers gathered in the port city of Marseilles, exploring their relationships, their quarrels, their arguments, and their music. A thread of continuity is provided between *Home to Harlem* and *Banjo* through Ray, who continues his journey from the first novel to find a proper place for himself and his art. In Marseilles, Ray finds opportunities for multiple, overlapping cultural identifications within the black diaspora and among other peoples of color. In a chapter entitled "Jelly Roll," invoking the language of an American barrelhouse blues song, McKay depicts a festive unity of all classes and colors of diasporic blacks at the aptly titled Café African: "All shades of Negroes came together there. Even the mulattoes took a step down from their perch to mix in. . . . The magic had brought them all together to shake that thing and drink red wine, white wine, sweet wine. All the British West African blacks, Portuguese blacks, American blacks, all who had drifted into this port that the world goes through."[61] As they share music and wine, the characters recognize a commonality and uncanny familiarity to their cherished folk musics: "They played the 'beguin,' which was just a Martinique variant of the 'jelly-roll' or the Jamaican 'burru' or the Senegalese 'bombé'" (46). McKay's paralleling these four musical variants reveals his awareness of a Black Atlantic triangulation between Africa, the United States, and the West Indies: a pattern that was rarely recognized by New Negro authors in the U.S.

Beyond celebrating a paradoxical sense of diasporic community, McKay uses the multicultural port setting of Marseilles to stage a highly dialogic novel in which a wide range of African-descended characters, as well as other people of color (and several interested whites), present distinct views about their futures, both on personal and geopolitical terms. The characters debate their own histories and the fate of the diasporic African community, as well as more charged questions of racial uplift, resistance to colonization, and the role of "high" culture versus folk culture in these processes. Toward this end, McKay gathers a multicultural and multiclassed cast of characters from the black diaspora. At the docks and "the Ditch" in Marseilles one finds southern African Americans (like the title character) comingling with British and French West Africans, British and French West Indians, and elite African Americans, as well as Syrians, Indians, and a few whites. Almost every single character has his or her own story of diaspora, as each has typically circulated between both the Old and New World, among various colonies of the European powers, and ended up in Marseilles as either a place of last resort or a place of refuge.

Although *Banjo* does not explicitly direct itself towards Caribbean-U.S. cultural crossings, it makes a significant intervention into framing the place of the United States in diasporic blackness. In many of the bar scenes, characters argue about the best place for Africans to find prosperity and freedom. In notable contrast to the centripetal spirit of *The New Negro,* the characters of *Banjo*—including the African American characters—perceive Harlem not as the center of global black culture, but as merely one part of the global diaspora. Banjo and others first engage this question in debating the value of Garveyism. Although the owner of the Café African and the Nigerian-born Taloufa value Garvey, most of the leading characters are skeptical, and Banjo effectively silences a Garveyite discussion by cutting him down to size: "He thought . . . that he was Moses or Napoleon or Frederick Douglass, but he was nothing but a fool, big-mouf nigger" (77).

The characters in *Banjo* are no more trusting of the African American elite than they are of Garvey. They are keenly aware of the limitations imposed on African Americans in the United States, not only by Jim Crow but also by the strictures of the black bourgeoisie. Ray, from *Home to Harlem,* rejects the U.S. black elite: "The best Negroes are *not* the society Negroes," he tells his friends at the bar (117), and he confesses that it was in Harlem that he first realized, "in a moment of bitterness," that "civilization is rotten" (163). Banjo himself, although "a child of the Cotton Belt," denies his national background in Marseilles: "They had all been thunderstruck when he calmly announced that he was not an American" (11). While a few, such as the Senegalese owner of the Café African, look to Harlem as the place of opportunity—"American is better every time for a colored man," he says (73)—most others (including Banjo himself) are skeptical of the opportunities afforded in the United States. Both Banjo and the more educated U.S. emigré, Goosey, refer to it sarcastically as the "You-whited States" (304) or "United Snakes," which "struck Ray's imagination, giving him a terrible vision or the stripes of Old Glory transformed into wriggling snakes and stars poisonous heads lifted to strike at an agonized black man writhing in the midst of them" (117). In this respect, *Banjo* decenters the United States as the privileged locus of black cultural production and opportunity.

While resisting the notion that the United States is the best "port of call" in the Black Atlantic, the characters in *Banjo* are keenly aware of the power of U.S. citizenship: "An American seaman (white or black) on the beach is always treated with a subtle difference by his beach fellows. He has a higher face value than the rest, his passport is worth a good price and is eagerly sought by passport fabricators. And he has the assurance that, when he gets tired of beaching, his consulate will help him back to the fabulous land of wealth and opportunity" (19). The freedom of some characters in *Banjo,* such as Goosey, comes in part because of what one might call "U.S. privilege"—a passport that gives him the ability to come and go as he pleases, with the protection of the U.S. consulate and the expectation that, in a pinch, he can always return to the States. Significantly, Banjo, in spite of his birth in the United States, has long since abjured his passport. No doubt because of his own difficulties with U.S. immigration (to which Du Bois alluded in his letter), McKay's text pays particular attention to those without those passport privileges. McKay is always careful to note the immigration statuses of the characters in Marseilles, and many are displaced because of U.S. legal strictures. From the first chapter the reader encounters "deportées from America for violation of the United States immigration laws" (6). More specific cases abound as well. The Nigerian-born Taloufa, for example, "lived in the United States until after the passing of the new quota immigration laws, when, the fact of his entering the country illegally getting known, he was arrested and deported" (101).

Banjo thus shows a keen sense of the unequal distribution of power among the Black Atlantic, not only in terms of geopolitics, but in the different experiences of diaspora (willing or unwilling) faced by its characters. In bringing together a community of Africans possessed of common culture but unequal rights of citizenship in a global context, one might argue that *Banjo* is paradoxically utopian and pragmatic at the same time, for it both presents a vision of fruitful multicultural and multinational black community unseen in any U.S. New Negro Renaissance text, and at the same time traces the specific legal impediments that inhibit the flow within that community. Moreover, one might argue that, to the extent that the United States has adopted harsh immigration and deportation laws, it cannot be the black Zion envisioned by the architects of *The New Negro*. Indeed, the most crucial plot development, by the end, is Ray's decision to join with Banjo in his wanderings and not to go "home to Harlem," in effect rejecting the centering principal that Du Bois argued McKay should follow.

5 Translation and Cultural Critique between the Caribbean and the United States after the New Negro Renaissance

THE ONSET of the Great Depression in 1929 is usually taken by cultural historians as the end of the New Negro Renaissance. Drastically changed economic conditions silenced the "roar" of the twenties, and along with it, much of the exchange of cultural capital between uptown and downtown Manhattan. At first glance, one would expect this change in circumstance to have had a parallel effect upon West Indian-U.S. collaboration, but this was not always the case. The combination of declining economic opportunities and increased immigration restrictions did slow the flow of West Indian immigration to the United States considerably in the 1930s and beyond, especially in comparison to the dramatic increase in immigration between the close of World War I and the Great Depression. At the same time, new opportunities for cross-cultural exchange and collaboration arose during this period, born of several factors. Roosevelt's "Good Neighbor" policy, which granted increased respect to the independence of Caribbean and Latin American nations and reduced interventionist practices, cleared the way for cultural contact to occur under less militarized auspices. The end to U.S. occupation of Haiti in 1934 and the nullification of the Platt amendment that same year removed two of the major obstacles to sovereignty in the region, and literary crosscurrents shifted accordingly. While the United States still maintained considerable influence in the Caribbean (and would still produce resistance to that influence), U.S.-Caribbean literary exchanges expanded in directions beyond the recent controversies of the occupation. Indeed, the removal of direct U.S. intervention seemed to clear the way for comparative investigations into the history of the Caribbean, along with considerations of its future.

Laying a Foundation for Revolutionary Partnerships: C. L. R. James's *The Black Jacobins*

One of the most notable historical studies produced in the post-occupation period was undoubtedly C. L. R. James's *The Black Jacobins: Toussaint L'Ouverture and the San Domingo Revolution* (1938). Building upon a rich variety of primary and secondary sources, James constructed the most thorough history to date of the roots, details, and outcomes of the Haitian revolution. Focused primarily on the revolutionary period itself from 1791–1803, James's study was not explicitly comparative or cross-cultural with respect to the United States; he would achieve that end with *Mariners, Renegades, and Castaways,* which will be addressed in the conclusion of this book. James locates his conclusions about the Haitian revolution within a global context to stake a claim for its importance in world history, particularly in the New World. More broadly, James uses *Black Jacobins* to explore the complex interrelations of race, nation, and capital among Europe, Africa, and the Americas, as well as to position Haiti as a touchstone for decolonization.

James lards his historical commentary with prescient observations about how the Haitian struggle for independence parallels and anticipates other revolutionary struggles. At the start of *Black Jacobins,* James compares the music of voodoo to other revolutionary songs of the past and future: "For over two hundred years the slaves sang it at their meetings, as the Jews in Babylon sang of Zion, and the Bantu today sing in secret the national anthem of Africa."[1] The comment sets the stage for an account of Haiti's history that, while intensely focused on the minute and complex details of race and class conflict on the island, locates the struggle in a continuum of political movements for freedom and human dignity. As *Black Jacobins* develops, James uses the revolution to illustrate continuities between eighteenth-century imperial politics and those of the early twentieth century, including the rise of fascism. He compares Haitian mulattoes' complex internal position at the time to that of German Jews in the present (41).

James also finds parallels in the competition between imperial powers. As the fratricidal war developed on the island among whites in the wake of the French Revolution, "he [Toussaint] and his brother slaves only watched their masters destroy one another, as Africans watched them in 1914–1918, and will watch them again before long" (82). James's use of Haiti as a synecdoche of imperial geopolitics is supported by the varied strains of European and American involvement as the revolution unfolded, with France obviously struggling to preserve its dominion, but Spanish, British, and U.S. interests also backing different factions in hopes of gaining a foothold in San Domingo. For James, competition for hegemony still resonated in the 1930s, both within the Caribbean and in Africa, and he makes clear to his readers that they should not forget these lessons of history. One of the crucial edicts he offers is that in spite of the struggles against France, it is the Anglophone tradition that offered the most dire consequences for blacks—then and now: "From no classes of people have Negroes suffered more than from the capitalists of Britain and America. They have been the most pertinacious preachers of race prejudice in the world" (227). At the same time, like Martí and Firmin in their political critiques, James has high praise for notable patriots from the United States like Thomas Jefferson and Thomas Paine, and he compares Toussaint L'Ouverture's struggle to keep Haiti together to Lincoln's challenges during the Civil War (290). By the end of *Black Jacobins,* James uses the Haitian revolution as a predictor of future decolonization, and he clearly intends to strike fear into the heart of the British empire: "The blacks of Africa are more advanced, nearer ready than were the slaves of San Domingo" (376). Given such predictions, James's study resonated most powerfully in the pan-Africanist circles in London, particularly with his friend George Padmore. Within the United States, the immediate impact was not as widely disseminated, but scholars have found that Arna Bontemps used James as a historical source for his novel of the Haitian revolution, *Drums at Dusk* (1939).[2] Later in this chapter I will offer an examination of how Hughes and Bontemps adapted Haitian history, as their works show not only their increased interests in the Caribbean but also how the island had become a capacious symbol for a range of conflicting black perspectives on uplift and progress.

Revisiting the Caribbean in the 1930s and 1940s

Overall, the younger generation of U.S. authors after the New Negro showed a stronger interest in the history and culture of the Caribbean than predecessors like Locke and DuBois had, and they pursued it via both travel and translation. The effects of the New Negro Renaissance upon Anglophone Caribbean writing and the Francophone negritude movement have been well explored by scholars, and Caribbean writers have been explicit in acknowledging their debts to their U.S. literary kin. For the scholar interested in cultural connections between the United States and the Caribbean, this period brings the exchanges traced at the start of this book full circle. I argued in my first chapter that a significant but relatively unrecognized body of Caribbean writers contributed a range of perspectives toward fin-de-siècle debates about pan-Africanism, U.S. hegemony, and the Monroe Doctrine. In succeeding decades, West Indian immigrant writers shaped U.S. discourse more directly by contributing to the New Negro movement. Between 1933 and 1945, that movement, in turn, shaped a new generation of West Indian writers who did not immigrate to the United States, but were nonetheless connected to the U.S. via strong bonds of translation, communication, and collaboration, including Nicolás Guillén, Léon Damas, Aimé Césaire, and René Depestre. These crosscurrents would be shaped subsequently by an expanded U.S. presence in the region. During World War II the United States procured a lease from Great Britain to establish a wide range of military bases on Commonwealth islands in the Caribbean. The postwar boom period in the United States resulted in an increase in tourist travel from the U.S. to the islands (especially African Americans seeking an escape from Jim Crow), as well as Caribbean immigration to the U.S. because of renewed economic opportunity there. Tensions during the cold war and U.S. hostility to Fidel Castro would bring much of this collaborative potential to a close, but the years between the New Negro Renaissance and the end of the Cuban Revolution (1959) showed the rise of some of the most productive and reciprocal literary partnerships between the United States and the Caribbean.

One of the most important artists to complete such partnering work during this period was the dancer and choreographer Katherine Dunham. Dunham, the founder of the Ballet Nègre in Chicago, was already an important figure in the dance world by the 1930s. Winning a Julius Rosenwald Fellowship gave her the opportunity to complete her bachelor's degree in social anthropology through fieldwork in Haiti, Jamaica, Martinique, and Trinidad. Dunham published some of her observations in *Esquire* in the 1930s under the pseudonym of Kaye Dunn; she recounted her observations in greater detail much later in the books *Journey to Accompong* (1946), *Dances of Haiti* (1947), and *Island Possessed* (1969). Throughout these writings, Dunham observes and notates dances with a structuralist interest in body and ritual. While Dunham does lapse into some conventional tropes in her writing about the islands, such as embracing a primitivist view of island cultures or discussing the pros and cons of "going native," she dissented strongly from the hypersexualized tropes imposed on the Caribbean body by most U.S. visitors. Writing of the Maroons in Jamaica, Dunham notes that the hip-shaking shay-shay between men and women is done in reverence of village, tradition, and the elders: "Old women are still the favorites. . . . The Maroons do not dance for the sex thrill as we Americans do."[3] Similarly, in tracing the steps of the béguine (from Martinique), Dunham describes the dance not as sexual but as something deeper, purer, and "more fundamental": "Only occasional white visitors to the island misunderstand the pure love for dancing behind the *béguine*" (195). Dunham relates the story of a sailor from the United States who misreads his participation in a dance with a beautiful woman as holding out the promise of a sexual liaison:

> The sailor thinks that they will leave the floor together to meet in a moment on one of the dark porches off the balcony. He watches them greedily as the music finishes and the floor clears. . . . The dance ends there for them. They have enjoyed it. They are satisfied in the accomplishment of an artistic feat—in matching techniques. Now it is a new conquest of another dance, another partner. The sailor is disappointed, but he is new here. (198)

Dunham's account of this scene offers a cautionary tale regarding outsiders' expectation of a sexualized Caribbean and validates the folk dances on aesthetic terms that are "purer" than the motives of the sailor. In this light, it is the tourist who is the primitive, and the native the "civilized" aesthete. Dunham's work as a choreographer and dancer further served to validate the cultural depth of the islands for American audiences. After completing her degree, Dunham used her fieldwork as the basis for most of her subsequent career. In 1938, Dunham presented her first extended ballet piece, *L'Ag'Ya,* based upon her observations of the Martinican dance of the same name. That same year, Dunham presented *Tropics,* another Caribbean-inflected ballet, and she appeared in her first film, *The Carnival of Rhythm.* Dunham achieved tremendous success as a broker between Caribbean and U.S. cultural traditions. Her ballets were well-reviewed by highbrow dance critics, such as Edward Barry from the *Chicago Tribune* and Frederick Orme from *American Dancer,* and they were popular enough to keep her touring. The ballet that she further developed from *Tropics,* entitled *Tropical Revue,* toured nationally for two years (1943–45), and she subsequently toured Mexico and Europe as well. As Dunham's career progressed, she became more and more committed to educating audiences about the Caribbean, moving away from programs in the manner of a "revue" towards programming intended to give audiences a rich sense of historical and cultural context for each dance she had observed in the region. For example, Dunham's program entitled *Caribbean Backgrounds* (presented at Howard University in 1947) offered the audience more than a dozen specific dances from Cuba,

Haiti, Trinidad, Martinique, and Jamaica, each with annotations regarding its origins, evolution, and current cultural function. Kate Ramsey has demonstrated that such exchanges, which were often promoted by the U.S. government under Roosevelt's Good Neighbor policy, were not merely aesthetic, but also had a political aim: to offer a bulwark against communist influence by "spotlight[ing] . . . cultural relations" between the United States and the Caribbean.[4] For the purposes of my study, an even greater concern is the possibility that Dunham's work appropriated, if not "purloined," Caribbean cultural resources, but her approach to Caribbean dance stands in notable contrast to the exoticizing that characterized most U.S. views on Caribbean culture. Moreover, unlike the leaders of the New Negro movement, Dunham did not nationalize the dances or claim them as part of an extended African American canon, but introduced them on their own cultural terms to U.S. audiences.

The Increasing Demand for New Negro Texts in the Caribbean

Cultural influence and inspiration during the post-occupation period flowed in both directions and more freely than before. Dissemination of texts from the New Negro Renaissance contributed to a shared cultural conversation between the United States and the Caribbean. Book clubs, schools, and philological societies from Anglophone islands like Jamaica, Barbados, and Trinidad sought out New Negro texts, often via personal letters to James Weldon Johnson, Claude McKay, and others. Rupert Meikle, founder of the Quill and Ink Club in Jamaica, wrote to McKay not only to commend his work, but to ask for him to return to be honored:

> To us Postwar Jamaicans Claude McKay has been more or less a legend and we very much long for the day when he will visit his native land and let us see and hear and honour him. After reading your latest work the desire to know you is stronger than ever and I do so wish you would come on a visit. Why don't you?[5]

The Jamaican Women's Liberal Club, for their part, wrote to Johnson to thank him for his inspiration:

> Your work and worth have reached the far shores of Jamaica, B.W.I. and thru men like Professor Hamilton of Elmira College and W. A. Domingo of New York City, we have been given knowledge of you. . . . As a group of Negro women, we are keenly interested in the achievements of men and women of

> the race and we thank you for your contributions. You are helping to make a place for us "in the sun."[6]

The Jamaican poet and teacher Una Marson also wrote to Johnson to comment upon the effect of the New Negro upon Jamaica, with concerns as well for how to gain access to their works:

> It is now a case of "Jamaica Aroused." People are thinking and waking up to find themselves very much behind. It is really quite telling to be in the middle of it. . . . I wish your books and those of other writers were on sale here. But alas, few of our people who would like to read them can run to the prices. I have founded a Reader's and Writer's club here.[7]

Outside the Anglophone islands there was an increasing demand for translation of New Negro works, particularly those of Langston Hughes, into Spanish and French. Hughes himself was perhaps the most important U.S. conduit for cultural traffic between the islands and the United States in the 1940s and 1950s, as his work was not only championed in the Caribbean by colleagues like René Piquion (from Haiti) and Gustavo Urrutia (from Cuba), but he himself translated modernist Cuban poetry (notably, that of Nicolás Guillén) for American audiences.

Hughes's attitudes towards the Caribbean ranged widely across his career, from relative inattention to it early on, to interest in revisiting its revolutionary history, to use of the region as a foil for race relations in the United States, to colonialist exoticizing. In spite of Hughes's substantial involvement in the region, most scholars have paid scant attention to the importance of his Caribbean activities. With the exception of Vera Kutzinski's examination of the relationship between Hughes and Guillén (which will be discussed later in the chapter), most scholars scarcely mention the Caribbean in their consideration of Hughes. Hughes's most thorough biographer, Arnold Rampersad, gives scant attention to Hughes's visits to the Caribbean, and when he does attend to them, it is usually with disdain for the Caribbean intellectuals with which Hughes was in conversation.[8] Edward Mullen offers a good primer to Hughes's time in Cuba and Haiti in "The Literary Reputation of Langston Hughes in the Hispanic World and Haiti," but, as the title suggests, Mullen's primary concern is Hughes's literary influence upon the region, and not vice-versa.[9] R. Baxter Miller's well-known examination of Hughes's evolving aesthetics, *The Art and Imagination of Langston Hughes*, mentions the Caribbean only once, in a quick reference to *Emperor of Haiti* (1936), Hughes's play on the Haitian Revolution.[10] Even criticism attuned to questions of geography in Hughes, such as William Hogan's "Routes, Roots, and Langston Hughes's Hybrid Sense of Place," overlook both Hughes's time in the region and the symbolic importance it accrued in his work.

A key reason why scholars may not have explored Hughes's Caribbean connections in depth is that the author himself did not dedicate much time in his autobiographical writings to his time in the region. Hughes offers surprisingly few details about his literary relationships with Caribbean authors in his autobiographies, although he does describe his time in Spain with Guillén. In the first volume of his autobiography, *The Big Sea* (1940), Hughes mentions his two trips to Cuba, but only in passing, at the end of the book. He gives more attention to the Caribbean, including visits to Cuba and Haiti, in *I Wonder as I Wander* (1956), but those reflections occupy a very small portion of the book in comparison to his writings about Russia, Europe, and the Spanish Civil War. I will address Hughes's reflections on the Caribbean in *I Wonder as I Wander* later in this chapter, as they emerge in tandem with key pieces of travel writing from Hughes on the region.

For both Hughes and his friend Arna Bontemps, their primary encounter with the Caribbean emerged in their treatments of the Haitian revolution in fiction and drama in the late 1930s. Bontemps wrote a historical novel entitled *Drums at Dusk* (1939), and Hughes developed a play (*Emperor of Haiti*) and an opera (*Troubled Island* [1937]) focused on that historic event. Bontemps and Hughes had each written about Haiti earlier in the 1930s, but largely in passing. Hughes completed a pair of short articles reporting upon the U.S. occupation for the *New Masses* and the *Crisis* (which he later incorporated into *I Wonder as I Wander*).[11] Together, Hughes and Bontemps had used Haiti as the setting for a slight, comic children's novel (*Popo and Fifina* [1932]). Representing the Haitian revolution necessarily produced a more substantive engagement with the Caribbean and its implications than Bontemps and Hughes had achieved in their previous writings. Neither author was as historically accurate in rendering the revolution as C. L. R. James was in *Black Jacobins,* but Hughes's and Bontemps' works reveal an increased recognition of Haiti as a historical resource and inspiration for African American literature and culture. At the same time, it is clear from the details of each text that Haiti was less important as a subject of investigation in its own right than as a screen for projective aspiration.

The editors of the authoritative edition of Hughes's *Emperor of Haiti,* Leslie Catherine Sanders and Nancy Johnson, note that while the play is clearly well-researched, "Hughes departs from the historical" record to suit his dramatic purposes. Dessalines, for example, emerges as the single hero, and "the brutal slaughter that perpetuated the Haitian revolution is little in evidence in the play."[12] His American audience was likely challenged by his respectful attitude towards voodoo in the play. When questioned as to whether or not she should risk her soul by participating in a violent revolt, the slave Lulu declares, "Hell's a place for Christians, ain't it? Not for us"—a statement met with general approval. A man named Antoine proudly states that "Voodoo Gods ain't mixin' with the white gods"; the fellow slave Celeste asserts, "Legba's better" (5:292). In exchanges like this, along with the careful rituals orchestrated in the script, voodoo is clearly represented not as barbaric, but as a fruitful alternative to Christianity. At the same time, Hughes skillfully holds these skeptical questions about Christianity at a safe distance, as both the historical and cultural setting are remote from that of the Cleveland audience that witnessed its premiere at Karamu Theater.

Hughes's handling of questions of racial and color conflict in the play, whether among the revolutionaries or between blacks and whites, shows a desire to fit the revolution into a progressive, multicultural vision. Although Hughes gestures towards the complex racial strata on the island, he does so in order to make a call for black unity across all colorist lines. Dessalines, for example, counsels his black friend, who bears the heavy-handed name "Congo," that they must overcome their distrust of mulattoes: "They're not alike, Congo. Some we can trust" (5:290). The elderly advisor Martel extends this inclusion, offering to Dessalines a textbook vision of progressive internationalism: "There are still whites in the world, Jean Jacques. And we have need of them, as they once needed us. You've often heard me say, it's time to stop turning our guns against them now. . . . Jean Jacques, I'm an old man. But in my old age, I dream of a world where no man hurts another. Where *all* know freedom, and black and white alike will share this earth in peace" (5:302). As inspiring as Martel's words may be, they emerge in jarring juxtaposition to even the most basic facts of the revolution. Only by keeping the brutal racialized violence of the revolution offstage can Hughes lend any plausibility to Martel's vision. While Hughes's *Emperor of Haiti* certainly has a more tangible connection to the Caribbean than O'Neill's *Emperor Jones,* each play is alike in embodying a U.S. fantasy of what the islands represent, albeit for distinct political and aesthetic purposes.

Bontemps' *Drums at Dusk* was less overtly political than *Emperor of Haiti* and more historically nuanced in representing tensions among varied cultural and racial factions on the island. For example, unlike Hughes, Bontemps paid attention to the differences among *blancs, petit blancs, mulattos,* and *negres.* Toussaint L'Ouverture appears as a character and plays a historical role comparable to that in the revolution, although he is curiously in the background for much of the novel. Instead, Bontemps focuses on the romantic and political entanglements of a white aristocrat sympathetic to the black revolution, Diron Desautels. In their introduction, Michael Bibler and Jessica Adams suggest that this choice of protagonist accounted, in part, for the novel's muted reception.[13] The focus on a white protagonist in the midst of a black revolution may have made it less attractive for African American readers. Bibler and Adams also note that in terms of genre expectations, the violence and dissipation depicted within *Drums at Dusk* put it outside the comfortable boundaries of recent historical romances of the U.S. Civil War, like Stark Young's *So Red the Rose* (1934) and Margaret Mitchell's *Gone With the Wind* (1936).

Bontemps' choice to focus on a white protagonist may have reflected his commitment to a broader progressive agenda that was not confined to strict racial lines. As in Hughes's *The Emperor of Haiti,* it seemed vital for the author to show that there could be a fruitful political partnership between blacks and whites during and after the revolution. Thus Diron, although an aristocrat, gradually develops a sympathetic political consciousness and cooperates both with Toussaint and with the Amis de Noirs [Friends of the Blacks] as the revolution takes hold. No doubt because of his desire to forge a multicultural partnership on the island, Bontemps exaggerates the importance of white participation in the brewing revolution there. The Amis des Noirs was an important radical political group, with a multiracial membership ranging from French notables like Condorcet, Lafayatte, and Abbé Grégoire to members of the Haitian mulatto elite like Léger Félicité Sonthonax and Jacques Vincent Ogé, but its most effective advocacy took place not inside Haiti, but outside it. Indeed, the rebellion instigated by Ogé in 1790 failed and resulted in his execution. More pointedly, Diron himself is a historical improbability of the highest order: there is no evidence of effective white partnership in Haiti with the Amis, nor of whites cooperating significantly with Toussaint, Dessalines, or any of the other Black Jacobins. Indeed, according to James, in the wake of Ogé's revolt, "All white San Domingo, pro-independence and anti-, were united on one common ground—the maintenance of slavery" (75). Nevertheless, Diron develops and voices a revolutionary consciousness that is uncanny in its progressive class politics: “Diron was not sure just where his allegiance belonged, and he cared much less. For how unimportant was the quarrel between ten thousand aristocrats, thirty thousand lower-class whites, and forty thousand mulattos in Saint Domingue when there were five hundred thousand—half a million—slaves on the island still in chains of unspeakable bondage! Nature was being thwarted and opposed by perverse and corrupt man” (37). One might anachronistically argue that Diron’s presence constitutes a gesture of “affirmative action” within a narrative of black revolt, an inclusion that Bontemps wished to make for a broader political agenda, but that had little plausible connection to the Haitian Revolution itself.

Subtle details of Bontemps’ renderings of Diron and Toussaint seem to reflect the author’s conflicted feelings about Diron’s role in the novel. In one of the few genuine complications of his character, Diron joins in counter-revolutionary violence when he is in a convoy with other planters and is ambushed by a band of escaped slaves: “Diron had a momentary feeling of sick revulsion. His pistol still smoked in his hand. He, the Friend of the Blacks, had fired with the others. Of course, there were ways to rationalize his action. The slaves had leveled their aim against him as well as the others” (157). As much as Diron had thought of himself as separate from the oppression of blacks, he nonetheless, in a moment of crisis, joins in the violence against them. With this episode Bontemps fruitfully suggests a cautionary tale, perhaps, to “right minded” white readers about the nature of violence and mobs, and the possibility of their complicity in violence within the United States. Bontemps also may bring that violence “home” to his readers by periodically showing slaves hung from trees (“Before the men stretched a line of swinging corpses, one to a tree” [86]), a practice that was less typical for Haiti at the time of the revolution, but is clearly evocative of lynching in the United States in Bontemps’ context.

Interracial tensions soon dissipate for Diron, however, as he leaves his convoy in search of his beloved, Celeste. Only a page after the violent confrontation, Diron encounters one of Toussaint’s patrols, and when challenged, he confidently declares, “I am Diron Desautels, Friend of the Blacks. . . . Here is my horse. And here is my pistol. *Vive la liberté*” (158). He is permitted to pass, and his moral equanimity returns: “He walked with zest when he left them. In his conscience he felt purged” (159).

In parallel to Diron’s journey to find Celeste in Le Cap, Toussaint escorts his former master and mistress, M. and Mme. de Libertas, to the city, and parts with them forever. As he does so, Toussaint provides a sense of continuity between the French Revolution and the struggle ahead, and offers a final vision of solidarity: "The Revolution in Paris was fought by Friends of the Blacks. Tonight the blacks take up arms, such arms as they have. This is a continuation, not a new conflict. You and I are not opposed" (160). Having acquitted himself of his duties to the Libertas family, Toussaint rides off into the night, and Bontemps offers one of his only lyrical renderings of Haitian mysteries in the ensuing passage:

> Blacker and blacker grew the night into which his horses galloped, a night peopled by demons and witches, a night charged with jungle sorceries and voodoo incantations, a night haunted by frightful masks and screaming ghosts, a night throbbing with drums. Once, at least, Toussaint had the strange feeling that time itself was slipping past him as his horses raced. Now again he was in tune with things. The black wonders, the mysterious shades, were with him, not against him. It was as if he had returned to the sweet age in which leaves were born. (161)

Toussaint's night ride is all the more powerful in contrast with the general tenor of *Drums at Dusk*. As Bibler and Adams note, in spite of the title, drums and voodoo are relatively silent in the novel, so Toussaint's supernatural developments emerge in even bolder relief in this passage. Perhaps most notable is the passage's conjoining the typical tropes of voodoo with a political and personal empowerment that is positively Edenic: Toussaint slips out of time and has "returned to the age in which leaves were born" (161). This metaphorically nationalist moment—"blacker and blacker grew the night"—stands in stark contrast to the panracial progressive discourse professed not only by Diron but by Toussaint himself on that same page. In this light, Bontemps' projected vision of the Haitian revolution is itself dialogically divided, as one strain of discourse upholds a fantasy of black-white collaboration in Haiti, while another indulges in a fantasy of black nationalism so potent as to have reversed time and restored a (golden) Black Age. The resolution of the Libertas and Diron plots is similarly conflicted. Toussaint's white friends all leave the island at the end, in time to avoid the greatest violence ahead, but do not ultimately dissociate themselves from the island. When Toussaint asks, "And you will return?" M. de Libertas says, "Not as a master of slaves" (160).

Bibler and Adams resolve these complexities in favor of a progressive agenda, perceiving the twinned focus on Toussaint and Libertas/Diron as a gesture of coalition building: "Bontemps tries to provoke a mixed audience to imagine a society in which whites and people of color might join together in the common cause of liberty and equality—a notion that was truly revolutionary in 1939 and remains so today" (xxxv). While agreeing with Bibler and Adams's account of Bontemps' agenda, I do not share their unproblematic enthusiasm for the author's choice to use the Haitian revolution as the locus for such a "common cause." Bontemps can succeed in depicting Haiti in this light only by significantly dehistoricizing the details of racial conflict on the island, sacrificing the historically specific achievement of the black revolution in favor of a utopian ideal that has little to do with Haiti and much to do with Bontemps' own progressive politics.

One might argue that the tension between progressive republican and black utopian aims in *Drums at Dusk* reaches an aporia, and the next Caribbean collaboration between Hughes and Bontemps seems designed to escape that tension. Together they authored the light musical *Tropics after Dark* (1940) for the Chicago American Negro Exposition. Although it was never staged due to financial constraints (some of the songs were sung at a revue at the exposition, however), it reveals a very different approach to the islands—one that would later emerge in Hughes's postwar travel writing. If *Emperor of Haiti* and *Drums at Dusk* each appropriated the Haitian revolution for dialogic explorations about the future of race relations and class solidarity, *Tropics After Dark* returns to far more conventional representations (such as Johnson's "Down by the Carib Sea") of the Caribbean as a humorously exotic, drunken, and highly sexualized place. As the editor of the manuscript in Hughes's *Collected Works* observes, it is "a period piece replete with stereotypes" (6:159). Indeed, a casual reading of *Tropics After Dark* might lead one to suspect that this was a fantasy piece by Carl Van Vechten, extending his vision of *Nigger Heaven* southward. The dramatic tension of the play resides in competition between two African American men, Buddy (from Harlem) and Billy (from Chicago), for the attention of island women, who are rendered as exotic and silly, speaking in a pidgin of English, French, and Spanish. The sexualized tone of the discourse emerges early in the first scene when Billy asks the female fruit vendors, confrontationally, "Ain't none o' you-all got no cherries?" (6:161). Questions of sexual conquest and competition abound between the men, and the real heart of the play lies in a game of dozens between them, with each insulting the other's hometown. Thus the exotic island locale becomes a place for domestic competition between two African American metropoles: the urbane and cultivated Harlem versus the robust and industrial Chicago. When the islands and their women are mentioned by the men, it is to describe their prowess at seduction, albeit through different tactics. While the island women declare that they "no savvy" what he wants from them, Billy declares, "I'll make you savvy," and testifies to his ability to win whatever he wants from the islands:

> You know I'm a sailor and I get around the world,
> And I got a way of meeting every situation, girl.
> If I get to Cuba and I want to eat,
> I just pinch the waitress and holler "Meat!"
> If I get to Haiti and need a drink,
> I point to my empty glass and wink.
> If I get to Martinique and desire a bed,
> I just nod my sleepy head.
> If I get to the Virgin Islands and want a gal—
> My Chicago jive will solve that, pal!
> Cause when I want something, I always want it now.
> But if you no savvy, I'll make you savvy somehow. (6:166)

Although this text is lighthearted, its humor is predicated upon the servility of the islands and their women. As much as one might like to read Billy as an object of satire or critique, he is central to the play and seems to be admired, even by his rival, for his exuberant and possessive spirit. Buddy is more romantic, as he declares his love for one woman: "In a tropic bower/I found a flower" (6:167). But he is nonetheless a stock character of the United States condescending to a simple peasant beauty: "Dusky Rio Rita!/Chocolate Carmencita!/How I'd like to meet ya,/You cute little baby" (6:172). More stock scenes emerge in the play, including a consultation with a Voodoo Man and a Devil Dance (6:175). By the end, both men succeed in making their paramours "savvy," and marriage is ahead for each couple. There is a closing irony in the sense that these men who came as conquerors have "fallen" for the islands, but this moment of "going native" is utterly conventional and still rendered as a kind of sexual competition between the islands and the United States. Billy notes, "Won't them chicks in Chicago be mad when they hear about this! Done lost sweet Billy Mitchell—down in Rumba Land" (6:178).

Representations of the United States in Nicolás Guillén's Poetry

Beyond his theatrical representations of the Caribbean, Hughes had a substantive connection with the poets of Cuba and Haiti, particularly the poet Nicolás Guillén, whose works he translated during the 1940s. Before turning to those translations, it is important first to consider Guillén's poems in their original Spanish, particularly because Hughes's choices in translating him were relatively narrow. In comparison to his large output of poems focusing on Cuba and the Caribbean, comparatively few of Guillén's poems reflected upon the United States, but those that did so made significant aesthetic and political interventions into the question of U.S.-Caribbean relations. Although Guillén never visited the United States (he was denied an entrance visa in 1941 because of his leftist politics), he witnessed the cultural, political, and economic effects of the hegemonic U.S. presence in Cuba, and grew to fear its expanding influence throughout the Caribbean. In addition, as Guillén grew more explicitly political in his poetry in the 1940s and 1950s, he kept himself informed about developments in the United States with regard to racial justice, and his poems directly addressed injustices in the U.S.

Guillén's collection *Motivos de son* (1930) inaugurates his *negrismo* [blackness] project of capturing Afro-Cuban folk idioms, rhythms, and traditions in poetic form. Consequently, there is relatively little mention of the United States, except insofar as it threatens the Cuban language. For example, the satiric poem "Tu no sabe inglé" [You don't know English] teases the putative addressee, Bito Manué, for his attempts to learn English (presumably to ingratiate himself with the Yankees).

Con tanto inglé que tú sabía,
Bito Manué,
con tanto inglé, no sabe ahora
desí: ye.

La mericana te buca,
y tú le tiene que huí:
tu inglé era de etrái guan,
de etrái guan y guan tu tri . . .[14]

[With as much English as you know,
Bito Manué,
with so much English, you still don't know
how to say: "ye."

The American woman kisses you,
and you have to run after her:
your English is still no better than "guan"
no better than "guan" and "guan, tu, tri."]

Linguistically, this poem treats English in crude dialect form, rendering "one, two, three" as "guan, tu, tri." This choice not only mocks the inadequacy of Bito's pronunciation and, by extension, his failed attempt to mimic the neocolonial master, but also serves as a counter to the American tradition of deformed Spanish dialect in poems about the islands (evident, for example, in James Weldon Johnson's "Down by the Carib Sea" or Hughes's and Bontemps' *Tropics After Dark*). The depiction of Bito's romance also shows a reversal of the U.S. cliché of the Latin lover preying on an innocent American woman; here, it is the American woman who is the sexual predator and dangerous object of desire.

Guillén treated the United States and its neocolonial presence much more extensively in his subsequent collection, *West Indies, Ltd.* (1934). The title prophesies an Anglo-American corporatization of the Caribbean islands, and the collection explores the confrontation between Caribbean and "Yankee" cultures in vivid and evocative detail. In the central poem of the volume, also titled "West Indies, Ltd.," Guillén emphasizes the multiracial character of the islands—"Here there are whites, and blacks, and chinos, and mulattoes"[15]—which serves to prepare his critique of the monoculture imposed by U.S. corporations. The central sections of the poem offer a primer explaining the Yankee as an invasive, alien species. In contrast to the beautiful natural scenes in the preceding sections, the imperial presence evokes a hellish landscape of labor and exploitation: "This is the grotesque seat of companies and trusts./Here are the lake of asphalt, the iron mines, the coffee plantations."[16] Turning to the visitors themselves, the poem offers a litany that is largely grotesque. While the poem accords some respect to the musically-inclined visitors ("dancers of the fox trot, the boys of the jazz band"), the most ornate (and damning) language is directed towards the wealthy heads of corporations and their dissipated scions.

> Here are the servants of Mr. Babbit,
> those who send their children to West Point
>
> . . . .
>
> Here are the absurd syphilitic young men,
> Smokers of opium and marijuana,
> Showing off, as if in glass cases, their lesions,
> Having new suits cut for them each week.[17]

"The absurd" aptly characterizes the entire presence of the Yankees evoked here; Guillén's rendering shows them to be possessed of great power but unworthy of it. The Yankees' culture is banal (hence the reference to

Sinclair Lewis's *Babbit*), but they are able to spread it because of their military might (due to "West Point"). Similarly, the young Americans, in contrast to the mighty laborers celebrated elsewhere in the poem, are diseased and afflicted, seeking crass pleasures, while possessing the capital to purchase new clothes every day. In this light, Guillén reaches back to the traditions of Martí, Sylvain, and other Caribbean intellectuals who situated savagery and cultural decay not in the tropics, but in the United States.

In counterpoint to these critical depictions of the U.S. presence in Cuba, Guillén incorporates into "West Indies, Ltd." the folk songs of a character named Juan el Barbero, who sings of the need for men to take action to free themselves. These songs are skillfully rendered as performances that offer an interruption to the framing voice in the poems. Often, they reveal Guillén adapting traditional forms for new political purposes. The fifth part of "West Indies, Ltd.," for example, takes the form of a *son* that pays homage to the hard work of harvesting cane, with a crucial twist when the subject of a knife appears. The central stanza to the poem avows, "Men, when they are men, have to carry a knife."[18] In the context of preceding stanzas describing the sugar harvest ("From the cane comes sugar, sugar for coffee"[19]), this central stanza appears to refer to the harvest, which is the work of men with knives. Subsequently, however, the question of armament and power takes on a political dimension, as Juan sings, "When I became a man, I picked up a knife, and they threw me in prison [presidio]."[20] The term "presidio" is crucial here, as it refers not simply to a civilian prison (which would be more likely rendered as "prisión"), but to a military prison that typically houses political prisoners. Indeed, in 1931 the Cuban dictator and U.S. ally Gerardo Machado had recently completed the famous Presidio Modelo, a huge prison (six-thousand-inmate capacity) with the help of loans from Chase National Bank of New York.[21] Thus, in Guillén's context, mention of a "presidio" would almost certainly evoke this new, repressive space financed by neocolonial interests. In spite of this punitive setting, this section of the poem closes with the possibility of liberation, as Juan sings that he would be happy "if I would die right now," because "I will give you, I'll give you, I'll give you/yes, I will give you freedom."[22]

West Indies, Ltd. constituted Guillén's most sustained meditation on the presence of the United States in the Caribbean and the need for the West Indies to reject that hegemony, and he periodically returned to the subject in subsequent poems. In *Cantos para soldados y sones para turistas* [Songs for soldiers and tunes for tourists] (1937), Guillén puts his poems' speakers in implicit dialogue with a range of North American visitors, whether soldiers or tourists, and in a variety of moods and tones. Some, like "Yanqui con soldado" [Yankee with soldier], project an aura mixing tension, intimacy, and latent violence. The poem's speaker watches a soldier guarding the U.S. embassy, and when questioned about his business there, declares that "I walk in search of a soldier who wants to be my friend."[23] This moment of imagined communication extends into a piece of advice from the speaker to the young soldier, warning him that his sacrifice in the islands will not benefit him, but will enrich the old men and fathers back home, who profit from the interventions in Cuba: "your father . . . / who yesterday was a beggar, / gets fat today with the young blood that is spilled from you."[24] More playfully, a long poem entitled "José Ramón Cantaliso," much in the manner of the later verses of "West Indies, Ltd.," offers a series of *sones* sung to visiting tourists. The *son* gently mocks the hot, sweating tourists—"All these red yankees / are sons of a shrimp"—but makes clear the inequality in opportunity José faces in contrast with that of his listeners: "You live, / I die / you eat and drink / but not me."[25] In contrast to this distinction between himself and the tourists, José establishes an imaginative link to the poor musicians of "Nueva York" who are "poor like I am . . . //. . . To them I give my hand / and with them I will sing, because the song they / know is the same that I know."[26]

Guillén's poems in the postwar decades, particularly leading into the Cuban Revolution, became even more politically directed towards the United States. "Mi patria es dulce por fuera" [My country is sweet from the outside] (1947), for example, situates Cuba's struggle for independence in a historical continuum of domination—"Today Yankee, yesterday Spanish"—but closes with a violent gesture of independence: "an American marine / laid hands on me . . . / . . . but there he lies dead."[27] Guillén's poems about the United States not only comment upon the problematic interactions between the U.S. and Cuba, but also comment upon crises and failures within the U.S. republic itself, much as Martí did with his essays. In the collection *Sátira política* (1949–53), for example, Guillén critiques the United States from a variety of satiric perspectives. In "Yankee Dog," he compares the United States in the Caribbean to a scavenging dog running free without a collar or license. "U.S.A" comments ironically upon the "grace" and hospitality of white "savages" in the United States, who welcome African Americans into their communities with trampling, spitting, and burning.[28] Guillén also extends his eye towards U.S. imperialism in the East. Reflecting on developments in Asian independence movements after World War II, he imagines that MacArthur must be frightened because the people there can now "walk on their own feet,/without Yankees and without the Mikado."[29]

Two collections published on the eve of Castro's revolution (while Guillén was in exile, barred from entering Cuba by the Batista government in 1953), *La paloma de vuelo popular* [The will of the people] (1958) and *Elegías* [Elegies] (collected from 1948–58), explicitly link Caribbean and U.S. subject matter. Some of the poems, like "Canción puertorriqueña" ["Puerto Rican Song"] return to the questions of cultural nationalism posed early on in *Motivos de son.* Addressing his Caribbean brethren in Puerto Rico and reflecting upon the island's status as a U.S. protectorate ("arm in arm with Uncle Sam"), Guillén asks, "in what language, at last, can I speak to you?"[30] Guillén concludes by claiming kinship with Puerto Rico and lamenting its partnership with the United States, which grasps the island in a fatal manner: "New York City with San Juan,/Manhattan and Borinquen, rope and neck."[31] Guillén also addresses the Red Scare in the United States, celebrating the death of Senator McCarthy in the poem "Pequeña letanía grotesca den la muerte del senador McCarthy" ["Short Grotesque Litany on the Death of Senator McCarthy"]: "McCarthy is dead,/good and dead and dead,/Amen."[32]

In his later collections, Guillén addresses questions of racial justice and civil rights that extend throughout the Americas. In the poem "Sports," for example, Guillén celebrates black athletes throughout the hemisphere who had challenged the racist status quo, reflecting upon the pan-American community of black boxers. His honor roll ranges from Jack Johnson from the U.S. ("the mountainous black man" that "infuriated Lynch"), to Sam Langford from Canada (who brought "glory in his gloves"), to Kid Charol from Cuba ("the great king without a crown").[33] Guillén paid particular attention to the struggle to end Jim Crow segregation in the United States, as well as the backlash against the civil rights movement that was rapidly emerging in the U.S. South. Referring to the site of key conflicts over school integration in the 1950s, Guillén's poem "Little Rock" not only considers the specifics of racial violence in the U.S. South, but richly employs the school as a metaphor to investigate the "lessons" of Little Rock. Describing the South as an extended "escuela de miedo" [school of fear], Guillén writes that "Jim Crow will be the teacher,/the sons of Lynch will be your classmates,/and there will be in each black child's desk/ink of blood, pencils of fire."[34] In co-figuring an image of quintessential innocence and promise (the schoolhouse) with images of racial violence (ink as blood, pencils of fire), Guillén effectively transforms expectations surrounding the cold-war consensus, situating the United States not as a beacon of liberty, but as an exceptional teacher of injustice and racial inequality. Consequently, he concludes the poem with a fearful warning to the world about what "Americanization" would mean: "now think about what it would be/One world all the South/The world all blood and all whip."[35]

Guillén also deployed a similar mixture of cultural criticism of the United States and outreach to fellow West Indians in *Elegías*. This collection juxtaposes elegies to notable heroes, statesman, and artists from the Caribbean, ranging from Jacques Roumain of Haiti, whose works were discussed in chapter 2, to the Cuban labor leader and revolutionary Jesús Menendéz. In honoring the latter, Guillén imagines a celebratory witches' sabbath held in the United States:

> The eagle flying like a vulture,
> looks from one sea to another;
> hooded men dance funeral dances.
> They beat a funeral drum
> and burning the three fateful letters
> with which they announce the Ku Klux Klan,
> they let out from the South a unanimous shout:
> he is dead and gone, dead and gone![36]

Guillén boldly compares the American national symbol to a scavenging vulture, with clear political implications for its imperial designs upon Cuba. Even more pointedly, he displaces both bird images with a new national emblem—the dancing Klansmen—to represent violence and racial animosity as the core of U.S. politics. No doubt many U.S. readers would have chafed at having the Klan be seen as representative, but that is precisely Guillén's point: that these Klansmen's ideology was not an aberration, but representative of a dominant strain of U.S. political life, particularly in the eyes of the Caribbean. Another crucial aspect of this portrait is the tribal savagery embodied in the dancing Klansman—a primitivist portrait that the United States would more traditionally associate with the Caribbean. Indeed, such a strategy of reversal is central to what is perhaps Guillén's most searing poem for a U.S. reader, his "Elegía a Emmett Till." Guillén prefaces the poem by citing an article from the *Crisis* describing Illinois native Emmett Till's murder in Greenwood, Mississippi, by a white mob. Guillén begins by addressing the Mississippi River itself. Much in the manner of Hughes's "The Negro Speaks of Rivers," Guillén establishes a sense of kinship between the river and

African Americans of the South, born of the blood spilled into it: "Oh old river, brother of the blacks, / with their veins opened into the water."[37] While Till as a specific figure is commemorated and venerated in the elegy, Guillén also uses the river as a vehicle for considering the shape of culture and race in the U.S. South. In an anaphoric sequence of lines, each introduced by "the Mississippi passes," Guillén takes the reader on a virtual tour of southern violence and debauchery, ultimately arriving at "the nocturnal bonfire / by whose cannibal light / the white men dance."[38] As in his elegy for Jésus Menéndez, Guillén renders the U.S. southern male as the horrifying "other," but with an extra reversal, as he likens them to cannibals—the sensational image that white supremacists had applied to Caribbean "primitives" during the 1920s and 1930s.

Francophone Caribbean Poets' Engagement with the United States

Francophone poets from the Caribbean were also engaged in a dialogue with the United States during this period, and the crosscurrents took several forms. First of all, New Negro Renaissance writing was an important influence on Francophone Caribbean poets during the post-occupation period, including Aimé Césaire (from Martinique), Léon Damas (from French Guyana), and René Depestre (from Haiti). These poets' range of responses to New Negro literature, and to the United States more generally, recapitulates significant trends in Caribbean discourse from the turn of the century. Like Guillén, these poets embraced a pan-Africanist sense of hemispheric and global black culture (termed negritude in their circles), while maintaining keen concern for changing relations of power and domination in the Caribbean region. Within their poetry, their cross-cultural dialogue with the United States is evident in a range of manifestations, from dedications to U.S. poets with whom they felt kinship, to gestures of solidarity towards their African American brethren in the U.S., to direct critique of U.S. imperialism and neocolonialism.

The development of Léon Damas's career provides an apt illustration of the cross-cultural influences circulating between the United States and the Caribbean in the wake of the New Negro Renaissance. Known in many circles as "the founder of negritude" (though he did not claim that title for himself), Damas used a variety of genres—poetry, short fiction, and essays—to consider both the colonial condition of his native Guyana and the broader experience of African and African-descended peoples in the face of Western imperialism. Damas's direct references to the United States in his writings were comparatively few, but his experiences in the U.S., as well as his encounters with New Negro writers, profoundly shaped his philosophy and sense of geopolitics. Reflecting on negritude in an autobiographical essay, Damas commented upon the productive inspiration that New Negro writings provided to him and his fellow West Indians during his time in Paris in the 1930s: "We were determined to follow in the footsteps of Langston Hughes, Countee Cullen, and likewise Jean Toomer, Sterling Brown, Claude McKay, the author of *Banjo,* who realized in 1930 (a date to remember) a merited success."[39]

Damas crafted his first (and best-known) collection of poems, *Pigments* (1937), in the context of these Parisian encounters with fellow West Indian and U.S. writers. In that spirit, Damas used a quote from Claude McKay's "To the White Fiends" as an epigram to the collection:

> Be not deceived, for every deed you do
> I could match, outmatch: am I not Africa's son.
> Black of that black land where black deeds are done?[40]

The poems in *Pigments* take a cue both from McKay's militant spirit and from his reclamation of a diasporic connection between America and Africa. Thematically, Damas's poems look to African heritage as a source of strength for black West Indians and as an alternative to assimilation into European cultures and values. At the same time, Damas uses his poems to claim kinship in other geographic directions as well. In addition to gesturing towards fellow authors from the Caribbean, such as Alejo Carpentier and Césaire, Damas includes references to African American figures and culture from the United States. The poem "Hoquet" [Hiccup] is dedicated to Mercer Cook, a distinguished professor of Romance languages from Howard University (who would later become an important U.S. ambassador to West African Francophone nations) whom Damas had met in Paris in 1934 and with whom he had started a lifelong friendship.[41] Playing upon Cook's family's history as accomplished musicians (Mercer's father, Will Marion Cook, was a violin prodigy and an accomplished composer; his mother, Abbie Mitchell Cook, was an acclaimed soprano, and she originated the role of Clara in George Gershwin's *Porgy and Bess*), Damas uses a wide range of musical references in "Hoquet" to explore to whom Cook and Damas (and others, by implication) owed cultural allegiance. It concludes with an evocative anecdote describing Cook setting aside the violin in favor of the banjo:

> I remember that you never went back
> To your v-i-olin lesson

A banjo
You said a banjo
How you said
A banjo
You said, definitely,
A banjo
No, sir,
    You knew that one could not suffer with us
Neither ban
Nor jo
Neither gui
Nor tar
The mulattoes could not do that
Therefore let them become blacks.[42]

In fondly recalling Cook's rejection of his father's European instrument (the violin) in favor of an African-descended folk instrument (the banjo), Damas shows negritude not as a static, essentialist concept but as a process of generational change and becoming. Like McKay, he reaches for a banjo as an emblem of mutual recognition and celebration that can connect diverse descendants of the African diaspora—spanning from Africa, to Guyana, to Washington, D.C. The formal structure of "Hoquet" shows that Damas is engaged in another kind of bridging, as the three-fold repetition ("you said," "how you said," "you said, definitely") and other musical references evoke the blues generally and the forms of Langston Hughes more specifically.

Musical references provide the center of gravity for the two other poems directed towards the United States in *Pigments:* "Trêve" and "Shine." "Trêve" begins with an exhortation about the blues in general and an apparent rejection of them: "Enough of the blues/of the hammerings of the piano,/of the muted trumpet."[43] As this litany develops, Damas shifts from an ekphrastic representation of blues music towards a broader sense of what causes the blues. The poem offers an expanding litany of rejections, from "the foolish stomping of feet," to "the sounds that drown out the cries of beasts," to "a hyper-assimilated attitude," to, finally, "individual egotisms."[44] Like Hughes, Damas experiments with the question of what the blues expresses and what it masks; unlike Hughes, however, he perceives the blues as being limited by an escapist impulse, something that provides "la satisfaction du rythme" [the satisfaction of the rhythm] while drowning out the "cris" [cries] beneath.

Setting aside the question of whether or not this is a fair assessment of the cultural role of the blues, Damas's use of the blues, and consideration of its limitations, shows an important reversal of cultural privilege. Although Damas draws upon New Negro sources and techniques in *Pigments,* in this poem he also argues for the limitations of perhaps the most popular New Negro cultural export at the time. Indeed, by the end of the poem, which calls for a setting aside "of desires, of needs, of individual egotisms,"[45] Damas implies that collective action is needed to end the conditions that produce "the blues." In philosophical terms, one might say that Damas finds that "listening" (literally and figuratively) to the blues is a necessary but not sufficient condition for moving forward the cause of negritude.

The poem "Shine" is dedicated to Louis Armstrong, and the title bears a careful double entendre, referencing the famous Tin Pan Alley song performed by Armstrong while also evoking a racist epithet. "Shine" begins with a proud declaration of allegiance to African spiritual symbols: "I have in the top of my head/protected there/the ancestral conic faith."[46] The poem then gestures towards another traditional motif in poetic references to Africa—"masques" [masks]—but deploys that trope to figure whites as having "the automatic arrogance/of masks/of masks of living chalk."[47] By depicting white identity as a mask, Damas evacuates the ontological primacy of whiteness (it is an illusion, a false imposition) and reverses the African American poetic tradition (epitomized in Paul Laurance Dunbar's "We Wear the Mask") of representing black identity as a masking. In contrast to the resonance of concealment born by the image of a mask, the remainder of the poem uses images of a shining face (alluding not only to Armstrong's song but also perhaps to Armstrong himself) as a gesture of revelation:

> And my face shines with the horrors of the past
> and my frightful laugh is made to repel the spectre of the hounds
> tracking the fugitives
> and my voice that sings for them
> is sweet to capture
> their sad soul.[48]

This passage provides a doubled moment of representation within the poem, as the speaker's face bears witness to the travails of fugitive slave ancestors, while the poetic description offers an ekphrastic homage to Armstrong's music and performance style, with deep respect for the serious work accomplished by Armstrong in giving a depth to an otherwise "innocent" song.[49] The bright face in the poem is not a mask of concealment, but a mirror of enduring revelation; the bright laugh not a denial of the past, but an exorcism. Damas's overall linkage between past and present suggests that the sweetness of a song like "Shine" does not represent a turning away from the pains of the past (as later critics of Armstrong would argue), but a loving tribute to those lost to the horrors of that past. In addition, Damas's poem offers testimony to the survival of the descendants of those fugitives—in spite of the hounds and the other horrors visited upon them.

Besides his specific engagement with the cultural work of U.S. African American literature and music in his poetry, Damas cites the U.S. more broadly in his essays as an object lesson (and cautionary tale) for the Caribbean and other peoples of color seeking paths for development in the twentieth century. Like Firmin and Sylvain, Damas clearly recognized the United States as a powerful expansionist presence in the New World. In some cases, he uses the specter of U.S. hegemony as a rhetorical tool to argue for better investment in the black West Indies (especially his native Guiana) by France. At several points in his travel memoir, *Retour de Guyane* [Return to Guiana] (1938), he criticizes France for denying sovereignty to the Guyanese while simultaneously withholding capital that could help them (and France) develop their native resources. Damas notes that even the United States, during its occupation of Haiti, extended loans to the country and invested in it: "It is difficult not to make a comparison between the disinterest evident in the French government's timid refusal [to offer loans to Guyana], and the energy deployed by the U.S. government to enrich Haiti by force, to whom it [the U.S.] forced a loan against the will of the American public."[50] Damas is certainly not writing to defend the U.S. occupation of Haiti for the sake of its economic development; rather, he uses the United States as an extreme example to illustrate a political point. If the United States, a neocolonial hegemon that made no claims about spreading "civilization" and whose occupation of Haiti was so clearly an infringement of proper sovereignty in the region, managed to provide capital, then how could the French government, which represented itself as an avatar of superior Gallic culture, fail to provide even a minimum level of investment in Guyana? Beyond issues of comparative justice, Damas also hints that France's sluggishness would redound to the benefit of the United States and harm Paris. Noting the untapped gold and other mineral reserves in Guyana, Damas comments, "What most tempts Uncle Sam will be less the people than the soil, and in particular, the soil of Guyana. . . . To add to everything that has been said, at the risk of repeating the point: one must develop Guyana for its gold, so that the Metropole [i.e., Paris] can avoid having to purchase that metal."[51] To add even greater urgency to his case, Damas finishes *Retour de Guyane* with the warning that if the French do not develop Guyana for their mutual benefit, they "risk seeing, in this same Guyana, already suffering, the beginning of collapse of the French Empire."[52]

As much as Damas sought economic capital from France for Guyanese and other Caribbean development, he was much less sanguine about an importation of cultural capital. A central component of *Retour de Guyane* is his engagement with the question of whether or not Guyana and the French Caribbean should aspire toward their own separate cultural autonomy from France (beyond the questions of economic and political dependency) or seek to remake their native cultures in the image of Paris. As in his discussion of questions of economic development, Damas uses the United States as a useful foil for his argument. In a chapter aptly titled "Pour ou contre l'assimilation" [For or against assimilation], Damas looks to the United States as "une expérience de laboratoire" [a laboratory experiment] and offers a number of conclusions. Damas praises the extraordinary achievements of African Americans, citing Langston Hughes, Alain Locke, Booker T. Washington, Paul Robeson, Marian Anderson, Louis Armstrong, Duke Ellington, and Cab Calloway as exemplars of global black culture. Damas notes, however, that these achievements have emerged not because of assimilation into a majority white culture, but in spite of U.S. assumptions about white cultural supremacy. Damas poses several rhetorical questions about the source of these achievements: "Who would dare claim that it is thanks to massive assimilation that the territory of the United States has produced the most beautiful specimens of the black race that exist in the world? What do they [the 'specimens'] owe to complete assimilation?"[53] Damas's careful choice of words in these questions is crucial. Above all, it is not "des États-Unis," but "le territoire" that has produced these racial exemplars. Damas denies the United States credit as a nation for these achievements, reserving them for the land and the people, namely "la race noire" [the black race], that have produced them. Damas also mentions that these figures are "le plus connus en Europe" [the best known in Europe], hinting at the fact that during the New Negro Renaissance, African American cultural production was, in many cases, better appreciated in Europe than in the United States. Damas amplifies his case in this chapter by citing a short poem that Langston Hughes gave to him when they met in Cuba:

I'm makin' a road
Makin'! A road through the palmetto thicket
For light and civilization to travel on—
Makin'! A road for the rich old white men to travel over their big cars
And leave me standin' here
Rich folks ride—
And I get to see 'em ride
I aint never seen nobody ride so fine before[54]

Damas uses Hughes's poem as an exemplary and ironic evidence of the value of assimilation. The poem's speaker naively assents to the tropes of progress via assimilation, taking pride in how his taming the wild "palmetto thicket" provides a path of "light and civilization." In contrast to that claim, the road serves a more bathetic need, a conduit for "rich old white men" and "their big cars." More pointedly, the speaker does not have a chance to share in the fruits of his labors; he toils to make a path to be enjoyed by others. In this light, the United States provides a doubled example for Damas against assimilation. First, neither integration nor assimilation has been responsible for the achievements by African Americans in the United States that Damas most admired. Second, one of these admired poets himself had written a poem about the dangers of naïvely laboring on behalf of a "civilizing" project from which one will be excluded. Damas thus cautions that embracing assimilation and working on behalf of Western civilization does not assure a place within that civilization or a fair share of the fruits of those labors on behalf of it.

The works of René Depestre provide an equally complex case of cross-cultural dialogue between the Caribbean and the United States in the years after World War II. Depestre is best known for his militant defense of Afro-Caribbean culture and sovereignty against U.S. domination in his poetry of the 1960s, such as *Un arc-en-ciel pour l'occident chrétien* [*A Rainbow for the Christian West*] (1967),[55] but he was similarly committed to exploring the relationship with his northern neighbor in his earlier collections, such as *Étincelles* [Sparks] (1945), *Gerbe de sang* [Spray of blood] (1946), and *Traduit du grand large* [Translation of great length] (1952), and *Minerai noir* [Black ore] (1956). Depestre frequently cites U.S. poets in his dedications or epigraphs, including Walt Whitman, Edgar Allan Poe, Langston Hughes, and Carl Sandburg.[56] In some cases, Depestre uses such epigraphs for a relatively simple gesture of literary and poetic kinship, such as quoting a translation of Whitman's famous lines from *Leaves of Grass*—"Camerado, this is no book,/Who touches this touches a man"—as an epigraph to *Traduit du grande large.* In most cases, however, the engagement is more pointed and complex. One of the most important poems in *Étincelles,* for example, "Piété Filiale" [Filial piety] is dedicated "á Langston Hughes." The poem apostrophically addresses Africa and her extended family in a manner reminiscent of Hughes's African-themed poems from the 1920s:

> O African land
> I wander the route of your misfortunes
> the long march without paths of flowers
> the long marine wake of sweat
> Of tears and of blood[57]

As the poem develops, it avows both militancy ("I bring the bearing of a soldier/into the darkness of your suffering") and fraternity ("lights yellows blacks the skin matters little/the blood and the distress have the same color").[58] In this regard, Depestre uses "Piété Filiale" to claims kinship at multiple levels, not only as a son of Africa, but also to fellow brethren of the diaspora. In the context of the dedication, the title itself has another resonance, as it evokes a sense of either filial or fraternal piety for Hughes as literary precursor and kindred artist.

Besides gestures of literary affinity with writers from the United States, Depestre directly addresses interrelations between the U.S. and the Caribbean in the decades between World War II and the Cuban Revolution. Much as Anténor Firmin projectively explored U.S.-Caribbean relations in his essays following the Spanish-American War, Depestre's poetry about the United States during this period expressed concerns about U.S. power (which was of signal concern to Depestre as an avowed communist) and posed questions about what hemispheric partnerships might emerge in the post–World War II era. Despestre's earliest poems about the United States in *Étincelles* express an optimistic hope that the U.S. under the second Roosevelt administration might become a better partner to Haiti and the Caribbean. In some cases, this sentiment emerges from a small gesture or turn of phrase. For example, in "Dialogue sur les ondes de 1945" [Dialogue on the waves in 1945], Depestre imagines a series of heartening radio broadcasts after World War II, including a transmission from the United States: "Radio Washington: Roosevelt's four liberties are standing beside you."[59] The allusion to "four liberties" refers to President Roosevelt's famous "four freedoms" (freedom of speech and expression, freedom of religion, freedom from want, and freedom from fear) articulated in 1943.

In "Coups de téléphone dans l'après-guerre" [Telephone-coup after the war], Depestre shifts from the radio to the telephone to imagine a scene of reciprocal international communication and to investigate further the potential of Roosevelt's "four freedoms." Depestre imagines a series of phone conversations between himself as a representative of the Caribbean and leaders in Paris, Washington, D.C., and Moscow. Depestre first portrays an exchange with Washington, D.C.:

—Hello Hello the White House yes
A Negro is speaking
The black people of the world have caught wind of
Mr. Roosevelt's freedoms
—You can see all the people's celebrations.[60]

The optimism in this stanza rests on a careful balance of reciprocal communication and good faith: the "Maison Blanche" listens to the "Nègre" who has heard (and put new faith in) declarations by the United States about global freedoms for all people. As the poem continues, the speaker contacts Moscow and Paris as "camarades," concluding with a hope that in the postwar period "a new world will arise from the war" and that "the united nations will begin / to dance in peace their history / the joyous wave floods all the shores."[61] Depestre obviously does not envision an exclusive U.S.-Caribbean partnership of peace here; rather, he focuses on an internationalist vision of cooperation and unity. Nevertheless, his choice of Roosevelt in "la Maison-Blanche" as the first place to "call," figuratively, in the poem, suggests an awareness of the dominant role of the United States in the Caribbean, as well as the fact that U.S. support of "libertés" is the necessary starting point for a renewed sense of global justice for all people. Lest one think that Depestre's poem is overly naïve in its hope, the poem recognizes the difficulty of realizing such cooperative unity. The very fact that it is titled a "coup" suggests Depestre's awareness that it would be, paradoxically, a revolutionary upending of the world order (and a new kind of revolution—by phone, no less) for such a sense of unity and respect to emerge. Moreover, the poem is subtitled "Utopie 1945" [Utopia 1945], a phrase that acknowledges the slim chances of these hopes being realized.

The expectations of utopian cooperation with the United States that Depestre expressed in *Étincelles* did not carry forward into his subsequent poetry, although he continued to position himself in a dialogue with the U.S. In his next collection of poems, *Gerbe de sang*, Depestre claims literary kinship in a much more unexpected direction in an epigraph translated from Poe's *The Narrative of Arthur Gordon Pym* (1838): "And 'blood,' too, that word of all words—so rife at all times with mystery, and suffering, and terror—how trebly full of import did it now appear—how chilly and heavily (disjointed, as it thus was, from any foregoing words to qualify or render it distinct) did its vague syllables fall, amid the deep gloom of my prison, into the innermost recesses of my soul!"[62] Poe's passage suggests the rich resonance of blood as a signifier, with implications ranging from identity ("the innermost recesses of my soul") to violence ("suffering and terror"). Such an epigram forms an apt preface to *Gerbe de Sang,* as Depestre's collection explores the interconnection between heritage, poetic expression, and militant antifacism. Indeed, Depestre dedicates the volume "to the fight of the antifascists, to the young nonconformists of Haiti."[63] In this political context, Depestre deploys Poe's words in a direction cannily distinct from the plot development of *The Narrative of Arthur Gordon Pym.* In contrast to the "prison" setting of Poe's passage, which is written by the character Pym as he is trapped in the hold of the *Penguin,* the very title of Depestre's collection speaks of outpouring, expression, and violent struggle. Depestre's use of Poe is all the bolder considering the overall plot of *The Narrative of Arthur Gordon Pym.* By the end of Pym's narrative, he will be terrorized by (and barely survive) an eruption of unexpected black militancy (the revolt by the mysterious Antarctic natives). While this revelation functions essentially as a horror story for Pym, the prospect of such liberatory violence (for which Haiti provides an exemplum) is one of the goals that Depestre hoped to foster in this very collection.

In this spirit of liberation, Depestre concludes one of the most militant poems of *Gerbe de sang,* "Ressourcement 1946" ["Restoration 1946"], with a declaration of the regenerative power of war: "for our thirst the rifle can be a fountain/the stone offers a bed for our fatigue."[64] The title of the poem refers to the Revolution of 1946 in Haiti, which, while not a direct revolt against U.S. hegemony, was an indirect one. The revolution ended the authoritarian regime of President Élie Lescot, who had been in power since 1941 and was closely allied with not only the United States, but also with the Dominican dictator Rafael Trujillo, who had very strong U.S. support, was an avowed enemy of Haitian blacks, and had perpetrated ethnic cleansing against black Haitians within the Dominican Republic during the Parsley Massacre of 1937. This revolution was also significant because it was not merely an internecine coup within the military and political elite, but was joined by many students, intellectuals, and striking union workers, who aimed to wrest cultural and political sovereignty back from President Lescot's regime. Accordingly, Depestre closes the poem by avowing his own role as an artist in the struggle: "I descend in a boat within this poem."[65] In this closing image, Depestre effects a poetic refiguration of gunboat diplomacy and naval intervention, imagining himself as returning to Haiti for liberation (rather than invasion, which has been the usual role of boats in Haitian history), with his poem as the figurative vehicle for that struggle. The literary-militant tenor of the conclusion of this poem is consistent with Depestre's comment in an essay published in the same year as *Gerbe de sang* that it was vital for Haitian writers to sustain a literature of resistance in the wake of the U.S. occupation: "What did these artists there [Haiti] realize was their ideal? It would be necessary, one day, to reflect rigorously upon the work of the writers who attempted the first literary resistance during the nineteen years of the military occupation by the United States."[66] In Depestre's poetry from the 1950s, such as *Traduit du grande large* and *Minerai noir,* the militancy of his poetry developed in an even more resistant direction. Much as Guillén did in his later poetry, Depestre began to engage the United States directly on questions of justice and race *within* its borders, establishing a coalition between black West Indians and U.S. African Americans to combat the horrors of lynching and Jim Crow. In some of these poems, Depestre comments on issues in the United States from a relatively abstract perspective. In "Nuits d'un lyncheur" [Night of a lyncher], for example, Depestre draws a lyric portrait of a young man and woman in love and the nights they spend together. Although the United States is never directly referenced, both the title and the young woman's name, Jessie, strongly evoke a sense of the U.S. South. The poem develops by offering a series of contrasts addressed to the young woman about the two sides of her lover. He leaves her in the middle of the night for a mysterious errand, while she slumbers on. The poet comments on the man's dual nature: "On the one side of his heart / Sleeps a baby . . . / . . . On the other . . . / An obsession directs the hungry eyes / Of a wolf."[67] Three more times the poet discusses the "wolf" side of the apparently tender young man, closing with a revelation to the reader (and to the young woman, by implication) of the hideous object of the man's errand: "One hundred meters from there / A black man / Burns out his last drop / Of blood beneath the stars."[68] In comparison to the scenes of racial violence in Guillén, which depict lynching as a ritual openly enacted by the community, Depestre's conclusion moves in a less spectacular but perhaps even more disturbing direction, suggesting that even the seemingly loving and caring white men of the South have the bloodlust of the "wolf" within. Depestre skillfully suggests that the racial violence of the South gains power (and is so horrifying, in retrospect) precisely because it can be perpetuated in relative secret and without disturbing the calm of the white family. Depestre's poem implies that even when racial violence is not seen in the South, it is steadily, stealthily occurring, underwriting the peace of this young white couple. The silence and faith of the young Jessie in the gentleness of her "baby," then, are not only sorely misplaced, but tacitly underlie and abet the violence outside.

Within *Traduit du grande large,* Depestre addresses questions of violence and race in more explicit detail, commenting directly upon a cause celebre within the United States. Section 4 of the title poem is an elegy for Willie McGee (mistakenly named Willie Mac Chee in the poem), an African American from Mississippi who was electrocuted in 1951 for the alleged rape of a white woman. The case was widely regarded by progressives and civil rights activists as a "legal lynching," as the jury took only two and half minutes to reach its verdict. In some respects, this poem still bears a spiritual connection to "Nuit d'un lyncheur," as it also focuses on exposing racist violence under another cover, this time within the justice system itself. Depestre's tribute to McGee takes the form of an intricate, layered litany, with anaphoric repetition and refrains. At the start of this section, Depestre directly addresses "you": "For you I have said goodbye to Willie McGee."[69] In the overall context of *Traduit du grande large,* the "you" addressed is Haiti, to which the entire poem is dedicated.[70] In the local context of this section, this use of "you" evokes a sense of direct address to the reader as well, drawing him or her into a relationship of twinned responsibility—both to McGee, as a sacrifice, and to the poet, for having commemorated him for us. The gravity of this obligation quickly becomes apparent as Depestre vividly evokes McGee's violated body: "Goodbye to an innocent that the Yankee jackals, out of racism/Burned like a hated match."[71] Despestre's image of the burning match makes a powerful link between this legal execution (burning by electrocution) and the extrajudicial lynching (burning by match and gasoline). Moreover, in figuring the Yankees as jackals, he depicts the white jury and community as subhuman, canine scavengers. Besides stripping the whites of their figurative privilege (they are compared to dark African animals), Depestre suggests that outcomes, for black men, in the justice system in the United States are equivalent to the savage lynchings from which respectable whites (e.g., the judge and jury) wished to distance themselves.

As the poem develops, Depestre articulates a connection among the poet, McGee, and black peoples more generally: "He was like you o my people/He was like me."[72] In order to fathom further these interrelationships, Depestre offers a series of anaphoric stanzas predicated upon the statement "one recognizes us by . . . ," listing common features among diasporic black people and concluding, "One recognizes us/By the high grade of our ore/By our songs stamped with pain and misery/Like medals of shadows."[73] These images unite a recognition of shared suffering among African peoples with an appreciation of their bittersweet achievement (songs) and rich potential (high grade ore). The image of ore resonates doubly as well, both validating the quality of his people and suggesting their status as an exploited resource. This image takes on an especially haunting resonance when one remembers that ore is heated and burned to produce purer metals—a process that recalls, imagistically, the burning vividly described at the outset of the McGee section (indeed, this image must have been especially powerful for Depestre, as it gave the title to his next collection of poems, *Minerai noir*). As this section concludes, Depestre appropriates burning imagery for militant purposes of his own, calling for "feu feu feu!" [fire fire fire] against "lyncheurs" and "racisme" and beseeching black voices from around the world (including "la robuste harmonie de Paul Robeson" [81]) to unite in commemoration of McGee.

As *Traduit du grand large* continues, Depestre extends his critique of the United States beyond Jim Crow and lynching towards a broader depiction of the problems of capitalist excess, consumerism, imperialism, and nuclear proliferation. Anticipating the broadly critical vision of the U.S. role in geopolitics in *Un arc-en-ciel pour l'occident chrétien,* Depestre deplores the hegemonic spread of U.S. power through corporate interests (such as Coca-Cola), U.S. weaponry (napalm), and cold-war militarism (such as the Korean War): "The blessed gaze of General MacArthur before the horrors reaped by his armies."[74] In turning his attention to the internal politics of the United States, Depestre critiques what would later be known as the cold war consensus, arguing that for him, there was not a significant difference between "the 'Democrat' anger of Truman" and the "'Republican' smile of Eisenhower." Instead, Depestre describes both political parties of the United States united as "the atomic party of the White House."[75]

In keeping with the epigraph from Whitman prefacing *Traduit du grande large,* Depestre offers his critique in the spirit of a "comrade."

Like Whitman, Depestre seeks to collapse apparently fundamental differences between himself and his implied reader (for Depestre, his race and his communist affiliation): "You who are perhaps my worst enemy . . ./I address myself to you in spite of it all/You are nonetheless my brother."[76] Depestre's attempts to establish such connection hearken back to the utopian dimensions of the poems in *Étincelles,* but *Traduit du grande large* deploys the ideal of fraternity to put a burden of responsibility on the citizens of the United States. After offering his litany of the global wrongs perpetuated by the U.S., Depestre takes the tone of a scolding sibling, or even a Jeremiah, seeking to turn the U.S. away from its unrighteous path: "O my brother you cannot endorse the check of so many crimes."[77] This metaphor is especially resonant because it uses the language of capitalist exchange (the question of whether or not to endorse a check) to represent the problematic relationship between the poet and the United States, as if he is translating morality into the only language his brothers from the U.S. can comprehend. Within that figuration, however, Depestre effects a striking reversal, as he presents himself in the position of depositor or banker, sitting in economic/moral judgment of how to handle the "check" from the United States—an especially ironic twist, given that U.S. banking interests spurred the occupation in the first place. Depestre ultimately represents fraternity with the United States not as fait accompli but as a work-in-progress that can be completed only when U.S. citizens cast aside their prejudices and presuppositions: "You cannot be my brother until I have seen that/You have freed yourself from your prison of indifference."[78] This figuration is particularly potent in the context of his prior discussion of Willie McGee. Earlier in the poem Depestre lamented the plight of McGee and other African Americans held in the U.S. penal system, while here he represents the U.S. everyman as imprisoned as well. In this respect, his call for the United States to abandon its indifference would resound not simply as a moral act that benefits victims of U.S. hegemony, but also a liberation of U.S. citizens themselves into a more global perspective of fraternity and justice.

Aimé Césaire also sought to confront the United States with a catalogue of its injustices, and he eventually used his poetry to offer an even more militant set of confrontations than did Damas and Depestre. Although Césaire's literary relations with the United States were not as extensive as those of Damas and Depestre, he was a crucial (and perhaps the most self-conscious) participant in the collaborative hemispheric dialogue about blackness, colonialism, and resistance that emerged in the wake of the New Negro Renaissance. According to Césaire's friend and fellow poet, the future president of Senegal Leopold Senghor, they first encountered the writers of the renaissance between 1929 and 1934, during their time in Paris salons hosted by Paulette Nardal (co-founder of the influential *Revue du monde noir*), where Césaire and Senghor met Claude McKay, Jean Toomer, Langston Hughes, and Countee Cullen.[79] According to A. J. Arnold, Césaire felt the strongest connection, for reasons of class and region, to McKay, although he would subsequently translate works of all three of them. With regard to the African American writers in the Paris salons, "He considered them too bourgeois, too *mulatto*—a term that described quite perfectly the Martinican middle class at the time—and too Catholic."[80] At the same time, Césaire clearly admired all of these writers, as he included substantial translations of Johnson, Toomer, and McKay in the second issue of *Tropiques* (the journal he cofounded with Suzanne Roussi in 1941), and also wrote an introduction to their work for Francophone readers in that same issue. In terms of cross-cultural influences, it is clear from reading almost any of Césaire's poems that he was not strongly influenced by the stylistic techniques of New Negro poetry, though he did seem to sense a literary kinship, particularly with Hughes and McKay, in their mutual desire for black literary expression to turn away from the bourgeoisie and to embrace "primitive" and lower-class subjects. As Clayton Eshleman and Annette Smith note in their introduction to his *Collected Poetry,* "His own poetry does not draw on their forms of expression. As a writer who had repressed his own Creole background and was at this time being influence stylistically by the imaginative synthesis promised by French surrealism, he responded to the Harlem Renaissance mainly as a new collective black voice."[81] Indeed, Césaire's introduction to his translations of New Negro writers in *Tropiques* reveals his hesitancy to embrace the stylistics of the movement, while nonetheless valuing its philosophical and conceptual orientation. Césaire faults the poetry for its being "written only to the rhythm of a juvenile spontaneity," but finds it invaluable in elevating the previously neglected subject of the "common" Negro: "The ordinary Negro, the everyday Negro, whose grotesque or exotic aspect an entire literature is bent on finding, the black poet makes him a hero."[82]

Césaire's first major work, *Cahier d'un retour au pays natal* [*Notebook of a Return to a Native Land*] (1939), works towards a sense of black solidarity, and does so not only with reference to Martinique and fellow Caribbean islands, but also with reference to African Americans. Putting his "pays natal" [native land] in a broader context, he comments, "And my unbounded island, its bright boldness standing behind this Polynesia, before it, Guadeloupe cracked in two along its spine and with the same misery as us, Haiti, where negritude rose up for the first time and said that it believed in its own humanity and the funny little tail [queue] of Florida where they are finishing the lynching of a black man."[83] In the context of U.S-Caribbean connections, Césaire's sweeping vista of the islands is notable for two key assertions of ownership: first, of negritude itself, which he quite reasonably traces to Haiti, and second, of Florida, which is rendered as part of his greater Caribbean. With the grotesque twist on the "queue" of Florida as a means and locus of strangulation, Césaire anticipates his depictions of U.S. racial violence elsewhere in *Cahier* and in subsequent poems. Indeed, in the aftermath of this haunting evocation, Césaire celebrates his island as a space where blackness can flourish, especially in contrast with the United States:

> Who can brag of having it better than I? Virginia.
> Tennessee. Georgia. Alabama.
> Monstrous putrefactions of fruitless
> revolts
> marshes of putrid blood
> trumpets absurdly stopped up.
> red lands, bloody lands, brethren lands [terres sanguines,
> terres consanguines].[84]

Césaire's simple rhetorical question retropes and rephrases notions of American exceptionalism, arguing that, for descendants of the African diaspora, it is the islands, not the United States, that serve as the locus of opportunity in the hemisphere. Beyond offering images of the United States as stained land and barbaric swamps, Césaire makes a significant transition in the original French at the end of this passage by shifting from "sanguines" to "consanguines." The denotation of the first word is clear, as it evokes the sense of "bloody land" from the violence in the U.S. South. To assert that the land is "consanguines," however, is to claim a cultural linkage between his islands and the United States. Thus while Césaire takes pains to distinguish his "pays natal" from the scarred landscape of the U.S. South, he nonetheless extends a hand to his African American brethren in the north—a gesture that will take on more militant connotations in subsequent poems.

In *Cahier*, Césaire charted the Caribbean islands as a sanctuary from the violence of the United States and treated the questions of racial injustice in passing; in subsequent poems like "Mississippi" and "State of the Union," he places questions of U.S. injustice at the center of his work and, even more boldly than Guillén, Damas, or the early Depestre, figures the Caribbean as an imposing ally for African Americans. In these poems, Césaire puts into practice the politics he advocates in "Discourse on Colonialism." Although the bulk of "Discourse" is directed towards questions of European colonialism and its legacy, Césaire calls into question the possibility of the United States as providing an alternative. He situates the Caribbean islands as a crucial bulwark against expanding U.S. neo-imperialism, describing them as "at the gates of America," and exhorts his fellow West Indians not to look "upon that country [the United States] as a possible liberator. . . . [For] American domination [is] the only domination from which one never recovers."[85]

Césaire's poems addressing the United States make clear how that country could harm the Caribbean irrevocably—namely through its racism and racial violence—and argue that instead of being liberated by the U.S., the islands need to help their black brethren in the north be liberated from Jim Crow. In "Mississippi," for example, Césaire offers a critique of the United States in four relatively short anaphoric stanzas, each beginning with the phrase, "Too bad for you men who don't see."[86] At first, the poem appears to focus exclusively on witnessing and remembering violence, in contrast to those men "who don't see": "my eyes remember slingshots and black flags/that kill with each blink of my eyelids."[87] The poem then evokes a sense of gestating militancy, pitying the men of Mississippi for not noticing that "there is a buffalo who waits, sunk to its eyes in the swamp."[88] Césaire's "buffalo" is an apt image for black power, not only because of its color, patience, and strength, but because the term hints at the U.S. slang term "buffalo soldier," which refers to the African Americans regiments of the U.S. army who helped conquer the West and who fought in the Spanish-American War. In this poem, however, the buffalo will fight the expanding power of the United States rather than abet it: the black power upon which the U.S. has depended for support will turn against it. Most powerfully, the poem closes with a description of how the poet's words will establish a linkage between the waiting buffalo and Mississippi: "you cannot stop me from building plenty/of islands, like egg-heads, out of the blazing sky/under the calm ferocity of the huge geranium of our sun."[89] Césaire's combining of "calm ferocity" with an image of a geranium offers a richly paradoxical image of flowering militancy, deploying as its vehicle a metaphor of an otherwise innocuous flower. The image of justice-in-waiting reveals the mistake of viewing the Caribbean as merely a source of tropical beauty, and instead recaptures its history as a space of liberation and insurrection. In doing so, Césaire resurrects the revolutionary potential of the islands, no doubt with an aim to play upon older U.S. fears about black militancy in the Caribbean. Moreover, Césaire's metapoetic claim that his words build more "islands" for the lurking buffalo, suggests an imposing propinquity—that the Caribbean thirst for justice is leaping, island by island, towards the United States itself.

Césaire's most direct poem regarding racial violence in the United States, " . . . sur l'état de l'Union" [. . . on the state of the Union], deploys a similar vision of prophetic justice, lamenting the murder of Emmett Till and using it as a cause for investigating the "state of the Union," in the U.S. Césaire begins with a catalogic enumeration of the material resources of the United States (years worth of minerals, ores, etc.) but concludes that, in contrast, there is "Nothing, zero" in the nation's heart.[90] In contrast to this hollowness, Till is celebrated for his blood and his spirit. Césaire compares Till's eyes to a sea conch and his blood to wine as the poem develops. The first image produces a sensation of resounding depth and evokes a sense of kinship for Till with the islands. The second image hints at a more sacred connection, and Césaire ultimately renders the kinship between Till and the Caribbean on biblical terms, evoking both the Old and New Testament by hinting first at Cain and then at the communion of the Last Supper: "and as for your blood, let it hide the sun from me, let it be mixed with my bread."[91] The poem closes with a grotesque refiguration of the U.S. eagle as engaged in the "limp flight of a vampire that suddenly glides,"[92] and a question that poses the paradoxical suggestion that those vampiric enterprises have left the nation bloodless: "what, nothing, zero,/not even a drop/of blood in the sterile flesh of the white heart?"[93] In tandem with his indictment of the vampiric United States, Césaire continues his catalog of resources, in diminishing numbers of years left. This litany not only suggests that the days of material prosperity for the United States are numbered, but even more damningly, that it lacks a functioning heart—a critique that reaches back to Martí and Sylvain's concerns at the turn of the century.

Langston Hughes's Poetry on the Caribbean and Translations of Guillén

In comparison with Caribbean poets' significant literary engagement with the United States, Langston Hughes touched only very lightly on the Caribbean in his poetry. In the enormous corpus of his poems only six make reference to the islands, and only four directly address the region. Sometimes Hughes addresses his neighboring region as a gesture of solidarity. "Always the Same" (1932) mentions Haiti alongside Sierra Leone and Alabama; "Prelude to Our Age" (1951) places Toussaint L'Ouverture in a continuous lineage of black patriots like Crispus Attucks and Nat Turner. "Havana Dreams" (1933) continues the exotic and erotic tropes he deployed in *Tropics after Dark,* as the speaker celebrates the tempting "dreams" of the island: cocktails, flowers, and a mysterious woman.[94] Hughes's use of tropical clichés to figure island "dreams" stands in marked contrast to the gravitas with which he represents, in a wide range of poems, African Americans' "dream deferred." Other short poems from Hughes reckon with the past and future of the islands through imagistic gestures. In "Caribbean Sunset" (1926), for example, Hughes evokes the history of violence in the Caribbean by comparing its sunset to a "hemorrhage" (98). "To the Little Fort of San Lazaro on the Ocean Front, Havana" contemplates whether or not the fort, constructed to withstand pirate raids, can endure the expanding threats of U.S. imperialism. The poem offers a clever historical jab by finding a piratical continuity between the corsairs of the past and U.S. neocolonial capitalists in the present, such as National City Bank. At the same time, even as the poem offers a critique of U.S. imperialism, it is invested with a reductive pity, as it concludes with the suggestion that the fort might "tumble down, / Stone by helpless stone" (136). Hughes's vision of the "helpless" fort, even if laced with irony, renders the Caribbean impotent. Guillén, Damas, Depestre, and Césaire, in contrast, express faith in the capacity of Caribbean islands to resist the United States and to intervene in questions of racial justice to the north.

Hughes's longest poem on the Caribbean emerged from his participation in antifascist propaganda from the left as World War II developed. While Hughes, along with many leftists, at first opposed U.S. entry into World War II, he changed his stance once Hitler broke the German-Soviet Non-aggression Pact, and he then turned his creative energies to support the war. Because of his important stature as an African American poet with a reputation in the islands, the *People's Voice* asked Hughes to write a poem for an issue to be disseminated in the Caribbean. Hughes's poem, entitled "Broadcast to the West Indies," was published in August 1943, and while it is by no means one of his best poems in terms of technique, it is powerfully revealing of the anxious points of unity between the Caribbean and the United States. The poem begins in the manner of a radio address, saying "hello" to a large list of Caribbean spaces—Jamaica, Haiti, Cuba, Panama, St. Kitts—and then speaks for Harlem, "island too," as kindred to the Caribbean (273).

As the poem develops, Harlem explores this kinship with the islands —"You are dark like me/Colored with many bloods like me"—but also recognizes that racial conflicts in the United States might cause the Caribbean to turn away from helping the U.S. during the war. To answer this concern, the poem asserts a shared history of subjugation for Harlem and the West Indies, as well as a common cause to end it:

In common certain things we know:
    We are tired!
    Those things
    Must go! (274)

The poem closes with a chant of resistance in support of the war: "FOR FREEDOM!/WE PREPARE!" (275). Throughout the poem, Hughes establishes an intimate "imagined community"[95] between Harlem and the Caribbean ("a direct line/From your heart to mine"). There are, of course, problems with this metaphor. Beyond the fact that diaspora, colonization, and immigration make the assertion of a "direct line" precarious, the idea that the West Indies (or Harlem, for that matter) has one "heart" seems to fly in the face of the diverse range of islands cited in the poem. At the same time, as a piece of war propaganda the poem is skillfully wrought, and Hughes's slogan "for freedom we prepare" is richly resonant. This exhortation implicitly links the global and the local, connecting the struggle for freedom from fascism to other struggles for freedom in both the United States and the islands, such as calls for civil rights in the U.S. and demands for independence in the West Indies.

Hughes may not have written extensive poetry about the Caribbean, in part, because he was engaged in substantive translations of the works of Caribbean writers and may have wanted to let them speak on their own terms. Throughout the 1940s, Hughes translated important poems by Cuban modernists like Nicolás Guillén, Gustavo Urrutia, and Regino Pedroso, as well as fiction from the Haitian novelist Jacques Roumain. In addition, Hughes gathered a body of Caribbean poetry for an anthology he coedited with Arna Bontemps entitled *Poetry of the Negro* (1949). In the process of translating and collecting the works of these authors, Hughes appeared to gain a new understanding of the islands' potential as a site for art and activism, as his subsequent essays on the West Indies would reflect his respect for Caribbean cultural authority and autonomy.

At the same time, as Vera Kutzinski has well traced, Hughes's choices in translating Cuban poets, and Guillén in particular, have the effect of (mis)appropriating (one might even say annexing) *afrocubanismo* poetry into the African American blues tradition.

Hughes's translation of Guillén's poetry, prepared in collaboration with Ben Frederic Carruthers and entitled *Cuba Libre* (1948), drew upon two decades of Guillén's poetry to offer a putatively representative selection of Guillén's work. Many of Hughes's choices show an implicit desire to make a cultural translation of Cuban idioms into poetic tropes that would have been familiar to U.S. audiences. Hughes's translation of "Tu no sabe inglé," under the title "Don't Know No English," is an apt microcosm of his methods in representing Guillén's verse to a U.S. audience. Hughes imposes an ungrammatical, double negative title on the poem, one that is not reflected in the Spanish grammar. In addition, Hughes inflects the poem with heavy phonetic dialect that is not present in Guillén's original: "dat," "L'il," "fo'," "jes," "yo'," "'Merican." Guillén uses some dialect gestures in the poem, such as dropping the final "s" or initial "a" from some words, but his Spanish is much more normative and grammatical than Hughes's translation implies. Moreover, the words that Hughes translates into dialect have no irregular construction or spelling in Guillén's original that would suggest he intended to convey a vernacular pronunciation. Indeed, in Guillén's poem, the language that is represented in the most estranged manner is English itself: "one two three" is phonetically rendered as "guan, tu, tri." Hughes's dialect choices thus reverse the linguistic thrust of the poem. He regularizes the English of Manué, which is rendered dialectically in Guillén, while making the speaker's voice estranged and non-normative. In this translation and elsewhere in *Cuba Libre,* Hughes uses putatively African American dialectical forms with even heavier force than in his own vernacular poems. In addition, Hughes often adds extra, repeated lines to Guillén's stanzas so that he can fit them into blues structures akin to his own blues-inflected poetry. According to Kutzinski, the result of these choices is to produce "an *effect* of cultural homogeneity" that conflates Afro-Cuban culture with conventional representations of African American poetry.[96]

In addition, one might argue that the act of rendering Cuban dialect via African American dialectical clichés invokes troubling traditions of minstrelsy and dialectical misrepresentation. Kutzinski suggests that Hughes and Carruthers were aware of the complex relationship that their educated African American readers would have had with such dialectical choices. Writes Kutzinski:

> Not turning them into Negro dialect poems would have made them too alien to African American readers, while using dialect made them potentially all too familiar. Hughes no doubt speculated that if the black bourgeoisie and the black intelligentsia were hostile to American Negro dialect poetry as a suitable literary vehicle for representing their own lives, they might be more accepting of this mode when it was used to represent other parts of the African diaspora.[97]

I would further add that Hughes's choices in dialect allowed him a paradoxically doubled effect of distancing and (false) intimacy. To render Guillén's poetry in conventional dialect situated his poetry as that of a naïve if not primitive "other," while also permitting Guillén to be read as an extension of a U.S. tradition. Whether or not his readers liked dialect poetry, the fact that Hughes positioned his translation within a recognizable U.S. tradition served to uphold a sense that the legitimating forms of representing black culture (whatever one's stance) remained fixed in a U.S. context.

Hughes's use of a blues format would have also furthered a familiarizing aim, but it must be noted that it was Hughes's friends in Cuba, not Hughes himself, who first suggested a parallel between the blues and the *son*. For example, as Hughes prepared for his first visit to Cuba, Gustavo Urrutia wrote to Hughes and described the poetry of Guillén in parallel to the vernacular poetry of the United States:

> They are real Cuban negro poetry written in the very popular slang. They are the exact equivalent of your "blues." The language and feelings of our dear negroes made most notable by the love and talent of our own poets. I am only sorry that you will be unable to translate, and even understand what these poems mean, but you must know that the spirit of them is same as the blues, some are sad, some are ironical, others are sociological.[98]

Urrutia continues, in that same letter, to explain how Hughes's own poetry and stature was inspirational to his Cuban brethren: "You know how much we appreciate you, this explains why I communicate with you in this exciting manner before I do with any other of my friends." Indeed, when Hughes traveled to Cuba in 1930, the local literary and cultural journals were abuzz with commentary about him, and many of them placed blues-inflected work in parallel with new Cuban poetry based in the *son* form. The leading literary critic of the younger generation in Cuba, José Antonio Fernández de Castro, gave readers an introduction to Hughes in *Revista de la Habana,* along with translations of some of his poems,[99] and Salvador Novo published a small survey of the historical emergence of black poetry in the United States to prepare his readers for Hughes's work.[100] Guillén published an interview he conducted with Hughes and praised him not only for the musicality of his poetry—"He, more than any other poet in his idiom, has succeeded in incorporating in North American literature the most pure manifestations of popular music in the U.S. so influenced by the Negroes"—but also suggested, playfully, that Hughes could "pass" as Cuban: "He seems truly a 'mulatto' Cuban."[101] Fernández de Castro also made ample comparisons between Guillén and Hughes in terms of the blues in private correspondence. Writing to James Weldon Johnson, he observed that "Guillén, by the way, is the literary sensation down there at the moment with his Cuban 'Blues.' Has two full pages in *Social,* the Havana *Vanity Fair.*"[102] Fernández de Castro even humorously referred to Guillén as "the Cuban Langston Hughes."[103] Guillén himself wrote to Hughes to express confidence in Hughes's translations, although he regretted that he did not know English sufficiently well to judge them: "I lament that I do not know sufficient English to judge the translations: but with you being responsible, I am sure that they have surpassed my originals."[104]

Colleagues in Haiti also looked to Hughes for inspiration and solidarity during the 1940s. René Piquion, of Haiti, published a monograph on his work, and traveled to the United States in 1945 to prepare a book to introduce Haitian and Francophone West Indians to African American life there.[105] I mention these details of correspondence not to argue that Hughes deserved carte blanche in his translations, but to show that his Cuban and Haitian colleagues put him and his poetry in parallel with their own and trusted his ability to translate their works effectively for a U.S. audience.

For the purpose of cross-cultural comparison of U.S.-Caribbean representations of one another, it is not only the details of translation in *Cuba Libre* that are revealing, but even more so Hughes's choices of *what* to translate, or, perhaps more pointedly, what *not* to translate. Kutzinski notes that Hughes promoted *Cuba Libre* as an "ideal gift for lovers of . . . our good neighbor to the South," and argues that he and Carruthers framed the volume to uphold that sense of equivalence and collegiality. Their approach, she writes, "constructs for *Cuba Libre*'s readers a domesticating fiction of easy access to another nation's culture."[106] I agree, and would add that their choice of poems shows a commitment to sustaining that fiction. One might rightly expect that a translator of Guillén's poetry for a U.S. audience would pay particular attention to his poems that touched on the United States, especially given the ongoing debate about cultural and political relations between the countries. In *Cuba Libre,* however, Hughes includes only two poems that touch on the U.S., "Tu no sabe inglé" and "Cantaliso en un bar" ("Song in a Havana Bar," a section of the long poem "José Ramón Cantaliso" discussed earlier in this chapter). Both are both humorous in tone and do not contain the substantive examination of U.S.-Caribbean relations found in "West Indies, Ltd.," for example. Hughes does not comment in correspondence as to how he made his selections, so it is impossible to divine his intent, but he clearly excluded Guillén's poems that addressed the United States most directly. The challenging nature of Guillén's representations of the United States may have dissuaded Hughes from including such poems, particularly if one of Hughes's goals was to make Guillén palatable to a U.S. audience.

Questions as to where the Caribbean fit into a continuum of global blackness would also surround Hughes's ambitious collection of poetry of and about blacks, the anthology entitled *Poetry of the Negro: 1746–1949* (1949). Produced in collaboration with Arna Bontemps, this volume attempted to be the most encyclopedic anthology yet of poetic representations of black life. Spanning over two-hundred years, *Poetry of the Negro,* at least in its original conception, had a profoundly cross-cultural and cosmopolitan emphasis. The volume included not only African American poetry from Phyllis Wheatley to Gwendolyn Brooks, but also extensive selections from Caribbean poets, white poets writing about "the Negro" (e.g., Walt Whitman, Muriel Rukeyser), and the work of one African poet. From the standpoint of Caribbean-U.S. cultural crosscurrents, Hughes offered a significant representation of the West Indies in the first edition of the anthology. The Caribbean section occupied about one quarter of the anthology and included forty poets, categorized by island. This section was a veritable who's who of the Caribbean, encompassing six different islands (Jamaica, Trinidad, Barbados, Haiti, Cuba, and Martinique) and also treating three Latin American countries (Honduras, British Guiana, and French Guiana) as part of that geographic space. Beyond the range and depth of this selection, Hughes's extensive discussions with Bontemps about the Caribbean section, and the elaborate pas de deux of correspondence in obtaining rights to all those poems, well speak to his commitment to represent the Caribbean in the anthology. It is all the more surprising, then, that in plans for a subsequent edition of the anthology, Hughes was willing to jettison the Caribbean section altogether. In correspondence with Bontemps regarding a second edition, he related his plan to make room to include the latest poems by and about African Americans: "To keep to approximately the same number of pages, but at the same time adding twenty or so new Negro poets, and adding samples of those white poets who have written significantly about the Negro since 1950, I proposed dropping in its entirety the 'Caribbean' section, and placing Claude McKay in the U.S.A. group, our first section."[107] In his handling of McKay, Hughes echoed the appropriative gestures of *The New Negro,* which valued McKay's contribution but minimized his island background. In terms of the broader editing choice, anyone who has edited an anthology can sympathize with Hughes's dilemma—what to fit in, what to cut—but it is striking that he did not propose eliminating what would seem a relatively obvious choice (at least, from the standpoint of diasporic solidarity): the large body of poems by white writers (almost all from the United States) about African Americans. It was less important to Hughes to preserve the Caribbean voices of his original anthology than to maintain a critical mass of U.S. writing, whether by whites or blacks. Hughes thus built on the New Negro tradition of privileging U.S. African Americans as the legitimating voice of "the Negro," but pushed that tradition in an even more nationalistic and "patriotic" direction by suggesting that U.S. writers, whether white or black, were the relevant authorities on the subject. Perhaps Hughes was contributing to the cold-war consensus privileging U.S. exceptionalism, or perhaps he wanted to legitimate the United States as the source for representing "the Negro," but the effect was that Hughes's domestic interests trumped the cosmopolitan ones that characterized his previous representations.

Langston Hughes Abroad: Travel Writing from the Caribbean

Hughes's complex contradictions in his choices of how to represent the West Indies in his poetry and drama were paralleled by conflicted dimensions in his travel writing about the islands in the 1940s and 1950s. In the decade after World War II, Hughes contributed essays to a number of African American magazines, such as *Jet* and *Ebony,* that were campaigning to increase tourism to the Caribbean and to boycott vacation spots in the United States that did not afford equal respect to African Americans. In an ironic reversal of some of the discourse of *The New Negro,* places like Jamaica and Haiti, rather than Harlem, emerge in the travel writing of this period as racial utopias for African Americans.

Hughes's first travel writing about the Caribbean in the 1940s focused on Jamaica, and he effectively portrays it as a utopic escape for African

American men in particular, who could escape not only Jim Crow but domesticity in vacationing to the island. Hughes commends Jamaica as the "perfect prejudice-free vacation spot" and praises Jamaicans for being "delighted to entertain visitors of their own color" (Hughes, *Collected Works* 9:282, 284). Hughes notes the excitement of being in a country where blacks were in the majority: "Some 98 per cent of the population is descended from African slaves. Not until we got to the center of the town did I see any white people at all, and then not many" (9:285). In taking stock of the population in this manner, Hughes reveals to his readers the prospect of a nearby island where white is "other," and where the civil order is in the hands of black men, rather than white police, praising "the handsome tall dark traffic cops in blue trousers, white jackets, and white helmets" (286). Hughes takes particular care describing the women of the country, and on this subject, he plays into U.S. stereotypes of exotic sexuality in the islands. The second half of the article is effectively a catalog of feminine beauties: "luscious brown" beauty queens, "coolie girls" (Chinese-East Indian women) "golden with lustrous hair and dreamy eyes," and "willing young ladies from chocolate browns to peaches-and-creams" (9:287).

Beyond celebrating the beauty of the women, Hughes renders them as exotic commodities for consumption. Besides the language of appetite already cited (e.g., "luscious"), Hughes, almost projects a sense of early ripeness for his male readers: "It seems that girls mature early in the tropics and at sixteen they are ready to be kissed" (9:287). Central to the pleasures of island romance is the close proximity of nature. He conjures an imagined scene for his readers, pointedly placed in the second person:

> With a girl and a car you drive through the starry night perhaps to the Wickie Wackie on the open ocean seven miles from town. . . . Here you dance on a little raised dance floor, or drink at the tiny thatched bar. When the late moon rises, if the mood strikes you, leave your shoes under the table, take the girl's hand and run barefooted through the trees down to the sea and across the sand into the warm surf. In the golden moonlight with the lights and music of the club farther and farther away you wander down the beach. The night, the sand, the sea, the stars. (9:287–88)

Hughes effectively creates a miniature anecdote of urban escape in this passage. Notably, Hughes shows a sense of romance on the islands as untainted not only by the city, but by domesticity itself, as he suggests that the women of the islands are invested in the magic of the moment, rather than angling for marriage. Describing the close of an imagined assignation, Hughes assures the "you" that "just because a girl calls you 'darling' you don't *have* to stay" (9:288).

Hughes returns to a more polemical and political tone at the end of the article, albeit figured in a description of the pleasant natural environment of the island: "Although Jamaica has perpetual summer, in the towns there are almost no flies or mosquitoes. In the country snakes are just about unheard of, because the mongoose has eaten them up. Jamaica is a calm and beneficent land with few if any plagues. Certainly it is not plagued by Jim Crow, which is a very great blessing for colored vacationists" (9:289). Hughes's closing comments hinge upon a clever turn on the concept of "plague," which reverses traditional expectations of island perils. Whereas many colonial descriptions of Cuba, Haiti, and Puerto Rico traditionally offered cautionary tales of tropic lassitude and disease, here it is the United States that emerges as a contaminated space in comparison to Jamaica.

Hughes's most extensive travel writing emerged in several articles written for the *Chicago Defender*, which was sponsoring a trip to Haiti as a prize for a popularity contest for female readers. Hughes discussed the extensive cultural resources and traditions on the island, both of the elite and of the folk, including voodoo, and he even provided a bibliography for his readers who wished to read more about Haiti. Hughes focused upon the social and political landscape of the island, with particular emphasis on distinctions between Haiti and the United States:

> If the Defender's Popularity Contest winners are "race" women, they will love Haiti because it is truly a Negro country from the President down. Haiti is nobody's colony. Colored people own it and run it. And there is no Jim Crow. It is true that there are social levels, classes, and caste, which we have in the U.S.A., too. But there are no FOR WHITE ONLY signs in the entire country.[108]

The praise of Haiti as a "truly Negro country" has its most obvious political resonance in a nationalist sense of pride, combined with a vision of autonomy that casts the Jim Crow U.S. in a comparatively shameful light. Hughes's attention to the revolutionary history of the island also shows, perhaps, his sense that the island has a message for his African American readers beyond a critique of Jim Crow: "But more thrilling than its scenery and more stirring than its music, is its history. Haiti has a great and noble past. Toussaint, Dessalines, and Christophe dignify the history of the New World. And the Haitians, under their leadership, were the first Negroes in the Americas to free themselves from slavery. Nobody set the Haitians free. They freed themselves."[109] Hughes offers a useful lesson regarding the accomplishments of Haitian patriots, and he may also have been aiming to nudge his U.S. readers in a more militant direction by recalling this heroic history.

It may have also been important to Hughes to impress upon his relatively bourgeois readers that the United States was not the sole model for uplift and cultural development. Speaking to the questions of culture, both high and low, in a follow-up article, he commented,

> Most Haitians have never left their native island. And to visitors from the United States, the customs of the peasantry will seem picturesque and quaint, the rhythms of the congo drums infectious, and the dancing amazing. But many educated Haitians speak English. And the manners and the customs of their upper classes will seem no wise strange or quaint. In fact their poise and sophistication often surpasses that of persons of comparable stations in life in Negro America.[110]

Even as Hughes notes that some customs of the island will seem "quaint," the general tenor of this passage serves to de-exoticize the Haitian classes, by referencing their mastery of English, as well as their "poise and sophistication." In stating that the educated classes of Haiti "often surpass" comparable persons in the United States, Hughes confronts his own educated readers with the possibility that they are part of a broader New World black educated class, and not necessarily the pinnacle of it, as had been supposed in the discourse of the New Negro.

Several years after his visits to Haiti, Hughes reported again for the *Chicago Defender* from the Caribbean, this time from the Bahamas. Because the Bahamas are much closer to the United States and have been a more habitual destination for white U.S. tourists, these islands offered Hughes an object lesson for considering a cross-cultural hybrid, where black West Indian traditions and U.S. traditions cohabited. As in previous accounts of U.S. influence in Haiti or the canal zone, Hughes's article represents the U.S. presence as an invasive culture whose impact is *un*-civilizing the islands and spreading racial division that threatens to harm their social fabric. Hughes writes that on Nassau "there is a color line . . . since it is so near our American South. The deluxe hotels, restaurants, and beaches are not open to Negro patronage."[111] As in his writing on Jamaica, the Jim Crow color line is figured as a kind of expanding contagion, governed by proximity to the United States. At the same time, using a kind of differential diagnosis, Hughes still describes the islands in a favorable light compared to the U.S: "But there are no WHITE or COLORED signs such as Florida has, only an hour away, and no Jim Crow buses or taxis, and none of the red-necked rudeness in public services common to our mainland."[112] As in his handling of Haiti and Jamaica, Hughes repositions the Caribbean islands—even those influenced by Jim Crow—as more civilized than the United States, which has yet to overcome its "plagues" and "red-necked rudeness." Indeed, in a subsequent article on Nassau, in which Hughes offers more explicit criticism of the "color line" in the Bahamas and suggested that wealthy African Americans visit Haiti, Jamaica, or Cuba instead, he complains that "Nassau is quite Americanized."[113] Thus Hughes deploys the term "Americanization," a label usually deployed in U.S. discourse with a sense of approbation and cultural progress, and converts it into a badge of dishonor. Indeed, right after this description of Nassau, he faults the island for lacking the cultural depth and resources of Jamaica or Haiti: "There is nothing like the Myrtle Bank Hotel in Kingston or the Splendide in Port-au-Prince, where the silver is heavy, the table linen rich, and the wine steward will bring you whatever vintage you have the taste and intelligence—plus the money—to order."[114] In addition, Hughes argues that the wealthy U.S. hotels fail to include the vibrant vernacular culture of the island:

> At the fashionable Nassau hotels, like the British Colonial, I'll bet they never serve conch salad. And they probably drink the same drinks as at the Waldorf-Astoria in New York, the Ritz in Paris, or the Savoy in London—and never heard of Vat 19—which is maybe why the tourists from these hotels come "over the hill" to the night clubs at night to hear calypso bands and watch the Negroes dance—because only folks who drink Vat 19 and eat conch salad could dance with so much vigor.[115]

Hughes's critique of the stale bar cultures in the white hotels anticipates the late-twentieth-century concern that Americanization means standardization. In this regard, the traveler at the "Americanized" hotel has the worst of both worlds: neither the sumptuous culture of an elite Haitian or Jamaican hotel, nor the vibrant vernacular culture of the neighborhoods.

At the same time that Hughes was commenting upon the Bahamas in his articles, he made a similar case for the damaging effects of the United States upon Cuba in the opening chapters of *I Wonder as I Wander.*

Hughes describes a dichotomous experience within Cuba. Institutions and businesses that primarily served Cubans proved to be essentially color blind for Hughes: "Purely Cuban hotels, with no eye out for tourists, cater to guests of all shades of complexion and the service is most courteous."[116] Those places that had become Americanized had started to maintain Jim Crow, however: "The use of Havana as a winter playground for American tourists has, of course, brought its quota of Southern racial prejudice from the mainland. Hotels that formerly were lax in their application of the color line now discourage even mulatto Cubans, thus seeking the approval of their American clientele" (46). Hughes relates a particularly galling incident of being denied access to a beach club, even though he was invited by an influential member, his friend José Fernández de Castro (who had introduced him to Guillén). Barred from entering the beach by an American bouncer, Hughes exclaims, "Do you mean to tell me that you're drawing the color line on a *Cuban* beach against *American* citizens—and you're an American yourself?" (47). This single sentence captures the paradoxical, multinational (and perhaps antinational) implications of Jim Crow. The enforcement of a U.S. color line on the Cuban beach represents an infringement upon Cuban customs and culture, and the bouncer's threatening an American citizen on foreign soil reveals that his sense of national loyalty is compromised by his racism. Indeed, when Hughes and his friend Zell are arrested for refusing to leave, he realizes that he cannot count on any help from the U.S. consulate. Instead, it is the local police and a judge who provide aid to Hughes and an apology. The judge admonishes the beach attendants: "What you have done is against all the tenets of Cuban hospitality and against Cuban law, which recognizes no differences because of race or color" (49). The judge's twinned critique of Jim Crow on the basis of authority both official (the law) and unofficial (the culture of hospitality) positions Cuban society as possessed of an enlightenment and civilization that is being undermined by the U.S. presence.

Taken together, one might argue that Hughes's travel writings not only celebrate the islands for their richness, but also make the case that, at least in terms of cultural and social development, the U.S. presence furthers a "bad neighbor" policy in the region, whether from its spreading of Jim Crow or its denaturing of both elite and vernacular island cultures. Moreover, one might argue that the positive examples Hughes cites of national autonomy and black majority power might provide a "good neighbor" example for the United States to emulate and for which the black upper classes should advocate.

A Miraculous Similarity? George Lamming and Richard Wright Assess the Parallels between the United States and the Caribbean

At the same time that Hughes was presenting lessons from the Caribbean to his North American readers, a subsequent generation of Caribbean writers—notably George Lamming and Paule Marshall—wrestled with the model that the United States provided for race relations. Although Lamming and Marshall found different paths in their lives and in their works, each was alike in using the United States as a foil to consider the strengths and limitations of the Caribbean for black opportunity. Whereas prior black West Indian writers had critiqued the United States for its racial failings and looked to the islands—even in their colonized state—as a fruitful alternative, Lamming and Marshall used an analysis of the overt system of discrimination in the U.S. to expose the covert methods of exclusion in the Caribbean islands.

In terms of cross-cultural influence, the careers of Marshall and Lamming form ideal case studies for the 1950s. Each acknowledged the influence of African American literature on their works, and each benefited from the help of an African American mentor in entering the U.S. literary marketplace. Lamming has described the shaping role of Richard Wright's autobiography *Black Boy* on his autobiographical novel *In the Castle of My Skin.*[117] More directly, Wright found a U.S. publisher for the novel and wrote an introduction for it, in which he praised Lamming as a kindred spirit—"One feels not so much alone when, from a distant witness, supporting evidence comes to buttress one's testimony."[118] Marshall writes extensively of having been inspired by and mentored by New Negro Renaissance writers in her memoir *Triangle Road.* She describes Hughes as "my benefactor" for his encouragement of her work and for inviting her to join him as a cultural ambassador for the United States Information Service during the cold war.[119] Because the connections between these authors are so explicit, critics have generally been aware of this cultural traffic, particularly the ways in which Caribbean writers were influenced by Wright and Hughes. At the same time, critics have not fully reckoned with some of the significant components of the cross-cultural dialogue between these writers, such as the elements of Lamming's and Marshall's works that treat the United States as "other," or instances where the West Indian writers influenced their U.S. colleagues.

Richard Wright's small but illuminating body of writings on the Caribbean provides a model example of how African American dialogue about the region evolved over the course of the 1940s and 1950s. Considering Wright's vast body of travel writings, which touch on almost every region of the United States and the world at large,[120] he was comparatively reticent about the Caribbean. His Caribbean writings encompass a number of *Daily Worker* articles from 1937 and an unfinished travel narrative from 1950 entitled *Haitian Biographies*. Overall, Wright's writings move from pity for the oppressed brethren in the Caribbean to a respect for the revolutionary potential in the islands.

The four articles that Wright wrote for the *Daily Worker* over the course of 1937 treated the Caribbean as a more primitive parallel to the political landscape of the United States. Wright placed the suppression of trade union uprisings in Barbados and Trinidad that year by the British colonial authorities in parallel with the Scottsboro case, an oddly forced comparison that depicts, in microcosm, the problems Wright faced in applying models of racial conflict in the United States to the Caribbean. The young men in the Scottsboro case were literally innocent bystanders made into victims, whereas the trade unionists were engaged in an incipient class revolt against the holders of capital in the colonies. Oddly enough, Wright makes no attempt to place the trade union activities in parallel with domestic events like the Pullman strike. Indeed, Wright uses a rhetoric of victimhood that underrates the agency of West Indians. He represents the activists as hapless "victims" of "feudalism" and endorses a fellow Harlem activist's call that U.S. citizens should "render every possible aid to the helpless natives of Trinidad and Barbados in their struggle."[121] Wright's language, although sympathetic, is condescending and sounds almost unwittingly imperialistic, especially in the use of the term "natives," as if West Indians were an innocent tribe in need of rescue. Like their predecessors in the New Negro movement, Wright and his fellow U.S. communists claimed a monopoly on political agency: they had tools to export to the Caribbean, but not the other way around.[122]

Wright's unpublished manuscript from his travel to Haiti, entitled *Haitian Biographies*,[123] is undated, but both internal and external evidence demonstrate that it must be from 1950, when he spent two weeks on the island. Wright's interviewees refer to 1949 as the preceding year and consider their prospects in relation to the 1947 revolution. Wright's opening paragraph to this manuscript, with corrections, provides dramatic insight into the conflicted nature of his reactions to the region:

> On a recent visit to Haiti I was struck less by the exotic nature of its drums and Voodoo religion than by the sense of perturbation that lay behind the

> words and actions of its young people. The majestic contours of the Haitian landscape were much less appealing to my sensibilities than the chronic poverty of its millions of black peasants who are seeking so valiantly to rise from the dirt which chains them to their station in life. Between the ~~light-skinned elite which wields so much influence in Haitian life~~ educated minority and the voiceless peasants there is emerging a middle group whose lives are moving ~~upwards from the folk anchored superstitions of the past~~ towards a freer and less traditional conception of life and individual action.[124]

This text-in-process embodies a microcosm of Wright's conflicted views on the Caribbean. His replacing "the light-skinned elite which wields so much influence in Haitian life" with "the educated minority" shows his discomfort with the issue of the color hierarchy in the region and a desire to excise reference to the horizontal exercise of power in Haiti. Wright's editing also suggests that he is unsure of how to handle the conflicts between folk culture and modernity in the Caribbean. His prognosis of a "freer and less traditional conception of life" shows his belief that the "peasantry" must move forward, even as he retreats from writing dismissively of the local culture, deleting his description of "folk anchored superstitions of the past." Wright's conflicted perspective echoes his own description of his complex attitude toward the folk culture of Mississippi in his journal writings and in his poetic-ethnographic study *12 Million Black Voices* (1944).[125]

More broadly, Wright struggles with the question of how Haitian life might change in the future, and how this may or may not be part of a general pattern of revolution he observes throughout the world:

> The aim of the "emotional landscapes" that follow is not to value or judge the validity of such ~~revolts~~ or attempts at altering the rituals of Haitian life; my desire is to present to American readers in terms and concepts familiar to them a few intense life-problems or questions as lived by ~~black~~ Haitians, my conviction being that the color of their skins is of far less moment than the astounding identity which exists between Haitians and other peoples. One of the most startling aspects of life, to my mind, is not the differences which exist between people, but the miraculous similarity which links life on its deepest levels into one vast reservoir of human consciousness and experience.[126]

The small emendations within this passage are quite revealing, as they get to the heart of what may have most confounded Wright in his encounter with the Caribbean. His deletion of "revolts" literally edits out any reference to the social upheaval in Haiti, which parallels his minimizing of the violence in descriptions of Barbados and Trinidad in his *Daily Worker* articles. Even more complex is his deletion of the word "black" in reference to Haitians. One could argue that, given the racial makeup of the island, Wright is deleting a redundant piece of description (i.e., all Haitians are black, so there is no need to say so), but the elision seems to have a deeper resonance, tied into both his reckoning with the color hierarchy in the island and into his desire for universalism in revolutionary activity. This deletion, combined with his elimination of reference to the "light-skinned elite" shows Wright attempting to avoid any substantial reference to racial color at all in this description of Haiti. It is as if he is seeking textually, in his editing of the paragraph, to enforce his claim that there is "a miraculous similarity" between Haitians and other peoples he has observed in the world.

Indeed, a tension between racial consciousness and class consciousness, which had been at the heart of Wright's complex relationship with the American Communist Party, animates the bulk of this manuscript. The body of *Haitian Biographies,* which is largely a collection of portraits of young people discussing the future of Haiti, shows a pastoralizing tone that hearkens back to the language of the "peasant" in New Negro writings about the region, although this time one may detect a note of envy. Wright approvingly notes that there are "no Freudian complexes" in Haiti and that the family dysfunction he experienced as a child was not present: "Family tradition may flow smoothly for generations."[127] Given Wright's progressive interests, he expects those traditions to change and, in keeping with his internationalism, he titles one section the manuscript "The Dawn of Class Consciousness in Haiti," with unintended irony. Most would argue that that "dawn" occurred in 1791 with the Haitian Revolution. Wright's conflicted descriptions, elisions, and emendations in this manuscript show the degree to which the "miraculous similarity" between Haiti and the United States that he had asserted in the opening paragraphs was not readily present. Indeed, most of Wright's deletions have the effect of eliding the complex specifics of the Haitian power structure, shaping it to fit more familiar dynamics that he had observed in the United States and elsewhere. In this respect, it is significant that *Haitian Biographies* is one of the only uncompleted manuscripts among Wright's papers. His integration of the Caribbean into an internationalist worldview would remain an uncompleted project, a perpetual work in progress.[128]

Beyond Wright's observations regarding Haiti, there are substantive and reciprocal influences evident when one considers Wright's *Black Boy*

(1945), Lamming's *In the Castle of My Skin* (1953), and Wright's late novel *The Long Dream* (1958) as part of a hemispheric dialogue about home, identity, and diaspora. *In the Castle of My Skin* shows clear conceptual debts to *Black Boy.* Sandra Pouchet Paquet rightly observes that in addition to sharing an overall frame of "an autobiographical novel of return and reconnection," "Lamming repeats and revises many tropes and rhetorical strategies that Wright used in representing a reality that is historically different from that of *Black Boy.*"[129] Wright's exploration of double consciousness and the existential pressures produced by Jim Crow provided Lamming models for understanding and depicting his protagonists' sense of dislocation and alienation in the British colonial system. Connections between Barbadian and U.S. systems of race are explicitly foregrounded by Lamming's character Trumper, who has come to understand himself and Barbados with a new racial consciousness derived from his experience of Jim Crow. Lamming's novel, in turn, seems to have inspired Wright to take a different approach to understanding race and community in the South. Several years after writing the introduction to *In the Castle of My Skin,* Wright would revisit the U.S. South in his fiction for the first time in more than a decade, penning a novel of childhood development strikingly parallel to Lamming's. Not only does Wright replay crucial scenes of *In the Castle of My Skin,* he also draws upon Lamming's understanding of the self-hatred imposed by the British system as a way of probing more deeply into the psychology of community and class division in the African American South. In contrast to Wright's writings on the Caribbean, in which he tried to incorporate the region into his leftist international vision of uplift, Wright allowed his encounter with the region to transform his novel. One might say that Wright eventually started to see the Caribbean in his U.S. South.

This pattern of mutual inspiration and transformation well illustrates Lamming's vision, articulated in *The Pleasures of Exile* (1960), that writers from the Caribbean and the United States should place themselves in a reciprocal dialogue. Lamming explains that West Indian writers have looked to writers from the U.S. canon as literary brethren, while nonetheless aiming to erect their own tradition:

> We are not afraid to accept those necessary tools which America can offer, but we would like to build our own Pequod. Our desire for dialogue through the sole process of honest talking should not be interpreted as anti-American. It is rather because we are pro-American that we speak in this way. We are pro-Whitman and pro-Melville and pro–Mark Twain. We don't mind worshipping

> in that kind of cathedral; for there is a kind of possibility—indeed, more than a possibility—that we will introduce new psalms.[130]

Lamming establishes this metaphor of a greater cathedral not for the sake of accepting neocolonial dominion; indeed, he warns in that same essay that "we can be colonised by the pleasures that enter with foreign aid."[131] Rather, he aims to reposition the United States into a broader hemispheric model of Prospero and Caliban. As much as he finds that the United States has offered "necessary tools" for writers like himself, Lamming also argues that the U.S. has much to learn from the Caribbean: "America is one island only; and we are used to living with many islands. . . . A large chunk of Africa, that is also a part of us, has always been the conscience of America. And America can learn, by her presence in the Caribbean, how we have lived with that dilemma."[132] Lamming's comment is simultaneously decentering and linking, but not in a contradictory manner. By untethering the United States from its sense of singular mastery ("America is one island only"), he suggests that it can be freer to understand itself in a new context and receive new insights from regions it had thought of as separate and alien.

At first glance, it might seem surprising to use *Black Boy* and *In the Castle of My Skin* as a starting point for reciprocal hemispheric dialogue, as they seem almost philosophically opposed in their conceptions of community. Although the young Wright affirms a feeling of "fraternity"[133] with African American adolescent males, he is generally suspicious of the community as a whole and expresses dismay at the "bare, bleak pool of black life" in which "the people were alike, their homes were alike, and their farms were alike." Lamming's characters, by contrast, consistently articulate a feeling of security within their village. The narrator's friend Trumper (who, ironically, will be the most militant and racially conscious character by the end of the novel) expresses this peace: "'Tis always like this at home. The way we is here. My mother over yonder in that corner, an' my father down there in that corner, an' me somewhere else. An' you get the feelin', you know that everything's all right" (120).

It would be hard to find any passage in *Black Boy* in which there is such a sense of "everything being all right." In fact, Lamming seems most interested in appropriating Wright's vocabulary in describing what is *not* right. In *Black Boy*, the oppressiveness of the Jim Crow system is clear, but equally troubling for Wright are the more subtle effects on his consciousness. Wright describes the whites as "form[ing] a kind of super-world" under which "floated a latent sense of violence" (270). At the end of *Black Boy,* Wright flees not because of any one particular wrong (there is no galvanizing lynching scene, as there is in his story "Big Boy Leaves Home") but because of a generalized anxiety, a need to escape "the pressure" of the South (495). In *In the Castle of My Skin,* the problems are subtler—there is no explicit Jim Crow system, for example—but there is a nameless unease that afflicts many of Lamming's characters, and the author addresses it using a conceptual vocabulary closely linked to Wright's. Significantly, in Lamming these descriptions of mental oppression emerge from scenes not of exclusion (as is the case in Wright), but in scenes of forced inclusion. The ubiquity of the Union Jack, symbol of Barbadians' "privileged" status as "Little England," exerts a profound influence on the narrator: "The colours though three in number had by constant repetition produced something vast and terrible, a kind of pressure or presence of which everyone was a part" (36). Similar to Wright in his sense that there was a "super-world" above him, Lamming's characters feel an omnipresence of white authority ready to discipline them, emblematized in the colonial castle: "The world of authority existed somewhere along the fringe of the villagers' consciousness. . . . The obedient lived in the hope that the Great might not be offended, the uncertain in the fear it might have been" (28–29).

More specific evidence of Lamming's interest in Wright emerges in his revisiting two key scenes from *Black Boy:* Wright's childhood bath scene with his grandmother and Shorty's "earning" a quarter from a white man. Wright's bath scene marks a familial divide, namely between his grandmother and himself. As his grandmother washes his behind, Wright shocks her with an unexpected command: "Before I knew it, words—words whose meaning I did not fully know—had slipped out of my mouth. 'When you get through, kiss back there,' I said" (48). The outcome of this verbal misstep is a beating, but more significantly, exposure and humiliation before the family: the naked Wright runs through the house dodging his grandmother and mother, ultimately fleeing into the backyard "blindly in the dark, butting [his] head up against the fence, the tree" (49). Lamming also renders his narrator's bath a scene of exposure and humiliation, but with a different audience. Rather than fleeing into the backyard, the narrator is bathed there; his punishment arises not because of an insult within the family, but because he remains outside too long, drawing the attention of the neighbors: "The sun had dried me thoroughly, and now it seemed that I had not been bathed, but brought out in open condemnation to be jeered at" (19). When the mother comes out to punish him, the narrator flees inside for safety, which is a telling reversal of Wright. Whereas Wright's family is the grounding point for his alienation, Lamming's home is the grounding point for his safety.

Lamming and Wright each pen powerful scenes of black men abasing themselves for whites' coins, but with a noticeably different tenor in terms of social interaction with other blacks. In *Black Boy,* Wright observes the sad scene of Shorty doing whatever it takes to wheedle a quarter from white folks, culminating in his promise to the white hotel guests that "you can kick me for a quarter" (269). As one might expect, Wright admonishes Shorty, "A quarter can't pay you for what he did to you" (270), but surprisingly, Shorty gets the last word in the argument: "My ass is tough and quarters is scarce" (270). As debasing as this scene may be, Shorty seems to have taught Wright a lesson about material survival in Memphis, and it seems one of the rare scenes of reciprocal communication in the narrative.

Lamming's variation on the coin scene is one of the few places where *In the Castle of My Skin* presents a grimmer scenario than *Black Boy.* Lamming's young boys earn quarters from white men by diving into the water and competing to fetch the coins: "The boys dived and the white men watched the sprawling black limbs in their scramble" (116). The white spectators enjoy the struggle so much that they shift the game into a battle royal between the boys, and use the coins to reward the successful fighters: "The splash was their weapon, and the fight went on until one surrendered, unable to bear the stinging salt of the sea in his eyes. Then the white men tossed a coin, and the winner caught it" (116). This scene of boyhood competition ties into a broader strain of Lamming's portrait, the observation that white society holds power in Barbados by pitting the black West Indians against themselves in a competition to outdo one another. In this respect, Lamming builds upon Wright's scene to address an issue that Wright does not explore in equivalent detail in *Black Boy,* the role that competition among black people plays in aiding white hegemony.

Lamming's exploration of self-division born from the British system demonstrates some of the most important cultural work from which Wright will later learn. As much hostility as Wright shows towards fellow African Americans in *Black Boy,* there is little sense of the black community as upholders of Jim Crow, and the whites are clearly Wright's main enemy. He writes, "A dread of white people came to live permanently in my feelings and imagination" (85). Lamming's novel strikes out in very different terrain by exploring the way that Barbadians oppress themselves on the basis on their internalization of British mores.

Lamming explores, in brilliant indirect discourse, the self-hatred taught by the British: "The image of the enemy, and the enemy was My People. My people are low-down nigger people. My people don't like to see their people get on. The language of the overseer. The language of the civil servant" (27). Such angry language is rarely directed against whites in *In the Castle of My Skin,* largely because the British system has maintained a kind of "secret" hegemony while displacing responsibility for social limitations or exclusions onto the people themselves.

Wright's novel *The Long Dream* shows an appreciation for Lamming's subtle sense of how intraracial competition abets white authority in their communities. After reviewing and introducing *In the Castle of My Skin,* Wright appears to have figuratively "returned home" in *The Long Dream* to make a parallel investigation in his own home region. In its design as a novel of a rural childhood that concludes with a departure from that originary space, *The Long Dream* echoes not only the substance of *Black Boy* but the structure of *In the Castle of My Skin.* In contrast to the perspective in each of the latter works, however, Wright uses *The Long Dream* to explore the consciousness of a person "elevated" above the community. As the son of the wealthy funeral director Tyree, who is supported by white police and politicians, Fishbelly (whose name and family profession are redolent of a gruesome whiteness) is comparable in the position of "the overseers" and "the civil servants" from Lamming's novel. Wright carefully orchestrates Fishbelly's evolving attitude toward blackness, and the reader sees him "educated" into this perspective, much as Lamming's characters are. His mother gives him the first indication that he ought to set himself apart from other African Americans with the comment, "Son, they your *color* but they ain't your *kind.*"[134] Fishbelly later declares to his friends, "*I* ain't no nigger" (32, emphasis added). When his friend Sam counters, "To the white folks, you a nigger," Fishbelly responds, "That only 'cause some of our folks act bad" (32). Fishbelly's primary enemy, in his mind, is not the whites, but "our folks," whose behavior casts him in a bad light. Wright demonstrates how this hatred of other blacks is partly a projection of Fishbelly's own self-hatred, epitomized in his attempt to cover his hands near the end of the novel, "trying vainly to blot out the shameful blackness on him" (407).

A corollary to the shame of "our folks" in *In the Castle of My Skin* is the desire to attain as much "Britishness" as possible, to live up to the privilege of being subjects of "Little England." Lamming thus depicts many of his characters engaged in imitation or repetition of white customs. For example, in the wake of a tea party held by the white landlords, the young boys reenact the scene: "When they had watched the landlord and his friends on the roof of the brick house, they reproduced the scene behind the fence in the open air. They made saucers and cups with a mixture of dirt and water and saliva, leaving them in the sun to bake dry. Then they served a cup of tea from the tap of a standing pipe nearby" (28). Although the resourcefulness of the young boys is impressive, the very fact that their play material is dirt, in comparison to the lavish tea set of the landlords, points out a significant material disparity. This scene seems to be the youthful correlative to the adults' anxieties about the "people as enemy," as the boys attempt to live up to the "tea party" standards of the landlords, rather than imitating their parents' customs.

Lamming's novel shows great awareness of the ways that villagers are engaged in different performances, and he uses the tools of a playwright to accentuate the performative quality of key dialogues. Some older boys, for example, drawing upon their schooling, discuss their desire to "make history," and Lamming renders the scene dramatically:

> *Fourth Boy:* We going to make hist'ry. I always want to make some hist'ry.
>
> *Second Boy:* Me too. I read 'bout all those who been making hist'ry, William the Conqueror an' Richard an' all these. I read how they make hist'ry, an' I say to myself 'tis time I make some too.
>
> *First Boy:* We going to make hist'ry by Foster Fence. Let's make hist'ry. (48)

The vocabulary of these boys shows the marks of their British schooling, and the dramatic form foregrounds the fact that they are repeating, to a great extent, scripts that they have been taught. The only model history-makers available to them are legendary British kings, like Richard and William—they certainly have not been taught about Toussaint L'Overture or Dessalines. The situation is not so hopeless as it may seem, however, for there is a nascent militancy in their language that anticipates the strikes and riots at the end of the novel. They may have learned British history better than their teachers intended, as they have drawn from their studies of William and Richard some lessons about power, and the history they are planning to make is the stoning of the head teacher, Mr. Slime.

Wright draws upon Lamming's exploration of performance in both style and substance, and with a similar suggestion that such performances are not mere mimicry, but can be powerful stepping stones to change. In *The Long Dream,* there are plenty of obvious moments in which either Tyree or Fishbelly seem to be imitating white models unproductively—most noticeably, of course, in their despising fellow blacks.

In other places, Wright explores more subtle performances among the young boys. In almost a direct echo of Lamming's technique, Wright foregrounds these performances through dramatic form, which he had never done in previous novels. As was the case with Lamming, these performances center around issues of power. In perhaps the best example of a Lamming-like moment, Zeke and Sam stage a confrontation between an imagined white man and black man:

> Zeke, *imitating a rich white man:* Sam, you said you wanted to see me? What you want, nigger?
> Sam, *acting with dignity:* I want to talk to you about justice for black folks—
> Zeke, *amazed:* Nigger, what you mean talking to me like that? What do you want with justice? You gitting along awright, ain't you?
> Sam, *indignantly:* I'm talking about gitting us good jobs, Mr. Zeke. We black folks—
> Zeke, *haughtily:* What you niggers always whining about? I ain't your master! Go get you a job! Goddammit, *make* a job! We white folks made ours, didn't we? (109)

Although Wright's characters are engaged in a far more self-conscious performance than Lamming's boys—they are deliberately parroting white arguments for their debate—the cultural work of the performance seems akin to that of the boys who want to "make hist'ry." Wright's boys do not plan any violence, but they enact a kind of imaginative rehearsal of resistance, and Sam pretends to shoot Zeke to conclude the debate.

Wright's use of the boys in *The Long Dream* as sounding boards for debates about economic and political power parallels Lamming's orchestration of the boys' conflicts in *In the Castle of My Skin.* In this regard, I would argue that Wright has adapted and adopted what Pouchet Paquet terms the "polyphonic design"[135] of Lamming's novel: using the boys, in dramatic dialogue, to explore substantive questions of race, nation, and identity. Zeke and Sam, in *The Long Dream,* play roles quite similar to those of Trumper and Bob. Sam, like Bob, seems the voice of authority among the friends, and each is usually the leader in arguments among them. Two of the most parallel debates between these novels center around the question of America. In *In the Castle of My Skin,* Bob, Boy Blue, Trumper, and the narrator struggle to understand America's place in their sense of geography and history:

> "But what about America?" Trumper asked.
> "America?" Bob got up from the rocks.

> "You talking about the olden times," he said. "You talkin' about a way back in 1492. But Barbados wus discovered by the English in 16 something or the other, an' that is modern times."
>
> "An' who discover America?" Trumper asked.
>
> "The English too," Bob said quickly.
>
> "An' where these English come from?" Boy Blue asked.
>
> "From England," Bob said, making the question seem ridiculously simple. (156)

> [Trumper says:] "I want to go away."
>
> "Where you want to go to?" Boy Blue asked. "You always talkin' 'bout you want to go away."
>
> "I don't know," said Trumper, "p'raps to America. They say things good there." (168)

This staccato exchange of questions and answers seems almost like a school drill or quiz. Though Bob's sense that the English are responsible for discovering everything in the Americas is clearly wrong, it is precisely the "right" answer to offer in his English school, presumably. Trumper's desire to go to America (which is somewhat surprising, as he was so secure in his home at the outset of the novel) articulates a different sense of New World geography, as he looks outside the Commonwealth for opportunity. Indeed, it is Trumper who, after visiting the United States, reports back to his friends with a new vision of their northern neighbor and new lessons for life in Barbados. Part of Trumper's descriptions echoes traditional tropes of the U.S. as a place of singular energy and opportunity: "The United States is a place where a man-can-make pots-of-money. . . . 'Tis p'raps the only place in this God's world where there ain't got night an' day" (282–83). Trumper is also unsparing in relating the travails of race prejudice and violence in the United States: "In America I have seen as much as a man get kick down for askin' a question, a simple question. Not here" (295). Trumper learns from this example not that the British system is kinder and better, but that its power is subtle and covert. Commenting on the efficiency of the English as "great administrators," Trumper cites the example of a country club to illustrate the point to his friends:

> There be clubs which you an' me can't go to, an' none o' my people here, no matter who they be, but they don't tell us we can't. The put up a sign, "Members Only," knowin' full well you ain't got no chance of becomin' a member.

> An' although we know from the start why we can't go, we got the consolation we can't 'cause we ain't members. In America they don't worry with that kind o' beatin' 'bout the bush. (295–96)

By seeing the violence of Jim Crow in its most naked form, Trumper is able to establish a comparison with the operations of racist power in Barbados, perceiving that the English have held their power so successfully because it is unspoken and the black Barbadians do not have to confront overt and codified racism. Lamming reflects on this same issue in *The Pleasures of Exile:* "The West Indian, however black and dispossessed, could never have felt the experience of being in a minority. For the black faces vastly outnumber the white or expatriate white. This numerical superiority has given the West Indian a certain leisure, a certain experience of relaxation among white expatriates; for the West Indian has learned, by sheer habit, to take the white presence for granted. Which is, precisely, his trouble."[136]

Trumper's experience in the United States breaks that habit of relaxation and also produces a sense of positive racial identification that his friends did not embrace earlier in the the narrative. Trumper uses the phrase "my people," which is so vilified in the mouths of overseers and civil servants, as a gesture of connection and embrace. Relating his experience of hearing Paul Robeson sing "Let My People Go" (294), Trumper makes the phrase "my people" an emblem of political might. He calls Robeson "one o' the greatest o' my people" and puzzles his friends with his nascent pan-African identification. Trumper also gives a closing comment about the future rise of racial consciousness in Barbados: "The blacks here are my people too, but they don't know it yet" (297).

In Wright's novel, Sam, Zeke, Tony, and Fishbelly participate in a similar debate about where they can find fulfillment when they grow up. Like Bob, Sam speaks in authoritative terms among his friends, but rather than sustaining the sense of geography taught to him, he radically undermines it, in a conversation that refracts discussions of America in Lamming:

> "I want to stay where I am," Fishbelly confessed finally.
>
> "Okay," Sam agreed sarcastically. "Nobody wants to go to Africa . . . Awright. Who wants to go to *America*?"
>
> The three boys stared incredulously at Sam.
>
> "Sam's done gone stone crazy," Tony moaned.
>
> "We awready *in* America, you fool!" Zeke yelled.
>
> "Aw, naw, you ain't!" Sam cried hotly. "You niggers ain't *nowhere*." (31–32)

The setting, substance, and flow of this conversation echo that of Lamming's boys, but it provides an opposite conclusion. Rather than affirming their place within a national or colonial framework (as Bob does in his connecting everything to England), or situating America as a place of opportunity (as Trumper does), Sam argues that they essentially have no place within the nation itself, that they live in a no-man's-land. Trumper's parallel in Wright's novel would seem to be Zeke. Like Trumper, he is at first confident of his place—he shouts at Sam, "I'M AN AMERICAN!" (32)—but later chooses to leave for another country, France. From France, Zeke reports back to Fishbelly in a manner analogous to Trumper's reports to the narrator, and he advises him, "Shake the dust off your feet and don't look back once" (397).

Where to Look Homeward? Dilemmas of Culture and Place in Paule Marshall's *Brown Girl, Brownstones*

The question of whether to "not look back" anticipates the central dilemma of migrancy and diaspora in Paule Marshall's *Brown Girl, Brownstones* (1959). In contrast to the male bildungsromans of Wright and Lamming, in which the protagonists make a choice to migrate at the end of their narratives, Marshall's protagonist begins her narrative with that choice already having been made for her. At the start of the novel, Selina's parents have moved from Barbados to Brooklyn, and the entire family struggles with the challenge of ascending economically and socially in New York while still maintaining a fruitful connection to their homeland and Barbadian culture. The first description of the brownstones places their migration in the historical context of previous immigration to New York: "But now in 1939 the last of them [European immigrants] were discreetly dying behind those shades or selling the houses and moving away. And as they left, the West Indians slowly edged their way in. Like a dark sea nudging its way onto a white beach and staining the sand, they came."[137] This image offers a powerful double figuration of the Barbadian immigration both as something natural and inevitable—the latest in a series of waves—and as something transformative and possibly threatening, in "staining" the "white" with its coming. The dramatic tension in the novel centers around a similarly equivocal sense of the family's destiny. Selina's father, Deighton, envisions building a house back on the family land in Barbados once he has made enough money as an accountant: "I gon wait till they send the real facts and study them. Then a job making decent money and we gone" (9). Her mother, Silla, in contrast, yearns for a brownstone of her own, and fears both Deighton's improvidence (of which he has a notable history) and returning to the harshness of the island's agricultural labor. She reminds Selina that far from being "sweet," her childhood in Barbados was literally marked by serving in the "Third Class," the children's shift to pick grass from the cane field under the eyes of a whipping Driver (39).

The question of where the family "belongs" is made more complex by the question of how Barbadian identity intersects with competing national identities, both inside and outside the United States. While almost all of Marshall's characters are proud to be "Bajan," their identity acquires extra complexity by either their self-identification as British or their "passing" as African American. Although Deighton plans for a proud homecoming to Barbados, he sometimes fears that his foreignness will not allow him to blend into the culture of New York successfully. Notably, he flees Suggie's cooking cod upstairs because he is "afraid that the smell would insinuate itself into his clothes and he would carry it with him all night as the undisputable sign that he was Barbadian and a foreigner" (18). One of Silla's friends, in contrast, actively disavows an identification with the United States, explaining that she would never let her son (if she had one) fight for the U.S., but she would "if he was gon fight for England and the Crown." Silla tartly replies, "What John Bull ever did for you that you's so grateful? You think 'cause they does call Barbados 'Little England' that you is somebody? What the king know 'bout you—or care?" (57). Much as Lamming did in *In the Castle of My Skin,* Marshall's Silla undermines the aggrandizing concept of "Little England" as a bolster to Barbadian identity, seeing it, instead, as an inflating illusion. Given that many of the Barbadians seeking work (including Deighton) do not have visas or other papers, there is a strategic reason for not being overtly Barbadian around whites: to maintain legal work status. This invisible status conveys some advantages. Deighton does not need to fear being drafted, for example, because, as he says, "As far as the record goes I ain even in this country since I did enter illegally. Y'know that's a funny thing when you think of it. I don even exist as far as these people here go" (54). In other contexts, the white Americans' ignorance is an asset to Marshall's characters when they need to hide their illegal status. When it is time to apply for a job, Deighton reassures Silla, "When it says citizen on the application I gon put yes. They ain gon bother searching up the birth certificate. Besides, these white people here does think that all colored people is from the South" (68).

Commenting upon the complex identifications with which Selina and her family wrestle, Heather Hathaway aptly notes that the first part of the novel sets up a series of polarities through a "tone of irreconcilabity . . . between white and black, fusion and fission, 'femininity' and 'masculinity,' leisure and labor, individuality and conformity."[138] The evolution of these complex oppositions, whether of culture, gender, or otherwise, are well traced by Hathaway and other scholars, so I will not follow out their development in the novel. For the purpose of my argument, it is more important to observe that there is a consistent tendency on the part of U.S. critics to "reconcile" these oppositions, typically in favor of an optimistic reading of a new, "dual" West Indian/African American identity produced by the novel. Hathaway herself describes the progress in *Brown Girl, Brownstones* as a movement "from dislocation to dual location" (86). Although it is true that many of the apparent oppositions at the start of the novel grow less prominent as Selina grows up, optimistic visions of the novel's resolution belie the book's unyielding sense that some dualities cannot fully be bridged, especially as the political and economic demands of living the United States jeopardize Barbadian family or community traditions.

To be sure, crucial aspects of the novel reveal characters having some success at negotiating these cultural binaries. The joyous calypso celebration in the center of the novel suggests that the Barbadians have succeeded in transplanting key elements of their culture to the United States. As their song proclaims, "carnival has come to New York" (126). At a more personal level, Silla's posture shows that she has successfully imported the bearing taught by her mother:

> For she was handsome, as the women from the hills of Barbados sometimes are, a dark disquieting beauty. . . . Silla had learned its expressions early from her mother and the other women as they paused in the cane fields and lifted their sun-blackened, enigmatic faces to the sea, as they walked down the white marl roads with the heavy baskets poised lightly on their heads and their bodies flowing forward in grace and restraint. (115)

This beautiful description of the traditional gestures and postures shared by Barbadian women well supports Hathaway's contention that Marshall affirms a matrilineal descent of cultural traditions (117). One might argue that these powerful links to Barbadian culture provide a virtual connection, giving Selina and others, in effect, the Barbadian portion of Hathaway's "dual location." Indeed, many of the most powerful and poetic passages in the narrative—such as Selina's italicized reverie imagining her father's return to Barbados after his death (161)—suggest that

Barbados, in her mind's eye, provides a resource that can counter her winter of grief and loss.

At the same time, discussions at a meeting of the Barbadian Association in *Brown Girl, Brownstones* suggest an anxiety about the immigrants' ability to preserve their culture. For example, when one member of the Association, Claremont Sealy, proposes a change in their title—"You need to strike out the word *Barbadian* and put *Negro*. That's my proposal. We got to stop thinking about being Bajan. We ain't home no more" (190)—he is met with a figurative storm from the audience: "Then, as rain comes in the West Indies—without warning, to lash the earth in a helpless hysterical deluge—their indignation broke with the same fury" (191). Although Hathaway argues that the Barbadians are threatened by this change because of their hesitancy to be known as "Negro" (which would mean "willful identification with the oppression that African Americans suffered during the interwar years" [99]), substantive evidence within and beyond that passage suggests otherwise. As already noted, many Barbadian men in the novel are happy to "pass" as southern when it is strategically valuable. More broadly, I would argue that the association fears a more basic loss: that of community and culture itself. Indeed, the angriest dissenter from the change in name, Iris Hurley, complains that the proposer is "nothing but a commonist [communist]" (99). With that complaint, Iris indicts Claremont not as a black nationalist who collapses African American and West Indian identifications, but as an internationalist radical who ignores cultural lines altogether in favor of class divisions.

One of the reasons why Marshall's characters may find such a loss especially threatening is that the United States itself, although abounding in multiple ethnic groups, is represented as essentially cold and cultureless. Beyond the problems of racism and discrimination that the Barbadians face (which are the case whether they identify as "American," African American or West Indian), New York itself is consistently depicted as a dead, confining place in itself. When Selina travels to visit her father in the hospital, she sees the ugly underbelly of the metropolis: "She had never seen streets like these. The trolley might have taken her to another city, some barren waste land gripped by a cold more intense than winter's and raw with wind, a place where even the falling snow was a soiled brown. Factories stretched unending down the streets, towering blackly into the sky, their countless lighted windows offering no promise of warmth inside" (81). Selina's only solace in that journey is the passing by of a cat rubbing against her legs, "the one warm gesture in a cold country" (82).

Almost every passage describing New York City is charged with similar coldness and absence. New York City in Marshall's novel thus fails to be an integrated community at several levels. Besides the lack of racial equality (which is usually referenced off-stage in the novel—there are few moments of overt contact with whites at all), there is a profound lack of basic human connection. Critics have recurrently failed to note Marshall's unflattering portrait of New York (beyond the bare fact of discrimination), perhaps because, in assigning priority to immigrant cultures, she threatens U.S. identity by essentially treating it as a *non*-identity. One might argue that in the political model of dual location, Selina faces the challenge of living in a *non*location, a place haunted by absence and mechanization. Indeed, her mother herself, when destroying Deighton's trumpet in retaliation against his spendthrift ways, is figured with a curious dual image: "Repeatedly, Silla's body rose and dropped into a threshing rhythm. She might have been a cane-cutter wielding a golden machete through the ripened cane or a piston rising and plunging in its cylinder" (112). This bicultural image is powerfully asymmetrical: in the West Indian side of the figuration, Silla acts like a human laborer; in the New York side, she is part of a machine. This image suggests that Silla's relentless drive for social and economic ascent has caused her to become a cog in the engine of capitalism.

It is worth bearing in mind these complex failings of New York and the United States because they provide a serious complication to Hathaway's optimistic model of dual identity. Hathaway argues that Selina is ultimately empowered by the end of the novel and emerges as an "individual who can be intimately linked to both worlds" (118), but it is not at all clear that the United States provides a world into which she—or perhaps anyone—can yet be intimately linked. Having fought with her mother for perhaps the last time, Selina strolls by herself in the night air at the end of the novel. She listens to the sounds of the city and recalls family and friends with a decidedly mixed resonance: "Those faces, those lives touching hers had ruined her, yet, she sensed . . . they had bequeathed to her a small strength" (266). As Selina walks on, she gradually moves further and further away from the inhabited part of the city, through Fulton Park and towards a demolished block of brownstones:

> The song led her to a vast waste—an area where blocks of brownstones had been blasted to make way for a city project. A solitary wall stood perversely

> amid the rubble, a stoop still imposed its massive grandeur, a carved oak staircase led only to the night sky. . . .
>
> The project receded, and she was again the sole survivor amid the wreckage. And suddenly she turned away, unable to look any longer. For it was like seeing the bodies of all the people she had ever known broken, all the familiar voices that had ever sounded in those high-ceilinged rooms shattered—and the pieces piled into this giant cairn of stone and silence. She wanted to leave something with them. (248)

Selina tosses one of her two silver bangles into the rubble, making a gesture of unity with the past and the community, even as she is preparing to make her way forward alone. It is undeniable that Selina has accrued a core of strength by the end of the novel, but it seems an overly optimistic reading of the concluding scenes to find "reconciliation," as Hathaway does (117). Selina's gradual drifting away from friends and family toward the ruined part of the city suggests that life will take her into isolation, for now. By concluding the novel with a scene of rubble and desolation, Marshall suggests not a sense of completed reconciliation but the need for renovation and reconstruction. Moreover, this painful ruin is not a natural loss: the brownstones have not decayed in any organic way, but have been torn down by the city for a new project, a pattern that suggests that New York devours homes and dreams as it reinvents itself. The oak staircase that survived the demolition is now a bridge to nowhere, showing that the old path of capitalist uplift pursued by Silla (who sought one of the very brownstones now demolished) is a dead end. Indeed, in Selina's emergence as "sole survivor amid the wreckage," New York City seems less a "location" to belong to, and more of a shattered community, physically and metaphorically, that needs to be rebuilt in a new image.

Hathaway's argument that Selina has reconciled her identity by the end of the novel not only overlooks the relative bleakness of the final scene, but also allows her to replace Marshall's trenchant depiction of a broken city and family with an optimistic reading of successful dual identity within the United States. In her own writings, Marshall has commented extensively upon her frustrations about the limitations of power and opportunity accorded to black Americans in the United States in comparison those given to black West Indians in their homelands. She notes in her memoir that when she lived in Barbados while completing the editing of *Brown Girl, Brownstones,* she was struck by the dissonance between the opportunities for Barbadians in their country and the relative lack of black enfranchisement back in the United States: "How

I envied them! Black people who could actually anticipate taking charge politically! Who could seriously contemplate running their own government! What black American could ever dream of exercising that kind of power."[139] To be sure, a struggle by African Americans to realize such dreams had been ongoing and would culminate in the decade ahead. Marshall herself would soon join in that fight, but she had already made a substantive intervention with her suggestion in *Brown Girl, Brownstones* that the United States was not yet a stable location of identity, not the Zion of the New Negro, but an incomplete project, a promise as yet unfulfilled.

Conclusion

Fidel Castro's defeat of Fulgencio Batista's forces in the Cuban Revolution in 1959 ushered in a radically different era of U.S.-Caribbean relations, and the relationship between the United States and the Caribbean became explicitly militarized during the cold war. Trade and travel regulations initiated by the United States enforced a separation from Cuba for the rest of the century and, in many cases, had a chilling effect on contact with other islands. New U.S. restrictions upon who could enter the country and who could leave drastically reduced cross-cultural traffic, particularly from Caribbean authors to the United States. Even writers who had previously been able to secure visas were now denied if they had any history of leftist tendencies. The experience of C. L. R. James at Ellis Island, where he was detained even before the Red Scare was fully fledged, may have offered a harsh lesson to Caribbean writers about the welcome they faced in the United States if there was any dimension of political critique in their writings. Claude McKay, had he been alive, would have likely faced similar detention if he traveled to the Caribbean and attempted a return.

On the U.S. side, general tourism obviously continued, but high-level cultural and political visits (such as those previously sponsored by the NAACP during the 1920s and 1930s) were largely conducted under state auspices. Paule Marshall and Langston Hughes, for example, joined the USIS (United States Information Service) tours to promote democracy abroad. In Hughes's case, such a move helped put a safe distance between himself and his radical past—a crucial goal for Hughes as the House Committee on Un-American Activities reached new levels of vigilance, even after the death of Joseph McCarthy in 1957. As Vera Kutzinski has documented, Hughes turned his back on his Cuban friends entirely in the changed political climate. Guillén attempted contact with Hughes for several years after Castro's rise, culminating in an urgent Western Union telegram to Hughes in the wake of the Bay of Pigs Invasion in 1961. Hughes never responded.[1]

The rise of Black Power and resurgent pan-Africanism returned Caribbean discourse to many of the same questions animating the works of Martí, Firmin, and Sylvain at the turn of the preceding century: what would be the fate of African-descended peoples in the Caribbean and beyond? A broad dialogue between African American and Caribbean authors about decolonization soon developed, which would shape their literary fields throughout the 1950s and 1960s.[2] The failure of the Bay of Pigs Invasion assured many West Indians that the threat of renewed occupation, as had happened in Haiti, had been averted. At the same time, expanding corporate power in the booming 1950s guaranteed that the threat of neocolonial dominion, if not explicit imperialism, would remain as expansive as ever. Indeed, even in Cuba, the model case for Caribbean independence and resistance to U.S. hegemony in the twentieth century, the United States maintained a foothold, an imperial residue dating back to 1903: Guantanamo Bay, held by the U.S. Navy. The ambivalent status of that space well prophesied the future of U.S. power in the Caribbean, which would become increasingly covert, dispersed, and corporatized. Guantanamo is leased, not owned; it is subject to U.S. military dominion, but is not a colony or commonwealth; it is not a sovereign Cuban space, but neither is it fully subject to U.S. law. Amy Kaplan has argued persuasively that the ambiguous nature of the U.S. presence in Guantanamo foreshadowed future patterns of U.S. global dominances, which would deploy "new imperial taxonomies, which rebound across national borders."[3]

It was in the similarly liminal space of Ellis Island that James authored one of the most powerful and innovative indictments of U.S. hegemony in the twentieth century: *Mariners, Renegades, and Castaways: The Story of Herman Melville and the World We Live In* (1953). On an island that was neither the United States nor the Caribbean, but a gateway between them, James not only critiqued U.S. imperialism but argued that American citizenship itself was an unaccomplished project, whose promise would only be fulfilled when the United States embraced a less parochial and more hemispheric sense of national history. Few figures are better suited for offering a closing consideration of the complex cultural traffic between the United States and the Caribbean than James. Born in Trinidad and educated at Queen's Royal College in Port-of-Spain, James traveled to England in 1932 and became part of the circle of diasporic black intellectuals in London. There, as discussed in chapter 5, James wrote and published the famous study of the Haitian revolution of 1791, *Black Jacobins.* In 1938, James traveled to the United States at the urging of Leon Trotsky, who sought him as an ally against the support for Stalinism that was flourishing in many leftist circles in the United States. James stayed in the United States for fourteen years, writing on various subjects, and developed an intense interest in the works of Herman Melville.

In 1952, James was sent to Ellis Island in preparation for deportation, ostensibly for an expired visa, but undoubtedly also because of his leftist activism. There he was detained, not quite incommunicado, but denied visits from friends, his wife Constance Webb, and legal counsel. Ironically, or perhaps most appropriately, it was there in that national legal limbo that James penned his most accomplished work about borders and nations, and the peculiar shape of power and citizenship in the United States. Part literary criticism, part political critique, and part petition for legal reentry to the United States, *Mariners, Renegades, and Castaways* represents one of the most important "recovered" classics of pan-American or diasporic discourse in recent years. Published privately in 1953, the book went in and out of various editions in succeeding years as James attempted to keep this wonderful and odd text in print—indeed, he was even attempting an expanded edition shortly before the end of his life in 1989.

Although *Mariners, Renegades, and Castaways* is back in print, thanks to the diligent work of Donald Pease, the full extent of James's refiguration of the United States and national identity remains largely underappreciated. Pease uses James's work as a key text in his own attempt to move from American studies to "transnational American studies," but the intellectual weight of national borders remains curiously intact in Pease's analysis of James. Pease rightly observes that James's text functions both as an "interpretive exercise" and a "juridical appeal," but seems hesitant to reckon with the full scope of James's interpretation of the United States, privileging instead a reading of the text as the author's "plea that the book be taken by the reading public as proof of his competence for U.S. citizenship."[4] While there is no doubt that James had that rhetorical goal—indeed, the last chapter is very much an "apologia" pleading for or demanding redress—James has another, larger target for his critique: the integrity of citizenship itself in the United States.

On the question of U.S. citizenship, James transmutes his position of detention on Ellis Island into a position of intellectual privilege. For James, only at the border (or "on the island," as it were) can one recognize that, paradoxically, U.S. citizens do not possess the citizenship they believe is theirs. In a move of great brilliance, James makes his critique not by a direct assault on J. Edgar Hoover or the House Un-American Activities Committee, but by examining Melville's *Pequod* and its crew from *Moby Dick* as a chronotope for apprehending the operations of power in the cold war United States and the world at large. James's critique takes on even more power in the context of *The Purloined Islands* because many of the faults that he finds in Ahab—his idealist hubris, his subordination of nature, his exploitation of the crew, his use of material lures to seduce them—are those that many Caribbean writers in this study found characteristic of the United States. Most of these writers consider these issues in order to ask whether or not an extension of U.S. culture and governance to the islands will benefit them; James makes the even bolder leap of asking whether or not American citizens themselves have benefited from U.S. democracy in the manner they believe.

James begins his exegesis with an introduction that brilliantly collapses literary and geographical time and space. His two grounding claims are simple: first, that Meville "painted a picture of the world in which we live"; and second, that "Ellis Island, like Melville's Pequod, is a miniature of the all the nations of the world and all sections of society" (3). James not only suggests a prophetic continuity between Melville's literary imagination and the actualities of world history, but also fruitfully combines literary, personal, and political issues, imaginatively positioning himself as part of the "crew" that extends from the *Pequod* to Ellis Island. In so doing, he refocuses the locus of political understanding away from official legal documentation towards literature, and he internationalizes an American space for the purpose of challenging U.S. ideas of what it means to be an American.

James's first step in using the *Pequod* to mount his challenge to the cold-war consensus is to collapse the dyadic opposition between Ishmael and Ahab that grounded readings of Melville in American studies at the time. According to James, "The voyage of the Pequod is the voyage of modern civilization seeking its destiny" (19). Most American literary critics in James's time would have agreed, but read a surprisingly optimistic destiny from Melville's ship. Pease well describes the nationalistic uses to which *Moby Dick* was put by American studies in a cold-war context: "The narrative provided the state with an image of itself as overcoming the totalitarian Other to which it defined itself as opposed" (xxix). Thus, in these accounts, Ahab stood as the "other," a philosophically powerful but nihilistic embodiment of tyrannical power that was associated with everything that America was not. For American studies in James's context, Ishmael represented a rationalist, reflective embodiment of higher democratic ideals. It is he, not Ahab, that connects so well to the crew; his survival at the end represents a triumph of democratic spirit over dictatorial power.

In contrast to this optimistic opposition of Ahab and Ishmael, James argues that they are profound doubles of one another, and that Ishmael complicitly facilitates Ahab's work. James makes clear that in his reading, Ahab and Ishmael are both idealists, and that U.S. idealism is precisely the problem. Ahab is not a materialist of any kind, but rather is concerned with a metaphysical pursuit of what lies behind "the pasteboard masks."[5] According to James, precisely because Ahab's goals are so transcendent in nature, so disconnected from work and the crew—indeed from physical reality of any kind—"He is the most dangerous and destructive social type that has ever appeared in Western civilization" (9). One might recall Firmin's belief that the greatest (and most dangerous) source of expansionist power in the United States was not its simple material interests, but its ideological and salvific commitment to spreading democracy in the hemisphere. In this typological reading of Ahab, James makes some of his boldest assaults on the Western tradition: "How deeply embedded is the totalitarian personality in Western civilization is proved by the fact that one embodiment of it was no sooner destroyed [i.e., Hitler] than the Stalinist state threatened to overwhelm not only Europe but the whole of the world. It is another branch of the same tree."[6] For James, what unites Hitler, Stalin, and implicitly much of what Pease calls the "national security state" is the devotion to an abstract ideal that is disconnected from, indeed indifferent to, the mass of humanity. As James argues, it is not material gain, not even political power, but "the Plan" (14) that makes these figures so dangerous. In the overall context of *The Purloined Islands,* one finds that many of the Caribbean authors I have examined, like the crew of the *Pequod,* have found themselves subordinated to or incorporated by "the Plan" of a U.S. "captain." While Locke and Du Bois certainly did not lead the New Negro movement to the *Pequod*'s fatal end, the multinational "crew" from the Caribbean that supported the movement was left out of their "captains'" narratives.

Ishmael's contribution to Ahab's regime is a passive abstraction that not only tolerates Ahab's metaphysics but is entranced by his actions. Bearing an overwrought "weight of consciousness and knowledge" (30), Ishmael refuses to commit either to the tyrannical work of Ahab or to a defensive solidarity with the crew. As James comments, "He does not want to be a commodore but he does not want to be a cook either" (37). For James, Ishmael "takes refuge in philosophical abstractions," preferring passivity to direct action (46). What makes Ahab tempting, then, is that he has the courage to act upon abstract ideals, providing wish fulfillment for the analytic Ishmael: Ahab "embodies in action the theoretical conclusions of the disoriented intellectual" (42). James sees Ishmael as an epitome of the disengaged intellectual, one whose passivity aids and abets the practices of Ahabs: "Ishmaels, we say, live in every block. His submission to the totalitarian madness is complete" (44). Indeed, Meville's rendering of Ahab's "madness" shows him not only opposed to humanity and God, but to nature itself, not merely as embodied in the whale, but in elemental forces: "I'd strike the sun if it insulted me" (167). Ahab's hubris, along with his insistence upon subordinating the world to his metaphysics, echoes Williams's depiction of Columbus's failures of imagination in *In the American Grain.*

Ahab's successful use of economic lures to seduce the crew to support his mission—a Spanish doubloon (166), a "little lower layer" (a better cut of the profits) for Starbuck (167)—suggest a geopolitical system where the greatest means to suppress revolt is not overt force but the temptation of money. Indeed, throughout this study, one of the most recurrent insights made by Caribbean authors, from Martí, to McKay, to Marshall, is that to accept the economic promises of prosperity from the United States, whether as an immigrant or a recipient of U.S. corporate influence, is to risk a Faustian bargain—trading a sense of community, culture, or history for a greater economic stake that may leave one an unrecognized cog in the neocolonial machine, at home or abroad. As Lamming comments in *The Pleasures of Exile,* "The gift of money is not the beginning of a relationship; for money is merely the name of a relation, and its fruits are only one part of the general atmosphere."[7]

In answer to the question of why the crew did not revolt against this madness, James sees the impractical but "virtuous" first mate as partly responsible: the crew are "morally enfeebled by the incompetence of mere unaided virtue or rightmindedness in Starbuck" (50). For James, Starbuck and Ishmael share a need to justify following Ahab: these characters reveal to James "how men rationalized their subservience to tyranny" (53). Lest we forget, Ahab and Ishmael are the two most "American" characters on the ship, the rest of which is populated by a far more multicultural cast of sailors. Ultimately, in James's readings, it is precisely the foreign crew members—particularly the harpooners Daggoo, Tashtego, and Queequeg (whose coffin literally saves Ishmael at the end)—who provide the democratic energy. Writes James, "The crew [are] the real heroes of the book" (18). James notes that the fraternal power of the motley crew (the mariners, renegades, and castaways) is so strong that it almost helps Ishmael break out of his consciousness, to "forget[] his preoccupation with himself" (44). Paradoxically, then, the truest "Americans" in the book, in the sense of those promoting democratic action and liberty (especially from the tyranny of mind that afflicts Ahab and Ishmael), are precisely the non-Americans on board. A key paradox the crew faces, however, is that a simple change in ownership would not solve anything, as it would leave the hierarchical political economy of the whaling system unchanged: "That the crew should revolt to save the society of Bildad, Peleg, and Starbuck makes sense neither as politics nor literature."[8] To seize the ship and return it to Bildad and Peleg (the owners) would simply reaffirm the exploitative economy upon which Ahab's tyranny depends. Both the ship and political economy must be remade for a truly democratic state to arise.

With this reading of Ishmael and Ahab as apparently opposed but ultimately united American types, James mounts a serious rebuttal to the conclusions of the nascent American studies canon from the 1950s, and as he does so, he inverts almost all the operations of privilege, power, and citizenship that dominated the status quo at the time. From his position of not-quite exile, James claims a privileged vantage point for understanding the contradictions of American society as prophesied by Melville and fulfilled in cold war politics. Pease perceives James as using his interpretation to mount a claim for "post-nationality," but James's argument suggests almost the opposite: that the very promise of American national identity—at least on the democratic terms of citizenship and consensus professed in the 1950s—was not yet fulfilled. If to be an American citizen is to be part of a social contract, then James, standing outside, showed that the contract was broken and unfulfilled—and could only be realized, paradoxically, when America embraced the "un"-Americans inside and outside its borders, the mariners, renegades, and castaways that give the title to James's study.

In mounting this sophisticated argument, James not only demonstrates his case for citizenship, as Pease observes, but reveals to his readers that they do not possess the citizenship they believe they have—that, insofar as they live in the shadow of Ishmael and Ahab, they are not yet Americans either. James succeeded in using his time in detention to reveal that the United States had failed its own citizens—and that they had failed themselves. It is doubtful that James would reach a different conclusion were he alive today. It has become a truism to observe that the national security state that has arisen in the United States post-9/11 has deeply compromised the civil liberties and the rights of noncitizens. James's vision of Ishmael's subservience to Ahab becomes all the more prescient in offering a recurrent model of U.S. culture and politics. The operations of the Bush administration over eight years epitomized not only an unprecedented expansion of executive power, but a reductive subordination of the citizenry and the state to an Ahabian "plan." Just as Ahab's pursuit of the whale flies in the face of nature and sense, the "liberation" of Iraq, as a war of choice, was the product of neoconservative "ideals" that ran counter to both strategic and evidentiary realities. The middle and upper classes of the United States were complicit in accepting this mission, in part, for "a little lower layer" in the form of tax cuts and rebates, and were spared the sacrifice of joining the U.S. Army (itself a deeply multicultural crew of mariners and soldiers) in pursuit of "the plan." In recent U.S. history, then, Ishmael chose the comfort of the shore.

Although the Caribbean writers examined in *The Purloined Islands* had a wide range of views about what the United States represented as a nation and as a neighbor, they shared certain common concerns about the U.S.: (1) that the economic opportunities in the U.S. came at the price of other values, such as community, culture, or nature; (2) that Jim Crow, racism, and other repressive measures threatened to maintain a perpetually unjust system in the U.S.; and (3) most problematically, that the expansion of U.S. power would export those exploitative mechanisms to other countries. Like James, they would find that many of their concerns still resonate today. The election of Barack Obama, the first African American president of the United States, is undoubtedly a watershed moment, but deep problems of unequal political and economic opportunity still persist. While Jim Crow is gone, other, subtler repressive mechanisms have taken its place and, in some cases, grown. Post-9/11, the practice of racial profiling, for example, has expanded from African Americans to encompass Arab Americans or other immigrants perceived as Muslim or "un-American." Government surveillance, pursuit of immigrants, and use of internal and international detention centers have expanded accordingly. Abroad, besides its explicit interventions in Iraq and Afghanistan, the United States continues to extend its neocolonial economic dominion, in tandem with the expansion of multinational corporations that have become geopolitical forces in their own right. The very fact that the nation has suffered a recent recession has not stopped that flow, but made it all the more tempting for corporations to seek competitive advantage by outsourcing their operations to non-U.S. spaces where they are not subject to U.S. laws.

As the United States, even under the Obama administration, continues to maintain its non-national penal space in Guantanamo Bay, the "gifts" of the islands take on an especially bitter resonance. It is precisely because Guantanamo provides a close military base in our hemisphere that is *not* U.S. territory that it has been a tempting quasi-national resource for a repressive penal colony. The U.S. government chose a perfect location to hide its work: in plain sight, geographically speaking, on lease from the island that is our closest noncontiguous neighbor.

It is hard to imagine a part of our hemisphere more forgotten to contemporary Americans than the Caribbean. The most likely avenue for U.S. citizens to encounter the Caribbean is a ship—not the *Pequod,* but a Carnival Cruise. Carnival itself is a hybrid, multinational corporation that caters primarily to U.S. tourists, while registering its vessels abroad to avoid U.S. regulation.[9] The dominant genius of the Carnival Cruise line is to offer a modicum of exotic difference while providing an oversaturation of quintessential American pleasures that can be enjoyed in the non-national space of the sea and at foreign ports of call. Less festively, as a nation, the United States continues to depend on undocumented immigrant labor, not only from Mexico, but extensively from Haiti and the Dominican Republic (whose immigrants now form the largest ethnic group in New York City).[10] The United States relies on this "invisible" economy, while the most visible recognition in public discourse are anti-immigrant screeds, which have reached a fever pitch comparable to nativism in the 1920s. Even for those who *are* U.S. citizens, unequal access to health care, public education, and economic opportunity suggests that the U.S. citizenry has more in common with the mariners, renegades, and castaways than it would like to imagine.

Perhaps the most terrifying testimony to the continued and expanding power of the Ahabian American state is the contrast between James's detention in 1953 and the terms of detention in Guantanamo and other secret prisons at present. For all the privations James experienced, he was permitted to write, and his text was released, even while he was still interned. In spite of his detention, James managed to offer a substantial "gift" from two islands—Trinidad and Ellis Island. Although James's gift was briefly lost to obscurity, it was subsequently restored. The vast majority of prisoners at Guantanamo Bay have not been permitted pen and paper for more than thirty minutes a week (and have not been able to keep what they did not finish during that period), so they have been denied even the most basic forms of expression that every writer in this book has been able to take for granted.[11] *Moby Dick* concludes with Ishmael's invocation of *The Book of Job*, "And I only am escaped alone to tell thee." One wonders what stories and narratives have not escaped Guantanamo Bay and have been purloined and silenced forever. Indeed, the presence of other secret detention spaces like Guantanamo Bay throughout the world suggests that the United States now owns a horrifying archipelago of its own making, with a new generation of "island" voices who need to be heard.

Notes

Introduction

1. Zeltner, "3-D Headache?"

2. See Savin, "Rituals of 'Rememory'"; Lock, "Building Up from Fragments," 109–20; Hawthorne, "Ethnicity and Cultural Perspectives in Paule Marshall's Short Fiction." Critics have also made a similar gesture with *Praisesong for the Widow,* a more recent novel from Marshall that nonetheless predates *Beloved* by six years. See Smith, "Women's Spiritual Geographies."

3. This phrase echoes Richard Brodhead's study *The School of Hawthorne,* which persuasively (and [chrono]logically) situates Henry James, William Dean Howells, and other canonical U.S. writers as building upon Hawthorne's innovations with the American novel.

4. Mary Helen Washington, as quoted in Trescott, "The Daughter of the Mother Poets."

5. The sources on this subject are numerous. For several classic studies in this regard, see Morrison's *Playing in the Dark,* Lott's *Love and Theft,* Sundquist's *To Wake the Nations,* and North's *The Dialect of Modernism.*

6. Cobb, *Harlem, Haiti, and Havana,* 6, 51.

7. The extensive body of "new Americanist" scholarship that emerged in the 1990s has fruitfully questioned the parameters of literary and historical interpretation in American studies since the 1960s, often revealing the field's complicity in imperial or cold-war enterprises, or expanding the canon of American literature or literary issues to encompass new terrain. At the same time, most of this scholarship has been primarily centripetal or U.S.-centric in focus. The seminal anthology *Cultures of U.S. Imperialism,* edited by Donald Pease and Amy Kaplan, for example, gives excellent attention to questions of empire in U.S. literary history, but has almost nothing to say about the Caribbean, which is certainly a space with considerable experience of the United States as an imperial presence. More broadly, it leaves the voice of the subaltern curiously muted. Of the twenty-six articles in the volume, only a handful reach beyond traditional

U.S. geographies or incorporate serious attention to the culture and literature of the colonized "other." A similar lacuna characterizes both Pease's *Revisionist Interventions into the American Canon* and *The Future of American Studies.* The former, as the title suggests, trains new methodologies (especially historicist ones) onto traditional American studies texts and issues, but does not expand the purview of study. In the latter, with the exception of Donald Pease's and Gunter Lenz's incisive work, the focus is even more centripetal; when "international" issues arise, it is largely in regard to questions of importing theory. The critical gaze of American studies, particularly with respect to the prospect of decentering the United States, remains unchanged in these collections. Whether exceptional model or exceptional villain, the U.S. remains central.

8. Coronado, "The Aesthetics of Our America," 213–14.

9. Two recent anthologies in this "new southern studies" direction are *Look Away! The U.S. South in New World Studies,* edited by Jon Smith and Deborah Cohn, and, more recently, *Just Below South: Intercultural Performance in the Caribbean and the U.S. South,* edited by Jessica Adams, Michael Bibler, and Cécile Accilien. Although the editors of both collections do not aim to "annex" new spaces for southern studies—indeed, they explicitly disavow that goal—most of the essays necessarily have a southern focus, which means that Caribbean-U.S. connections in northern cities (which are considerable) are not taken into consideration. More broadly, while the contributions in each volume fruitfully complicate prior monocultural or bicultural (black and white) accounts of the U.S. South, that region nonetheless remains reified as the central object of study in most of the articles.

10. Rather than viewing the Caribbean as merely an extension of the U.S. South, Glissant repositions (and perhaps de- or internationalizes) the U.S. South as part of the continuum of slaveholding cultures extending from Gorée Island, through the Caribbean, to the U.S. slave ports of New Orleans and Charleston. Glissant, *Faulkner, Mississippi,* 30.

11. Gillman, "The New, Newest Thing," 196.

12. Gillman, "Otra Vez Caliban/Encore Caliban."

13. Hathaway, *Caribbean Waves,* 84–85.

14. Harris, *The Womb of Space,* xviii.

1. Birth of a Hemisphere

1. For example, there is only one recent essay putting Anténor Firmin in the context of U.S. literature, Plummer's "Firmin and Martí."

2. See, for example, Belnap's and Fernández's *José Martí's "Our America."* This valuable anthology of sixteen essays effectively explores central tenets of Martí's political and cultural writings, but with a decidedly U.S.-centric emphasis: ten of the essays use Martí as a foil for canonical or reclaimed U.S. authors, particularly in the Latino studies field. As subversive of traditional Americanist categories as such an anthology might purport to be, "the national" emerges as

a much more decisive focus than the "hemispheric" in this collection. Plummer's article (see previous note above) is a notable exception in emphasizing a cross-cultural focus in the hemisphere.

3. Rowe, for example, cites Du Bois's early writings like *The Souls of Black Folk* and *Darkwater* as "forerunner[s] of contemporary cultural and poscolonial criticisms" (*Literary Culture and U.S. Imperialism,* 177). See also Mostern's "Postcolonialism after W. E. B. Du Bois." Mostern credits Du Bois with anticipating the whole of twentieth century postcolonial theory and cites 1903 as the dawn of that era: "*The Souls of Black Folk* fulfils the entire definition of postcolonialism in nearly identical ways as *The Location of Culture* itself" (259). While I agree with aspects of each of these assessments, they treat Du Bois as if he were operating in a near vacuum and creating postcolonial critique ex nihilo. As apt as they are in their accounts of Du Bois, neither Mostern nor Rowe mentions Caribbean intellectuals—clearly colonial subjects striving to create a postcolonial discourse as well—whose collaborative participation in the Pan-African Conference was seminal to Du Bois's globalized perspective.

4. Martí, *Obras Completas,* vol. II, 133.

5. Ibid., 487.

6. Ibid., 624.

7. "En los fastos humanos, nada iguala a la prosperidad maravillosa de los Estados Unidos del Norte. Si hay o no en ellos falta de raíces profundas . . . si la ausencia del espíritu femenil, origen del sentido artístico y complemento del ser nacional, endurece y corrompe el corazón de ese pueblo pasmoso, eso lo dirán los tiempos." Ibid., 311. Unless otherwise noted, English quotations from Martí are my translations; I will include the original Spanish within endnotes for readers' reference.

8. "Un boa no los dejaría como el verano de New York deja a los niños pobres, como roídos, como mondados, como vaciados y enjutos. Sus ojitos parecen cavernas, sus cráneos, cabezas calvas de hombres viejos, sus manos, manojos de yerbas secas. Se arrastran comon gusanos; se exhalen en quejidos. ¡Y digo que este es un crimen público, y que el deber de remediar la miseria innecesaria es un deber del Estado!" Ibid., 172.

9. "Harto lucen ya, en estos hijos de padres desgraciados por esclavitud, el carácter e inteligencia del hombre libre. ¡Se los debe, por supuesto que se les debe, reparación por la ofensa; y en vez de levantarlos de la miseria a que se les echó, para quitarles su apariencia antipática y míseria, válense de esta apariencia que criminalmente les dieron para rehusarles el trato con el hombre." Ibid., 770.

10. Ibid., 607.

11. "El indio es muerto, con este sistema vil que apaga su personalidad: el hombre crece con el ejercicio de sí mismo, como con el rodar crece la velocidad de la rueda; y cuando no se ejercita, com la rueda, se oxida y se pudre." Ibid.

12. See Karem, "On the Advantages and Disadvantages of Postcolonial Theory for Pan-American Study."

13. "Esta República, por el culto desmedido a la riqueza, ha caído, sin niguna de las trabas de la tradición, en la desigualidad, injusticia y violencia de los países monárqicuos." Martí, *Obras Completas,* vol. II, 796.

14. "¡Libertad, es tu hora de llegada! El mundo entero te ha traído hasta estas playas, tirando de carro de victoria. Aquí estás como el sueño de poeta, grande como el espacio, de la tierra al cielo. . . . Vedlos: ¡todos revelan una alegría de resucitados! ¿No es este pueblo, á pesar de su rudeza, la casa hospitalaria de los oprimidos?" Ibid., 716, 721.

15. "Sin los frenos del patriotismo que aún en los ruines puede tanto, esta mezcla de irlandeses, de escoceses, de alemenos, de suecos, de gente que come carne y bebe cerveza . . . va rápida y sin bridas, sin más bridas que las del miedo o intinto de conservación, a conquistar lo que cree suyo." Ibid., 663.

16. "Pero no augura, sino certifica, el que observa cómo en los Estados Unidos, en vez de apretarse las causas de unión, se aflojan en de resolverse las problemas de la humanidad, se reproducen, en vez de amalgamarse en la política nacional las localidades, la dividen y la enconan; en vez de robustecerse la democracia y salvarse del odio y miseria de las monarquías, se corrompre y aminora la democracia, y renacen, amenezantes, el odio y la miseria." Ibid., 987.

17. Ibid.

18. "Se echan en la arena, y se dejan cubrir, y golpear, y amasar, y envolver con la arena encendida, porque eso es tenido por ejercicio saludable y porque ofrece singulares facilidades para esa intimidad superficial, vulgar y vocingerla a que parecen aquella prósperas gentes tan aficionadas." Ibid., 311.

19. "Otros pueblos—y nosotros entre ellos—vivimos devorados por un sublime demonio interior, que nos empuja a la persecución infatitgable de un ideal de amor o gloria. . . . No así aquellos espíritus tranquilos, turbados sólo por el ansia de la posesión de una fortuna." Ibid.

20. For the most fully developed version of this approach, see Saldívar, *The Dialectics of Our America.*

21. "Do We Want Cuba?" in Foner, *Our America: Writings on Latin America and the Struggle for Cuban Independence,* 228. Subsequent references to this text will be cited parenthetically by page number.

22. "Es probable que ningún cubano que tenga en algo su decoro desee ver su país unido a otro donde los que guían la opinión comparten respecto a él las preocupaciones sólo excusables a la pólitica fanfarrona or la desordenada ignorancia. . . . Admiran esta nación, la más grande de cuantas erigió jamás la libertad; pero desconfían de los elementos funestos que, como gusanos en la sangre, han comenzado en esta República portentosa su obra de destrucción." Martí, *Obras Completas,* vol. III, 171.

23. "Pues, ¿quién es el hombre? ¿el que se queda con la madre a curarle en la enfermedad, o el que la pone a trabajar donde no la vean y vive de su sustento en las tierras podridas con el gusano de corbata, maldiciendo del seno que lo

cargó, paseando el letrero de traider en la epalda de la casaca de papel?" Martí, *Antologia Critica,* 245.

24. "A adivinar salen los jóvenes al mundo con antiparras yanquis o francesas, y aspiran a dirigir un pueblo que no conocen." Ibid., 247.

25. See Kutzinski, *Sugar's Secrets.*

26. "Pero otro peligro corre acaso nuestra América, que no le viene de sí, sino la diferencia de orígenes, métodos, e intereses entre los dos factores continentales, y es la hora próxima en que se le acerque, demando relaciones íntima, un pueblo emprendedor y pujante de la desconónce y la desdeña." Martí, *Antologia Critica,* 251.

27. Froude, *The English in the West Indies,* as cited in Thomas, *Froudacity,* 145. Subsequent references to this text will be cited parenthetically by page number.

28. It is vital to note that this "confederation" is not across the islands as much as it is within each island. Thomas uses this term to acknowledge the need for pluralistic participation within each colony, rather than a pan-island confederation as envisioned by Martí or a contemporary political bloc like CARICOM. C. L. R. James makes this distinction clear in his 1969 introduction to the text (Thomas, *Froudacity,* 44).

29. Ibid., 28–29.

30. Fluehr-Lobban, introduction to Firmin, *The Equality of the Human Races,* xiii. Subsequent references to this text will be cited parenthetically by page number.

31. Plummer, "Firmin and Martí."

32. Firmin, *M. Roosevelt,* iii.

33. "L'avènement du nouvel hôte de la Maison Blanche [ce sera] une menace pour notre autonomie nationale." Ibid., iii. English quotations from *M. Roosevelt* are my translations; I will include the original French within endnotes for readers' reference.

34. "Un grand peuple avec lequel nous avons tant points de contact, matériels, et moraux." Ibid., iv.

35. "Saisir comment un peuple se rend en digne de la liberté et de l'égalité, en y mettant une énergie constante a conquérir l'une et l'autre, sous l'empire d'une éclairée, y voyant la source de tout bien-être social et de tout progress." Ibid., v.

36. "Et ce serait un nouveau mérite pour Roosevelt si belle et saine énergie, après nous avoir inspire une peur salutaire, nous faisait retrouver enfin la voie depuis longtemps abandonée de notre destinée nationale." Ibid., x.

37. "Cet ideal pour Haiti c'est l'effort sublime d'un petit peuple en vue de la rehabilitation de toute une race d'hommes." Ibid., ix.

38. "Le nom Immortel [qui] éveillera toujours notre esprit des sentiments de respet et d'admiration"; "une chose sacrée." Ibid., 103, 105.

39. "Personne ne recula devant les sacrifices nécessaires à la défense d'une cause dont on avait reconnu la justice." Ibid., 103.

40. "Sans doute, une problem rest-t-il à résoudre, avant que le peuple américain puisse réellement assumer le role d'avant-garde des nations civilisées. Je veux parler de cette troublante question de des Afro-américans dont l'admission aux prérogatives des citoyens et à l'égalité sociale est si ardemment contestée dans tout le Sud d'États-unis." Ibid., 131.

41. "Est impuissante à créer, chez le blanc de la Caroline du Sud ou de l'Alabama, par exemple, la sentiment de la solidarité nationale, capable de dominer une [raciste] répulusion. . . . Le cerveau de ce descendant des anciens esclavagistes est à jamais muré dans le cercle étroit des doctrines surannées de Morton et de Gliddon." Ibid., 207.

42. "La question de race domine fatalement le problème de las destine d'Haiti." Ibid., vii.

43. "Aprés cette fameuse doctrine, ce qui intéresee le plus les Haitiens, dans leurs relations avec l'états-unis, c'est la question de race ou de prejugé de couleur." Ibid., 193.

44. "Je répéterais volontiers les paroles du président d'États-unis, «Je crois de tout mon âme, à la doctrine de Monroe.»" Ibid., 192.

45. "Il du sentir que c'était bien lui, le loyal chevalier, le Lohengrin, protecteur des faibles, que le poète, appelait au secours de Cuba désespérée." Ibid., 165.

46. "Le vrai Américain n'a jamais eu peur de courir des risques, quand le prix à gagner était d'une suffisante valeur." Ibid., 181.

47. "C'est le resumé d'un ensemble d'initiation intellectuelle, de discipline sportive et d'imprégnation morale, des plus difficiles a rècontrer dans un seul individu." Ibid., 182.

48. "Qui pourrait disconvenir que «le plus grand bien» pour le citoyen des Phillipines soit la liberté, avec les franchises politiques, et qu'on doive la préférer, pour lui, à une indèpendance perpetuant la mailfaisance d'une oligarchie nationale?" Ibid., 182.

49. "On y trouve toutes les conditions des tels antécédents presques renversées." Ibid., 289.

50. "Forcement étrangers . . . des divers points de l'Afrique, souvent aussi distant que l'espace qui s'etend du Portugal aux monts Ourals." Ibid., 233.

51. "Mais Haïti n'avait plus le premier des Noirs et les États-Unis n'avaient pas encore saisi leur destinée dans l'hèmisphère occidental!" Ibid., 291.

52. "Les états du Sud séront pénétré par une civilization [i.e., Haiti's] plus large." Ibid., 481.

53. "La bénéfice d'une telle acquisition" "en comparant . . . avec les efforts et les dépenses considérables, en vie humaines et en argent." Ibid., 471–72.

54. "La main dans la main, soyons prèts à nous adosser aux pans escarpés des nos montagnes protectices, en nous touchant par le coude, unis pour la prospérité commune, comme pour la defense commune." Ibid., 496.

55. Mathurin, *Henry Sylvester Williams.* Subsequent references to this text will be cited parenthetically by page number.

56. According to Fluehr-Lobban, Firmin attended, though not as a signatory or presenter. Introduction to *The Equality of the Human Races,* xxxix.

57. See Walters, *My Life and Work,* 255. Subsequent references to this text will be cited parenthetically by page number. See also Sylvain, *Du Sort des Indigènes,* 510.

58. Du Bois mentions the conference in passing: "We were in London in some somber hall where there were many meeting, men and women called chiefly to the beautiful World's Fair at Paris; and then a few slipping over to London to meet Pan-Africa. We were there from Cape Colony and Liberia, from Haiti and the States, and from the Islands of the Sea." Du Bois, *The Oxford W. E. B. Du Bois Reader,* 581.

59. Sylvain, *Du Sort des Indigènes,* 506.

60. Harrison, *A Hubert Harrison Reader,* 352. Describing Du Bois as a "guardian of the gate," Harrison argues that Du Bois was highly selective in acknowledging the work of fellow African American authors: "Yet you will search Dr. Du Bois's bibliography in vain for any mention of Chesnutt. . . . But that is nothing unusual for Du Bois. In his family magazine [the *Crisis*] for February 1927, he lists under 'The Looking Glass' an unusual article by a black West Indian author [Harrison] in a white magazine called *The Modern Quarterly*—but he studiously refrains from mentioning the writer's name, although it was and is perfectly well known to him. He did something similar with George Schuyler recently."

61. Du Bois, *The World and Africa,* 5. Subsequent references to this text will be cited parenthetically by page number.

62. Du Bois, *The Autobiography of W. E. B. Du Bois,* 42–43. Subsequent references to this text will be cited parenthetically by page number.

63. Marable, *W. E. B. Du Bois,* 39.

64. See Gilroy's chapter "'Cheer the Weary Traveler': W. E. B. Du Bois, Germany, and the Politics of (Dis)Placement," *The Black Atlantic,* 111–45.

65. Lewis, *W. E. B. Du Bois,* 248–49. Subsequent references to this text will be cited parenthetically by page number.

66. Marable has observed that Du Bois also underrepresented the role of West Indians at the congresses he called, pointing out that he never fully acknowledged the leadership role George Padmore (from Trinidad) played in developing the congresses (particularly the influential congress of 1945) (164).

67. "(1) esclavagistes conscients . . . [qui] sont des vampires plus ou moins bien costumé en hommes; (2) esclavagistes inconscients qui, sans maltraiter de parti-pris les indigènes, entendent les maintenir à perpétuité dans une condition sociale inférieure; (3) les rare apôtres de la vrai civilisation, qui ont du rôle des colinisateurs une conception juste et genereuse." Sylvain, *Du Sort des Indigènes,* 326. All translations from Sylvain are my own. I include the original French in endnotes following my translated citation.

68. "La civilisation est l'etat d'évolution, état essentiellement dynamique, qui permeet sux societés organisés de d'assurer la perfectionnement moral de l'homme." Ibid., 327.

69. "Quel est donc l'obstacle qui s'oppose l'application de ces principes d'equité et de haute sagesse politique? Les plus stupide et odieux des préjugés sociaux: nous on nommé le préjugé du couleur." Ibid., 417.

70. "Stowe a suffisement dramatisé les horribles scène d'esclavage pour nous dispenser d'insister sur les effets dépresifs de la servitude." Ibid., 245.

71. "Si au lieu d'avoir passé au sein d'esclavage les plus fecondes années de sa jeunesse, Frederick Douglass avait été elevée à l'Université de Cambridge, d'Oxford, ou de Westpoint." Ibid., 246

72. "Les craintes de civilisateurs démentent leur promesses." Ibid.

73. "Nulle part au monde il ne se manifeste avec une caractère de violence plus odieuse qu'aux États-unis; là, sous le nom de lynchages, se renouvellent presque journellement des scènes de d'une invraisable sauvagerie." Ibid., 470.

74. "En une generation, le contact des Americains a fait d'eux des citoyens." Ibid., 420.

75. "Cette assembleé d'Africains venant, au coeur de New York, dans une salle de conférences populaire destinée a l'instruction de la démocratie américaine, revindiquers leurs droits de citoyens." Ibid., 420.

2. Fear and Fantasy

1. Sundquist, *To Wake the Nations,* 184, 186.

2. Dash, *Haiti and the United States,* 1. Subsequent references to this text will be cited parenthetically by page number.

3. I borrow this concept from Hans Robert Jauss's reception theory. For his most thorough elaboration of this idea, see *Towards an Aesthetic of Reception.*

4. The critical literature on *White Zombie* and zombies in general is surprisingly rich. Two of the best pieces are Chu's introduction to her *Race, Nationalism and State in British and American Modernism* and Fay's "Dead Subjectivity: *White Zombie,* Black Baghdad." Chu explores how "*White Zombie*'s horrors are political," both in its implications regarding "conflicts between labor and industry" and in the figure of the "zombie bride," who calls into question "the idea of marital consent" (5). Fay sees an even more polemical role to the zombie, as it is a subtle reflection on the dangers of occupation: "Displacing politics with horror, the film also performs curious racial reversals that implicate Americans in a colonial economy and suggest that U.S. citizens may themselves be susceptible to America's degrading Haitian policy" (83).

5. Johnson, *Selected Writings,* vol. I, 230. Subsequent references to this text will be cited parenthetically by volume and page number.

6. On 1 November 1920, Johnson wrote to Mr. E. P. Pawley, of the West Indies Trading Co., Port-au-Prince: "This letter will serve to introduce you to Mr. James O'Donnell Bennett, European Correspondent of the Chicago Tribune,

who is in Haiti to find out the truth concerning the Haitian situation." Johnson wrote similar letters on behalf of Bennett to Seymour Pradel and B. Danache. All of Johnson's correspondence discussed in this chapter is from the James Weldon Johnson Papers at the Beinecke Library; subsequent references to this correspondence will be cited by date and correspondent.

7. James Weldon Johnson, "Haiti and Our Latin American Policy," in Wilson, *In Search of Democracy,* 112–14.

8. Holly wrote, "Your presence in the Republic of Hayti is a token of the full hearted solicitude the American Negro has for his Race. . . . Your departure affects me as that of an old and faithful friend." (Holly to Johnson, 10 August 1920). In a similar vein, Etienne Mathon wrote to Johnson, "Votre lumineux rapport, les articles de The Nation et ceux vous annocez pourront, nous, l'esperions, eclairer la conscience Americaine et server a delivrer un people faible qu'on asservit au nom des Etats-Unis" (Mathon to Johnson, 10 August 1920).

9. Much as did Mathon and Holly, Danache cited Johnson as Haitians' best advocate on the continent: "It was an anchor of safety thrown to me by a friendly hand. I do not know, but somehow I hung my hopes upon it, having no one in the United States but you to whom I can confide my patriotic distresses" (Danache to Johnson, 7 August 1920).

10. Johnson to Georges Sylvain, 26 August 1920; Johnson to B. Danache, 24 August 1920.

11. Johnson to Mary White Ovington, 21 September 1920.

12. "I have been instructed to write you regarding a proposed conference of certain prominent citizens of Haiti and certain American citizens, for the purpose of forming a body which shall look after Haitian interests in the United States" (Johnson to Emile Faubert, 21 September 1920).

13. Johnson to Mary White Ovington, 21 September 1920.

14. Johnson to Etienne Mathon, 23 September 1920.

15. Alfred Henriquez to Johnson, 27 September 1920. Johnson received simiar letters from Victor Delbeau and Danache. See also Danache to Johnson, 6 October 1920, and Delbeau to Johnson, 28 September 1920.

16. Arthur Holly to Johnson, 10 December 1920.

17. Johnson to Louis Borno, 5 November 1920. See letters of the same date to Rosemond, Henriquez, and Sylvain.

18. Johnson to Borno, 3 December 1920.

19. Holly to Johnson, 10 December 1920.

20. Johnson to Holly, 22 December 1920.

21. Ibid.

22. Pauleus Sannon to Johnson, 11 January 1921.

23. A letter to the editor on 14 May 1921 from Johnson commented on the president's dedicating a monument to Simón Bolívar as a liberator. Johnson noted Haiti's role in helping Bolívar, as well as its stature as the second free republic in the hemisphere. He noted the irony, then, that the United States was occupying

a fellow republic while commemorating a freedom fighter like Bolívar. "To the Editor."

24. For example, Johnson wrote to Lemuel Livingston and Mendill McCormick with regard to testimony about the occupation and the imprisonment of Haitian journalists who had criticized the U.S. force. See Johnson to Lemuel Livingston, 18 May 1921, and Johnson to Mendill McCormick, 13 June 1921.

25. Johnson to Josephe Jolibois *fils,* 21 September 1921.

26. Johnson to Pauleus Sanon, 14 October 1921.

27. "Address to the Patriots of Haiti," c/o Johnson to Ernest Gruening, 4 November 1921.

28. See Rosemond to Johnson, 4 December 1922.

29. Johnson to Jolibois, 27 March 1935.

30. Niles, *Black Haiti,* 83. Subsequent references to this text will be cited parenthetically by page number.

31. Like Johnson, Seabrook has considerable sarcasm for American "improvements": "The most interesting and pervasive of the American innovations is the belated lesson in race-consciousness which they have been at pains to teach the Haitian upper classes. . . . These urban Haitians, free, vain, independent, and masters in their own land for a long hundred years or more, had accumulated money, education, a literature, an aristocratic tradition, and had somehow forgotten that God in his infinite wisdom had intended the negroes to remain always an inferior race" (*The Magic Island,* 127). Subsequent references to this text will be cited parenthetically by page number.

32. Seabrook, introduction to Wirkus and Dudley, *The White King of Gonave,* xii–xiii. Subsequent references to this text will be cited parenthetically by page number.

33. Herskovits, *Life in a Haitian Valley,* 1. Subsequent references to this text will be cited parenthetically by page number.

34. Taft, *A Puritan in Voodoo-land,* 16. Subsequent references to this text will be cited parenthetically by page number.

35. Craige, *Cannibal Cousins,* 29, 48. Subsequent references to this text will be cited parenthetically by page number.

36. Craige, *Black Bagdad,* 1, 15. Subsequent references to this text will be cited parenthetically by page number.

37. See Rosaldo, "Imperial Nostalgia."

38. Some scholars have condemned Hurston as simply a tool of U.S. imperialism. Fischer-Hornung asks, "Could it be that Hurston simply didn't 'get it' in Haiti?" ("An Island Occupied," 160). Others have sought to rescue her from that charge. Duck, for example, argues that Hurston "severed" her political and cultural analyses of Haiti because "folklore was here linked with an authoritarian and racially essentialist political ideology"; thus, her divided perspective, while seemingly imperialist, is actually antifascist and aimed at saving Haiti from a homegrown Mussolini ("Rebirth of a Nation," 127, 140).

39. Hurston, *Tell My Horse,* chapter VII ts., 1. Subsequent references to this typescript will be cited parenthetically by chapter and page number.

40. Hurston, *Tell My Horse,* chapter VII holograph ms., 5. Subsequent references to this manuscript will be cited parenthetically by chapter and page number.

41. "It is widely believed that his sister bought a house in France for him on her recent trip there. It is official that he applied for six months pay in advance to the fiscal agents, but this was refused. He gave as his reason that he was ill and that he wished to consult foreign specialists. The request for the advance pay being denied, he has perhaps submitted his ailments to local treatment. Certainly he is not the popular figure he was two years ago. His outward show of internal peace and prosperity is a fraud. If he wishes to maintain [that] the picture his propagandists paint for visiting journalists is correct, I challenge him to permit any three fair-minded Americans to spend thirty days in Haiti and go wherever they will unescorted by the police. Or if it is said that my impressions are unfair to Haiti, then I say again, let a disinterested committee who speak French visit the country outside of Port-au-Prince and Cap-Haïtien and judge between us" (holograph addition to chapter VII ts., 12).

42. Hurston, *Tell My Horse,* addition to chapter VII ts., 8.

43. Hurston's dialogic handling of these moments of violence in *Tell My Horse* well illustrates Rowe's contention that she uses a double-voiced "coding" to appeal to multiple audiences in her narration (*Literary Culture and U.S. Imperialism,* 256).

44. The extensive passage on the Sect Rouge that Hurston deleted reads as follows: "But to look at the Sect Rouge more intimately. At the head of the national group is an emperor and a queen. The big group is made up of local bands, each of which is ruled by a president, but all of the members have their grades. There are the Ministers, the Officers, the servants, the cooks, the honorary members *and* the bourresouse, who are the advance guard of the society. The success of the whole matter rests upon the courage, discretion, and efficiency of this advance guard. The honorary members are those who are in sympathy with the society, but for one reason or another are not yet initiated. They participate in the dancing with the privilege of tasting the food. Also whenever the band is to pass the door of these honorary members they go out and join them with white candles burning on their heads and hands and feet and thus illuminated they go to the dance.

"Now, the members of the Sect Rouge (also called the Red Circle) begin by sending out the word by secret ways advising the adepts as to the time and place of meeting. [After deleting the following three sentences, Hurston subsequently marked them to be retained in her final manuscript.] The most celebrated meeting place in the Department of the West used to be the bridge across the lake at Miragoane. An awful sight to the late traveler! The bridge covered with candles, the brilliantly costumed figures, themselves bearing multiple candles and the little coffin that is their object of worship, in the center of the floor of the bridge, the sharp piercing voice of the little drums and the wildly dancing horde. Every member appears at the rendezvous dressed in a complete red robe or hood or in a complete white outfit according to the arrangement. All gathered at the place, they commence the ritual that frequently transforms them all into demons with the bodies of animals. They assume the personality of bulls, horses, goats, hogs, chickens, and *gray hogs.*" Hurston, *Tell My Horse,* chapter XIV ts., 8.

45. Bhabha, *The Location of Culture.*

46. Dash, *Haiti and the United States.*

47. "Mario revit tout cela fut son enfance. Tout le parfum de sa terre, des jours anciens vécus dans du beau soleil lui montait aux narines. Ce colouir obscure qui ouvre sur la mer, là, pour la première fois, il se souvient d'avoir connu la chair et étreint un soue dans l'haleine immonde des puanteurs marines une petite vendeuse d'oranges. Olive . . . Elle s'appelait Olive." Casseus, *Viejo,* 1–2. All translations from Casseus are my own; for readers' reference, I include the original French in the endnote citations.

48. "Mais des Casernes Dessalines une sonnerie éclata, qui s'éleva comme un rampart autour du pavillon flotant des quarante huit Etats. Alors seulement il se souvint: l'Américan était maître ici, mais pas lui. . . . Liberté ou la Mort! Ironie de son drapeau flottant dans le matin clair, et que d'en face les blancs gifflaient de leurs sarcasms." Ibid., 5.

49. "Oui, un colon, un colon encore, et à qui on ne marchanda meme pas le prix de la terre." Ibid., 7.

50. See Kutzinski, *Sugar's Secrets.*

51. "L'atmosphère oppressait les poitrines de l'odeur amère de tabac amèricain, de celle aussi âcre des aisselles mouillées." Casseus, *Viejo,* 33.

52. "Chèri, je vais me débarrasser de Cap, et revenir." Ibid., 41.

53. "Je ne savais de quelle manière j'allais pourvoir vivre avec cette pensée, là, dans ma tête, cette image continuellement devant mes yeux, d'Olive ma femme, que j'aime plus que tout au monde, couchant avec ce sale blanc." Ibid., 141.

54. "Camarade, il ne faudra plus revenir ici, car cet homme et sa femme c'est l'éternelle histoire du «cochon et de la boue»." Ibid., 145.

55. "Mario défaille, et sur son Coeur doit s'alourdir le poids d'un continent noir avec tous ses deserts, ses grains de sable, ses Pyramides, avec toute les ondes d'un Nil obscure, l'écume sale de Mississipis que gratta le banjo. Une main le soulève, le projette dans un air saturé de jazz band, de congo-paillette, de slow blues et de pignitte que dirige Mario en habit noir et gants blancs." Ibid., 15.

56. "La nuite s'est refermée, et glissée dans le tuyau des veines. Mario d'hier prisonnier du Mario d'aujourd'hui, nouvellement né." Ibid., 29.

57. "Chante, chante tambour de nègres! Allons, chante-moi ton couplet noir. Tu n'es pas la musique des blancs, la longue flût d'argent ni le violon verni. Allons, chanse la chanson qui grouille dans ton ventre. C'est ca, c'est ca! Je veux ton couer, car tes hoquets sont sombres comme une peau de nègre, et l'haleine

de ma Guinée. . . . Ah! tu es ma mere, tambour, tu es mon père, tambour, tu es mon frère, et c'est toi que je posséderai quand je coucherai tout à l'heure avec ma chérie noire." Ibid., 29.

58. "Afrique! C'est l'âcre puanteur des marais hume ce masque méconnaissable, tous ces corps hysteriques. Et Mario est une liaison!" Ibid., 52–53.

59. "La bruyante joie des faces ternes, bruyantes et douloureuse, plaisir sans claret, visage sans soleil, farde au charbon de bois, antichambre de l'Afrique piétinée, mais musique-hall d'une race folle de la joie qu'on lui refuse, poésie dynamique, sensuelle de douce d'Harlem, débauche de lumières et de couleurs, fête de l'arc-en-ciel tout au long de tes soirées et de tes nuits, Harlem!" Ibid., 66.

60. "Cependant, je suis revenue ici, camarade, car malgré toutes les richesses d'Harlem, tous les décors d'Harlem, il y a quelque chose à laquelle tu ne peux resister, et c'est l'appel impérieux de ta terre, lorsque ca te tient là, loge au milieu de ton Coeur, comme si ca frappait sur un gong sonore, chaque heure, chaque minute, chaque second, ah! c'est terrible cela, camarade!" Ibid., 63.

61. "Afrique! continent primitif où ta peau règne, desert infini sur lequel veillent les vielles Lois noires, Afrique, c'est en toi, et en toi seule qu'il puise le secret de sa revolt'e éternelle." Ibid., 156.

62. "La flame luit, nue brillante, sur le masque grimacant de Cap où le tranche est resté enfoncé jusqu'à la garde dans la carotid." Ibid., 158.

63. Thoby-Marcelin and Marcelin, *The Beast of the Haitian Hills,* xix.

64. Brodhead, *Cultures of Letters,* 107.

65. Roumain, *Masters of the Dew,* 29. Subsequent references to this text will be cited parenthetically by page number.

3. Expanding "Our America"

1. For a full account of this term, see Bakhtin, *The Dialogic Imagination.*

2. According to Bourne, "Already we have far too much of this inspidity, masses of people who are cultural half-breeds, neither assimilated Anglo-Saxons nor nationals of another culture. . . . It is not the Bohemian who supports the Bohemian schools in Chicago who is sinister, but the Bohemian who has made money and who got into ward politics" ("Trans-National America," 98).

3. Frank, *America Hispana,* 260, 267. Subsequent references to this text will be cited parenthetically by page number.

4. Stevens, *Collected Poems,* 29. Subsequent references to this text will be cited parenthetically by page number.

5. Conrad, *Heart of Darkness,* 9.

6. Kutzinski, *Against the American Grain.*

7. Williams, *In the American Grain,* 7. Subsequent references to this text will be cited parenthetically by page number.

8. Columbus, *The Journal of Christopher Columbus,* 47–48.

9. Crane, *Complete Poems,* 48. Subsequent references to this text will be cited parenthetically by page number.

10. Benítez-Rojo, tracing the uncanny repetition that marks the exploitative history of the Caribbean islands, describes it as a machine: "This machine, this extraordinary machine, exists today, that is, it repeats itself continuously. It's called: the plantation" (Benítez-Rojo, *The Repeating Island,* 8).

11. O'Neill, *Representative Plays of Eugene O'Neill,* 184.

12. Bradford, "The Knight and the Artist," 88.

13. Faulkner, *Collected Stories,* 896. Subsequent references to this text will be cited parenthetically by page number.

14. Stanchich, "The Hidden Caribbean 'Other' in William Faulkner's *Absalom, Absalom!*" 9. Subsequent references to this text will be cited parenthetically by page number.

15. Matthews, "Recalling the West Indies," 257. Subsequent references to this text will be cited parenthetically by page number.

16. Indeed, one could argue that the insistent critique of womanhood and virginity in the Haitian passages, along with the anxieties about fertility and sexuality, reflects not so much Sutpen's or Faulkner's vision of the island, but the shaping narrative perspective of the Compson men, who pursue these themes obsessively elsewhere in *Absalom, Absalom!* and *The Sound and the Fury.*

17. Stanchich, for example, argues that Sutpen "doubles for the American national conscience" (4). Matthews sees the Haitian passages as a source of "potential recognition about the South's obscured origins" (256). Both of these claims, as attractive as they are, make a leap in representation that is not supported by Sutpen's position in the novel as a quitessential outsider—wherever he is.

18. Kutzinski makes a persuasive case that it is Cuba, not Haiti, that is a more probable source of wealth and slaves for someone in Sutpen's position at that time. "Borders and Bodies," 55–88.

19. Langford, *Faulkner's Revision of Absalom, Absalom!* 255. All of my references to the original manuscript of *Absalom, Absalom!* are taken from Langford's collation. Subsequent references to this text will be cited parenthetically by page number.

20. Faulkner, *Absalom, Absalom!* 247. Subsequent references to this text will be cited parenthetically by page number.

21. Retamar observes that such justifying distinctions between Anglo-American colonialism and Latin colonialism (which invariably situate the Anglo-American as more civilized and humane) are foundations of the intellectual tradition of American exceptionalism. He effectively critiques this tendency in "Against the Black Legend," 56–73.

22. The film was directed by Tay Garnett and released as *Slave Ship* in 1937. The screenplay drafts retain the original novel title, *The Last Slaver.* Because it is those drafts I am analyzing in this essay, I will refer to the project by that title as well.

23. King, *The Last Slaver,* 21.

24. Faulkner, Hellman and Lehman, *The Last Slaver,* 24 September 1936, 57. Subsequent references to this text will be cited parenthetically by date (where needed) and page number.

25. Faulkner, Hellman and Lehman, *The Last Slaver,* 10 October 1936, 98. Subsequent references to this text will be cited parenthetically by (where needed) and page number.

4. Nationalizing Blackness

1. Hathaway observes that McKay "was adopted as a literary spokesman by large segments of the African American public" yet "too often has been monodimensionally read within the canon of . . . African American literature" (*Caribbean Waves,* 9, 46). Subsequent references to this text will be cited parenthetically by page number.

2. See Carl Van Vechten's novel *Nigger Heaven* for a key example of such white appropriation.

3. I am using the term "cultural capital" in the sense articulated by Pierre Bourdieu in his analysis of noneconomic exchange in his sociology. See *The Logic of Practice.*

4. See Lott's famous iteration of this pattern in U.S. cultural history in *Love and Theft.*

5. For a thorough history of the interactions between Caribbean and African American communities in New York, see Watkin-Owens, *Blood Relations.*

6. Lewis, *When Harlem Was in Vogue,* 130. Subsequent references to this text will be cited parenthetically by page number.

7. Harrison, *A Hubert Harrison Reader,* 252. Subsequent references to this text will be cited parenthetically by page number.

8. Pederson, "The Caribbean Voices of Claude McKay and Eric Walrond," 197. Also see Parascandola, *Look for Me All Around You.*

9. Baker, *Modernism in the Harlem Renaissance,* 76. Subsequent references to this text will be cited parenthetically by page number.

10. Douglas, *Terrible Honesty,* 303–12.

11. See Favor, *Authentic Blackness.*

12. "The Rise of the West Indian," 214.

13. Du Bois, *The Negro,* 110.

14. Du Bois, *Black Folk then and Now,* 129.

15. Garvey, *The Philosophy and Opinions,* 126. Subsequent references to this text will be cited parenthetically by page number.

16. Garvey to Du Bois, 25 April 1916, in Du Bois, *The Correspondence of W. E. B. Du Bois,* 214.

17. Garvey to Du Bois, 16 July 1920. Ibid., 245.

18. Du Bois to Garvey, 22 July 1920. Ibid., 245–46.

19. Du Bois to Domingo, 18 January 1923. Ibid., 263.

20. See Du Bois on Garvey in the *Crisis* 21 (December 1920): 58, 60; 21 (January 1921): 112–15; and 25 (January 1923): 120–22.

21. Du Bois, *The Oxford W. E. B. Du Bois Reader,* 265. Subsequent references to this text will be cited parenthetically by page number.

22. McKay, "Garvey as a Negro Moses," 8.

23. Walrond, *Winds Can Wake Up the Dead,* 126.

24. Du Bois to P. B. Young, 8 August 1925, in Du Bois, *The Correspondence of W. E. B. Du Bois,* 317–18.

25. Du Bois, *The Autobiography of W. E. B. Du Bois,* 185.

26. Padmore comments, "Although Dr. Du Bois was not the first Negro intellectual to have visions of a pan-African movement, the credit must go to him for giving reality to the dream and conserving its ideals until such time as it found acceptance as the basic ideology of emerging African nationalism." Padmore, *Pan-Africanism or Communism,* 117.

27. Du Bois, *Dark Princess,* 6. Subsequent references to this text will be cited parenthetically by page number.

28. See Perry's *A Hubert Harrison Reader* and *Hubert Harrison: The Voice of Harlem Radicalism.*

29. Perry, *A Hubert Harrison Reader,* 170.

30. Johnson, *Lift Every Voice and Sing,* 46. Subsequent references to this text will be cited parenthetically by page number.

31. Walrond, *Winds Can Wake Up the Dead,* 111.

32. Rogers, "The West Indies," in Wilson, *The Messenger Reader,* 371–72.

33. Johnson, "The New Frontage on American Life," in Locke, *The New Negro,* 296. Subsequent references to this text will be cited parenthetically by page number.

34. McKay to Locke, 1 August 1926, in Cooper, *The Passion of Claude McKay,* 143.

35. McKay, *Selected Poems,* 62. Subsequent references to this text will be cited parenthetically by page number.

36. Walrond, *Winds Can Wake Up the Dead,* 82–83.

37. Ibid., 91–92.

38. Walrond made clear in his critical writings during the Harlem Renaissance that Toomer was inspirational to him, describing him as "the strongest" of the New Negro writers and singling out *Cane* for particular praise (ibid., 130).

39. Ibid., 146.

40. Walrond, *Tropic Death,* 21. Subsequent references to this text will be cited parenthetically by page number.

41. African American journalists visiting the canal zone during the 1920s confirm Walrond's portrait of U.S. abuses. See Patterson, "American Democracy in the Panama Canal Zone."

42. Editorial, *Opportunity,* 334.

43. Frank, "In Our American Language," 352.

44. Escobedo, "Archival Conflicts," 96.

45. Jones, "West Indian-American Relations," 357.

46. Holstein, "The Virgin Islands," 344. Subsequent references to this text will be cited parenthetically by page number.

47. Domingo, "The West Indies," 341.

48. McKay, "My House" and "America in Retrospect," 342.

49. Johnson to McKay, 12 November 1926.

50. Du Bois to McKay, 16 March 1927.

51. See McKay to Du Bois, 18 June 1928. This case was not as clear cut as that of Johnson and *Opportunity.* McKay did submit five poems to Du Bois in October of 1925. After they were published, he later wrote to Du Bois that "I think I beseeched you over a year ago *not* to publish those poems I sent to the 'Crisis' towards the end of 1925," but it is not clear that he did so.

52. Johnson to McKay, 2 June 1927.

53. Schomburg to J. M. Boddy, as cited in Escobedo, "Archival Conflicts," 94.

54. Walrond to McKay, 14 February 1927.

55. Locke to McKay, 27 April 1927.

56. McKay to Jackman, 1 August 1927.

57. McKay to Jackman, undated.

58. McKay to Jackman, 12 December 1929.

59. McKay, *Home to Harlem,* 9. Subsequent references to this text will be cited parenthetically by page number.

60. McKay to Ivy, 20 September 1929, in Cooper, *The Passion of Claude McKay,* 143.

61. McKay, *Banjo,* 46. Subsequent references to this text will be cited parenthetically by page number.

5. Translation and Cultural Critique

1. James, *The Black Jacobins,* 18. Subsequent references to this text will be cited parenthetically by page number.

2. Bibler and Adams, introduction to Bontemps, *Drums at Dusk,* xvii. Subsequent references to this text will be cited parenthetically by page number.

3. Dunham, *Kaiso!* 57. Subsequent references to this text will be cited parenthetically by page number.

4. Ramsey, "Without One Ritual Note," 18.

5. Rupert Meikle to McKay, 19 January 1937.

6. Jamaican Women's Liberal Club to Johnson, 1 July 1937.

7. Una Marson to Johnson, 27 July 1938.

8. For example, in describing the Caribbean contributors to Hughes's *Poetry of the Negro,* Rampersad writes that "not all the West Indians were difficult"—a backhanded compliment, to be sure (*The Life of Langston Hughes,* vol. II, 155).

9. Mullen, "The Literary Reputation of Langston Hughes in the Hispanic World and Haiti," in Mullen, *Langston Hughes in the Hispanic World and Haiti,* 15–46.

10. Miller, *The Art and Imagination of Langston Hughes,* 94.

11. See Hughes, "People without Shoes," 12; and "White Shadows in a Black Land," 157.

12. Sanders and Johnston, introduction to Hughes, *The Collected Works of Langston Hughes, vol. 5,* 278. Subsequent references to this text will be cited parenthetically by volume and page number.

13. Bibler and Adams, introduction to Bontemps, *Drums at Dusk,* ix. Subsequent references to this text will be cited parenthetically by page number.

14. Guillén, *Obra poética,* vol. 1, 109. Unless otherwise noted, all translations of Guillén are my own. In subsequent citations of Guillén's poems, I include the original Spanish in endnotes for reader's reference.

15. "Aquí hay blancos y negros y chinos y mulatos." Ibid., 159.

16. "Ésta es la grotesca sede de companies y trusts./Aquí están el lago de asfalto, las minas de hierro,/las plantaciones de café." Ibid., 166.

17. "Aquí están los servidores de Mr. Babbit./Los que educan sus hijos en West Point. . . ./Aquí están los absurdos jóvenes sifilíticos,/fumadores de opio y de mariguana,/exhibiendo en vitrinas sus espiroquetas/y cortándose un traje cada semana." Ibid.

18. "Los hombres, cuando son hombres,/tienen que llevar cuchillo." Ibid., 165.

19. "De la caña sale azúcar,/azúcar para el café." Ibid.

20. "¡Yo fui hombre, lo llevé, /y se me quedó en presidio!" Ibid.

21. Ronald Segal very effectively describes how U.S. business interests were the largest supporter of the repressive dictator (*The Black Diaspora,* 229).

22. "si muriera ahora mismo;" "yo te daré, te daré/te daré, te daré,/ay, yo te daré la libertad." Guillén, *Obra poética,* vol. 1, 165.

23. "Ando en pos de un soldado que quiera ser mi amigo." Ibid., 188.

24. "tu padre . . . que ayer lo hizo mendigo,/engorda hoy con la joven sangre que a ti te exprime." Ibid.

25. "Todos estos yanquis rojos/son hijos de un camarón;" "Ustedes viven/me muero yo,/comen y beben,/pero yo no." Ibid., 201.

26. "pobres/como soy yo. . . .//A ellos les daré la mano,/y con ellos cantaré, porque el canto que ellos saben/es el mismo que yo sé." Ibid.

27. "Hoy yanqui, ayer española"; "un marino Americano,/me quiso dar con la mano, . . ./. . . pero allí se quedó muerto." Ibid., 226–27.

28. Ibid., 272–73.

29. "anda por sus propios pies,/sin yanquis y sin Mikado." Ibid., 278.

30. "brazo con brazo del Tío Sam"; "en qué lengua por fin te podré hablar." Guillén, *Obra poética,* vol.2, 21–22.

31. "New York City with San Juan,/Manhattan y Borinquen, soga y cuello." Ibid., 22.

32. "muerto McCarthy/bien muerto y muerto/amen." Ibid., 27.

33. Ibid., 10.

34. "Jim Crow será el maestro,/hijos de Lynch serán sus condiscípulos/y habrá en cade pupitre/de cada niño negro,/tinta de sangre, lapíces de fuego." Ibid., 23.

35. "ahora pensad lo que sería/el mundo todo Sur,/el mundo todo sangre y todo látigo." Ibid., 24.

36. "Aire de buitre removiendo el águila/mira de un mar al otro mar;/encapuchados danzan hombres fúnebres,/baten un fúnebre timbale/y encendiendo las tres letras fatídicas/con que se anuncia el Ku Klux Klan,/lanzan del Sur un alarido unánime:/¡Va por la muerte, por la muerte va !", Guillén, *Obra poética,* vol.1, 431.

37. "¡oh Viejo río hermano de los negroes!/con las venas abiertas en el agua." Ibid., 400.

38. "El Mississippi pasa"; "la nocturna hoguera/a cuya luz cannibal/danzan los hombres blancos." Ibid., 401.

39. Damas, "*Negritude* in Retrospect."

40. Damas, *Pigments,* 9.

41. Damas's friendship with the Cooks would continue and develop after World War II. He toured the United States in 1946, visiting Harlem, Washington, D.C. (where Cook was teaching at Howard University), and Florida (where he experienced Jim Crow on a segregrated southern train). In 1972, he began a lecture tour of U.S. universities at the suggestion of Cook. In 1974, Damas became a Distinguished Professor at Howard University, where he taught until his death in 1978.

42. "Il m'est revenu que vous n'etiez encore pas/à votre leçon de vi-o-lin/Un banjo/Vous dîtes un banjo/comment dîtes-vous/un banjo/vous dîtes bien/un banjo/Non monsieur/vous saurez qu'on ne souffre chez nous/ni ban/ni jo/ni gui/ni tare/les *mulâtres*ne font pas ça/laissez donc ça aux *nègres.*" Damas, *Pigments,* 36. All translations from Damas are my own; I include the original French in endnotes for readers' reference.

43. "Trêve de blues/de martèlments de piano/de trompette bouchée." Ibid., 21.

44. "de folie claquants des pieds"; "de rings/qu'énervent/des cris de fauves"; "d'une attitude/d'hyperassimilés"; "egoïsmes particuliers." Ibid.

45. "de désirs/et de besoins/et d'égoïsmes particuliers." Ibid.

46. "J'ai au toit de ma case/jusqui'ici gardé/l'ancestrale foi conique." Ibid., 63.

47. "l'arrogance automatique/des masques/des masques de chaux vive." Ibid.

48. "Et mon visage brille aux horreurs du passé/et mon rire effroyable est fait pour repousser le spectre des/lévriers traquant le marronnage/et ma voix qui pour eux chante/est douce à ravir/l'âme triste." Ibid., 64.

49. The lyrics of "Shine" exemplify the kind of naïve optimism attributed to African Americans by many Tin Pan Alley songwriters (in this case, Cecil Mack, Lew Brown, and Ford Dabney):

Oh chocolate drop, that's me
'Cause, my hair is curly
Just because my teeth are pearly
Just because I always wear a smile
Like to dress up in the latest style
'Cause I'm glad I'm livin'
Take troubles all with a smile
Just because my color shade
Is different maybe
That's why they call me "Shine."

Armstrong's famous recording in 1930 infused this song with a depth of pathos and expression belying the simple lyrics—a characteristic that Damas clearly recognized in his homage to Armstrong in "Shine." Indeed, one might argue that Damas's "Shine" represents a kind of gloss (no pun intended) on what Armstrong's performance evokes, in spite of the simple words. In the context of Damas's rendering, for example, the line "'Cause I'm glad I'm livin'" moves from an apparent celebration of "good times" towards an avowal of powerful cultural endurance and survival.

50. "Il est difficile de ne pas faire une comparaison entre le désintéressement dont fit preuve le goveurnment devant ce refus peureux, et l'énergie que déploya le gouvernment de U.S.A. pour enrichir de force Haïti, en lui imposant un emprunt contre le gré de la partie de l'opinion publique américaine." Damas, *Retour de Guyane,* 103.

51. "Ce qui tentera le plus *Uncle Sam* ce sera moins les hommes que le sol et en particulier le sol de la Guyane. . . . Qu'ajouter à tout ceci, que peut-on faire, sinon répéter: il faut exploiter la Guyane pour son or, pour la nécessité où se trouve la Métropole d'éviter l'achat de ce métal." Ibid., 155.

52. "Risquent de voir en cette même Guyane, déjà agonisante, commencer l'effrondrement de l'Empire français." Ibid.

53. "Qui oserait soutenir que c'est grâce a cette assimilation massive que le territoire des États-Unis a produit les plus beaux spécimens de race noire qui existent au monde? Que doivent á l'intégrale assimilation?" Ibid., 127.

54. This poem was later expanded into the poem "Florida Road Workers," published in 1930.

55. The first portion of *Un arc-en-ciel pour l'occident chrétien,* subtitled "poème-mystère vaudou" ["Voodoo Mystery Poem"], gives voice to a litany of voodoo gods, from Legba to Loko, and these gods frequently critique the United States, both for its internal racial politics and for its expansionist aims in the Caribbean. For example, in contemplating the operations of Jim Crow within the

U.S. South, Depestre faults "vous juge d'Alabama" [you judge of Alabama] for "vos mensonges" [your lies] (124) and calls out to "filles blanches d'Alabama" [white daughters of Alabama] to acknowledge "mon innocence" (154). Like Guillén and Cesaire, Depestre reverses the geographic axis of savage/civilized to fault the U.S. whites as "zombis" (152). In discussing the U.S. presence in the Caribbean, Depestre echoes many of the tropes and figures of Guillén's *West Indies, Ltd.,* addressing, for example "Le-fils-cadet-de-West-Point" [the cadet-son from West Point] (112) and "les-fils-futur-ambassedeur-a-Panama" [the son future-ambassador to Panama] (114) . This influence is not at all surprising given that Depestre completed two translation of Guillén's poetry (*Le Grand Zoo* [1966] and *Poésie cubaine, 1959–1966* [1967]) as he was writing *Un arc-en-ciel pour l'occident chrétien.* In the later portions of *Un arc-en-ciel,* Depestre offers an ode to Malcolm X (208) in tandem with a celebration of other black world leaders from history (from Makandal to Lumumba), and turns his attentions to the ultimate global threat posed by the United States, in the form of "Les Dieux atomiques d'Omaha" [The Atomic Gods of Omaha] (224). All quotations above are taken from Dyan's excellent bilingual edition of *Un arc-en-ciel pour l'occident chrétien.*

56. Depestre cites Sandburg in two epigrams and uses him as a title source in two key collections in the 1960s: *Journal d'un animal marin* (1964) and *Un arc-en-ciel pour l'occident chrétien* (1967). *Journal d'un animal marin* bears the following epigraph translated from Sandburg's *Poetry Considered:* "La poésie est le journal d'un animal marin qui vit sur terre et qui voudrait voler." [Sandburg's original reads, "Poetry is the journal of the sea animal living on land, wanting to fly in the air"]. Even with the scathing critique of the United States in *Un arc-en-ciel,* Depestre nonetheless identifies a kindred spirit in the U.S. poet, again citing a quotation from Carl Sandburg's *Poetry Considered* in the second epigraph to the volume: "La poésie est un document imaginaire qui explique comment on fait des arcs-en-ciel et pourquoi ils disparaissent." [Sandburg's original reads, "Poetry is a phantom script telling how rainbows are made and why they go away"]. See Depestre, *Rage de vivre,* 132, 176.

57. "Ô terre d'Afrique/je parcours la route de des malheurs/la longue marches sans allées de fleurs/le long sillage marin de sueur/de larmes et de sang." Depestre, *Rage de vivre,* 31. All translations from *Rage de vivre* are my own; I include the original French in endnotes for readers' reference.

58. "Je porte la tenue de combattant/dans l'episseur de at souffrance"; "blonds jaunes noirs peu importe la peau/le sang et la détresse ont la même couleur." Ibid.

59. "Radio-Washington: le quatre libertés de Roosevelt/sont debout à vos cotés." Ibid., 34.

60. "—Allô Allô la Maison-Blanch yes/—Un Nègre est à l'appareil/les libertés de Monsieur Roosevelt/serait-ce du vent pour les hommes noirs/—Voyez-y la fête de tous les peuples." Ibid., 33.

61. “un monde nouveau se lève de la guerre”; “les Nations unies vont se mettre/à danser en paix leur histoire/la ronde joyeuse inonde toutes les rives.” Ibid.

62. Ibid., 40.

63. “au combat de antifascistes/aux jeunes non-conformistes d’Haïti.” Ibid.

64. “pour notre soif le fusil peut être fontaine/la pierre offre un sommier à notre fatigue.” Ibid., 45.

65. “je descends en bateau dans ce poème.” Ibid., 46.

66. “Ces artistes-là ont-ils réalisé leur idéal? Il faudra, un de ces jours réfléchir avec rigeur sur l’oeuvre des écrivains qui ont essayé leurs premières armes littéraires durant les dix-neuf ans de l’occupation militaire des États-Unis.” Ibid., 23.

67. “D’un côté e de son coeur/dormait un enfant,” while “d l’autre” “un idée fixe pointait sex yeux/affamés de loup.” Ibid., 127.

68. “Cent mètres de là/Un nègre/Brûle sa dernière goutte/de sang sous les étoiles.” Ibid.

69. “Pour toi j’avais l’adieu de Wille MacChee.” Ibid., 79.

70. “Te voici ma petite Patrie.” Ibid., 68.

71. “L’adieu d’un innocent que les chacals yankees du racisme/Brûlerent comme une dérisoire allumette.” Ibid., 79.

72. “Il était comme toi ô mon peuple/Il était comme moi.” Ibid., 80.

73. “Comme on nous reconnaît”; “À la haute teneur de notre minerai/À nos chansons frappées de peine et de misère/Comme des médailles de ténèbres.” Ibid.

74. “le regard bienheureux du général MacArthur/Devant les horreurs moissonnées par ses armées.” Ibid., 92.

75. “de colère «démocrate» de Truman”; “le sourire «républicain» d’Eisenhower”; “l’atome parti de la Maison-Blanche.” Ibid., 94.

76. “Toi qui es peut-être mon pire ennemi. . . ./Je m’adresse malgré tout à toi/Tu es malgré mon frère.” Ibid., 92.

77. “Ô mon frère tu ne peux endosser le chèque de tant de crimes.” Ibid., 93.

78. “Tu ne peux pas mon frère devant ce que j’ai vu/T’enfermer dans la prison de l’indifference.” Ibid., 92.

79. Leopold Senghor, quoted in Eshleman and Smith, introduction to Césaire, *Collected Poetry,* 2.

80. Arnold, *Modernism and Negritude,* 53–54.

81. Eshleman and Smith, introduction to Césaire, *Collected Poetry,* 2.

82. Césaire, quoted in ibid., 2.

83. “Et mon île non-clôture, sa claire audace debout à l’arrière de cette polynésie, devant elle, la Guadeloupe fendue en deux de sa raie dorsale et de meme misère que nous, Haïti où la negritude se mit debout pour la première fois et dit qu’elle croyait à son humanité et la comique petite queue de la Floride où d’un nègre s’achève la strangulation.” Ibid., 46. All translations of Césaire’s poetry are my own. I have included the original French in endnotes for readers’ reference.

84. "Qui peut se vanter d'avoir mieux que moi? Virginie./Tennessee. Géorgie. Alabama/putrefactions monstrueuses de révoltes/inopérantes/marais de sang putrides/trompettes absurdement bouchées/terres rougues, terres sanguines, terres consanguines." Ibid.

85. Césaire, *Discourse on Colonialism,* 77.

86. "Hommes tant pis qui ne vous apercevez." Césaire, *Collected Poetry,* 172.

87. "Mes yeux souviennent/de frondes et drapeaux noirs/qui assassinent à chaque battement de mes cils." Ibid.

88. "Il y a qui attend un buffle noyé jusqu'à la garde des yeux du marécage." Ibid. Césaire employs a similar techinique in his poem "La Tornade," in prophesying that the United States will notice the gathering storm too late for it to protect itself: "Le temps que/le sénateur s'percut que la tornade était assise dans son assiette/et la tornade était dans l'air fourrageant dans Kansas City." Ibid., 183.

89. "Vous ne pouvez m'empêcher de batir à sa suffisance/des îles à la tête d'oeuf de ciel flagrant/sous la férocité calme du géranium immense de notre soleil." Ibid., 172.

90. Ibid., 342.

91. "et pour le tien [sang] qu'il me cache le Soleil, qu'à mon pain il se mêle." Ibid.

92. "Mou vol de vampire qui tout soudain plana." Ibid., 344.

93. "quoi, rien, zéro,/de sang pas une goutte/au carne blanc coeur désinfecté?" Ibid.

94. Hughes, *Collected Poems,* 173. Subsequent references to this text will be cited parenthetically by page number.

95. I am borrowing this term, of course, from Benedict Anderson. See *Imagined Communities.*

96. Kutzinksi, "Fearful Assymetries," 112.

97. Ibid., 122.

98. Urrutia to Hughes, 20 April 1930.

99. Fernández de Castro, "Presentación de Langston Hughes," in Mullen, *Langston Hughes in the Hispanic World and Haiti,* 169–71.

100. Novo, "Notas Sobre la Poesía de los Negroes en los Estados Unidos," in ibid., 176–78.

101. "Él, antes que ningún otro poeta en su idioma, ha conseguido incorporara la literatura norteamericana las manifestaciones más puras de la música popular en los E.U. tan influída por los negroes"; "Parece justamente un "mulatico" cubano." Guillén, "Conversación con Langston Hughes," in ibid., 172–75.

102. Fernandez de Castro to Johnson, 2 August 1930.

103. Fernandez de Castro to Johnson, 2 March 1931.

104. "Lemento no conocer el sufficient ingles para juzgar las traducciones: pero siendo ustedes responsables, estoy seguro de que ellas han superado los originales míos." Guillén to Hughes, 28 January 1949.

105. Langston Hughes wrote about Piquion to Arna Bontemps to gain support for a visa for an extended visit so that he could complete the volume: "Rene Piquion, International House, 500 Riverside Drive, wishes to remain in the U.S. throughout the summer to collect material for a book about Negro life here for publication in Haiti, a sort of New World A-Comin' book in French concerning ourselves for Haitian readers, as there is nothing of the sort up to date in French." Hughes to Bontemps, 29 March 1945.

106. Kutzinksi, "Fearful Assymetries," 121.

107. Hughes to Bontemps, 28 January 1965, in Nichols, *Arna Bontemps-Langston Hughes Letters,* 470.

108. Hughes, "'Magic Island' Of Haiti."

109. Ibid.

110. Hughes, "Defender Contest."

111. Hughes, "Nassau—A Flower Garden Island."

112. Ibid.

113. Hughes, "Nassau, Rum, Conch Salad."

114. Ibid.

115. Ibid.

116. Hughes, *I Wonder as I Wander,* 46. Subsequent references to this text will be cited parenthetically by page number.

117. See Lamming, interview by George E. Kent.

118. Wright, introduction to Lamming, *In the Castle of My Skin,* vi. Subsequent references to this text will be cited parenthetically by page number.

119. Marshall, *Triangle Road,* 28.

120. Domestically, in both *Twelve Million Black Voices* (1941) and *American Hunger* (1944), Wright addresses both northern and southern scenes, rural and urban settings, and white and black racial landscapes. On the basis of his experiences abroad, he published substantial pieces documenting his experiences in Africa (*Black Power* [1954]), Asia (*The Color Curtain* [1956]), and Mediterranean Europe (*Pagan Spain* [1957]). Given the comprehensive attempts Wright made to explore the shape of global uplift, his silence on the Caribbean is even more striking.

121. See "Plan Parley on Feudalism in West Indies"; "Harlem to Denounce Terror in West Indies"; "Plan to Aid Negroes in West Indies"; "Call Parley to Aid West Indian Negroes." Wright Papers. Because the articles were from the *Daily Worker,* they do not have a byline. They were kept by Wright in a clipbook dating from the time he wrote for that paper; the archival finding aids at the Beinecke Library attribute them to him.

122. The subsequent decade would show black revolutionary theory to be one of Trinidad's most important exports, and Wright would later become friends with two of Trinidad's most important intellectuals, C. L. R. James and George Padmore.

123. The title *Haitian Biographies* is an archival label, given by the Beinecke Library for cataloging the typescript. Wright did not give his typescript any title. In bibliographic citations the title is enclosed in brackets, but for the sake of typographic clarity and compactness I have omitted the brackets in the body of this chapter.

124. Richard Wright, *Haitian Biographies,* n.p.

125. In *12 Million Black Voices,* Wright observes of the urban African American workers in the north: "After working all day in one civilization, we go home to our black belts and live, within the orbit of the surviving remnants of the culture of the South, our naïve, casual, verbal, fluid folk life" (127). Writing of himself in a personal journal in 1945, Wright described himself as a man in a "contradictory circumstance, a plantation Negro living in New York, a peasant who is an artist of sorts" (Wright Papers, 13 February 1945).

126. Richard Wright, *Haitian Biographies,* n.p.

127. Ibid.

128. The very form of Wright's materials on Haiti is itself striking. It begins with a typescript introduction, which may or may not have been written during the visit, then shifts to longhand manuscript, and finally to shorthand notes that eventually trail off, incomplete.

129. Paquet, *Caribbean Autobiography,* 116.

130. Lamming, *The Pleasures of Exile,* 152.

131. Ibid., 153.

132. Ibid., 154.

133. Wright, *Black Boy (American Hunger),* 91. Subsequent references to this text will be cited parenthetically by page number.

134. Wright, *The Long Dream,* 16. Subsequent references to this text will be cited parenthetically by page number.

135. Paquet, *Caribbean Autobiography,* 124.

136. Lamming, *The Pleasures of Exile,* 33.

137. Marshall, *Brown Girls, Brownstones,* 2. Subsequent references to this text will be cited parenthetically by page number.

138. Hathaway, *Caribbean Waves,* 96. Subsequent references to this text will be cited parenthetically by page number.

139. Marshall, *Triangle Road,* 103.

Conclusion

1. Kutzinski, "Fearful Asymmetries," 3–4, 139–40.

2. Aimé Césaire's *Discourse on Colonialism,* first published in 1950, would thrust questions of decolonization into important circles of U.S. culture and left a contributing influence on the Black Arts movement of the 1960s and beyond. Indeed, Césaire's contributions to postcolonial discourse (along with those of fellow Martinican Frantz Fanon) would profoundly affect the shape of subsequent

generations of U.S. writers from the 1960s onwards. The civil rights leader Stokely Carmichael (born in Trinidad and raised in the United States), for example, opened his most famous manifesto, *Black Power: The Politics of Liberation in America,* with an extensive quote from Fanon's *The Wretched of the Earth,* which notes the perils of U.S. imperialism at home and abroad: "Two centuries ago, a former European colony decided to catch up with Europe. It succeeded so well that the United States of America became a monster, in which the taints, the sickness, and the inhumanity of Europe have grown to appalling dimensions" (xi). Césaire's politically inflected surrealism was also clearly an important influence on LeRoi Jones/Amiri Baraka, who self-consciously sought to distance his work from that of New Negro predecessors. Baraka also drew inspiration from Cuba in his work. He cites his visit to Cuba in 1960 as "a turning point in my life" and reported upon his visit in the essay "Cuba Libre." According to William Harris, "This trip was the beginning of Baraka's radical political art and his identification with Third World Artists" (introduction to *The LeRoi Jones/Amiri Baraka Reader,* xx).

3. Kaplan, "Where is Guantanamo?" in Dudziak and Volpp, *Legal Borderlands,* 261. Kaplan's article skillfully examines the recent legal and penal controversies surrounding Guantanamo in the context of its history as an imperial space for the United States.

4. Pease, introduction to James, *Mariners, Renegades, and Castaways,* xxxi, xiii. Subsequent references to this text will be cited parenthetically by page number.

5. Melville, *Moby Dick,* 167. Subsequent references to this text will be cited parenthetically by page number.

6. James, *Mariners, Renegades and Castaways,* ts., 11. I take this sentence from the original ts., as it is missing from reprinted editions. The recent reprint, in contrast, reads as follows: "Hitler was no sooner destroyed than the Stalinist state threatened to overwhelm not only Europe but the whole of the world. The type is the same" (14).

7. Lamming, *The Pleasures of Exile,* 154.

8. James, *Mariners, Renegades and Castaways,* ts., 56.

9. Although Carnival's corporate headquarters is based in Florida, not a single ship is registered under a U.S. port of call; they are almost all registered in either Panama or the Bahamas. Carnival has also been criticized for deceptive and exploitative labor practices, which escape restriction and regulation because of the multinational jurisdictions involved.

10. See Nguyen and Sanchez, "Ethnic Communities in New York City."

11. See Amnesty International, "Cruel and Inhuman."

Bibliography

Adams, Jessica, Michael Bibler, and Cécile Accilien, eds. *Just Below South: Intercultural Performance in the Caribbean and the U.S. South*. Charlottesville: University of Virginia Press, 2007.

Amnesty International. "Cruel and Inhuman: Conditions of Isolation for Detainees at Guantánamo Bay." 1 April 2007. http://www.amnesty.org/en/library/info/AMR51/051/2007.

Anderson, Benedict. *Imagined Communities: Reflections on the Origin and Spread of Nationalism*. New York: Verso Press, 2006.

Arnold, A. J. *Modernism and Negritude: The Poetry and Poetics of Aimé Césaire*. Cambridge: Harvard University Press, 1981.

Baker, Houston A. *Modernism in the Harlem Renaissance*. Chicago: University of Chicago Press, 1987.

Bakhtin, Mikhail. *The Dialogic Imagination*. Ed. Michael Holquist. Austin: University of Texas Press, 1994.

Belnap, Jeffrey, and Raúl Fernández, eds. *José Martí's "Our America": From National to Hemispheric Cultural Studies*. Durham: Duke University Press, 1998.

Benítez-Rojo, Antonio. *The Repeating Island: The Caribbean and the Postmodern Perspective*. Trans. James A. Maraniss. Durham: Duke University Press, 1996.

Bhabha, Homi. *The Location of Culture*. New York: Routledge, 2004.

Bontemps, Arna. *Drums at Dusk*. Ed. Michael Bibler and Jessica Adams. Baton Rouge: LSU Press, 2009.

Bourdieu, Pierre. *The Logic of Practice*. Stanford: Stanford University Press, 1992.

Bourne, Randolph. "Trans-National America." In *Theories of Ethnicity: A Classical Reader*. Ed. Werner Sollors. New York: NYU Press, 1996. 93–108.

Bradford, M. E. "The Knight and the Artist: Tasso and William Faulkner's 'Carcassonne.'" *The South Central Bulletin* 41.4 (Winter 1981): 88–90

Brodhead, Richard. *Cultures of Letters*. Chicago: University of Chicago Press, 1993.

———. *The School of Hawthorne.* New York: Oxford University Press, 1986.

Carmichael, Stokely, and Charles V. Hamilton. *Black Power: The Politics of Liberation in America.* New York: Random House, 1967.

Casseus, Maurice. *Viejo.* Paris: Editions La Presse, 1935.

Césaire, Aimé. *Aimé Césaire: The Collected Poetry.* Trans. Clayton Eshleman and Annette Smith. Berkeley: University of California Press, 1983.

———. *Discourse on Colonialism.* Trans. Joan Pinkham. New York: Monthly Review Press, 2000.

Chu, Patricia. *Race, Nationalism and the State in British and American Modernism.* New York: Cambridge University Press, 2006.

Cobb, Martha. *Harlem, Haiti, and Havana.* Washington, D.C.: Three Continents Press, 1979.

Columbus, Christopher. *The Journal of Christopher Columbus During His First Voyage.* London: Hayklut Society, 1893.

Conrad, Joseph. *Heart of Darkness.* New York: Bantam, 1981.

Cooper, Wayne F., ed. *The Passion of Claude McKay.* New York: Schocken Books, 1973.

Coronado, Raúl. "The Aesthetics of Our America." *American Literary History* 20.1–2 (Spring 2008): 210–16.

Craige, John H. *Black Bagdad.* New York: Minton, Balch, and Company, 1933.

———. *Cannibal Cousins.* New York: Minton, Balch, and Company, 1934.

Crane, Hart. *The Complete Poems and Selected Letters and Prose of Hart Crane.* Ed. Brom Weber. New York: Doubleday, 1966.

Damas, Léon. "*Negritude* in Retrospect." In *Léon-Gontran Damas, 1912–1978: Founder of Negritude: A Memorial Casebook.* Ed. Daniel L. Racine. Washington, D.C.: University Press of America, 1979. 259–60.

———. *Pigments.* Paris: Présence Africaine, 1956.

———. *Retour de Guyane.* Paris: Editions Jean-Michel Place, 2003.

Dash, J. Michael. *Haiti and the United States: National Stereotypes and the Literary Imagination.* New York: Palgrave, 1997.

Depestre, René. *Un arc-en-ciel pour l'Occident chrétien.* Trans. Joan Dyan. Amherst: University of Massachusetts Press, 1977.

———. *Rage de vivre: oeuvres poétiques complètes.* Paris: Seghers, 2006.

Domingo, W. A. "The West Indies." *Opportunity* 4.47 (November 1926): 341.

Douglas, Ann. *Terrible Honesty: Mongrel Manhattan in the 1920s.* New York: Farrar, Straus, and Giroux, 1995.

"Do We Want Cuba?" *Philadelphia Manufacturer* 16 March 1889. In *Our America: Writings on Latin America and the Struggle for Cuban Independence.* Ed. Philip S. Foner. Trans. Elinor Randall. New York: Monthly Review Press, 1977.

Du Bois, W. E. B. *The Autobiography of W. E. B. DuBois.* New York: Oxford University Press, 2007.

———. *Black Folk then and Now.* New York: Oxford University Press, 2007.

———. *The Correspondence of W. E. B. DuBois*. Vol. 1, *Selections, 1877–1934*. Ed. Herbert Aptheker. Amherst: University of Massachusetts Press, 1973.

———. *Dark Princess*. New York: Oxford University Press, 2007.

———. *The Negro*. New York: Oxford University Press, 2007.

———. *The Oxford W. E. B. Du Bois Reader*. Ed. Eric J. Sundquist. New York: Oxford University Press, 1996.

———. *The World and Africa*. New York: Oxford University Press, 2007.

Duck, Leigh Ann. "'Rebirth of a Nation': Hurston in Haiti." *Journal of American Folklore* 117.464 (2004): 127–46.

Dunham, Katherine. *Kaiso! Writings by and about Katherine Dunham*. Ed. Veve Clark and Sara E. Johnson. Madison: University of Wisconsin Press, 2005.

Editorial. *Opportunity* 4.47 (November 1926): 334.

Escobedo, John. "Archival Conflicts: The New Negro Movement and Caribbean as Other." *English Language Notes* 45.1 (Spring/Summer 2007): 93–102

Faulkner, William. *Absalom, Absalom!* New York: Modern Library, 1936.

———. *Collected Stories*. New York: Random House, 1950.

Faulkner, William, Sam Hellman, and Gladys Lehman. *The Last Slaver*. Ts. 24 September 1936. Albert and Shirley Small Special Collections Library. University of Virginia.

———. *The Last Slaver*. Ts. 10 October 1936. Albert and Shirley Small Special Collections Library. University of Virginia.

Favor, J. Martin. *Authentic Blackness: The Folk in the New Negro Renaissance*. Durham: Duke University Press, 1999.

Fay, Jennifer. "Dead Subjectivity: *White Zombie*, Black Baghdad." *CR: The New Centennial Review* 8.1 (2008): 81–101.

Firmin, Anténor. *The Equality of the Human Races*. Trans. Asselin Charles. New York: Garland Publishing, 2000.

———. *M. Roosevelt, Président des États-unis et La République de Haiti*. Paris: V. Pichon et Durand-Aurias, 1905.

Fischer-Hornung, Dorothea. "An Island Occupied: The U.S. Marine Occupation of Haiti in Zora Neale Hurston's *Tell My Horse* and Katherine Dunham's *Island Possessed*." In *Holding Their Own: Perspectives on the Multi-ethnic Literatures of the United States*. Ed. Dorothea Fischer-Hornung and Heike Raphael-Hernandez. Tübingen, Germany: Stauffenberg Verlag, 2000. 153–68.

Frank, Waldo. *America Hispana*. New York: Scribners, 1931.

———. "In Our American Language." *Opportunity* 4.47 (November 1926): 352.

Garvey, Marcus. *The Philosophy and Opinions of Marcus Garvey*. Dover, MA: The Majority Press, 1986.

Gillman, Susan. "The New, Newest Thing: Have American Studies Gone Imperial?" *American Literary History* 17.1 (2005): 198–214.

———. "Otra Vez Caliba/Encore Caliban: Adaptation, Translation, American Studies." *American Literary History* 20.1–2 (Spring 2008): 187–209.

Gilroy, Paul. *The Black Atlantic: Modernity and Double Consciousness*. Cambridge: Harvard University Press, 1993.

Glissant, Édouard. *Faulkner, Mississippi*. Trans. Barbara Lewis and Thomas C. Spear. Chicago: University of Chicago Press, 2000.

Guillén, Nicolás. *Obra poética, 1920–1972*. 2 vols. Ed. Angel Augier. Havana: Editorial de Arte y Literatura, 1974.

Harris, William. Introduction to *The LeRoi Jones/Amiri Baraka Reader*, by Amiri Baraka. New York: Thunder's Mouth Press, 1991.

Harris, Wilson. *The Womb of Space: The Cross-cultural Imagination*. Westport, CT: Greenwood Press, 1983.

Harrison, Hubert. *A Hubert Harrison Reader*. Ed. Jeffrey B. Perry. Middletown, CT: Wesleyan University Press, 2001.

Hathaway, Heather. *Caribbean Waves: Relocating Claude McKay and Paule Marshall*. Bloomington: Indiana University Press, 1999.

Hawthorne, Evelyn. "Ethnicity and Cultural Perspectives in Paule Marshall's Short Fiction." *MELUS* 13.3–4 (Autumn-Winter 1986): 109–20.

Herskovits, Melville. *Life in a Haitian Valley*. New York: Alfred A. Knopf, 1937.

Hogan, William. "Roots, Routes, and Langston Hughes's Hybrid Sense of Place." *Langton Hughes Review* 18 (Spring 2004): 3–23.

Holstein, Casper. "The Virgin Islands: Past and Present." *Opportunity* 4.47 (November 1926): 344.

Hughes, Langston. *The Collected Poems of Langston Hughes*. Ed. Arnold Rampersad. New York: Knopf, 1994.

———. *The Collected Works of Langston Hughes*. 16 vols. Ed. Leslie Catherine Sanders and Nancy Johnston. Columbia: University of Missouri Press, 2001–2003.

———. Correspondence. Langston Hughes Papers. Beinecke Library. Yale University. New Haven, CT.

———. "Defender Contest Will Introduce Winners to World of Haitian Charm and Culture." *Chicago Defender* 20 May 1950.

———. *I Wonder as I Wander*. Columbia: University of Missouri Press, 2003.

———. "'Magic Island' Of Haiti Is a Wonderful Prize for Defender Contest Winners." *Chicago Defender* 29 April 1950.

———. "Nassau—A Flower Garden Island Just For Tourists." *Chicago Defender* 19 June 1954.

———. "Nassau, Rum, Conch Salad, Calypsos and Night Clubs." *Chicago Defender* 26 June 1954.

———. "People without Shoes." *New Masses* 12 (October 1931): 12.

———. "White Shadows in a Black Land." *Crisis* 39 (May 1932): 157.

Hurston, Zora Neale. *Tell My Horse*. Addition to ts. Hurston Papers. Beinecke Library. Yale University. New Haven, CT.

———. *Tell My Horse*. Holograph ms. Hurston Papers. Beinecke Library. Yale University. New Haven, CT.

———. *Tell My Horse.* Ts. Hurston Papers. Beinecke Library. Yale University. New Haven, CT.

James, C. L. R. *The Black Jacobins: Toussaint L'Ouverture and the San Domingo Revolution.* New York: Random House, 1989.

———. *Mariners, Renegades, and Castaways: The Story of Herman Melville and the World We Live In.* Hanover, NH: University Press of New England, 2001.

———. *Mariners, Renegades and Castaways: The Story of Herman Melville and the World We Live In.* Ts. 1953. C. L. R. James Papers. University of the West Indies. Aruba, Trinidad.

Jauss, Hans Robert. *Towards an Aesthetic of Reception.* Minneapolis: University of Minnesota Press, 1982.

Johnson, James Weldon. "Address to the Patriots of Haiti." James Weldon Johnson Papers. Beinecke Library. Yale University. New Haven, CT.

———. Correspondence. James Weldon Johnson Papers. Beinecke Library. Yale University. New Haven, CT.

———. *Lift Every Voice and Sing: Selected Poems.* Ed. Sondra Kathryn Wilson. New York: Penguin, 2000.

———. *The Selected Writings of James Weldon Johnson.* 2 vols. Ed. Sondra Kathryn Wildon. New York: Oxford University Press, 1995.

———. "To the Editor." *Chicago Tribune* 14 May 1921.

Jones, Eugene Kinckle. "West Indian-American Relations: A Symposium." *Opportunity* 4.47 (November 1926): 357.

Kaplan, Amy. "Where is Guantanamo?" In *Legal Borderlands: Law and the Construction of American Borders.* Ed. Mary L. Dudziak and Leti Volpp. Baltimore: Johns Hopkins University Press, 2006. 239–66.

Karem, Jeff. "On the Advantages and Disadvantages of Postcolonial Theory for Pan-American Study." *CR: The New Centennial Review* 1.3 (February 2002): 86–116.

King, George S. *The Last Slaver.* New York: Putnam's, 1933.

Kutzinski, Vera. *Against the American Grain.* Baltimore: Johns Hopkins University Press, 1987.

———. "Borders and Bodies: The United States, America, and the Caribbean." *CR: The New Centennial Review* 1.2 (Fall 2001): 55–88.

———. "Fearful Asymetries: Langston Hughes, Nicolás Guillén and *Cuba Libre.*" *Diacritics* 34.3–4 (2004): 112–42.

———. *Sugar's Secrets: Race and the Erotics of Cuban Nationalism.* Charlottesville: University of Virginia Press, 1993.

Lamming, George. *In the Castle of My Skin.* Ann Arbor: University of Michigan Press, 1989.

———. Interview by George E. Kent. *Black World* 22.5 (1973): 4–14, 88–97.

———. *The Pleasures of Exile.* Ann Arbor: University of Michigan Press, 1960.

Langford, Gerald. *Faulkner's Revision of Absalom, Absalom! A Collation of the Manuscript and the Published Book.* Austin: University of Texas Press, 1971.

Lewis, David Levering. *W. E. B. Du Bois: Biography of a Race.* New York: Henry Holt and Co., 1993.

———. *When Harlem Was in Vogue.* New York: Penguin, 1997.

Lock, Helen. "'Building Up from Fragments': The Oral Memory Process in Some Recent African-American Written Narratives." *College Literature* 22.3 (October 1995): 109–20.

Locke, Alain, ed. *The New Negro.* New York: Boni and Liveright, 1925.

Lott, Eric. *Love and Theft: Blackface Minstrelsy and the American Working Class.* New York: Oxford University Press, 1995.

Marable, Manning. *W. E. B. Du Bois: Black Radical Democrat.* Boulder: Paradigm, 2005.

Marshall, Paule. *Brown Girls, Brownstones.* Mineola, NY: Dover, 2009.

———. *Triangle Road: A Memoir.* New York: Perseus Books, 2009.

Martí, José. *Antologia critica.* Ed. Susana Redondo de Feldman and Anthony Tudisco. New York: Las Americas Publishing Co., 1968.

———. *Obras completas.* 4 vols. Caracas, 1964.

"Massive Earthquake Reveals Entire Island Civilization Called 'Haiti.'" *Onion* 25 January 2010. http://www.theonion.com/content/news/massive_earthquake_reveals_entire.

Mathurin, Owen Charles. *Henry Sylvester Williams and the Origins of the Pan-African Movement.* Westport, CT: Greenwood Press, 1976.

Matthews, John T. "Recalling the West Indies: From Yoknapatawpha to Haiti and Back." *American Literary History* 16.2 (Summer 2004): 238–62.

McKay, Claude. *Banjo.* New York: Harcourt Brace, 1957.

———. Correspondence. Claude McKay Papers. Beinecke Library. Yale University. New Haven, CT.

———. "Garvey as a Negro Moses." *Liberator* 5 (April 1922): 8–9.

———. *Home to Harlem.* Boston: Northeastern University Press, 1987.

———. "My House" and "America in Retrospect." *Opportunity* 4.47 (November 1926): 342.

———. *Selected Poems.* Ed. Max Eastman. New York: Bookman, 1953.

Melville, Herman. *Moby Dick.* New York: Oxford University Press, 1988.

Miller, R. Baxter. *The Art and Imagination of Langston Hughes.* Lexington: University Press of Kentucky, 2006.

Misrahi-Barak, Judith, ed. *Revisiting Slave Narratives.* Montpellier, France: Université Paul Valéry, 2007.

Morrison, Toni. *Playing in the Dark: Whiteness and the Literary Imagination.* New York: Vintage, 1993.

Mostern, Kenneth. "Postcolonialism after W. E. B. DuBois." In *Postcolonial Theory and the United States.* Ed. Amritjit Singh and Peter Schmidt. Jackson: University of Mississippi Press, 2000. 258–76.

Mullen, Edward J., ed. *Langston Hughes in the Hispanic World and Haiti.* Hamden, CT: Archon Books, 1977.

Nguyen, Pauline, and Josephine Sanchez. "Ethnic Communities in New York City: Dominicans in Washington Heights." Voices of New York. New York University. 2001. http://www.nyu.edu/classes/blake.map2001/dominican2.html.

Nichols, Charles H. *Arna Bontemps–Langston Hughes Letters*. New York: Dodd, Mead, and Co., 1980.

Niles, Blair. *Black Haiti*. New York: Grosset and Dunlap, 1925.

North, Michael. *The Dialect of Modernism: Race, Language and Twentieth-Century Literature*. New York: Oxford University Press, 1998.

O'Neill, Eugene. *Representative Plays of Eugene O'Neill*. New York: Liveright, 1927.

Padmore, George. *Pan-Africanism or Communism: The Coming Struggle for Africa*. London: Denis Dobson, 1956.

Paquet, Sandra Pouchet. *Caribbean Autobiography: Cultural Identity and Self-Representation*. Madison: University of Wisconsin Press, 2002.

Parascandola, Louis, ed. *Look for Me All Around You: Anglophone Caribbean Immigrants in the Harlem Renaissance*. Detroit: Wayne State UP, 2007.

———, ed. *Winds Can Wake Up the Dead: An Eric Walrond Reader*. Detroit: Wayne State University Press, 1998.

Patterson, Harvey T. "American Democracy in the Canal Zone." *Crisis* 20.2 (1920): 83–85.

Pease, Donald, ed. *The Future of American Studies*. Durham: Duke University Press, 2002.

———, ed. *Revisionist Interventions into the American Canon*. Durham: Duke University Press, 1993.

Pease, Donald, and Amy Kaplan, eds. *Cultures of U.S. Imperialism*. Durham: Duke University Press, 1993.

Pederson, Carl. "The Caribbean Voices of Claude McKay and Eric Walrond." In *The Cambridge Companion to the Harlem Renaissance*. Ed. George Hutchinson. New York: Cambridge University Press, 2007. 184–97.

Perry, Jeffrey B., ed. *A Hubert Harrison Reader*. Middletown, CT: Wesleyan University Press, 2001.

———. *Hubert Harrison: The Voice of Harlem Radicalism*. New York: Columbia University Press. 2008.

Plummer, Brenda Gayle. "Firmin and Martí at the Intersection of Pan-Americanism and Pan-Africanism." In *José Martí's "Our America": From National to Hemispheric Cultural Studies*. Ed. Jeffrey Belnap and Raúl Fernández. Durham: Duke University Press, 1998. 210–27.

Rampersad, Arnold. *The Life of Langston Hughes*. 2 vols. New York: Oxford University Press, 1988.

Ramsey, Kate. "Without One Ritual Note: Folklore Performance and the Haitian State, 1935–1946." *Radical History Review* 84 (Fall 2002): 7–42.

Retamar, Roberto Fernández. *Caliban and Other Essays*. Minneapolis: University of Minnesota Press, 1989.

"The Rise of the West Indian." *Crisis* 20 (September 1920): 214.

Rosaldo, Renato. "Imperial Nostalgia." *Representations* 26 (1989): 107–23.

Roumain, Jacques. *Masters of the Dew.* Trans. Langston Hughes and Mercer Cook. Portsmouth, NH: Heinemann Press, 1978.

Rowe, John Carlos. *Literary Culture and U.S. Imperialism.* New York: Oxford University Press, 2000.

Saldívar, José David. *The Dialectics of Our America.* Durham: Duke University Press, 1991.

Sanders, Leslie Catherine, and Nancy Johnston. *The Collected Works of Langston Hughes.* Vol. 5, *The Plays to 1942.* Columbia: University of Missouri Press, 2002.

Savin, Ada. "Rituals of 'Rememory' in Paule Marshall's *The Chosen Place, the Timeless People.*" In *Revisiting Slave Narratives.* Ed. Juditgh Misrahi-Barak. Montpellier, France: Université Paul Valéry, 2007. 177–98.

Seabrook, William. *The Magic Island.* New York: Literary Guild of America, 1929.

Segal, Ronald. *The Black Diaspora.* New York: Farrar, Straus, Giroux, 1995.

Singh, Amritjit, and Peter Schmidt, eds. *Postcolonial Theory and the United States.* Jackson: University of Mississippi Press, 2000.

Smith, Carissa Turner. "Women's Spiritual Geographies of the African Diaspora: Paule Marshall's *Praisesong for the Widow.*" *African American Review* 42.3–4 (Fall/Winter 2008): 715–29.

Smith, Jon, and Deborah Cohn, eds. *Look Away! The U.S. South in New World Studies.* Durham: Duke University Press, 2002.

Stanchich, Maritza. "The Hidden Caribbean 'Other' in William Faulkner's *Absalom, Absalom!:* An Ideological Ancestry of U.S. Imperialism." *Mississippi Quarterly: The Journal of Southern Culture* 49.3 (June 1996): 603–17.

Stevens, Wallace. *Collected Poems.* New York: Vintage Books, 1990.

Sundquist, Eric, ed. *To Wake the Nations: Race in the Making of American Literature.* Cambridge: Harvard University Press, 1993.

Sylvain, Benito. *Du Sort des Indigènes dans Les Colonies d'Exploitation.* Paris: L. Boyer, 1901.

Taft, Edna. *A Puritan in Voodoo-land.* Philadelphia: The Penn Publishing Company, 1938.

Thoby-Marcelin, Philippe, and Pierre Marcelin. *The Beast of the Haitian Hills.* Trans. Peter C. Rhodes. Intro. Philippe Thoby-Marcellin. New York: Time-Life Books, 1946.

Thomas, J. J. *Froudacity: West Indian Fables by James Anthony Froude.* London: New Beacon Books, 1979.

Trescott, Jacqueline. "The Daughter of the Mother Poets; Novelist Paule Marshall, Exploring the World of Black Immigrants." *Washington Post* 8 October 1991: C1.

Van Vechten, Carl. *Nigger Heaven.* New York: Alfred A. Knopf, 1926.

Walrond, Eric. *Tropic Death.* New York: Collier Books, 1954.

———. *Winds Can Wake Up the Dead: An Eric Walrond Reader.* Ed. Louis J. Parascandola. Detroit: Wayne State University Press, 1998.

Walters, Alexander. *My Life and Work.* New York: Fleming H. Revell, 1917.

Watkins-Owens, Irma. *Blood Relations: Caribbean Immigrants and the Harlem Community.* Bloomington: Indiana University Press, 1996.

Williams, William Carlos. *In the American Grain* New York: New Directions, 1956.

Wilson, Sondra Kathryn, ed. *In Search of Democracy: The NAACP Writings of James Weldon Johnson, Walter White, and Roy Wilkins.* New York: Oxford University Press, 1999.

———, ed. *The Messenger Reader.* New York: Random House, 2000.

Wirkus, Faustin, and Taney Dudley. *The White King of Gonave.* Intro. William Seabrook. New York: Doubleday, Doran and Co., 1931.

Wright, Richard. *Black Boy (American Hunger).* New York: HarperCollins, 1993.

———. [*Haitian Biographies*]. Richard Wright Papers. Beinecke Library. Yale University. New Haven, CT.

———. Journal. Richard Wright Papers. Beinecke Library. Yale University. New Haven, CT.

———. *The Long Dream.* New York: HarperCollins, 1986.

———. Scrapbook of *Daily Worker Articles.* Richard Wright Papers. Beinecke Library. Yale University. New Haven, CT.

———. *The Long Dream.* New York: HarperCollins, 1986.

———. *12 Million Black Voices.* New York: Viking Press, 1941.

Zeltner, Brie. "3-D Headache? *Avatar* Special Effects Might Not Be for Everyone." *Plain Dealer* 13 January 2010: A1.

Index

New World Studies

Vera M. Kutzinski, *Sugar's Secrets: Race and the Erotics of Cuban Nationalism*

Richard D. E. Burton and Fred Reno, editors, *French and West Indian: Martinique, Guadeloupe, and French Guiana Today*

A. James Arnold, editor, *Monsters, Tricksters, and Sacred Cows: Animal Tales and American Identities*

J. Michael Dash, *The Other America: Caribbean Literature in a New World Context*

Isabel Alvarez Borland, *Cuban-American Literature of Exile: From Person to Persona*

Belinda J. Edmondson, editor, *Caribbean Romances: The Politics of Regional Representation*

Steven V. Hunsaker, *Autobiography and National Identity in the Americas*

Celia M. Britton, *Edouard Glissant and Postcolonial Theory: Strategies of Language and Resistance*

Mary Peabody Mann, *Juanita: A Romance of Real Life in Cuba Fifty Years Ago* (Edited and with an introduction by Patricia M. Ard)

George B. Handley, *Postslavery Literatures in the Americas: Family Portraits in Black and White*

Faith Smith, *Creole Recitations: John Jacob Thomas and Colonial Formation in the Late Nineteenth-Century Caribbean*

Ian Gregory Strachan, *Paradise and Plantation: Tourism and Culture in the Anglophone Caribbean*

Nick Nesbitt, *Voicing Memory: History and Subjectivity in French Caribbean Literature*

Charles W. Pollard, *New World Modernisms: T. S. Eliot, Derek Walcott, and Kamau Brathwaite*

Carine M. Mardorossian, *Reclaiming Difference: Caribbean Women Rewrite Postcolonialism*

Luís Madureira, *Cannibal Modernities: Postcoloniality and the Avant-garde in Caribbean and Brazilian Literature*

Elizabeth M. DeLoughrey, Renée K. Gosson, and George B. Handley, editors, *Caribbean Literature and the Environment: Between Nature and Culture*

Flora González Mandri, *Guarding Cultural Memory: Afro-Cuban Women in Literature and the Arts*

Miguel Arnedo-Gómez, *Writing Rumba: The Afrocubanista Movement in Poetry*

Jessica Adams, Michael P. Bibler, and Cécile Accilien, editors, *Just Below South: Intercultural Performance in the Caribbean and the U.S. South*

Valérie Loichot, *Orphan Narratives: The Postplantation Literature of Faulkner, Glissant, Morrison, and Saint-John Perse*

Sarah Phillips Casteel, *Second Arrivals: Landscape and Belonging in Contemporary Writing of the Americas*

Guillermina De Ferrari, *Vulnerable States: Bodies of Memory in Contemporary Caribbean Fiction*

Claudia Sadowski-Smith, *Border Fictions: Globalization, Empire, and Writing at the Boundaries of the United States*

Doris L. Garraway, editor, *Tree of Liberty: Cultural Legacies of the Haitian Revolution in the Atlantic World*

Dawn Fulton, *Signs of Dissent: Maryse Conde and Postcolonial Criticism*

Nick Nesbitt, *Universal Emancipation: The Haitian Revolution and the Radical Enlightenment*

Michael G. Malouf, *Transatlantic Solidarities: Irish Nationalism and Caribbean Poetics*

Maria Cristina Fumagalli, *Caribbean Perspectives on Modernity: Returning the Gaze*

Vivian Nun Halloran, *Exhibiting Slavery: The Caribbean Postmodern Novel as Museum*

Paul B. Miller, *Elusive Origins: The Enlightenment in the Modern Caribbean Historical Imagination*

Eduardo González, *Cuba and the Fall: Christian Text and Queer Narrative in the Fiction of José Lezama Lima and Reinaldo Arenas*

Jeff Karem, *The Purloined Islands: Caribbean-U.S. Cross-Currents in Literature and Culture, 1880–1959*

The Purloined Islands

New World Studies

J. Michael Dash, *Editor*

Frank Moya Pons, and
Sandra Pouchet Paquet,
Associate Editors